STUDIES IN MEDIEVAL AND RENAISSANCE HISTORY

Volume I

STUDIES IN
Medieval and Renaissance
History

Volume I

Edited by
WILLIAM M. BOWSKY
University of Nebraska

UNIVERSITY OF NEBRASKA PRESS ● LINCOLN
1964

Publishers on the Plains
UNP

CONTENTS

INTRODUCTION

Studies in Medieval and Renaissance History is planned as a series of annual volumes designed for original major articles and short monographs in all fields of medieval and renaissance history.

The first impetus for the creation of this series came from a belief that there is a need for a scholarly publication to accommodate the longer study whose compass is too large for it to be included regularly in existing media but too small for it to appear in book form. The editors will consider articles in all areas of history from approximately the fourth through the sixteenth centuries—economic, social and demographic, political, intellectual and cultural, and studies that do not fit neatly into a single traditional category of historical investigation.

The editorial board hopes that the *Studies* will create another link between the work of medieval and renaissance scholarship; for many articles pertinent to both disciplines appear in publications consulted almost exclusively by either medieval or renaissance scholars.

While this series is devoted primarily to the publication of major studies it will contain occasional bibliographic essays and briefer articles dealing with unpublished archival or manuscript resources. The *Studies* will also make available in translation original articles by scholars who do not write in English.

Studies in Medieval and Renaissance History is not the official organ of any association or institution. Publication in the series is open to all historians whose research falls within its scope and fields of interest.

"STATUS REGIS"

by Gaines Post

University of Wisconsin

STATUS, ID EST, MAGISTRATUS; L'ETAT, C'EST MOI; AND STATUS REGIS: THE "ESTATE ROYAL" (1100-1322)[1]

IN STUDIES already completed or still under way, I have been interested in showing what *status regni* (or *reipublicae, imperii, civitatis*) meant in legal thought from the time of the great revival of Roman law to the age of Philip the Fair, Edward I, and Edward II.[2] It has become

1. I use the following abbreviations for the main sections of the *Corpus Iuris Civilis*, eds. Mommsen, Krueger, etc. (3 vols.; Berlin, 1889): *Inst.* (*Institutes*); *D.* (*Digest*); *C.* (*Code*); *Nov.* (*Novellae*). The references to the *Glossa ordinaria* of Accursius are in the Denis Godefroy edition (Lyons, 1604): to *D.,* Vols. I–III; to *C.,* Bks. 1–9, Vol. IV; to the *Tres Libri,* Bks. 10–12 of *C.,* Vol. V; to *Inst.* and *Nov.,* or *Authenticae,* Vol. V.

For the *Decretum* of Gratian and the *Decretals of Gregory IX,* I have depended on the edition by E. Friedberg, *Corpus Juris Canonici* (2 vols.; Leipzig, 1879–81). The references to the *Glos. ord.* of Johannes Teutonicus on the *Decretum* are in the Lyons, 1553, edition. But the *Glos. ord.* can be found in many editions of the sixteenth century—so also for the *Glos. ord.* of Accursius to the *C.I.C.*

A few words about *l'État, c'est moi* in the title. I had already been reflecting on it and using it, e.g., in my "*Ratio publicae utilitatis, ratio status* und 'Staatsräson' (1100–1300)," *Die Welt als Geschichte,* XXI (1961), 71 n. 54 (written in 1959), when I received in July, 1961, a reprint of an excellent article by Professor Michael J. Wilks of the University of London, "The Idea of the Church as 'Unus homo prefectus' and Its Bearing on the Medieval Theory of Sovereignty," *Miscellanea Historiae Ecclesiasticae* (Stockholm, 1960), pp. 32–49. Wilks, on the pope as the Church in theories of the late thirteenth century, says (p. 43) that this meant that the ruler "acts as the state itself: *l'État, c'est moi.*" He adds that "the term 'State' itself gradually evolved from the proposition that the pope, on behalf of the mystical personality, contains within himself . . . the complete good of the society." I will show in this study how the origin of the essence of *l'État, c'est moi* is to be found rather in the glossators of the Roman law in the twelfth century. But it is interesting that Professor Wilks and I have been thinking in similar ways about the rise of elements of the modern State in the middle ages. See below, nn. 56–70, on *status papae* and *status Ecclesiae.*

2. "The Theory of Public Law and the State in the Thirteenth Century," *Seminar* (An Annual Extraordinary Number of *The Jurist*), VI (1948), 42–59, was an introductory essay. I have also developed parts of the subject in the following: "*Plena potestas* and Consent in Medieval Assemblies," *Traditio,* I (1943), 370–83, 397–408; "The Two Laws and the Statute of York," *Speculum,* XXIX (1954), 417–32; "Two Notes on Nationalism in the Middle Ages," *Traditio,* IX (1953), 281–320; and "*Ratio*

clear, I think, that the "state" of a community was pre-eminently the
public and common welfare and safety both of the corporate body of
the State and of all the members in common. The "state" of an independent, sovereign kingdom was the subject of public law; and the
maintenance and preservation of the *status regni* was the highest duty
and the right of the king and his government. Indeed, the defense and
good ordering of the "state of the realm," of the realm itself, was in
accordance with the law of nature; for God and the natural law that
comes from God and participates in human reason approved human
society in general and the State in particular. The public law directly,
the natural law indirectly, therefore gave to the supreme magistrate
those powers of jurisdiction and coercion that were necessary for every
kind of business that pertained to maintaining the *status* or *utilitas
publica* of the kingdom—powers of commanding the army in defense
of the realm, of legislating, of interpreting and enforcing the law, of
judging and protecting the rights of subjects.

"Reason of State" itself was in fact in this period the art of reasoning about what should be done for the public "state" of the community.[3] It was the *ratio status* (or *ratio publicae utilitatis*) *regni*, the
"reason" of the public and common welfare and safety of the people
and of the *universitas* and *communitas regni*, of the *regnum* or *respublica*. Subject ultimately to the law of God and nature, but itself a
principle of the public law, it included and was the "right" reasoning
of the highest magistracy for the preservation of the *status regni*. It
was the reasoning about the just means needed ordinarily and extraor-
dinarily for maintaining law and order and preserving the peace and
safety of the State and its members. If it was the steady *ratio jurisdictionis et gubernationis*, it was also, in times of dire emergency, the

publicae utilitatis, etc.," *Welt als Gesch.*, XXI, 8–28, 71–99. A study of the theory of
the "naturalness" of the State, *ca.* 1100–1260, has been completed for publication
elsewhere.

I capitalize our word "State" in order to distinguish it from "state" as the *status*
or "state" of the State.

3. On medieval "reason of State" see my study, "*Ratio publicae utilititatis*, etc.,"
Welt als Gesch., XXI, 8–28, 71–99.

I find it amazing that W. Ullmann can still say that the "principle of *publica
utilitas* was . . . probably evolved from the *mundeburdum*, the supreme protection,
inherent in the theocratic king"; *Principles of Government and Politics in the
Middle Ages* (London, 1961), p. 133. Has he read no Roman law, not to mention
studies by Gaudemet and myself—and by many others? Of course the principle
that a ruler should "promote the public weal" (p. 133) is well-nigh ageless and
universal.

ratio necessitatis, the "reason" that was based on the already ancient maxim, "Necessitas legem non habet." In other words, the *raison d'être* of the State and its government demanded the use of reason for their welfare and safety.

So insistent were the terms *status regni, ratio status regni,* and their equivalents, that by the late thirteenth century *status* began to appear by itself. The word was about to designate the community which it had qualified, and it finally became the word we frequently use for any kind of independent political community, the State. This tendency, indeed, was strengthened by a strong emphasis on the prerogatives of the royal magistracy. Naturally the necessities of the "state" of the realm demanded a king and royal government to reason, command, judge, interpret, and act for the common and public welfare. Now the office and powers of the king (the prerogative in general) were subsumed under a variety of terms, such as *auctoritas, majestas, potestas, dignitas, honor,* and *corona. Imperium,* too, might be used, though perhaps with a slightly greater connotation of the actual powers of governing than of the more abstract nature of kingship. But quite frequently, especially from the second half of the twelfth century on, *status regis* (the king's "state" or "estate") appeared in royal documents and in legal and political thought. *Status regis* was as current in England as on the Continent. In the Statute of York, 1322, it became the *estat* of the king and his heirs, and the related *estat* of the royal household and *estat* of the crown.

What was the *status, estat,* of the king? Was it the same as the royal authority, majesty, dignity, power, honor, and crown? Or was it the private aspect of kingship, the estate of the king's "body natural," his private estate—an estate that was superior to the social status of any of his subjects, but private and personal all the same? The question needs to be answered, if an answer is possible, not only because the term has not been subjected to proper examination in the context of public law and kingship, but also because its meaning is still debated by students of the Statute of York. In Part I of this study, therefore, I propose to examine the legal ideas about the *status magistratus* and the *status regis* in order to show how the legists, canonists, and scholastic theologians began to use the word *status* for the powers of governing and even for the government itself. In Part II the results of Part I will be applied to the Statute of York in order to decide whether *lestat* of the king was public or private, and whether in England kingship was becoming the subject of public law or remained chiefly feudal, personal, and proprietary. Part III, on the Roman law and the coronation oath, is actually an appendix to Part II; but it too deals with the *status regis*.

Throughout I use the word "State" for medieval *Respublica, Imperium, Regnum,* or *Civitas,* for every community, that is, which was treated as virtually independent and as a subject of public law. After all, by the late twelfth century not only the kingdoms of England and France but some Italian communes were in fact, and frequently in legal theory, as sovereignly independent as the Empire. As for the other terms, such as *status, dignitas,* and *honor,* I do not feel that it is necessary to explain in detail what is obvious, that they each had several different meanings in the realm of private law and society. My interest here is in what they meant in the realm of public law.

I. STATUS, ID EST, MAGISTRATUS; L'ÉTAT, C'EST MOI

SINCE the State—whether as a legal or juristic person, a reality or a fiction—can do and suffer nothing except through the men who act in its name, it is sometimes defined as the government.[4] The most extreme statement of the definition is of course the famous "l'État, c'est moi," formerly attributed to Louis XIV. We know that while *le roi soleil* often acted as if he were in fact the State, he really thought of himself as the "dépositaire" of the public good, ruling with justice for its achievement.[5] Perhaps Napoleon was the first ruler to say in effect that he was the State: "La chose publique, l'État, ce fut moi."[6] Yet did he have the State in mind? "La chose publique" may have connoted the old *respublica*, which in earlier times meant the public business of government, even the constitutional order itself, almost as often as it stood for the Republic, the State. Further, as will be shown, *status* in its public meaning was used at times for *respublica* (*chose publique*), *utilitas publica*, and the powers of the magistracy—for the government itself. Thus the French emperor may have reflected the ancient and medieval idea that the *status* was in one of its usages the magistracy and the fullness of powers of the prince.

Whatever "l'État, c'est moi" meant to the first man who said it, historians assume that the idea is modern. And if it means "I am the State," it no doubt is chiefly modern. But if it means "I am the *state*," that is, "I am the final authority and therefore the real government," then we can no longer say that it is modern. Indeed, we shall find the idea in medieval sources, long before *lo stato* in Machiavelli was usually the prince or the prince's authority.[7] But again, the idea that

4. Louis L. Snyder, *The Meaning of Nationalism* (New Brunswick, N.J., 1954), p. 19, quoting Benedetto Croce and Harold Laski.

5. For a standard discussion of the statement attributed to Louis XIV see E. Lavisse, in Lavisse, *Histoire de France . . . jusqu'à la revolution* (2d ed.; Paris, 1911), VII, i, 131, 147. The best treatment, however, is by Fritz Hartung, "L'État c'est moi," *Historische Zeitschrift*, CLXIX (1949), 1–30.

6. Hartung, *HZ*, CLXIX, 17–23, 27, on Napoleon.

7. Historians of the Italian renaissance persist in starting modern ideas about the State with Machiavelli. For example, Federico Chabod, *Machiavelli and the Renaissance*, trans. David Moore (London, 1958), pp. 49, 116 f.; J. H. Hexter, "*Il principe* and *lo stato*," *Studies in the Renaissance*, IV (1957), 113–38; G. H. R.

the head of the government and his appointed officials were the essence of the public *status* could easily persuade a king that he was not only the indispensable ruler but also the essence of the territorial State which he ruled; and this may have contributed to the later absolutism implied in "L'État, c'est moi." (After all, it is not only in monarchies that the chief executive, after enjoying great prestige and authority for a number of years, can yield to the corruption of power and feel that he is the State because he alone knows what is essential to the welfare of State and people alike.)

Now, in the middle ages no prince was likely to say that he was the *status reipublicae*, the *status publicus*, or the *regimen, imperium,* or *magistratus;* nor that he was the *respublica (chose publique)*, much less the Republic, Realm, or State. Legists, canonists, and scholastic philosophers, however, sometimes came near saying it for the prince in speaking of his *status* as if it were far more than his well-being and private estate, as if, indeed, it were the fullness of public power invested in him and his magistracy or government. How could they not do so? For they studied and were inspired by Roman sources.

Status defined as the form of government or the constitution of the State occurs in Cicero and other classical Latin authors.[8] But it was Ulpian's use of the word (*D.* 1, 1, 1, 2) which chiefly inspired the legists of Bologna, who in turn influenced drafters of the public documents of princes and cities, and writers on government and politics. Ulpian defined the public law as that law which deals with the *status rei Romanae* and with those things that are necessary for this *status*, namely, with all *sacra* pertaining to religion and the cult, and with priests and magistrates—with all things that are "publicly useful."[9] Evidently, because of the emphasis on religion, the priesthood, and the magistracy (religion and priests being as essential as magistrates to

Parkinson, "Ethics and Politics in Machiavelli," *Philosophical Quarterly,* V (1955), 37–44. Chabod scorns the thought that there could be a medieval background of Machiavelli's political ideas (p. 238). Professor Hexter, however, does suggest a medieval background. Cf. my *"Ratio publicae utilitatis, etc.," Welt als Gesch.,* XXI, 8–10, 97–99.

8. For this meaning of *status* in the Latin classics one need only consult a good Latin dictionary, e.g., Lewis and Short, s.v. *status.*

9. *D.* 1, 1, 1, 2: ". . . publicum ius est quod ad statum rei Romanae spectat . . . ; sunt enim quaedam publice utilia, quaedam privatim. publicum ius in sacris, in sacerdotibus, in magistratibus consistit. . . ." For our purpose here it hardly matters that the words on public and private utility may be an interpolation of the sixth century. The glossators accepted them as Roman and not Byzantine.

the public and common welfare and the Empire), the *ius publicum* was here essentially the constitutional law.

In commenting on this passage the glossators and commentators most frequently defined the *status rei Romanae* as the public utility or welfare, which included the general common welfare of the people and the safety and peace of the whole State. It was sometimes the *respublica* itself, almost the State. For they explained that the public law dealt also with all the means needed for maintaining the *status*— "ad statum conservandum, ne pereat."[10] At any rate the public law pertained *inter alia* to the magistracy and its powers, for the prince and his subordinates were indispensable for interpreting and enforcing law and justice and defending the *status reipublicae*. As remarked above, "reason of State" was in part the "reason" or art of government for the end of preserving the common welfare and the State.

The early legists, in fact, began to identify this *status* with the *magistratus*. One glossator of the twelfth century equated the *ius publicum* itself with the magistrates: the public law is "the consuls or others."[11] Perhaps in this there is a suggestion of the modern Italian *diritto pubblico,* that is, the constitution and constitutional law of a State. But according to another gloss the *magistratus* simply has the "public right" (*ius publicum*) to command or execute court decisions.[12] More important are two or three early glosses which directly interpret Ulpian's *status rei Romanae* as the magistracy or public authority.

10. Accursius in the *Glos. ord.* to *D.* 1, 1, 1, 2, ad v. *Publicum ius.* Azo had already, ad v. *statum,* said: "Id est, existentiam, ne pereat. *Az.*"; gloss in the Paris, Bibliothèque Nationale, MS lat. 4451, fol. 9; and probably he was inspired by Hugolinus, ad v. *statum:* ". . . ne pereat"; Paris, BN, MS lat. 4461, to *D.* 1, 1, 1, 2. Important, too, is a fuller statement made by Accursius on the same words of Ulpian in *Inst.* 1, 1, 4, ad vv. *Publicum ius est quod ad statum rei Romanae spectat*: "Scilicet, principaliter, nam et singulorum est utilitas rempublicam salvam conservari. *Accursius.*" This indicates that he thinks of the *status* as not only the public welfare of the Republic, but as practically the same thing as the Republic. In the whole context of the *Glos. ord.,* no doubt, *status* as the object of public law does not yet mean the State; but it is clear that the early glossators and Accursius were approaching the idea of *status* as something over and beyond the welfare of the community and its members; it is almost an abstract or juridical person in itself.

11. To *D.* 4, 2, 23 Non est verosimile, ad vv. *ius publicum invocare:* "Id est, consules vel alios"; MS Vat. lat. 2511, fol. 33.

12. To *D.* 9, 2, 37 Liber homo, ad vv. *si homo ius imperandi habuit*: "Scilicet, publicum, ut magistratus in executiones"; MS Vat. lat. 2511, fol. 78ᵛ. The passage in *D.* states that if a free man inflicts a physical injury on another as a result of a command by one who has the *ius imperandi,* he is not guilty of a crime.

One glossator says that the *status* is, as it were, the *magistratus* in the city. In another version of this opinion the words, "Id est, ad similitudinem," indicate that the *status* has only a similitude, as it were, to the magistracy.[13]

In one manuscript a gloss of the twelfth century adds words which are difficult to interpret, for it is not clear whether they apply to *ius publicum* and *ad statum* or to the succeeding clause attributed to Ulpian, *D*. 1, 1, 1, 2, "privatum ius quod ad singulorum utilitatem." The gloss reads: "Nam hoc est ius est hoc confirmat et retinet civitatem."[14] The difficulty of interpretation is threefold. First, there is no doubt a needless repetition of *hoc* and *est*; and therefore I make the conjecture that the reading should be "Nam hoc ius confirmat et retinet civitatem." Second, the words are interlinear in the line immediately following "Id est, ad similitudinem, etc.," and thus may very well refer to the definition of *ius publicum* as that law which pertains to the *status rei Romanae*. Third, if the gloss is intended to explain *privatum ius*, which pertains to the utility of individuals, it may instead refer not only to private law but also to Ulpian's opinion, that private law derives from precepts from the natural law, the *ius genium*, and the civil law.[15]

What, then, is the meaning? Literally, the author of the gloss says that "this law establishes and preserves the city [State]." Perhaps he meant that it was the public law that maintained the State in dealing with the *status*, that is, the public welfare and the magistracy—but especially the magistracy, since without a government there could be neither State nor its public welfare. On the other hand, perhaps he meant that the private law, although it directly pertained to the private welfare of individuals, indirectly pertained to the public authority, and is as important as the public law for the strength and the survival of the community. Perhaps he had vaguely in mind the

13. MS Vat. lat. 2511, fol. 3, to *D*. 1, 1, 1, 2, ad v. *statum:* "Veluti magistratus in civitate"; and in the Paris, BN, MS lat., 4458-A, fol. 1ᵛ, ad v. *statum:* "Id est, ad similitudinem veluti magistratus in civitate." Both glosses are interlinear and clearly to *statum* in Ulpian's definition, "publicum ius est quod ad statum rei Romanae spectat." They stand in sets of glosses of the twelfth century on the *Dig. Vetus*.

14. Paris, BN, MS lat. 4458-A, fol. 1ᵛ. The gloss is interlinear, and while its position is just above the words of Ulpian, "Privatum quod ad singulorum utilitatem," it could easily be a continuation of the gloss to *statum* in the preceding line—the gloss quoted above, n. 13.

15. *D*. 1, 1, 1, 2: "privatum ius tripertitum est: collectum etenim est ex naturalibus praeceptis aut gentium aut civilibus."

general thought expressed by the glossators, that the public law primarily treated the things that were for the public welfare, but secondarily interested individuals, both in maintaining the general public utility and the security of all in peace, and in regulating the government needed to interpret the private law in courts. The private law, in turn, primarily pertained to private rights and the private welfare of the individual members of the community; but secondarily it was of public interest to the community that private rights be used justly; and of course it interested the government to enforce the private law, and to make new private laws for new situations. "Private law," said Azo and others, "is public by authority."[16] On the whole, however, I conclude that the words "hoc ius confirmat et retinet civitatem" seem logically to refer to *ius publicum* and *status rei Romanae*. That is, the public law in dealing with the magistracy and religion and priesthood deals with the maintenance of the *status* of the Republic. But above all it regulates the *status*; hence *magistratus* and *status* are in part equivalent terms.

In a sense, therefore, already in the twelfth century the idea had appeared that the public welfare, the *status*, of the Republic or city, of the State, was in part the public authority, the magistracy or government. But at the same time *status* in its public meaning was being associated with the idea of the powers of the head of the State and his magistracy. One glossator made *status* and *potentia* (that is, the *status* or *potentia rei Romanae*) mean the same thing; and he defined the *res Romana* as *dicio*, that is, sovereignty, rule, power, and the like. In other words, he was trying to explain Ulpian's *status rei Romanae* as the public power of the Roman government.[17] This was a stronger

16. See the *Glos. ord.* of Accursius to *D.* 1, 1, 1, 2. Azo says, ad v. *privatum ius:* "utilitate, sed pub[licum] autoritate"; in the Paris, BN, MS lat. 4451, fol. 9. Thus the private law is itself public because its interpretation and enforcement, for the common welfare of the people in the State, depends on the supreme public authority; and of course new laws in the realm of private law are made and promulgated by the public authority. This theory was repeated in detail by the legists and canonists of the thirteenth century.

17. British Museum, MS Royal II C. III, fol. 1, to *D.* 1, 1, 1, 2, ad v. *statum:* "Id est, potencia"; and ad v. *rei romane:* "Id est, dicionis." These glosses are interlinear, and clearly belong to the words indicated. In effect, therefore, the glossator was saying: "Id est, ad potenciam dicionis," or "Id est, ad potenciam dicionis reipublicae," or even "Id est, ad potenciam magistratus," since sometimes *respublica* and government were equivalent in our period.

This manuscript of the *Dig. Vetus* is extremely interesting, the early glosses in it differing remarkably from those in other manuscripts that I have consulted in the

way of saying that the "state of the Republic" was the magistracy and its power to preserve it—"lest it perish," said Hugolinus, Azo, and Accursius.[18] The public law was the law of the constitutional order and the public authority, and it demanded obedience to them.[19]

The gloss defining *status* as *potentia* stands in a late twelfth- or early thirteenth-century manuscript of the *Dig. Vetus* preserved in the British Museum, and the glosses (of the twelfth century) in this manuscript are frequently different from those I have noted in other manuscripts containing the *Dig. Vetus*. This does not mean that there is any evidence that the author of the gloss in question was an Englishman or an Anglo-Norman of the time of Henry II. Nevertheless it is interesting that in his *Dialogus de Scaccario (ca.* 1177), Richard Fitzneale, treasurer of the Exchequer under Henry II, and educated in some elements of Roman law, indicates a close relationship between the king's *status* and *potestas*—more will be said about this in Part II, on the *status regis*.[20] Perhaps this usage was more common than might be supposed. At least it is hinted in a document of Lothair III: since, the emperor said, monasteries strengthen the *potencia regalis*, privileges for them profit both the *status regni* and the king's eternal reward; they are "pro nostro et totius imperii statu."[21] And in 1212–1213, Frederick II declared that his public *status* was the powers of office which he wished to exercise for the *bonus status*, peace, and tranquility of the Empire.[22]

In the thirteenth century, as in the twelfth, the *status* of the State was most frequently defined as the public welfare, *utilitas publica*—sometimes as the common welfare and common good, although there was a technical, legal distinction between the public and the common utility.[23] But one also finds, as in the preceding period, the definition of *status* as the magistracy and constitutional order or accepted system of government. Thus Jacques de Révigny, a great French jurist of the

---

Bibliothèque Nationale, Paris, in the Vatican, and elsewhere. It demands thorough study—Savigny was not acquainted with it.

18. Above, n. 10.

19. Gloss to *D.* 1, 1, 1, 2, ad v. *magistratibus*: "obediendis"; in Paris, BN, MS lat. 4451, fol. 9.

20. W. Stubbs, *Select Charters* (9th ed.; Oxford, 1921), p. 200; see below, Part II, n. 9. Henceforth Stubbs will be referred to as *SC*.

21. *MGH, Dipl. Reg. et Imp. Ger.,* VIII, 25, No. 19; p. 58, No. 35; see below, Part II, nn. 25–27.

22. *MGH, Legum S. IV, Const.,* II, 54–56, Nos. 43–45.

23. See below, Part II, n. 24, for a brief explanation.

second half of the century, made the *status reipublicae* and the *regimen imperii* equivalent. Both were subjects of the public law, which included laws on churches, priests, and judges—judges specifically, since laws would be to no purpose unless there were magistrates to interpret and enforce them. Further, the public law indirectly included private law; for that law which pertained to private utility pertained to the public *imperium,* for the Roman law says that the *imperium* will prosper if it has wealthy subjects.[24] Here is a kind of confusion of *status,* government, and Empire and Republic.

Jacques de Révigny, again, stated almost the same thing in a farfetched definition of *majestas,* in a gloss on *D.* 48, 4 Ad legem Iuliam maiestatis, 1 (Ulpian on the crime of treason against the Roman people, Republic, and the magistrates). *Majestas,* he says, is, as it were, the *maior status,* whence the *magistratus* can be so called because they dwell in a greater and higher place.[25] Thus the *maior status,* the majesty of the prince, is in effect the *magistratus* of the head of the State.

He was able even to associate the crown with the common fatherland of the kingdom of France. King Philip Augustus in 1197 had already spoken of the defense of the *caput* and of the *corona regni.* A French legist, Jean de Blanot, had connected the defense of the crown of France with the good of the *patria* and the public good or public utility of the kingdom.[26] Jacques de Révigny, obviously having in mind the problem treated by Jean, assumed that the king of France was emperor in his own realm, and placed the imperial prerogative in

24. *Commentary* or *Lectura* on *Inst.,* in Paris, BN, MS lat. 14350, fol. 144ᵛ–145, to *Inst.* 1, 1, 4, ad vv. publicum ius est, quod ad statum rei Romanae spectat: "id est, ad statum rei publice. Unde ius quod pertinet ad regimen imperii ius publicum dicitur . . . Unde iura que loquuntur de ecclesiis, de sacerdotibus, de iudicibus pertinent ad ius publicum . . . Item iudices, quia frustra essent iura nisi essent magistratus qui iura redderent. . . ." The public law indirectly includes private law: "Sed videtur quod ius quod pertinet ad utilitatem privatam sit publicum, quia pertinet ad imperium, et tale est publicum. Dicit lex habundabit imperium, si locupletes habeat subiectos . . ." Jacques repeats, on the Empire and rich subjects, what had frequently been said by earlier legists.

25. Gloss to *D.* 48, 4, 1: "Maiestas dicitur quasi maior status; inde et magistratus dici possunt, quia in maiori loco at altiori morantur . . . Iac. R." It is in the Vatican, MS Pal. lat. 753, fol. 151; this manuscript contains the *Dig. Novum* and many glosses by legists after the time of Accursius and the *Glos. ord.*

26. See my "Two Notes on Nationalism," *Traditio,* IX, 289; on Philip Augustus, see J. R. Strayer, "Defense of the Realm and Royal Power in France," in *Studi in onore di Gino Luzzato* (Milan, 1949), p. 292; also Ernst Kantorowicz, *The King's Two Bodies* (Princeton, 1957), p. 340.

the crown; and he judged that like Rome and the Empire the kingdom of France was the *patria communis,* the independent common fatherland, of all subjects of the king. Therefore, in case of simultaneous, aggressive attacks, one on the local *patria* of Burgundy and the other on the common *patria* of France, should a vassal of the duke of Burgundy respond to the summons of the duke or to that of the king to fight the enemy? Jacques is in doubt and is inclined to favor the local *patria.* But significantly he furnishes these strong arguments, made by certain legists ("doctores legum"), for the king, crown, and the *patria communis:* the *tuitio reipublicae,* that is, of France and the crown, is a public utility that is to be preferred to the lower utility of a province; and the "corona regni est communis patria, quia caput." Because it is the head, the crown of the realm is the common fatherland.[27] It is also the *respublica,* which no doubt is the royal government as well as the kingdom.

Bracton, a contemporary of Jean de Blanot and Jacques de Révigny, associated with the crown all the king's rights of jurisdiction and

27. See my "Two Notes on Nationalism," *Traditio,* IX, 290 f. This comment is in the Paris, BN, MS lat. 14350, fols. 185–185ᵛ, to *Inst.* 4, 6, 13: "Sed pone Carses ingrediuntur Burgundiam . . . Ipsi [doctores legum] dicunt contrarium [to the first duty of the vassal to fight for the local *patria*] . . . quia Roma est communis patria, sic corona regni est communis patria, quia caput. . . ." He almost implies that Paris, seat of the royal government, is both crown and common fatherland.

Perhaps Jacques de Règivny was hesitant about choosing between the defense of the local *patria* and the defense of the *patria communis* because in the Roman law the necessity (or defense) of a province might be so urgent that the provincials should at once furnish supplies to the army defending it. In such a case it was presumed that the main duty fell on the people of the region immediately in danger, and not directly on the Empire as a whole or the *patria communis.* The provincial governor himself was duty-bound to act speedily and wage a defensive war without waiting for the approval of the emperor. In this situation of dire, urgent, immediate danger or necessity, then, the local *patria* demanded loyalty first to itself rather than to the common *patria.* Obviously, however, in the long run, since the danger to a province also threatened the Empire as a whole, local loyalty or patriotism was ultimately subordinate to the emperor and the Empire. In other words, local patriotism came first only momentarily, in cases of emergency and necessity; the interests of the Empire and the common fatherland were thus served. There was in theory no sacrifice of the superior patriotic loyalty to the State.

Perhaps, however, Jacques de Révigny did not fully accept this. But he does refer to legists who did, who understand how, when enemies threatened a local and the common *patria* at the same time, defense of the common *patria* came first, for only thus was the safety of the province or local *patria* assured. In such a case the common *patria* of the State as a whole demanded a loyalty that superseded local loyalties.

power in the realm, rights that pertained to the government and the defense of the *patria*. For, like Johannes de Deo, a distinguished canonist, who had (*ca.* 1245) explained that all things belonged to the prince in the sense that *omnia* are "in manu eius quo ad tuitionem et defensionem," Bracton held that the king in his *iurisdictio, dignitas,* and *potestas* possessed "omnia iura in manu sua quae ad coronam et laicalem pertinent potestatem et materialem gladium qui pertinet ad regni gubernaculum"; that, in brief, all businesses relating to justice and peace in the realm belonged to no one but the *corona* and *dignitas regia*. His concept of the crown was thus in the tradition of the equation of the royal *dignitas, status, potestas,* and *corona.*[28] French legists were going further: the crown stood for more than the king's public authority; it was not only the symbol of it, it *was* the *patria communis* of the realm; and thus also the king, by way of the concept in *corona-caput regni,* was, as it were, the State. The *pater patriae* was becoming confused with the *patria*. But we must not exaggerate. No doubt Jacques de Révigny was merely emphasizing the majesty of the king's power over the realm. Nevertheless the tendency that became more manifest in the jurists of the late thirteenth and the fourteenth centuries was already appearing in France. If the king and crown existed for the *status regni,* they were, as the head, the common fatherland of the realm.

In England itself, in the late thirteenth century, one finds a reflec-

28. It is interesting that before Bracton wrote his treatise Johannes de Deo connected the *omnia in manu principis* with the Roman law and the glossators (that all things belong to the prince not as his property but as subject to his *iurisdictio, protectio,* and *gubernatio*; see below, nn. 81 f.); and like Bracton he also reflected the early medieval tradition in Sacramentaries and in a Frankish coronation *ordo*—on this Kantorowicz, *King's Two Bodies,* p. 153 n. 192. Since the passage from Johannes de Deo is apparently unknown, I now give it from his *Libellus dispensationum,* Rome, MS Casanatense, 108, fol. 297, c. 2: "*De dispensatione principum vel regum qui non habent maiorem super se, nisi papam loco dei.* Et licet omnia sunt principis, quia per principes et reges deus distribuit humano generi omnia, ut testatur Aug. viii. di. quo iure [St. Augustine, quoted in the *Decretum,* Dist. 8, c. 2]; C. de quadrien. prescrip. bene a Zenone [*C.* 7, 37, 3] . . . ; tamen sic est intelligendum, scilicet, quod sint omnia in manu eius quo ad tuitionem et defensionem. . . ."

See Bracton, *De legibus,* ed. Woodbine, pp. ii, 160; and on Bracton, Kantorowicz, *op. cit.,* pp. 143–64. (Of course one recalls C. H. McIlwain's famous treatment of the meaning of Bracton's *iurisdictio* and *gubernaculum*; but there is no need of discussing the distinction here.) The crown is not the realm, but it includes the royal power necessary for the "defensio regni et patriae" (Woodbine, II, 28, 32). On the crown and the coronation oath see below, Part II, nn. 12, 25–33, 67–94, and Part III.

tion of the tendency to identify the royal magistracy with the realm. In the case of the dispute between John Baliol and Robert Bruce over the succession to the kingdom of Scotland, the argument was made in court that the "right of a realm is principally royal dignity and government of people."[29] At the same time, and in the following century, Neapolitan and Bolognese jurists were being more explicit. Andrew of Isernia held that the king and the *respublica regni* were identical: the king is in the kingdom and the *respublica* is in him as in the head.[30] The glossators and others had a century earlier noted that the prince was not only the *caput regni* but was also a *corpus* (the "body politic" of the sixteenth century?) which included the lesser magistrates and Senate as members.[31] The prince was both the head of the State and the head of the governing body of the State. It is therefore possible that Andrew of Isernia thought that the king was the *respublica* (*chose publique*) in the sense of the government rather than the Republic.

29. Barnaby C. Keeney, "The Medieval Idea of the State: "The Great Cause," *Univ. of Toronto Law Journal*, VIII (1949), 62 f., 63 n. 42, from the *Annales regni Scotiae*: "Kar dreit de reaume principaument est reale dignité e government de pople." I quoted above Keeney's translation. For crown as *regnum*, see H. G. Richardson, "The English Coronation Oath," *Speculum*, XXIV (1949), 50.

30. Quoted by E. Kantorowicz, "Mysteries of State: An Absolutist Concept and Its Late Medieval Origins," *Harvard Theological Review*, XLVIII (1955), 80; also below, n. 69.

31. *Summa Codicis* (Venice, 1584), p. 40, to *C.* 1, 26: "Dictum est supra de principe, qui caput est omnium magistratuum: nunc audiamus de aliis magistratibus qui sunt principis tanquam capitis membra. . . ." This kind of thought was expressed by other legists and also by John of Salisbury; Kantorowicz, *King's Two Bodies*, pp. 207, 208 n. 42. Thus the *princeps* was not only the *caput* of the State; he was a *corpus*, a corporation sole, so to speak, including the lesser magistracy and the Senators, who were all a *pars corporis principis*—see *C.* 9, 8, 5, and *C.* 12, 1, 5, and the *Glos. ord.* to these imperial laws.

Late twelfth-century glossators had already noticed this; so Placentinus (in his *Lectura* or *Com.*, published as Azo's to the *Tres Libri*, in the edition Paris, 1577), to *C.* 12, 1, 5: the *senatores* are "magna pars corporis imperii" (*imperium* here meaning no doubt the imperial government or powers); Pillius (Paris, BN, MS lat. 4429, fol. 170ᵛ), to *C.* 12, 1, 5, ad v. *curiam nostram*: "Ergo nec senatores, qui sunt magna pars corporis . . . p."; and Johannes Bassianus in his *Summa* on the *Authenticae* (Paris, BN, MS lat., 4542, fol. 185ᵛ): "*De senatoribus* . . . Ideo de officiis singulorum magistratuum tracta[tu]rus, premittit de senatoribus tanquam maioribus, qui pars corporis principis esse dicuntur. . . ."

It was not difficult, therefore, for legists to think in terms of the *curia regis* and king as a "body politic" and identify the corporate body of king and government with the State. See below, nn. 68 and 72, on the pope as a corporate body and even the Church.

This seems the more likely because he also said that where the prince is, there is the whole law.[32]

Lucas de Penna, too, avoided the danger of calling the king the State. In one place he does say that "the prince is the head of the realm, and the realm the body of the Prince";[33] in another, that the prince is in the *respublica* and the *respublica* is in the prince.[34] But even when he says that the prince is the *respublica,* and the *respublica* is in him, he probably means only that the king is the *chose publique,* the "body politic," the government; for the king is not the *utilitas publica,* rather his *honor* (office) exists for the public welfare.[35] Nor can we attribute the identification of the State with the prince to the great jurists of Bologna and northern Italy. If Alberico da Rosciate said that in obeying the *patria* one obeyed the magistrates who preside over the *regimen patriae,* this is not quite the same thing as saying that the *patria* is the government.[36] Bartolus reverted to the old literal way of defining the *status* of the Roman Republic as the *magistratus—* which, however, he calls the *regimen.*[37] And Baldus emphasized the familiar idea that the prince represents the people; and the prince is the *imperium* and the *fiscus,* because only in him does the Empire live, will, and act.[38] Again the prince is the government rather than the State.

Meanwhile, it is important to note, the scholastic theologians, partly inspired by Aristotle's *Politics* but partly continuing the legal tradition, identified *status* and *magistratus* perhaps as frequently as the legists did. Thomas Aquinas is above all important. To understand his treatment of *status* it is well first to recall his doctrine of "reason of State."

32. Francesco Calasso, *Gli ordinamenti giuridici del rinascimento medioevale* (2d ed.; Milan, 1949 and 1953), p. 268, and nn. 1 and 2.

33. Quoted by Kantorowicz, *King's Two Bodies,* p. 216 n. 66.

34. *Op. cit.,* p. 214 n. 60.

35. *Com.* on the *Tres Libri* (Lyons, 1697), to *C.* 11, 71, 5 (p. 622, c. 1, No. XXIIII): when the king is acting for the public utility, his apparent harshness must be endured "propter honorem principis, qui est res publica, et res publica est in eo." Cf. Kantorowicz, *King's Two Bodies,* pp. 215 f.; also Walter Ullmann, *The Medieval Idea of Law as Represented by Lucas de Penna* (London, 1946), p. 170.

36. *Com.* on the *Dig. Vetus* (Lyons, 1541), I, 12, No. 18, to *D.* 1, 1, 2 (Pomponius, on obedience to parents and the *patria*): ". . . dicit ergo hic parendum patrie: idest magistratibus qui presunt regimine patrie. . . .'

37. Bartolus, to *Inst.,* 1, 1, 4.

38. Otto Gierke, *Political Theories of the Middle Age,* trans. F. W. Maitland (Cambridge, 1900), p. 163 n. 216, quoting Baldus to *C.* 10, 1; also *Glos. ord.* to *D.* 49, 14, 3, 10: Caesar "pro fisco accipitur: cuius cesaris omnia sunt."

His *raison d'état* was the "reason" of the natural end of the city in the common good of the citizens and in its own welfare and safety; and it was the "right reason" used by the government for the attainment of the *ratio civitatis*.[39] So far as I know he did not literally speak of the "reason of the public welfare" as the lawyers did (*ratio publicae utilitatis*), nor of the equivalent "reason" of the *status civitatis, regni, respublica*—but his *ratio civitatis* is close to the same meaning. Nor did he often distinguish literally between the *status regis* or *principis* and the *status regni*. Once or twice, however, he treated the government as the *respublica*. That is, the public business of ruling the State is the government. For the whole *impositio ordinis* is in him who rules the city, and this is the *respublica* itself, the *ordinatio civitatis*.[40] But in one instance, in the Latin text of the *Politics*, the *communitas* itself is the *politia*, or form of government;[41] and therefore the citizen should have the virtue proper for participating in the *politia*. In general however, Thomas subordinates citizens and government alike to the community, since the necessity common to all is the *salus communitatis*. Yet at the same time the community, "consists in the order of the *politia*," and every good citizen works for the "conservatio politiae."[42] There is a certain assumption that the community, good government, and *respublica* are, for practical purposes, public aspects of the same thing, which we call the State. Roughly, therefore, Thomas's thought, although largely here in Aristotelian terms, is close to that expressed in the *status reipublicae* and *status regis et regni* of the lawyers and royal documents. Once at least, indeed, he advocates extraordinary taxation, in case of the necessity of defense against an enemy, either for the common utility, or "pro honesto statu principis conservando."[43]

39. See my study, "Ratio publicae utilitatis, etc.," *Welt als Gesch.*, XXI, 86 f.

40. *Com.* or *Expositio* on the *Politics*, ed. P. Fr. R. M. Spiazzi (Rome, 1951), p. 136 (III lectio 5, No. 385): "Et dicit [Arist.] quod respublica nihil est aliud quam ordinatio civitatis quantum ad omnes principatus qui sunt in civitate, sed praecipue quantum ad maximum principatum, qui dominatur aliis principatibus. Et hoc ideo, quia impositio ordinis in civitate, tota consistit in eo qui dominatur civitati; et talis impositio ordinis est ipsa respublica." See Thomas Gilby, *Between Community and Society* (London, 1953), p. 276 n. 1, where the first part of this passage is quoted. In another place Thomas says that *respublica* "est nomen commune omnibus politiis" ed. Spiazzi, p. 139, III lect. 6, No. 393.

41. Spiazzi, ed., p. 127, Arist. (Bekker 1276b 16 f.), No. 233: the need of individual citizens is the "salus communitatis," but the *communitas* "est politia."

42. *Ibid.*, p. 129, No. 366.

43. *De regimine Judaeorum*; in A. P. d'Entrèves, *San Tommaso d'Aquino, Scritti Politici* (Bologna, 1946), p. 47.

The *status communitatis* and the public *status principis* are closely related.

When he uses the word *status* in its public sense, only rarely is it the *status* of the State or city. If he does say once that a king is useful to the city in using his power so as to "conserve the state of the city" (*statum civitatis*), and thus may recall the words of the glossators, that the public law deals with the maintenance of the "state of the republic lest it perish," [44] normally he prefers to say "the good" and the "safety" (*salus*) of the city. Usually, therefore, the public *status* is not the common good or public welfare; it is the government itself, or the kind of *politia* in a State. It is the public magistracy of prince, aristocracy, or people necessary for achieving the end of the city. Examples of this usage are numerous. In one case the "*totus status civitatis*" might be altered by a change made by a new law; in the context it seems that here *status* means *politia*, although Thomas is close to making the *status civitatis* equivalent to the common good of the State.[45] Clearly, however, the *status* is the form of government in these meanings: the *status plebeius*, when the whole multitude of the people wishes to rule;[46] the good *status popularis*, the kind of mixed polity which Solon established in his *patria* in place of the *status paucorum* (oligarchy);[47] the *regius status* or *regia potestas*, the good kind of monarchy that governs for the common utility;[48] the *status optimatum*, or *politia*, of

44. To *D.* 1, 1, 1, 2, Ulpian, "publicum ius est quod ad statum rei Romanae spectat"; see above, nn. 10, 18. Thomas Aquinas says (*Com. on Politics*, ed. Spiazzi, p. 104, No. 316): "quia rex est utilis civitati, ut sua potestate efficaciter *conservet statum civitatis*."

45. *Com. on Politics*, ed. Spiazzi, p. 94, II lect. 12, No. 289: "Habebit enim transmutationem politiarum. Una enim lege transmutata, quandoque totus status civitatis mutatur." Such a statute, permitting innovations, might even lead to the annulment of good earlier laws (*patrias leges*). This would mean the dissolution of *leges* and of the whole *politia* "sub specie communis boni." In other words, specious reason of State cannot justify new laws that nullify good law and fundamentally change the constitutional order.

46. *Com.*, p. 80, II lect. 7, No. 242; also Nos. 246–49. Here the *status plebeius* is a bad kind, for plebeians are the lowest of the people, without virtues.

47. *Com.*, p. 115, II lect. 17, No. 342; also p. 122, III lect. 1, No. 350: "qui est civis in statu populari secundum quem populus principatur" is not a *civis* "in statu paucorum" (the oligarchy); p. 139, lect. 6, No. 393: the rule of the multitude when it is for the common utility "vocatur respublica, quod est nomen commune omnibus politiis."

48. *Com.*, p. 139, III lect. 6, No. 393: the *principatus* of one is called "regia potestas . . . si intendat communem utilitatem"; Peter of Auvergne, in his continuation of Aquinas's *Com.*, says (p. 184, III lect. 16, No. 524): "regius status est cui

the few when they "principantur propter bonum commune."[49] Finally, Thomas speaks of the *status politici gubernatio*. Perhaps in this instance, since he is referring to Aristotle and Plato on the Spartan military virtues, and remarks that the Spartans were not apt in those things "which pertain to the government of the political state," he means the government or "principate" in a good *politia*; hence *status politicus* may be translated "constitutional state."[50]

Ernst Kantorowicz is right, therefore, in saying that Thomas Aquinas "uses *status* in a descriptive fashion without any connotation of abstractness."[51] In this usage, apart from the word *politia*, Thomas carried on the tradition of the legists. For the State itself he preferred such terms as *communitas, civitas,* and *regnum*—sometimes *respublica* in the sense of Republic rather than the best kind of government.[52]

Some other scholastic theologians and philosophers accepted *status* in the same sense. Kantorowicz notes that William of Auvergne equated *status* and *status publicus* with the form of government.[53] Georges de Lagarde has found another example in Peter of Auriole, who stresses the necessity of the prince for the good of the community. But subjects should obey the law even more than the prince and magistrates. For since, as Aristotle says, as few things as possible should be entrusted to the prince, because men are prone to evil, "in omni statu pauciora sunt committenda arbitrio judicis et omnia deberent committi legi."[54] Tempting as it is to exclaim that already in the late thirteenth century the word *status* meant the State, probably Peter's words should be translated, "in every kind of government." Again the *status* is the magistracy. In particular it is the order that cannot exist except in the authority of the head, the *dux,* for the *dux* is a greater good than that of the city and its order, which is the discipline that

---

subiicitur multitudo quae nata est subiici secundum inclinationem naturalem alicui superexcellenti in virtute ad principatum politicum vel regalem."

49. *Com.,* p. 139, III lect. 6, No. 393.

50. *Com.,* p. 195, II lect. 14, No. 319: "Et ideo, quia bene se habebant in his, quae pertinent ad bellum, male autem in his quae pertinent ad status politici gubernationem." But the last words together seem to be equivalent to the *principatus* or government, for Thomas says that when the Spartans finally had a principate, many dangers threatened, since they did not know how to live in peace.

51. *King's Two Bodies,* p. 271 n. 235.

52. *De regimine principum* I, 4 (d'Entrèves, p. 12), and I, 15 (d'Entrèves, p. 40).

53. *King's Two Bodies,* p. 271 n. 235.

54. Lagarde, *Naissance de l'esprit laïque,* II. *Secteur social de la scholastique* (2d ed.; Paris and Louvain, 1959), p. 299 n. 106.

unites the city to its head. The unity of the community is in the unity of command. Nonetheless, the "reason of government" of this head is subordinate to the "right reason" of justice and the reason of the good of the city and its parts.[55]

The canonists naturally accepted much of the language of the Roman law and the legists. But if on this point, with respect to the papal government and the *status Ecclesiae,* they do not talk in the same way, a near equivalent appears in decretists and decretalists from the late twelfth century on. The author, perhaps French, of the *Summa* "Antiquitate et tempore" on the *Decretum* of Gratian, had Ulpian's definition of public law in mind when he said that the *ius publicum* pertains to the *respublica.* What is called *publicum* is derived not from the *populus* but from the *respublica,* and the public law is concerned with the prerogative of the emperor, priests, and others whose function is to protect the *respublica* and provide for it in *sacra,* priests, and magistrates.[56] He seems, therefore, to equate *respublica* both with the *status rei Romanae* of Ulpian (that is, the *status* or public welfare is the *respublica*) and with the magistracy. The magistracy is not quite, but almost, the *status reipublicae.* It is interesting, moreover, that this decretist hints at the thought that the public law was the magistracy. Another decretist stated it better (late twelfth century): since the public law is for the public utility (again Ulpian's *status*), whoever injures magistrates or other public persons is said to injure the *ius publicum.*[57] The famous Huguccio had said much the same thing, adding that sacred things (altars, *vasa,* vestments, etc.), magistrates, and priests pertain to all (in State and Church), and that by the public law these three subjects of it enjoy immunity and reverence. Further, it is a violation of the public law to damage or injure any *sacra,* priests, or

55. *Ibid.,* pp. 284 n. 74, 296–99.
56. Vatican, MS Pal. lat. 678, fol. 37, c. 2 (to Dist. 1, c. 11): "Sed ius publicum dicitur quod pretinet (ad) rempublicam; et sic non a populo sed a re publica dicitur publicum. Hoc autem est, quod est de prerogativa imperatoris et sacerdotum et aliorum, quorum precipue est tueri enim rempublicam et ei providere in sacris . . . et sacerdotibus . . . et magistratibus." Further, "magistri dicuntur, quibus precipua cura incumbit, et qui maiorem diligentiam et sollicitudinem debent rebus quibus presunt." On this *Summa* see Stephan Kuttner, *Repertorium der Kanonistik* (Vatican City, 1937), p. 178 f.
57. Vat., MS Reg. lat. 1061, fol. 1–1ᵛ: "est publicum quoque ad puplicam respiciat utilitatem. Unde si quod [read quis] ledat magistratus vel alias puplicas personas, dicitur ledere ius puplicum." On the *Summa Reginensis* see Kuttner, *Repertorium,* pp. 160–66.

magistrates, or to prevent, by any means, appeals to pope, king, or judge. For the public law protects both the public utility or *status rei Romanae* and all men or things that exist for the public welfare.[58] Still another decretist came even closer to *status-magistratus*. The public law, he says, pertains to the *status*, that is, the *dignitas* of the Roman *res(publica)*. Since he says elsewhere that the *dignitas* of the apostolic See is in part the papal authority in dispensing and legislating, and is one of the means of exalting the *majestas* of the Roman Church, he implies that the public *status* of the whole Church is practically the same as the papal government.[59]

No doubt Henry of Susa (Hostiensis) was reflecting this tradition when, in his *Lectura* or *Commentary* on the *Decretals* of Gregory IX, discussing the renunciation of his right as a cardinal to vote in a conclave of 1270 (in the long process of electing a pope in 1268–1271), he debated the legality of such a renunciation. The *ius eligendi papam* is a divine and public law, he says, public because it pertains "ad statum rei Romanae," (as in *D.* 1, 1, 1, 2) for the public law consists in *sacra*, magistrates, and priests. But insofar as the papacy is the highest (public office), the *ius eligendi* is "summe publicum." Since the public law cannot be changed by private agreements (as in *D.* 2, 14, 38), since renunciations must be approved by a superior, and since the *ius eligendi* belongs to the cardinalate, a cardinal cannot renounce his

---

58. *Summa*, to Dist. 1, c. 11: ". . . Est publicum quod ad publicam principaliter respicit utilitatem, vel ad statum rei romane: et consistit in sacris, etc. . . . Unde si quis ledat sacra vel sacerdotes vel magistratus, vel alias publicas personas, dicitur ledere ius publicum . . . ; nam sacra, sacerdotia et magistratus ad omnes pertinent. . . . Ius ergo quo ista tria gaudent immunitate et reverencia dicitur publicum. Et contra hoc ius facit quicumque aliquod istorum trium ledit; contra hoc ius facit quicumque appellantem ad papam vel iudicem vel regem quoquo modo impedierit, scilicet, vel verberando vel necando vel alio modo." There are many manuscripts of the *Summa* of Huguccio; here I have taken the text from the Paris, BN, MS lat. 3892, fol. 3ᵛ.

Related to this thought is a passage from the *Summa Parisiensis*, ca. 1160, ed. Terence P. McLaughlin (Toronto, 1952), p. 3: "*Jus publicum:* i.e. personarum publicae utilitatis curam habentium."

59. *Summa* (wrongly attributed to Rufinus in the ed. by J. F. v. Schulte [Giessen, 1892]), p. 9, to Dist 1, c. 11: "Ius publicum est, quod ad statum, i.e., dignitatem rei romanae principaliter spectat . . ."; and p. 375, to Causa 25: "Duo sunt maxime, in quibus romanae ecclesiae maiestas inaltatur [*exaltatur* in the manuscript]: potestas ligandi et solvendi, et ecclesias dispensandi, nunc autem subiungit, quantam sedes apostolica dignitatem habeat ecclesias dispensandi, ostendens, quomodo sua auctoritate quas voluerit potest ecclesias specialibus privilegiis munire et novos canones condere. . . ."

right (and duty) to vote. Again, a cardinal cannot renounce his office nor any right pertaining to the office, "maxime in his, quae publicum statum respiciunt." But in the election of the supreme pontiff "omnia sunt de iure publico"!

Actually the good cardinal bishop of Ostia was permitted (perhaps by the college of cardinals as a corporate body of the magistracy acting as the *caput Ecclesiae* when there was no pope) to retire from this particular enclave and thus renounce his right—after all he was old and ill, and the citizens of Viterbo were virtually imprisoning the cardinals and depriving them of proper shelter and food in order to make them hasten to elect a pope.[60] Nevertheless, Hostiensis here shows that the *ius publicum* and *status publicus* were the "constitutional" law and *ordo* of the Church, regulating *inter alia* the election of popes. The cardinalate and the papacy, essential for maintaining the *status Ecclesiae,* were in another sense the highest *status publicus* in the Church.

One finds this meaning of *status Ecclesiae* in at least two renowned scholastic philosophers and theologians of the late thirteenth and early fourteenth centuries. Henry of Ghent understood the "state of the Church" as the *ordo ecclesiasticus*—the ecclesiastical hierarchy, of which the pope was the head.[61] John of Paris still more specifically attributed to the pope a *status* that was public and meant the *plenitudo potestatis.* For, he says, the pope is the universal *dispositor* and *dispensator bonorum*; and, according to the "needs of his state" ("secundum exigentiam sui status"), he can make his own more of the revenues of churches than inferior prelates can, for only he has the *plenitudo potestatis.*[62] In

---

60. *Lectura* or *Com.* (Venice, 1581), I, 91ᵛ–92, Nos. 32–34, 42, 50; the comment is to *Decr. Greg. IX,* 1, 9, 10 Nisi cum pridem, ad vv. *humiliter obedire.* There is no need here to discuss the whole problem of renunciation in relation to public law; it was often debated by the canonists. For one treatment of it see Peter N. Riesenberg, *Inalienability of Sovereignty in Medieval Political Thought* (New York, 1956), pp. 59–80, 75, on Hostiensis and the *publicum statum* of the Church.

On the papal election of 1268–71 and the date of Hostiensis's *Lectura* see Ch. Lefebvre, "Hostiensis," in *Dict. de droit canonique,* Vol. V (1953), cols. 1220–21; also H. K. Mann, *Lives of the Popes,* XV (London, 1929), 339. On the cardinals as a corporate body and *caput Ecclesiae* see Brian Tierney, *Foundations of the Conciliar Theory* (Cambridge, 1955), pp. 74 f.

61. Quoted by Lagarde, *Naissance de l'esprit laïque,* II (2d ed.), 206.

62. Dom Jean Leclerq, *Jean de Paris et l'ecclésiologie du XIIIᵉ siècle* (Paris, 1942), pp. 174, 186 f.; Tierney, *Foundations of the Conciliar Theory,* pp. 157–78, 167, for a good discussion of John of Paris, but without specific reference to the papal *status.* This argument, that the pope is *dominus omnium* and can make full use of the

this thought of John of Paris the analogy to the older "reason of the estate royal" is evident.

No one, however, except John of Paris, so far as I know, said *status papae*; and no matter how great the *plenitudo potestatis* and *dignitas* and *majestas* of the pope, no canonist fully equated the pope with the *status Ecclesiae*. The "state of the Church," which will be examined in another study, was largely the public welfare of the Church and the faith. Yet the exalted position of the pope inevitably led to those statements which were close to holding that he was the Church, or the "state of the Church," in the sense that he was the law itself, and his magistracy was the public *status* for interpreting the law and the public welfare of the Church. Herein the pope was like the prince in the secular State. In the late twelfth century, for example, a decretalist, Honorius, said that the pope was the *magister* and *custos* of the canons of the Church, that he was the *canon* (*lex*), and that it was sacrilege to dispute what he did.[63] Another decretalist (on Innocent III's declaration that the pope is the vicar of God, exercising a divine authority when for necessity or utility he makes changes in the lands of churches) said that the papal power was beneath God but above man. If the secular prince had a "celestial power," so much the more had the vicar of Jesus Christ. Nor was the law (*lex*) made for him: he was the *lex*, and what was pleasing to him was *lex*.[64]

---

revenues of churches (naturally in accordance with the law, but also for the defense of the faith and the Church), is similar to the doctrine of the legists on the powers of the emperor; on this, see below, nn. 78–83.

63. *Summa decretalium quaestionum,* in the Paris, BN, MS lat. 14591, fol. 50. Treating the subject of papal rescripts, Honorius says: "Item ipse [papa] est magister et custos canonum, ut xxiii. Q. iii. cum quibus (c. 36). Item ipse est canon, ut ix. Q. iii. ipsi sunt. Item sacrilegii instar habet de facto pape disputare. . . ." If a rescript is contrary to natural law, "non est secundum illud procedendum"; "si vero iuri positivo . . ." the rescript is valid "ut causa necessitatis, id est . . . publico. . . ."

On this work see Stephan Kuttner and Eleanor Rathbone, "Anglo-Norman Canonists of the Twelfth Century," *Traditio,* VII (1949–51), 304–36.

64. Paris, BN, MS lat. 15398, fol. 112ᵛ, to Comp. III 3, 1, c. Quanto (*Decr. Greg. IX* 1, 7, 3), ad vv. *romanus pontifex, qui non puri hominis sed veri dei vicem gerit*: "Unde potestas eius ultra hominem et citra deum. Celeste enim dicitur arbitrium habere princeps secularis, nedum vicarius iesu christi . . . Nec ei lex posita est . . . ; ipse est lex . . . ; et quod placet ei lex est. . . ."

On the theory of the papal monarchy see in general Walter Ullmann, *Medieval Papalism* (London, 1949), who exaggerates the absolutism of the papacy; Tierney, *Foundations of the Conciliar Theory,* esp. pp. 23–36, 47–84; and Tierney, "Grosseteste and the Theory of Papal Sovereignty," *Journal of Ecclesiastical History,* VI (1955), 1–17. Of course the other literature on this subject is too abundant to refer to here.

To be sure no canonist meant this literally: in the general theory of the papal authority, the pope could not be the law to the extent of being completely unlimited and arbitrary in legislating and interpreting and judging. And if, like the emperor, the pope was presumed to have "iura omnia in scrinio pectoris sui," this again did not mean that he did not need to consult with the cardinals and legal experts in important matters.[65] No doubt, however, the theories of the pope as the supreme *auctoritas* in his *plenitudo potestatis,* and as the head of the corporate body of the Church, had their connection with the idea that in his being the head of the sacerdotal magistracy, of the *ordo ecclesiasticus,* the pope was the essential *status Ecclesiae* in the sense of his being the *status, id est, magistratus.* St. Cyprian, in a well-known passage quoted by Gratian in the *Decretum,* had said: "The bishop is in the church and the church in the bishop.[66] On this, before 1220, a decretist remarked that "here the Church is called the bishop," and that the Church is the clergy (*ecclesiastici viri*). But he preferred to say that the Church is the *congregatio fidelium.*[67] In general, however, if the Church was treated as the mystical body of Christ and the corporate body of all the faithful, the definition of the Church as the clergy, particularly the prelates, surely led to the extreme statement of Aegidius Romanus, that the pope, as the head, can be called the Church. Or as Alvarus Pelagius was to say, "the mystical body of Christ is where the head is, namely, the pope." Indeed, St. Jerome had declared that the *salus Ecclesiae* depended on the *dignitas* of the pope. The logical conclusion was drawn by Augustinus Triumphus that the good of the pope was greater than that of the Church, since the good of the Church could not exist without that of the pope. Such ideas, of course, were analogous to the theory of the glossators, that the magistracy, as a *status* subject to public law, was a necessity, for otherwise there could be no administration of law and justice for the sake of the *status Reipublicae* (to D. 1, 1, 1, 2). In one sense, then, the pope was the Church; he was a "corporation sole" and was absorbing into it the

65. On *iura omnia* see Fr. Gillmann, "Romanus pontifex iura omnia in scrinio pectoris sui censetur habere," in *Archiv f. kathol. Kirchenrecht,* XCII (1912), 3–17, and CVI (1926), 156–74.

66. Quoted by Ernst Kantorowicz, "Mysteries of State," *Harvard Theol. Rev.,* XLVIII, 79; *King's Two Bodies,* p. 215; referring to *Decretum,* C. 7, q. 1, c. 7 Scire.

67. *Glos. ord.,* to C. 7, q. 1, c. 7: ". . . Hic dicitur ecclesia episcopus: alibi est idem quod ecclesiastici viri, ut supra .lxiii. dist. ca. 1." To Dist. 63, c. 1, one finds this gl. ad v. *ecclesia*: "Ecclesiam hic vocat viros ecclesiaticos. Quandoque vocatur congregatio fidelium . . . De hoc dixi vii. q. 1. scire."

corporate body of the Church. At least he was the *status Ecclesiae* in the sense that the lawyers had long been speaking of the king's *status* as both the government and the *status regni*.[68]

This development resulted, too, no doubt, from the frequent claim that the local Roman Church, the pope and cardinals, was the universal Church. *Urbs et orbis* in reality were often absorbed into the one *Urbs* as the *urbs* extended its power over the world. The analogy with ancient Rome and its absorption of and into the world is clear. Thus one cannot but think of the fact that, apart from the prevailing theories of the papal government and the Church, the supreme magistrate acted at times as if his authority was indeed the Church, or at any rate the public *status Ecclesiae*. Let it be emphasized again, however, that the thought was rarely expressed, and never outside the context of the doctrine that the pope was subordinate to the faith and the law of God. But again, as the final interpreter of all laws, even under the limitations of tradition and the faith and the necessity of the faith and the Church (the *ratio status Ecclesiae*), the pope in substance was both the head and in his office the public welfare of the Church. The *justa causa* and the *casus necessitatis* increased the powers inherent in the *status papae*, which was deemed necessary for preserving the *status Ecclesiae*. The *ratio status papae* must be exercised *ratione status Ecclesiae*.[69] We can now understand how Pope Clement VI could denounce Cola di Rienzo for trying "primatum ecclesie prefate [Romane] subvertere ac tocius orbis statum . . . conturbare."[70] The primacy of the Roman Church and the pope was practically equivalent to the State of the World, another way of expressing the State of the Church, *urbe et orbi*.

A development similar to that in the Church had long been going on in theories of the *status* of secular princes. Professor Ernst Kantorowicz has treated it so well that I need only call attention to how the

68. Kantorowicz, *King's Two Bodies*, pp. 194–206, 204 n. 32; Wilks, "Idea of the Church," *Miscel. Hist. Eccles.*, pp. 41–43. See above, n. 1.

69. See my *"Ratio publicae utilitatis, etc.," Welt als Gesch.*, XXI, 24–28, on the papal authority and *justa causa*, necessity, and "reason" of the *status Ecclesiae*.

70. Quoted by Eugenio Dupré-Theseider, *L'idea imperiale di Roma nella tradizione del medioevo* (Milan, 1942), p. 335. Clement VI goes on to say (p. 336) that Rienzo unlawfully pretended to have rights in the election of the emperor "et de statu Romani imperii ordinare." In a word, the pope was making *status* equivalent to the government according to the constitutional *ordo* of the Empire. This strengthens my interpretation of *tocius orbis status* as essentially the papal authority, which of course the pope held was superior to the *status Romani imperii*.

prince was the soul, the *lex animata,* of the State, and the *vigor iusti-tiae* and *pater legum.* As Lucas de Penna said, quoting Seneca, the emperor is the soul of the *respublica,* and the *respublica* is his body; and, in his own words, "the Prince is the head of the realm, and the realm the body of the Prince."[71] But in the theory of the State as a corporate body the head was likely to coincide with or absorb the whole. "The estate of the king (*status regalis*)," said Ptolemy of Lucca, "has by nature a certain universality, because it is common to the people subject to him." Moreover, as noted above, the prince, like the pope, was, in a general sense, the law, having "omnia iura in scrinio pectoris sui."[72]

John of Salisbury and the glossators, however, generally avoided such identification by resorting to the theory of representation. John held that the prince was neither the public utility (*status*) nor the State, but its minister, the bearer of the "public person" and of the whole body (*universitas*) of his subjects and their community. He was the *potestas publica* whose duty it was to reason and act for the public and common welfare. In the legists, too, one finds that the prince represented the State. Yet, by changing the theory of consent in an ordinary corporation into a theory of *ex officio* representation, without any active consent of the members, in the corporate State, Azo helped prepare the way for identifying ruler and community. The *universitas,* he says, cannot consent, either because of its multitude (it was a com-

71. *King's Two Bodies,* pp. 214 f., 99; see Index s.v. *Lex animata.* Interesting also are *Auth.,* Coll. 6, 2 (*Nov.* 73), and Coll. 8, 6, 1, 4, and the *Glos. ord.* thereto: ". . . Nec mirum si imperator novit, ut dicit: quia omnia sunt in pectore suo . . . Item est pater legum . . . Item est anima legum"; and "No. principem esse ipsam legem animatam in terris . . . Acc." Cf. Calasso, *Ordinamenti giuridici,* pp. 267 f.

72. Ptolemy (Tholemy) of Lucca quoted by Wilks, "Idea of the Church," *Miscel. Hist. Eccles.,* p. 43 n. 41, from the *De regimine principum,* II, 7. On *iura omnia,* see above, n. 65. The maxim came from the Roman law and was often repeated for the powers of sovereign princes in the thirteenth century. The legists, like the canonists, held that the prince had only a presumptive general knowledge of the law. He must consult with his counselors and legal experts before making new laws and interpreting the law, for only the experts could know the law in detail. And if they did not know the law for a particular case they should go to the documents in the archives—the *scrinium* is occasionally called the *registrum* or archives. Hence we can say that the prince's possession of *iura omnia in scrinio pectoris sui* really meant that he was the final authority in deciding cases and interpreting the law on the basis of research and consultation. Besides n. 65 above, see the *Glos. ord.* to C. 12, 20, 3, and Lucas de Penna to C. 12, 19 (p. 715, No. 2), where the *scrinia legum* are *iurisperiti.*

mon saying that a corporation could not easily consent), or, "quod est verius," because the members conferred "consensum suum omneque ius et potestatem in magistratus"; and therefore "quod faciunt magistratus videtur ipsa universitas facere."[73] But this is agency in private law applied to the representation (without recall of the representatives and without consent to new ones) of the State by the magistracy, by the prince himself; for Azo has in mind the *Lex regia* (*D*. 1, 4, 1) and the *universitas* of the people in the State. Perhaps this explains why at this point he departs from the standard theory of consent in the ordinary corporation, that while it is difficult for the members to consent, consent is possible by means of the *maior pars*. As for the State, Azo apparently holds that the membership is too great for any effective practice of consent; hence all consent along with powers that had belonged to the people was surrendered to the government—whether council in the Italian commune, emperor and his magistracy in the Empire, or king in a realm. As a result it was easy to speak of the *magistratus* as the *universitas* of the State itself, or at least to think in similar terms, and to forget that the magistracy represented people and State while acting for the common safety and public welfare. If therefore the idea that the prince was the law, and the soul of the body of the State, was not an actual identification of State and magistracy, it encouraged, along with the theory of *ex officio* representation, the ultimate appearance of the concept that the head of the corporate body of the State was in a sense the State itself, and not merely the representative and minister of it and its *status*.

Moreover, still another trace of this kind of identification appeared in the late thirteenth and early fourteenth centuries. As we noted above, the legists sometimes thought of the ruler as the *imperium*,

---

73. *Policraticus* IV, ii, iii; quoted by J. E. A. Jolliffe, *Angevin Kingship* (London, 1955), p. 16; also in Antonio Rota, "L'Influsso civilistico nella concezione dello stato di Giovanni Salisberiense," *Rivista di storia del diritto italiano*, XXVI–XXVII (1953–54), 220.

Azo's theory is expressed in a gloss to *C*. 1, 53 De contract. iudicum (in the Paris, BN, MS lat. 4536, fol. 26—this manuscript contains many glosses of the twelfth century): ". . . Hic nota ipsa universitas consentire non potest, et propter sui multitudinem, ut ff. de libertis uni. 1. i [*D*. 48, 3, 1]; aut, quod est verius, quia consensum suum omneque ius et potestatem in magistratus contulerunt; et ita quod faciunt magistratus videtur ipsa universitas facere, nec potest ut supra media persona intervenire. *Az*." But Accursius, *Glos. ord.*, to *C*. 1, 53, 1, ad v. *Provincias*, says, "Ipse magistratus universitatem repraesentat"; however, the whole gloss shows that he has in mind lower magistrates only.

respublica, fiscus, or even the *regnum.* In all probability they understood these terms in the sense of government or *regimen,* the public *status* in his magistracy. The prince was the *status-respublica.* So, to repeat, Andrew of Isernia said that the king and the *respublica regni* were the same; for whoever was the head in the kingdom, the *respublica* was in him as in the head; and where the prince was, there was *totum ius.*[74] Lucas de Penna essentially agreed, holding that any apparent harshness of the king, if he was acting for the public utility, must be endured "propter honorem principis, qui est res publica et res publica est in eo."[75] These legists, then, understood what we might express in the words "l'état, c'est le roi," meaning that the "state," *respublica,* was the public welfare and also the magistracy of the king. But the State was not the king, nor the king the State. They did not say that the *rex* or *princeps* is the *regnum.* Even when they identified prince and *imperium,* as Baldus did, probably *imperium* meant the supreme power or authority, not the Empire.

Status est magistratus, then, was seldom expressed literally, but in some legists and canonists, and in Thomas Aquinas, in varying degree the word *status* bore the meaning both of the public welfare of the community and of the necessary government. Perhaps this meaning was derived in part from an age-old habit of princes and other chief magistrates, the habit of saying "my administration," "my authority," "my government," and indeed "my *imperium*" (either as power or as Empire), or "my kingdom." Such expressions were often casual, as unimportant as "my country," "my fatherland," "my State," whether said by a public official or by a private citizen. As remarked earlier, however, a head of State accustomed to great prestige and power might succumb to the thought that both government and the State were his personal property. By an easy transition he might identify his private person both with his public office and with that entity called the State.

74. Kantorowicz, *King's Two Bodies,* pp. 215 f.; "Mysteries of State," *Harv. Theol. Rev.,* XLVIII, 78–80; Andrew of Isernia, *Lectura* on the *Const. Regni Sicilae,* p. xxvi, col. 2: ". . . quia fiscus et respublica Romanorum idem sunt, sicut Imperator et respublica, ut ff. de bon. poss. non est ambigendum [*D.* 37, 1, 12]. Rex ergo et respublica regni sui idem sunt, sicut Imperator et respublica Romanorum, qui est in regno, sicut caput, respublica in eo [*ea* here], sicut in capite, dicit Seneca. I. de clementia, hoc modo. . . ." Calasso, *Ordinamenti giuridici,* p. 268, quotes Andrew thus: "princeps et respublica idem sunt," and "ubi est princeps, est totum ius." See also above, nn. 27–38.

75. *Com., Tres Libri,* to C. 11, 71, 5 (p. 622, c. 1, No. XXIIII); cf. Kantorowicz, *King's Two Bodies,* pp. 215 f.

No doubt an emperor or king, if he thought about it at all, was conscious only of his duty when declaring that the State and its government were his. Political and legal theorists, too, generally intended only to say that the State and its administration belonged to the prince *ratione publicae et communis utilitatis, ratione status regis et regni.* But in this feeling of ownership, which was not the same thing as feudal proprietorship, and in the very failure to separate his public and private "bodies," the ruler's identification of himself with the State was at least possible. In any case possessiveness was present. Thus Frederick Barbarossa was surely claiming that the essence of the Empire was his when, replying to Arnold of Brescia and the citizens of Rome, he exclaimed: "Behold our republic!"—"Nostram intuere rem publicam!" In his power, he continued, was the glory of Rome, the senatorial dignity and the consuls (members of his "body politic"?) and the *imperium*. Then, after telling how he prescribed laws for the people, not the people for him, and how he protected the rights of possessors of property, he declared that he was not obligated to take oaths to confirm old laws and customs or to defend at the risk of life the *patria*. For how could he not defend the *patria,* and especially the "See of my imperium"?[76] Frederick was virtually saying, "This is *my* Republic, *my* Empire, *my* Fatherland." Neither Arnold of Brescia nor the pope could tell him what his duties were! In fact, his *respublica* and *imperium* were more than his powers of government; they were the whole territorial extent of the Empire: *reipublicae curam gerere,*[77] *Romani imperii gubernacula* (at Roncaglia, 1158—but also *legittimum imperium,* i.e., lawful power),[78] *bonus status imperii nostri* (1177), and "Ex debito imperialis officii tenemur per universum imperium nostrum pro necessitate et statu provinciarum pacem ordinare" (1179).[79]

76. Otto of Freising, *Gesta Friderici, MGH, SS. Scholarum,* pp. 109 f. Does this mean that Frederick maintained that only kings took coronation oaths, as he did at Aachen in 1152, but that as emperor he was above taking oaths? See below, Part III, nn. 7, 21, 38; also text, after n. 13.

77. *MGH, Legum S. IV, Constitutiones* I, 207, No. 148, *an.* 1154: "Imperialem decet solertiam ita rei publicae curam gerere et subiectorum commoda investigare, ut regni utilitas incorrupta persistat et singulorum status iugiter servetur illesus." This is in the famous *constitutio* against the alienation of fiefs, confirmed at Roncaglia in 1158. Compare with Richard Fitzneale's words on the *sollertia* of the king's officials in the Exchequer; below, Part II, n. 95. Is it possible that, besides the Roman law, Macrobius, *Saturnalia,* I, 11, was of influence in such a formulation? "Alii putant eundem Priscum cum statum ciuium sollertia providi principis ordinaret...."

78. Speech reported by Otto of Freising, *Gesta Friderici,* p. 188.

79. *MGH, Legum S. IV, Const.* I, Nos. 263, 277.

This kind of royal or imperial possessiveness, however old and customary, was of course the more vigorous in the twelfth century because of the revival of the Roman law. Frederick Barbarossa's advisers, some of whom had been disciples of Irnerius at Bologna, were familiar with Justinian's usage of the terms *respublica nostra* and *nostrum imperium*.[80] As is well known, Martinus took Justinian at his word and therefore asserted that the Empire and everything in it were the emperor's property. Bulgarus, however, made the important distinction which all the legists of note were to follow, and which made possible the steadfast theoretical separation of the public office from the personal property of the prince.[81] Against Martinus he argued that the Empire belonged to the emperor only with respect to jurisdiction and protection. It was the emperor's, other glossators said, solely *ratione jurisdictionis et gubernationis*.[82] Since according to this theory

80. Mommsen and Krueger, eds., *Digest,* p. 8 ("Deo auctore nostrum gubernantes imperium"), 10 ("Omnem rei publicae nostrae sanctionem"), 13 ("Tanta circa nos . . . usque ad nostri imperii tempora . . ."). In the second and third examples the meaning is government and power, or administration.

81. An early gloss states this, in Vat., MS Pal. lat. 763, fol. 113, to *C.* 7, 37, 3 Bene a Zenone, 1, ad vv. *omnia principis esse intelligantur*: "Quantum ad iurisdictionem; vel dic omnia quantum ad proprietatem secundum ea, scilicet, que procedunt [tam] ex suis rebus quam ex fiscali substantia. . . ." Of course the fisc is treated by the legists sometimes as the public treasury of the State, sometimes as the treasury that belongs to the prince but normally is used for all expenses of his position and government.

82. The gloss in Accursius's *Glos. ord.* to Justinian's words in the *Prooem.* to the *Digest* sums up the conflicting opinions; also to *C.* 7, 37, 3 Bene a Zenone, 1, ad v. *omnia principis*. I quote the first gloss, ad vv. Omnem reipublicae nostrae sanctionem: ". . . Et quod hic dicit, 'omnem totius reipublicae nostrae,' id est totius imperii, quod est suum, et res in eo contentae, ratione iurisdictionis vel protectionis, ut hic; non proprietatis, secundum Bul. Sed M. etiam proprietatis. . . ." (*Totius* is an interpolation made by the glossator in the text of Justinian's introduction.) See also my "*Ratio publicae utilitatis,* etc.," *Welt als Gesch.,* XXI, 79.

Odofredo, one of the first great Commentators (mid-thirteenth century), offers an interesting discussion to *D.* 50, 17, 66. On the argument that the emperor "potest absorbere ius meum in totum," because "omnia sunt principis," and that St. Paul said that every soul is subject to "potestatibus sublimioribus" (Rom. 13:1), Odofredo replies that "quod competit mihi naturali ratione, et equitate, ut dominium rei mei, et exceptione competenti, pacto non potest tollere: quia iura naturalia sunt immutabilia. . . ." Nor can the emperor issue a rescript to one man which injures another. *Omnia* belong to the prince "quo ad protectionem." *Fiscalia* do belong to him; but if all things did, no one could claim anything as his own. As for St. Paul, that every soul is subject to the higher powers, this is true only "quantum ad obtemperandum in his, que sunt iurisdictionis." The prince can punish only for *justa causa.* (In the *Lectura* on the *Dig. Novum* [Lyons, 1552] p. 193, No. 2.)

the prince enjoyed no proprietary right either to the State or to the highest public office, except insofar as they were his for governing justly and defending against enemies, a weakening of the feudal emphasis on the private, personal character of kingship was to result. Yet the very exemption of the royal government from private law may have brought about the danger that the king could claim that if the *status* of his public powers and the *status* of the realm were his in a purely public sense, he really was the State. So in the Church, as we have observed, the pope did not own the properties of churches and the clergy, nor the Church. But since the supreme authority was his, *ratione status Ecclesiae,* it was easier for extremists to declare that in effect he was the Church.[83]

Possessiveness and some identification with the State, then, could and did develop. Justinian, again, helped the process along with a pious statement (*C.* 6, 51 [50], 1, 14a). On the claims of the fisc to property of persons dying intestate and without heirs, he said that he would not exercise this imperial privilege to the injury of his subjects. For *"imperialiter* we judge that the welfare [*commodum*] of subjects is our own"; and "what profits all in common, this we think should be preferred to the utility of our private affairs."[84] The glossators quickly made the connection between the emperor's possession of the public welfare and his possession of the jurisdiction for maintaining it.[85] In other words, "what profits all" was public and above the prince's private utility. But the common welfare itself belonged to the prince. It was another way of saying *quod omnes tangit:* "what touches all" in effect touched the prince too as the head of the State; and thus the maxim became a principle of public law.[86] (We shall note in Part II

83. Above, nn. 59, 65, 62; Tierney, *Conciliar Theory,* p. 167 f., and *passim,* on the *plenitudo potestatis* (see Index); Guido de Baysio, *Rosarium* (Venice, 1577), to *Decretum, C.* 23, q. 8 c. Tributum, Nos. 6 and 7, where the theory is applied to the French monarchy.

84. *C.* 6, 51 (50), 1, 14a: "Tantum et enim nobis superest clementia, quod scientes etiam fiscum nostrum ultimum ad caducorum vindicationem vocari, tamen nec illi pepercimus nec Augustum privilegium exercemus, *sed quod communiter omnibus prodest, hoc rei private nostrae utilitati praeferendum esse censemus, nostrum esse proprium subiectorum commodum imperialiter existimantes."*

85. For example, a pre-Accursian gloss to *C.* 6, 51 (50), 1, 14a, ad v. *subiectorum commodum:* "Et cum omnia imperatoris esse censentur, ut j. de quadri, prescrip. bene a ze[none]"; MS Vat. lat. 11152, fol. 141ᵛ, c. 1. The reference is to *C.* 7, 37, 3, 1; cf. above, nn. 81–82. A later gloss adds, fol. 141ᵛ, c. 1: "Nota imperatorem extimare subiectorum utilitatem suam propriam."

86. A special study will be devoted to *quod omnes tangit* in its various public

how the business of the *status regni* was the king's business, touching the royal *status*.)

Azo, on Justinian's words about the *commodum* of subjects as his own, briefly referred to a *Novella* in which the emperor condemned the exploitation of subjects in the provinces by any magistrates, and ordered his agents and governors to collect no more than was owed to the fisc. Immoderate exactions, said Justinian, diminish the *imperium* and injure subjects.[87] Lucas de Penna, more than a century after the time of Azo, also directly connected these two laws of Justinian with his own statement that the emperor thought of the *commoda provincialium* as his own, and that Cicero held that the property and wealth of individuals belonged to the *civitas*.[88] Writing with the same passages in mind, Alberico da Rosciate said that the *Novella* of Justinian meant also that if a man tried to purchase high office that carried with it both *dignitas* and *iurisdictio,* he was burdening the *respublica.* Indeed, the prince should appoint only worthy and virtuous men to "dignitates et honores," "judging imperially that the public utility is his own."[89]

Thus in their different ways both Justinian and the legists held that not only the State (*Respublica* or *Imperium*) and its government (*respublica* and *imperium*) were the prince's, but also the public welfare and *commodum* and common utility of his subjects were his to maintain. This obviously was connected with the public duty of the magistracy to be just to all private persons in exercising *iurisdictio,*

---

and private meanings. There is no need of referring to the already abundant literature on it. Here I need only point out that "what profits all" and "what endangers all" belong to discussions of "what touches all."

87. To *C.* 6, 51 (50), 1, 14a, ad v. *existimantes*: "I.[nfra] aut. ut iud. sine quoquo suf. § cogito. *Az.*" The reference is to *Auth.*, Coll. 2, t. Ut iudices, etc., § cogitatio, or *Nov.* 8 Praef., § 1 cogitatio. See the *Glos. ord.* also to these passages.

88. *Com.* in *Tres Libros Codicis* (Lyons, 1597), p. 866, No. 1: "Provincialium, quorum commoda propria reputat imperator, supra. de cadu. toll. 1. i. prope fi. Nam tunc et imperium et fiscus abundabit, cum subiecti locupletes sunt, ut iudi. sine quoquo suffra. §. 1. unde tullius 3. de offi. Singulorum facultates et copiae divitiae sunt civitatis [Cicero *De officiis* iii. 15 (63)]." This is to *C.* 12, 37, 8.

89. *Com.* on the *Code* (2 vols.; Lyons, 1545), II, 195ᵛ, c. 1, to *C.* 9, 26, 1 Nullus: no purchase of office, "quia lex presumit quod rempublicam gravaret, in aut. ut iudices sine quoquo suffra. §. j. et. §. cogitandum"; and "princeps cessante pecunia et precibus solum dignis et virtuosis daret dignitates et honores utilitatem publicam imperialiter estimans propriam, ut supra. de cadu. tol. l. unica circa fin. . . ." He adds that, alas! the prince today often yields to money and entreaties; he is *legibus solutus.*

and with the right of subjects to receive protection and justice. And it was connected with the frequent association of these principles with the *status* both as the public welfare and as the government, and with *quod omnes tangit* as a principle of public law: the *status regis* and *status regni* touched the welfare of all. What touched the common interest and utility of all touched the public welfare of king and realm. But first such a public business touched and demanded the exercise of the *potestas-status regis*.

Some of this was expressed by German emperors of the eleventh and twelfth centuries, some of it by Philip Augustus,[90] much more of it increasingly by kings of France and England in the following century, and by the lawyers. John of Salisbury already understood the essence of it when he said that the prince is the public power, an image of the divine majesty on earth, obeying the law and accepting all the burdens of ruling. Hence the power over all subjects was conferred on him in order that he might be able to achieve the utility of all, individually and in common, and best maintain the "state of the human Republic." For each is a member of the others; they are members of each other. Herein, John continues, *natura* leads: nature placed in the head of the community the universal *sensus*; thus all members are subject to the head, and the people must carry out and obey the needs of the prince.[91] If John thought of the Republic or State as a body, a *universitas*, like the glossators he also viewed the prince and other

90. Examples in H. Fichtenau, *Arenga. Spätantike und Mittelalter im Spiegel von Urkundenformeln*, in *Mitteilungen des Instituts für osterreichische Geschichtsforschung, Ergänzungsband*, XVIII (1957), 80, No. 154: Conrad II, *an.* 1030, "Publice rei et communi hominum utilitati in omnibus et per omnia consulendum fore consemus . . ."; from *MGH, DL*, III, 105, No. 155, Lothair III, *an.* 1136: "Imperialis benevolentie proprium iudicamus commoda subiectorum investigare et eorum diligenti cura mederi calamitatibus simulque *publicum bonum statum ac dignitatem imperii* omnibus privatis commodis preponere"—this in the famous feudal law promulgated by Lothair; *MGH, DL*, III, 105. Philip Augustus, in his provision for the government of the realm while he was crusading (Fichtenau, *Arenga*, p. 80, No. 156; also in H. F. Delaborde, *Recueil des actes de Philippe Auguste*, I [Paris, 1916], 416, No. 345): (*an.* 1190) "Officium regium est subjectorum commodis modis omnibus providere et sue utilitati private publicam anteferre." This obviously reflects the words of Justinian in *C.* 6, 51 (50), 1, 14a, and the maxim that the public welfare must always be preferred to any private welfare.

91. *Policraticus*, ed. Webb, I, 235 (IV, i): "Est ergo . . . princeps potestas publica et in terris quaedam divinae maiestatis imago. . . . Unde merito in eum omnium subditorum potestas confertur, ut in utilitate singulorum et omnium exquirenda et facienda sibi ipse sufficiat, et humanae rei publice status optime disponatur, dum sunt alter alterius membra. In quo quidem optimam uiuendi ducem naturam sequi-

magistrates or "judges" as the public head, possessing the real public mind or "reason" of the State in the public and common welfare of all—of all as one body and of all as individuals.[92] Naturally—by the sanction of nature—the prince as head possessed the magistracy and the supreme authority over the body. The common opinion was that as the head he represented the community. Almost, however, he was the community, for practically speaking it was in him more than he was in it.

Now we can sum up. Professor Percy Ernst Schramm has remarked that in the middle ages the king was the *Zeichen* of the State, that consequently scepter, crown, and other symbols of monarchy are better sources for understanding medieval kingship than chronicles, documents, and treatises.[93] But in this study it has become clear, I hope, that the legal ideas are by no means unimportant. Perhaps the doctrine of the royal *status* as the king's power and magistracy, and as the rights and duties of the crown, is as important as a symbol; the concept of the *corona* as the *ensemble* of those rights which pertained to and were the royal estate and dignity is as important as the material crown. Perhaps the *status regis* is as positive an indication of the royal majesty as any other expression.

To be sure, the "state" of the king was not the State; but it was not only the royal *potestas,* it was also the whole magistracy, the government. For as early as the latter half of the twelfth century the glossators were beginning to revive the ancient Roman understanding of the *ius publicum* as the "constitutional" law that was concerned both with the *status,* public welfare, of the State and with the indispensable *magistratus.* Without the magistracy of prince and lesser administrators and judges, how could the state of the Republic be maintained? So it was that, as in antiquity, the public *status* became in one sense the *magistratus,* the constitutional order. Furthermore, *status* and *magistratus* were at times equivalents of the *respublica,* in the sense of the *regimen, gubernatio,* or *politia*—"la chose publique."[94] And the scholastic theologians agreed that the *status* of the State was, as it were, the *magistratus* of prince, king, or any sovereign government.

Almost, but not quite, the jurists of the late thirteenth and the

---

mur, quae microcosmi sui, id est, mundi minoris, hominis scilicet, sensus universos in capiti collocavit, et ei sic universa membra subiecit, ut omnia recte moveantur. . . ."

92. Cf. Kantorowicz, *King's Two Bodies,* pp. 207, 208 n. 42; also Rota, "L'Influsso civilistico," *Riv. stor. dir. ital.,* XXVI–XXVII, 213–26.

93. *Herrschaftszeichen und Staatssymbolik,* III (Stuttgart, 1956), 1067.

94. This has been noted occasionally, above, nn. 32, 35, 40, 56–59.

fourteenth centuries made the transition from "state" to "State." They were approaching the identification of the State (Republic or Realm) with the supreme authority vested in the government of the prince. Yet neither they nor those who equated *magistratus* and *status* really had in mind the kind of absolutism attributed to *l'État, c'est moi.* The prince might be the public *status,* but he was not the State. As the public *status* he was included in the whole body of his realm, and therefore the prince as the *status* was subordinate to that end—the public welfare, commonweal, of the community as a whole, the *status regni.* If he was subordinate, however, to the State and the public and common welfare, he had the right to interpret and practice that *ratio status* (*ratio publicae utilitatis*) which was the necessary reasoning for the achievement of the end of the State, its well-being and safety, and the common welfare of its members. *Ratio status magistratus* and *ratio status Reipublicae* became inseparable. Quite naturally, though never saying it, a powerful king might think to himself that he was not only the *status* or government, not only the head of the State, but the State itself.

In this small essay the main emphasis has been placed on the theme of *status, id est, magistratus.* But in passing we have noted that in the twelfth century, both in the glossators and in the *Dialogus de scaccario,* the word *status* occasionally meant the public authority and powers (*potestas* and *potentia*) of the chief magistrate, the head of the State. Most frequently, in fact, we find that the ruler, rather than being the *status,* possessed a *status—status regis* was a frequent term in royal documents, chronicles, and the writings of the jurists. In the second section of this study, therefore, we shall examine the importance and meaning of the "state" of the king. The *status regis* no doubt became the more important because of the assumption that the "state" of the king was also in essence the government of the realm, and because the *status regis* was necessary "ad statum [regni] conservandum, ne pereat."

Once more, it is clear, the twelfth and thirteenth centuries contributed important political ideas to the Italian renaissance and the modern age. Even if he did not study them, Machiavelli perhaps owed his emphasis on *lo stato* as the Prince to the medieval legists and to Thomas Aquinas. No doubt more directly he got this definition from current usage in the Italy of the fourteenth and fifteenth centuries. When in 1315 the people of Mantua made a Gonzaga the head of the city, it was because the care of the "status reipublice" belonged "especially to those whom the *status* itself touched."[95] That is to say, in effect, in public law *quod omnes tangit* meant that the public welfare chiefly touched or was the chief concern of the Gonzaga, and the care of this *status* belonged to him. In consequence, as the *magistratus*, the Gonzaga held the "status" and was the substance of it if not completely identical with it. In Giovanni Villanni's *Cronica* the *stato* is often the government of Florence. Another example comes from Ludovico de Corthosiis (de Padua), 1418. In his *De principibus,* if in one instance *status* is almost our State, it is in other instances the "state" of the prince perhaps in the sense of public office or government.[96] About the same time the famous Coluccio de' Salutati, writing on the subject of the tyrant, seems clearly to have used *status* for the magistracy.[97] The medieval background is evident.

Perhaps the medieval background, or at least the continuing terminology and the meaning which became current in the middle ages, is also evident in the sixteenth century, in England as well as Italy. These words of Sir Philip Sidney remind one both of *status-magistratus* and Justinian's identification of the emperor and the public welfare of his subjects: "The Princes persons . . . in all monarchall governmentes are the very knot of the peoples welfare, and light of all their doinges to which they are not only in conscience but in necessitie bounde to be loyall."[98] Plowden, the Tudor jurist, surely had the medieval royal

95. A. Marongiu, *L'Istituto parlamentare in Italia dalle origini al 1500* (Milan, 1949), p. 78 n. 42, quoting from V. Vitale, *Il dominio di parte guelfa in Bologna, 1280–1327* (Bologna, 1901) pp. 237 f. :". . . illis status rei publice cura spetialior comitatur quos tangit sinipse status."

96. The *De principibus* seems to be unedited; I consulted it in the Paris, BN, MS lat. 4612, fols. 229–68: (fol. 229ᵛ) the pope cannot depose a prince for burdening his subjects if the prince is acting "cum causa, puto pro iusta deffensione status"; (fol. 243ᵛ) on the confiscation of the property of those who are guilty of treasonable acts "contra statum suum. . . . Barones facientes contra statum principis debent magis puniri quam alii cives. . . ." Even the first example could mean that the prince acting for the security of his public power could, e.g., collect extraordinary taxes. The second example indicates that treason against the "state" of the prince is treason against the State—as in the Roman law, *D.* 48, 3, 1.

As for Villani, see VI, 39, 87; VII, 16, 79; VIII, 1 (in ed. C. Durando [Turin, 1880], II, 127, 206; III, 46, 163; IV, 3).

97. *De tyranno,* ed. F. Ercole (Bologna, 1942): c. 2, art. 21, "statum . . . ordinavit"; c. 3, art. 7, the *status reipublicae* in Caesar; c. 4, art. 6, on recovering the *status* and *dignitas.* Coluccio also speaks of the *status civitatis* (c. 4, art. 8).

98. In the *Arcadia,* quoted by A. H. Gilbert, *Machiavelli's Prince and Its Fore-runners* (Durham, 1938), p. 3.

status in mind when he said: "But his Body politic is a Body that cannot be seen or handled, consisting of Policy and Government, and constituted for the Direction of the People and the Management of the public weal"; and to the "natural Body" of the king "is conjoined his Body politic, which contains his royal Estate and Dignity."[99]

Perhaps, finally, had Louis XIV actually said, "l'État, c'est moi," he might possibly have intended that a small *é* (*l'état*) be understood, meaning that he was the supreme *potestas* and magistracy, existing for the *commun profit*. And when Napoleon declared that he had been *la chose publique, l'état,* was he departing radically from the old tradition of *status, magistratus, respublica, potentia, potestas* of the prince as the *lex animata* and the soul of the *respublica*?[100] The classical and medieval Roman legal thought on the public law and the State was not unknown in the new Empire, and Napoleon had possibly absorbed some of its spirit with respect to the *status principis*.

99. Quoted by Kantorowicz, *King's Two Bodies*, pp. 7, 9; cf. n. 30 above.

100. See above, nn. 55–59. In the fifteenth century Jean-Juvenal des Ursins wrote of the king as the soul and principle of life of the *chose publique*; Gilbert, *op. cit.*, p. 3, from Ch. Petit-Dutaillis in Lavisse, *Histoire de France*, IV, ii, 207— where one also finds that Jean-Juvenal said that the king's own soul is the soul of, or belongs to, the crown. Therefore, in effect, whereas in the Canon law the salvation of one's soul was a right more important than the common welfare, here the king's private soul is so identified with the life of the *chose publique*, the State in this case, that its eternal salvation is less important than the salvation on earth of the public soul of king-crown-realm-people. Moreover, the State is the king and the king is the State. Perhaps this idea resulted from another principle stressed by the canonists and popes: ordinarily the right of the private soul was superior to the common welfare; but in the case of great prelates, who were subjects of the public law and in turn administered their churches in the public and common interest, they must remain in office even at the risk of their personal immorality, for the sake of the public and common welfare in the work of saving souls.

II. *STATUS REGIS, LESTAT DU ROI,* AND THE STATUTE OF YORK

IN THE first section of this study we followed the development of the concept of the *status* of a State as in part the magistracy and its powers. At times, indeed, the *status publicus* was *la chose publique,* the *respublica,* again in the meaning of the "constitutional" *ordo, politia,* or government. It was logical that since the public law was concerned primarily with the *status magistratus* as the necessary means of preserving the *status* of the political community, the word *status* itself should come to designate the supreme powers of the head of the State. Quite early in fact, the *status* of a king was at times the royal *potestas.* But I did not develop this aspect of kingship. It is important now to do so, not only because the emphasis on the *status* or estate of the king as well as on the *status* of the kingdom led to the word's becoming a common term, State, for any politically organized society, but also because there is still no agreement on the meaning of *status regis, lestat du roi,* and *lestat de la coronne* in the Statute of York, 1322.

Perhaps my method—that of offering, so to speak, a Romano-canonical commentary on these and related terms in a few English sources up to and including the Statute—will seem absurd to those scholars who are masters of medieval English legal and constitutional history. Nevertheless I hope that the deliberate repetitiousness involved in the method—because of the need of showing how *status* in the context of public law must be understood in other terms too, such as *majestas, dignitas, honor, potestas,* and *corona*—and the application of the continental legal and political thought to what is often assumed to be purely English, will support a few scholars who have, without studying the Roman tradition of public law, come to a like conclusion.

What, now, according to the drafters of the Statute of York, was the *estat* of the king? And was it different from the *estat* of the crown? Influenced perhaps by the common assumption that medieval kingship belonged to feudal and private more than to public law,[1] the late G. T.

1. For example, F. Pollock and F. M. Maitland, *History of English Law* (2d ed.; Cambridge, 1898), I, 512–18, and II, 2–5; and recently, J. E. A. Jolliffe, *Angevin Kingship* (London, 1955), and R. S. Hoyt, "Royal Taxation and the Growth of the Realm in Mediaeval England," *Speculum,* XXV (1950), 40. Professor Hoyt also believes that *status regni* came to have the sense of "state of the realm" only in the late thirteenth or early fourteenth century.

Lapsley decided that the king's estate was largely personal, closely related to the royal household and its revenues and administration, while the estate of the crown was public, signifying the inalienable public powers of the king in his courts. Quite recently John H. Trueman has supported this interpretation.[2] George L. Haskins, whose conclusions were criticized by Lapsley, held that the king's estate was principally his properties and revenues and was the same as the estate of the crown. S. B. Chrimes assumed that the estate of the king was the mass of rights and duties and attributes which constituted the kingship; the estate of the realm was probably the "state or good condition" of the kingdom and the people as a whole, and it involved taxation more than legislation. Joseph R. Strayer, however, emphasized legislation as the main concern of the king and Parliament in dealing with both estates.[3] Several years ago I joined in the battle of interpretations, but did not develop what I said in passing about the *status regis,* which I defined as the public *status* of the king as head of the realm, an estate which existed for the end of the *status regni.*[4] Much more needs to be said!

Following the example set by Ernst Kantorowicz in his excellent book, *The King's Two Bodies,* I quote first from the English sources of the sixteenth century in order to state the theme. Let Henry VIII begin our interpretation of the Statute of York: "We be informed by our judges," he said, "that we at no time stand so highly in our estate

2. See the summary of various interpretations given by Trueman, "The Statute of York and the Ordinances of 1311," *Medievalia et Humanistica,* X (1956), 64–69, and Trueman's own conclusions, pp. 75–81. For Lapsley, whose interpretation is defended by Trueman, see his long article, "The Interpretation of the Statute of York, 1322," *EHR,* LVI (1941), 22–51, 411–46; it is reprinted in *Crown, Community and Parliament in the Later Middle Ages,* eds. H. M. Cam and G. Barraclough (Oxford, 1951), pp. 153–230. My references are to the older printing in the *EHR.* B. Wilkinson, *Constitutional History of Medieval England,* Vol. II (London, New York, Toronto, 1952), chap. iii, does not discuss the problem of *status regis.*

3. Haskins, *The Statute of York and the Interest of the Commons* (Cambridge, Mass., 1935), pp. 98–104; Chrimes, *Constitutional Ideas of the Fifteenth Century* (Cambridge, 1936), pp. 91–93; Strayer, "The Statute of York and the Community of the Realm," *American Historical Review,* XLVII (1941), 1–22—but Strayer's study, excellent though it is, does not treat the meaning of *estat,* for his emphasis is on the "community of the realm" and on consent.

4. "The Two Laws and the Statute of York," *Speculum,* XXIX (1954), 425, 432. Trueman, "Statute of York," *Med. et Human.,* X, 79, observes that I did not clearly explain what I meant by "estate" of the king. He is right, because I was interested chiefly in the "estate of the realm" and merely reflected briefly on the *status regis,* the central idea in many of the sources presented here and in other studies.

royal as in the time of parliament, wherein we as head and you as members are conjoined and knit together in one body politic." Moreover, he declared that England was an Empire "governed by one supreme head and king, and having the dignity and royal estate of the imperial crown of the same."[5] In the later sixteenth century, we learn from Edmund Plowden's *Reports,* the "body politic" consisted of policy and government and was "constituted for the Direction of the People and the management of the public weal." To the natural body of the king was "conjoined his body politic which contains his royal Estate and dignity"; the "body natural" was "adorned and invested with the Estate and Dignity royal"; and the "body natural" and the "body politic" were indivisible and incorporated in one person.[6]

What Henry VIII thought of the royal estate is not clear, but in the first statement it was certainly an attribute of his headship in Parliament. Presumably he was describing the supreme authority which he most fully exercised when he and Parliament constituted the governing body of the realm. He was not the "body politic" itself, but he, as head, and the members of Parliament constituted it; and thus in a way his words remind one of the glossators' *corpus principis,* a body which included the emperor, his greater magistrates, and the Senate.[7] At any rate the "estate royal" was no private aspect of kingship, for in the second statement Henry attributed to the head the "dignity and royal estate of the crown"; and indeed the royal estate was assimilated to the crown. Plowden seems to identify the king and his estate and his dignity still more closely with the "body politic," as if the king and his *status* were the whole government, not including Parliament. But again the estate or dignity of the king was public, standing for the royal authority. The "estate royal" belonged to the "body politic," not to the "body natural."

Yet the "body politic," consisting of policy and government, and containing the royal estate, dignity, and office, could not be separated from the body natural. They were two aspects of one public person. How this may be analogous to the Chalcedonian doctrine of the two natures of Christ has been shown by Kantorowicz. What is significant

5. The first passage is quoted by G. L. Haskins, *The Growth of English Representative Government* (Philadelphia, 1948), p. 125; also by Kantorowicz, *King's Two Bodies,* p. 228. The second passage is quoted by Kantorowicz, *loc. cit.*

6. Kantorowicz, *King's Two Bodies,* pp. 7, 9

7. Above, Part I, n. 31.

for the present purpose is that while the public body was essentially
the royal estate and dignity, or contained these, it was manifestly
impossible to separate completely this estate from the body natural.
But it was different, for it was a public estate, closely related to the
royal office and dignity and to the crown.

In Shakespeare, too, as Kantorowicz reminds us, the king's "state"
was his public office. Richard II says (Act IV, scene 1, lines 192–93):

> You may my glories and my state depose
> But not my griefs, still am I king of those.[8]

The royal "sacred state," moreover, was virtually the crown and was
closely tied to the king's "pomp and majesty," his "manors, rents,
revenues," and his powers of legislating and administering (Act IV,
scene 1, lines 208–13):

> With mine own hands I give away my crown,
> With mine own tongue deny my sacred state.
>
> . . . .
>
> All pomp and majesty I do forswear;
> My manors, rents, revenues I forgo;
> My acts, decrees, and statutes I deny.

Both in Shakespeare and in the crown lawyers, indeed, and in
Henry VIII, the concept of the royal *status* as something connoting the
public authority, crown, power, dignity, and majesty and glory of
the king, an estate supported by "manors, rents, revenues," strongly
reminds us not only of the early legists and canonists, but also of Richard Fitzneale's words in the *Dialogus de Scaccario*. We have encountered the *Dialogue* already, but it is so significant as the work of a
great public officer who long served Henry II that we must again examine it for the meaning of the royal estate. For Richard speaks of those
dignitates by which the *gloria regiae potestatis* shines forth; even ecclesiastics should serve kings and their *jura,* above all in maintaining the
material wealth which belongs to or touches kings *ratione sui status*;
and the *potestates principum* are measured by the *mobilium copia.* In
a word, the royal estate is the king's power, not his revenues; it is supported, however, by his wealth in revenues. Furthermore, the *status
regis* participates in the Exchequer, where royal officers administer and
judge in fiscal matters both for the *utilitas* and *status regis* and for the

8. Quoted by Kantorowicz, *King's Two Bodies,* p. 37.

status regni.[9] In the Exchequer as in the royal government in general, therefore, the *ratio publicae utilitatis (status) regni* is the principal *ratio potestatis (status) regis.*[10] Thus Richard Fitzneale was in fact

9. Stubbs, *SC*, pp. 200, 205. See also the text in the edition by Charles Johnson, *Dialogus de Scaccario* (Nelson's Medieval Classics: London, etc., 1950), pp. 1, 14. Johnson's translation of *status ratione* is not satisfactory, given Richard's possible reflection of the Roman law and the glossators. The text reads (ed. Johnson, p. 1): "Oportet autem hiis servire non in conseruandi tantum dignitatibus per quas gloria regie potestatis elucet, uerum in mundanarum facultatum copiis que eos sui status ratione contingunt. Ille enim illustrant, hec subueniunt. Porro mobilum copia uel defectus principum potestates humiliat uel exaltat." His translation reads: "And we ought to serve them by upholding not only those excellencies in which the glory of kingship displays itself but also the worldly wealth which accrues to kings by virtue of their position. Those confer distinction, this gives power. Their power indeed rises and falls as their portable wealth flows and ebbs." (It is interesting that Cicero *De officiis* iii, 15 [63], quotes Hecaton of Rhodes thus: "Singulorum enim facultates et copiae dviitae sunt civitatis.")

In my opinion the words *potestas* and *status* are here virtually equivalent in meaning; therefore *status* is weakened by the translation "position." And "by virtue of their position" weakens too much the literal "by reason of their state" or "power." "Portable" wealth suggests to me rather the wealth in money (which the Exchequer collects) that is necessary if the king's "state" of power is to be sufficient for defense against enemies, as the next sentence suggests: "Quibus enim hec desunt hostibus preda fiunt. . . ."

And the passage in Bk. II, c. 10 (ed. Johnson, p. 100; Stubbs, *SC*, p. 234), on how "ratione publice potestatis" the king can confiscate the property of a usurer who has injured a loyal subject, illustrates again how the translation is weakened by the lack of regard for the current legal thought and terminology. For Johnson has for the key words: "because as head of the executive he [the king] is to receive all the goods of the creditor, or rather usurer, who has enriched himself by ruining one of them" (i.e., one of the king's faithful subjects). Obviously, a literal translation is better: "by reason of his public power," or "by reason of his *status* or estate" the king receives the goods of the usurer. To be sure the "reason" of the king's public *status* or power is related to his being the "head of the executive"; but why not put it in the sense of the words in the twelfth century?

Finally, in the edition of the *Dialogus* by A. Hughes, C. G. Crump, and C. Johnson (Oxford, 1902), the editors (p. 163) say that Hugh of Fleury, *De Regia Potestate* (*ca.* 1100), uses almost the same language. This is only partly true. I find nothing like *ratione status sui* and the words about kings' powers and wealth in Hugh, although in general Hugh stresses the royal power which comes from God and the duty of ecclesiastics to be obedient to the king. See Hugh's *De regia potestate* in *MGH, Libelli de lite*, II, 466–94.

R. L. Poole, *The Exchequer in the Twelfth Century* (Oxford, 1922), does not discuss the problem of the influence of Roman law.

10. Stubbs, *SC*, p. 234: if a usurer has enormously injured a subject, the king "ratione publicae potestatis" can confiscate the usurer's property.

As for the Exchequer, the king's revenues, and the demesne, and problems con-

reflecting the legal thought of contemporary glossators, that the public powers of the supreme magistrate and his judges were the *status* that existed to maintain *(conservare)* the *status Reipublicae,* "lest it perish."[11] Obviously, as Shakespeare said, the king must have his public property and revenues in order to exercise the powers that belonged to and were the royal estate.

If a twelfth-century authority on English kingship presents a concept of the public estate of the king which fundamentally agrees with that of the sixteenth century, many sources between the two periods show that the tradition was no doubt continuous. To be sure Bracton says only that the public *iura* of the king, the royal powers of jurisdiction and government for the protection of private rights and for keeping the peace, pertain to the crown and the royal dignity. These powers belong to the *iurisdictio ordinaria* and cannot be alienated by the king.[12] Bracton does not mention the *status regis*. Nonetheless his doctrine of the rights of king and crown essentially puts in different words Richard Fitzneale's description of the royal authority or powers as the *status regis*. And because his theory of kingship belongs in substance to the context of the main current of thought in the legists, one can say that he too was really talking about the public estate of the king.

But it was the legists and canonists, and the scholastic theologians, who from about 1150 carried on a steady, continuous theory of the public *status* of prince or king. We need recall now only the opinion of the legists, that the public law dealt both with the *status principis et magistratus* and with the *status Reipublicae*. By reason of his public *status,* by reason of his jurisdiction and government, the prince could say that the Republic or Empire belonged to him. The *status Reipublicae* was indeed his own; the common and public welfare of his subjects and of the State was his; and his welfare, his *status,* in the powers of governing, was itself necessary for the state of the Republic. The

nected with the king's private as opposed to his public revenues and expenditures, see in general R. S. Hoyt, *The Royal Demesne* (Ithaca, 1950). On the public character of the imperial and royal fiscs see Kantorowicz, *King's Two Bodies,* pp. 164–91, 342–46.

11. Above, Part I, n. 10.

12. Stubbs, *SC,* p. 413; Bracton, *De legibus,* ed. Woodbine, II, 166–67 (fol. 55b); Kantorowicz, *King's Two Bodies,* p. 149. In general on Bracton's idea of kingship, see C. H. McIlwain, *Constitutionalism, Ancient and Modern* (Ithaca, 1940), pp. 71–94; Kantorowicz, *King's Two Bodies,* pp. 143–64; and, for the influence of Roman law, Fritz Schultz, "Bracton on Kingship," *EHR,* LX (1945), 136–76. Cf. above, Part I, n. 28.

ratio status principis was also the *ratio status Reipublicae*. Both estates, the public authority and the common welfare, were public, complementing each other—sometimes, indeed, the confusion of both resulted in the prince's being the public *status* if not the State.[13]

Obviously, since the prince needed revenues in order to govern and defend the Republic, his fisc, or treasury, was public; it was necessary to and a part of the *status Reipublicae*. Therefore, as Justinian said, the imperial fisc should act not against but for the common profit ("quod communiter omnibus prodest"; *C.* 6, 51, 1, 14a); and the *proprium commodum subiectorum* was also the emperor's good or profit. It follows that the revenues of the prince in his fisc were both for the public state of his office and for the state (public and common welfare) of his subjects and of the State.[14] The prince of course enjoyed a private patrimony that was his private estate, but the revenues that came into the fisc were certainly not his private but a part of his public estate. Rather, these public revenues supported his public estate. Both the estate of the prince and the means to support it, therefore, were businesses that concerned the prince and the people's welfare in common.

It has been argued, however, that the business of the king of England was different from that of the realm.[15] But, in fact, just as in Justinian's ideal, any important *negotium* that touched the state of the realm touched the king and was his business; and the public business of the king in his public estate was sometimes the business of the *populus* (i.e., the greater men), or of the *universitas regni*. So, for example, Innocent IV held that a king could not debase the coinage "sine consensu populi" or of the *maior pars regni*, "for the business of the king is the business of the *unviersitas*."[16] Normally, of course, the king's

13. See my *"Ratio publicae utilitatis, etc.,"* Welt als Gesch., XXI, 8–28, 71–99; and above, Part I, esp. nn. 68, 74f.

14. Above, Part I, nn. 84–91; also Kantorowicz, *King's Two Bodies,* pp. 173–230.

15. Trueman, "Statute of York," *Med. et Human.,* X, 69; cf. below, n. 36. But W. Ullmann, *Principles of Government and Politics in the Middle Ages* (London, 1961), pp. 175–78, notices that some *negotia* are common to king and realm.

16. *Com. on Decr. Greg. IX* (Venice, 1578), p. 118, to 2, 24, 18 Quanto. This decretal was the basis of the standard theory developed by the canonists, that any debasement of the coinage, or any change in its value, required the consent of the people (the *populus* usually meaning the greater men of the realm). It is well known that Nicholas of Oresme was to emphasize the theory of consent to changes in the coinage of the realm.

On the meaning of *populus,* while sometimes it meant all the people, including

estate as the supreme power and magistracy for maintaining law and order, although it vitally touched the *status regni*, required no consent except what was often presumed to be the original consent of the people to the transfer of the *imperium* to him and his heirs. With regard to his normal powers of ruling, however, the *populus* which counted, chiefly the great lords of England, sometimes questioned the wisdom of the king and his advisers and tried to control the powers that properly belonged to the royal *status* and crown. Indeed, to anticipate, the Statute of York was the royal government's reply to such an attempt in the early fourteenth century. But any *negotium* that required the king's action because of his public estate and at the same time touched the rights and well-being of his subjects, and therefore the *status regni,* was a business that was common to king and "people" and required *tractatus* and consent in Parliament. In such matters *quod omnes tangit* was sometimes consciously applied as a principle of public law, although the king had in fact a greater right to demand and get consent to any action necessary for the safety of the realm and "people" than the "people" had to refuse it. What touched the *status regni* was, then, definitely the king's business; and, as we shall observe, it touched his public *status* too. Head and members were interested in any important business that touched both and affected the all-embracing *status regni.*

There were two businesses of the greatest importance (*ardua negotia*) that were of vital interest and concern to king and realm in common—the defense of the public and common welfare, of the *status* of the realm, against enemies threatening the safety of the State, and the maintenance of justice and law and order, *ratione communis et publicae utilitatis,* again *ratione status regni.* "Regis namque officium pugnare est bella populi sui, et eos rectissime iudicare" (I Kings 8). Justinian declared in well-known words that the imperial majesty should be decorated with arms and armed with laws in order to van-

---

the *plebs* as well as the nobility, generally it was assumed that the greater men were the *populus.* So a decretist of the early thirteenth century expresses quite well the difference between *populus* and *plebs,* in the *Summa* "Antiquitate et tempore" on the *Decretum* (in Vatican, MS Pal. lat. 678 fol. 37ᵛ), Dist. 2, c. Lex est: ". . . Nota quod ea[dem] differentia est inter populum et plebem, que est inter animalem et hominem, inter genus et speciem. Nobiles enim, et in nobiles simul collectum, sunt populus. Ple[b]s est ubi non sunt senatores et viri consulares . . . ; id est, universus populus maiores natu tribus modis dicuntur, nobilitate, dignitate, antiquitate." Cf. *Inst.* 1, 2, 4.

quish enemies in battle and do justice in the courts. As an early glossator said, the office of the emperor was twofold, that of peace and war, of "expelling the iniquities of false accusers" and of fighting enemies and conquering and triumphing—in time of peace fighting with laws is to hold trial and give sentence.[17] The war of defense and justice, of course, concerned subjects also, the subjects in varying degree as fighters and taxpayers and as interested parties in the courts. Each was a business common to the *status regis* and the *status regni.* Legists and theologians held that extraordinary subsidies levied for the defense of the realm were levied also for the maintenance of the *status regis*—so, for example, Thomas Aquinas and Lucas de Penna.[18] The royal estate must be the stronger for waging war and providing justice for subjects.

This development had its roots not only in the early history of kingship but in the Canon and Roman law of the twelfth century. Popes and decretists agreed that a king who refused or was too *fainéant* to defend the *patria* should lose his royal *status* and *dignitas.* As a decretist said, *ca.* 1169, if the *status* of a king changed for the worse because he would no longer fight in defense of the realm, the pope had the right to absolve the king's vassals from the oath of fealty. Hence Pope Zachariah released the Franks from their oath taken to the king "intuitu regie dignitatis," and deposed the last of the Merovingians because he was *inutilis* in the exercise of the royal *potestas.*[19] The

17. *Inst., Prooem.,* "Imperatoriam maiestatem"; and gloss to this in MS Vat. lat. 8782, fol. 49: "Officium imperatoris duplex est diversarium, id est, pacis et belli. . . ." There is no need of quoting the whole gloss; the idea is also in the *Glos. ord.* of Accursius—also in English sources, e.g., Glanville and *Fleta.*

18. Above, Part I, n. 43, for Thomas Aquinas; Lucas de Penna says, *Com.,* to *C.* 10, 18, 1 (p. 83, c. 1, No. 10): ". . . si aliquis casus de novo emergat in quo oporteat multa expendere pro utilitate communi ,vel *pro honesto statu principis conservando,* ad quae non sufficiunt redditus proprii, vel exactiones consuetae, puta si hostes terram invadunt. . . ." Clearly Lucas holds that the *status regis* is the royal, public power, directly serving the *status regni.*

19. Paris, BN, MS lat. 14997, fol. 109, *Summa Coloniensis* ("Elegantius in iure divino"), to *Decretum,* C. 15 q. 6, c. 3 Alius item: "Status quoquo mutatione interveniente, a iuramento fidelitatis absolvere ecclesia consuevit. Unde Gelasius [actually Gregory VII, in a letter of 1080]: Zacharias papa regem francorum, non tam pro suis iniquitatibus quam quod tante potestati inutilis esset, a regno deposuit, omnesque francigenas a iuramento fidelitatis absolvit. Hoc intelligendum est de iuramento quod prestitum fuit intuitu regie dignitatis. Nam quod intuitu persone fit, relaxari nequit, nisi is, cui factum est, ab ecclesia separetur. . . ." (On this *summa* see Kuttner, *Repertorium,* pp. 170–72.) The papal letter and a gloss to the above gloss show that the Merovingian king was accused of failure to fight in defense of the *patria*; see my "Two Notes on Nationalism," *Traditio,* IX, 283 f.

French (*Francigenae*), said a decretist, were absolved from their oaths of fealty "ratione dignitatis . . . non ratione personae." Furthermore, still another decretist associated the *corona* with the royal estate and dignity: the *corona regni* should go to that man who was successfully waging war *pro commune salute*.[20] The French king and legists, indeed, were making the war of defense a business so important to king and realm alike, that they tended to confuse *rex, regnum, corona,* and *patria*; the *defensio patriae et coronae* was also the defense of the *bonum commune* or *bonum publicum regni*.[21] The royal estate, dignity, and crown, therefore, existed chiefly for the defense of the kingdom and the public welfare.

Because of the vital necessity of the king's *status* for defending the realm, clearly his estate included the public right to meet necessities or emergencies. Since such necessities touched or concerned both king and subjects, the king of England frequently claimed that every necessity of defending even an overseas possession that was not in the territory of the kingdom touched the *status regni* and the crown as well as his own feudal rights. The defense of the realm of England was involved in the defense of Normandy or other fiefs in France, even though such fiefs really pertained to the king as a feudal lord and not to the realm of England proper. In fact, these overseas possessions, in spite of being the king's private feudal rights of lordship or *dominium,* belonged also to the *imperium* of the king and were subject to the royal jurisdiction and administration in the Chancery and the Exchequer. They were a part of a feudal empire, and they were subjects of the crown.[22] By the time of Edward I, Wales, like Ireland under Henry II, was also treated as a part of the Empire that belonged to the

20. Johannes Faventinus, in *Glos. ord.* of Johannes Teutonicus, to C. 15 q. 6 c. 3; Paris, BN, MS lat. 14997, fol. 109; and my "Two Notes on Nationalism," *Traditio,* IX, 284 n. 15.

21. Jean de Blanot and Jacques de Révigny, quoted in my "Two Notes on Nationalism," *Traditio,* IX, 289 f.; also Guillaume Durantis, *Speculum Iuris,* IV, Part iii, 2, No. 31, as quoted by Kantorowicz, *King's Two Bodies,* p. 251 n. 180—on king and crown, pp. 340 f. See also J. R. Strayer, "Defense of the Realm and Royal Power in France," *Studi in onore di Gino Luzzato* (Milan, 1949), p. 292; and above, Part I, nn. 26, 27.

22. See Julius Goebel, Jr., "The Matrix of Empire," introductory essay in Joseph Henry Smith, *Appeals to the Privy Council from the American Plantations* (New York, 1950), pp. xiv–xxii, xliii–lii; also Barnaby Keeney, "Military Service and the Development of Nationalism in England, 1272–1327," *Speculum,* XXII (1947), 542 f. On an early thirteenth-century claim that England was an Empire, see Kantorowicz, *King's Two Bodies,* pp. 345 f.

crown.[23] It is therefore not surprising that the king's *status* was public even for the defense of territories that properly had nothing to do with the *status regni*. The *universitas regni Angliae* itself, the community of the realm represented chiefly by the magnates, admitted in 1294–1295 that Edward I in fighting a just war in defense of Gascony was also defending the *regnum* and the *status regni*.

Thus the king's business of defending both the kingdom and his feudal "empire" was also the business of the people in the community of the realm. Whether stated as *necessitas regis et regni* or *negotia regis et regni,* in time of war—which the king on his side naturally said was a just one of defense—the necessity or business that touched the king touched the kingdom; what touched the head touched the members; what touched the *status regis* touched the *status regni.* Conversely, the necessity of preserving the *status regni* was a public business that directly concerned the public *status* or duties and powers of the king, powers exercised for the "common profit" (*publica* and *communis utilitas*) of the realm. In other words, we see again that the *ratio status* of the king, the reason and necessity of his public *potestas,* existed *ratione utilitatis publicae et communis regni,* or *ratione status regni.*[24]

I have anticipated the final conclusion, which is based on the pre-

23. Goebel, "Matrix of Empire," in Smith, *Appeals,* pp. xliii–lii. It is particularly interesting that in 1278 counsel for Llewellyn, while arguing that every province "sub imperio Regis" should have its own laws and customs in its own language, admitted that each province and its customs existed for the *ampliacio corone* rather than the *diminucio corone*; p. xliv n. 131. It is interesting, too, that this is a possible reflection of the contemporary theory of provinces or kingdoms within the Roman Empire, a theory transferred to the "Empire" under the king of England.

24. I cannot treat the subject here, but it should be remarked that some glossators tried to explain that the *utilitas publica* was the *status* of the whole Republic or State as a corporate entity, *universitas,* including the head and the members; that the *utilitas communis* was the common welfare of the members viewed individually. In a fashion the public welfare was the subject primarily of public law, the common welfare the subject of the private law that was made for private rights. But since private law depended on the authority of the government for its enforcement, it was subordinate to public law; it was "public by authority," private in its application to the private rights and welfare of individuals. Hence the common welfare of the individual members of the State depended on the public welfare of the State and its government, else private law and rights could not exist. But the glossators could be inconsistent, and frequently *public* and *common welfare* were used without distinction, although the *public* looked more to the State as a whole than to the members viewed either individually or collectively. In the French of English royal documents *commun profit* stands for *public* and *common welfare* alike, and for *status regni et populi.*

sentation of much more evidence. But before turning again to English sources it is interesting and useful to notice briefly some indications of the equivalence in meaning, on the Continent, of the terms *status, dignitas, honor,* and *corona,* in connection with the authority of the prince and with the *status regni.* Lothair III declared that the *regalis potentia* was strengthened by monasteries; privileges for them profited both the *regni status* and the eternal reward of the king, and they were "pro nostro et totius imperii statu." Louis VII associated the *honor regis* with the protection of all subjects, including monasteries. In the documents of Philip Augustus one finds that any injury done to the rights of the metropolitan of Tours was an injury to the *status corone* and the realm, and that Pope Innocent III should be favorable to "nos et regnum nostrum et negocia honorem nostrum contingentia" and to "regni nostri proficuum."[25] To be sure, the king's salvation was a private matter; but just as in the Roman law, so in the twelfth century *sacra* (*inter alia* monasteries, churches, and religion) were subjects of the public law, and it was the duty of the prince to aid religion and churches for the public and common welfare in the salvation of souls—so the *Glos. ord.* to *D.* 1, 1, 1, 2. (As late as the seventeenth century Oxenstierna, justifying Gustavus Adolphus's invasion of Germany, said that "it was a question not so much of religion, as of the *status publicus,* in which religion is comprehended."[26] Privileges and gifts to

---

25. Lothair III, in *MGH, Dipl.,* VIII, 25, No. 19, and 58, No. 35; Louis VII, letter quoted by H. Fichtenau, *Arenga. Spätantike und Mittelalter im Spiegel von Urkundenformeln,* in *Mitteilungen d. Inst. f. österreichische Geschichtsforsch., Ergsbd.,* XVIII (1957), 44; for Philip Augustus, see H. F. Delaborde, *Recueil des actes de Philippe Auguste,* I (Paris, 1916), 179 f. (to Pope Lucius III, against the papal injury to the Church of Tours, the *regnum,* and the *corona*), and 165 f. (letter composed by Stephen of Tournai, to Lucius III, on the peril to the *status corone*); and Philip Augustus in letters to Innocent III (*Recueil,* II [1943], 144 and 246, Nos. 593 and 685); against the pope's favoring Otto of Brunswick as emperor; again Philip speaks of the *corona* as if it were the "crown of the realm," not simply the royal crown: the invasion of *terra nostra* by the count of Flanders is "in damnum corone," and the king asks for aid "tum pro capite nostro, tum pro corona regni defendenda," and "pro defensione capitis nostri et corone regni" (*Recueil,* II, 115 f., No. 566). On the French crown in this period, see Strayer, "Defense of the Realm and Royal Power in France," in *Studi in onore di Gino Luzzato,* I, 289–96.

More examples could be given from our period. But let one from 1034 suffice: Conrad II and Henry III, in a privilege for the bishopric of Bamberg, that it belongs "ad imperialem nostram maiestatem . . . totius regni curas statumque imperii precipueque omnium sanctarum dei ecclesiarum commoda considerare . . ."; Fichtenau, *Arenga,* p. 118, No. 238. See also n. 28 below.

monasteries and churches therefore enhanced the public and royal power because they also increased the *utilitas publica, status regni.* So the canonists sometimes argued in the thirteenth century: royal gifts and privileges to churches were not alienations that injured the rights of king, crown, and realm and thus violated the coronation oath. Donations to God, said Johannes de Deo (*ca.* 1243), do not injure the Empire, because the Empire is better defended by the prayers of the Church than by arms and physical labor. But a donation can be revoked, he admitted, if by it the Empire or a kingdom, duchy, or county is "enormously injured—unless, however, prescriptive right defends the gift and the donee."[27]

Frederick Barbarossa's advisers and his chancery understood quite well the public nature of the imperial *status, dignitas,* and *majestas,* and how this *status* existed to prevent injury to the rights and *status* of people and Empire. At the Diet of Roncaglia (1158), Frederick asserted that his powers of jurisdiction and coercion belonged "ad statum eius dignitatis" and to the office of the imperial majesty. Perhaps the *bonus status imperii nostri* was the "good state" of his *imperium* or authority as well as that of his Empire.[28] Moreover, the *status Romani Imperii* and the *status* of the illustrious princes who maintained the glory of the Empire should be "preserved unharmed"; and in 1162 the emperor declared that he was the *defensor ecclesiarum Dei,*

26. See the glosses in the *Glos. ord.* to *D.* 1, 1, 1, 2. Legists and canonists constantly stated that religion and the Church, and the maintenance of the faith, belonged to the public law and vitally interested the State. Of course this theory was not forgotten in the modern age. For Oxenstierna and Sweden, see M. Roberts, "The Political Objectives of Gustavus Adolphus in Germany, 1630–1632," *Trans. Royal Hist. Soc.,* Ser. 5, VII (1957), 22. Professor Stuart Hoyt, therefore, on the same problem in England, needs correction, *Speculum,* XXV, 40 (see n. 1, above).

27. *Questiones de facto,* in the Vat., MS Borghes. 260, fols. 132–61; this *questio* fols. 132–32v.

28. Otto of Freising, *Gesta Friderici, MGH, SS. Scholarum,* p. 188; *MGH, Legum S. IV, Const.* I, Nos. 161, 205, 211, 263, and 277. The documents of Conrad III are also interesting: *an.* 1152, the *dignitas imperii nostri* adorned by works of piety; and to cultivate justice and engage in piety "sic nostro convenit honori" (Fichtenau, *Arenga,* pp. 39 f.); *an.* 1139, "ad nostre dignitatis spectat coronam, boni operis dare et relinquere posteris suis exemplum" (Fichtenau, *Arenga,* p. 52). Such formulas were already ancient; for example, in the *Formulae imperiales* of the Carolingian age one finds the *regia et imperatoria dignitas* associated with doing justice; Fichtenau, *Arenga,* pp. 41 f., from *MGH, Formulae,* p. 291. On *corona* and *honor* see also Peter Rassow, *Honor imperii. Die neue Politik Friedrich Barbarossas 1152–59* (Munich and Berlin, 1940), pp. 78–80, 90–93, 107 n. 176.

"ut eas et earum iura integra et illesa sub nostro imperiali protectione defendamus."[29] So the imperial chancery was recalling laws of late Roman emperors on the oath of judges and magistrates and on the rights of the public fisc and the rights of subjects and churches, using famous words derived therefrom ("publicum illaesum," "privilegia . . . illibata," "ita eius patrimonium iugiter servetur illaesum"), and connecting them with the *status principis* and *status Reipublicae*. Particularly important is the wording of the famous feudal law promulgated by Frederick in 1154:

Imperialem decet solertiam ita reipublicae curam gerere, et subiectorum commoda investigare, ut regni utilitas incorrupta persistat, et singulorum status iugiter servetur illaesus.[30]

If this law directly prohibited the alienation of fiefs, indirectly it prohibited the alienation of the *iura regis et regni (imperii)*, since it aimed at preventing the loss of *debita servitia* and the consequent injury of the *honor imperii* and of the military power of the emperor.

We shall encounter this terminology again when we consider the English coronation oath and observe how, like the rights of the fisc and of subjects in the Roman law, the rights of king and crown, subsumed in the *status* and *dignitas regis* and in the *status coronae*, should be maintained *illibata* or *illaesa*. Indeed, the so-called inalienability clause which may have been added to the English coronation oath as early as 1154, originated in part in the oaths of Roman magistrates in the time of Justinian.[31]

But we must return to the terminology in imperial documents on the powers of the prince. Two more examples will be sufficient to our purpose. In 1212 and 1213, Frederick II piously subordinated his public *status* to the *decor et potestas imperii* and the *bonus status pacis* throughout the Empire.[32] This was another way of saying what his grandfather had said in 1165: "The *dignitas* of the Empire and the imperial *honor* demand that the emperor should always have before his eyes and in his hands the *necessitates reipublicae*; the *honor (imperii)* uses the right method, and its *status* is made the stronger, when the *salus totius patriae* and the *necessitates* of the poor are usefully

29. *MGH, Legum S. IV, Const.* I, Nos. 231 and 217.

30. *MGH, Legum S. IV, Const.* I, No. 148 (also in the *Libri Feudorum*, Book 2, chap. 55).

31. See below, Part III, for a full treatment of the subject.

32. *MGH, Legum S. IV, Const.* II, Nos. 43 and 45.

and mercifully provided for."[33] Here, surely, the *status* of the emperor was the *honor imperii,* or powers of office.

In the two laws, then, and in the documents of emperors and kings on the Continent, *status, honor, dignitas,* and *corona* often stood for the public authority, or for those powers of the prince which were deemed necessary for the maintenance of the *status* of the realm. Therefore such important businesses as defending the State and doing justice for the protection of the lawful rights of subjects were common to, or interested in common, the *status regis* and the *status regni.* But of course the conduct of such *ardua negotia* belonged primarily to the estate royal, to the crown. How they were conducted sometimes touched the *status populi et regni;* but the *negotia* themselves always touched, because they were for, the *status* of the realm and all its members. Altogether, in the twelfth century, kings and their administrators and judges were advancing, if slowly in the midst of feudal habits and concepts, toward the theory and ideal stated in an edict of Louis XV in 1717: "Notre couronne n'est a nous que pour le bien et salut de l'État."[34]

We can now understand how in England, as early as the twelfth century, there was a similar appreciation of the *status regis et regni.* In the so-called *Leges Henrici (ca.* 1109–1118) we find the idea that the *imperium* of the king was strengthened by the establishment of courts at certain times and places. *Placita* were not to be held more often unless the *"propria regis necessitas vel commune regni commodum"* demanded them.[35] The king's own necessity, no doubt, could be different from the common good of the realm, but in this case it was the necessity and common good of the realm too.[36] Again, just as Emperor Lothair III felt that privileges for monasteries strengthened the *status* of the Empire, so King Henry II granted lands to churches not only

33. *Op. cit.,* I, No. 228; cf. Rassow, *Honor imperii,* in general, for the background in the twelfth century; cf. below, nn. 69–74.

34. Quoted by Fichtenau, *Arenga,* p. 202, No. 448—from A. Babeau, "Les préambules des ordonnances royales et l'opinion publique," *Séances et Travaux de l'Académie des Sciences Morales et Politiques,* Compte Rendu, 56ᵉ année, N.S., Part 46 (1896), p. 853.

35. Stubbs, *SC,* p. 123.

36. Trueman thinks that this is evidence for a distinction between *negotia regis* and *negotia regni.;* "Statute of York," *Med. et Human.,* X, 69; above, n. 15. But of course *vel* can mean "or" in the sense of "and" and "what is the same thing" or "or rather." In any case, the business of the common welfare of the realm was the king's business, and it belonged to his office, crown, dignity, and estate to conduct it.

for the salvation of his own soul and the souls of his grandfather, Henry I, and of his sons, but also *pro statu regni mei*.[37] Unlike Lothair, Henry did not stress the strengthening of the royal *potentia*, but no doubt that aspect of the *status regis* was closely related to the king's spiritual welfare. Ralph de Diceto says that Henry II was acting as the *pater Anglorum* when, solicitous for the common safety, he used the *publica potestas* in the shires to reform the sheriffs, who had not been doing justice and had abused the fiscal rights of the king and injured (*laedere* is the verb) the *majestas principis*.[38] In the assize of Northampton, c. 7, if justice belonged "ad dominum regem et ad coronam suam" and "ad commodum domini regis," it also belonged, in the context of the ideas and terminology of the century, to the public *status regis* and to the crown alike.[39] Justice belonged to the estate of the king for the maintenance of the estate of the realm; and it was as profitable and useful for the king's *status* as it was for the public and common welfare.

The *Dialogue of the Exchequer* shows that the important public business of war was common to king and realm. A knight's horses and armor, says the author, should normally be left to him if he is an insolvent debtor, so that in case of necessity he can serve in the *negotia regis et regni*. But if he fails, when summoned, to heed the *necessitas regis vel regni*, his creditors shall leave him one horse so that he can retain his knightly dignity and fight in the king's service.[40] The necessity common to king and kingdom, then, was above all the necessity of the king's authority both for good government and for war in defense of the realm.

We find increasingly abundant evidence of this in the thirteenth century. King John identified his own *magna et ardua negotia* of the war against Philip Augustus with the *utilitas communis* of the kingdom. Further, he declared that it was just that all the members (of the realm) should hasten with their aid to the *defensio capitis*.[41] Thus quite early the corporate theory of the realm appears in a royal document (of course John of Salisbury had already fully stated the old doc-

37. Quoted by Hoyt, *Speculum*, XXV, 40; above, nn. 1 and 26.

38. Stubbs, *SC*, p. 155. On *majestatem laedere*, see below, Part III, nn. 7 and 38.

39. Stubbs, *SC*, p. 180. On the early development of the concept of the crown in England in relation to the public law and kingship see Kantorowicz, *King's Two Bodies*, pp. 342–46; also Ullmann, *Principles of Government and Politics*, pp. 178–80.

40. Stubbs, *SC*, p. 239; *Dial.*, II, chap. 14, p. 111. Note again how *et* and *vel* are used.

41. Stubbs, *SC*, p. 277; Rymer, *Foedera*, I, 87.

trine of the body of the Republic and its head and members). If the *status regis* is not mentioned, it is implied in that it was the public business of the king as head to defend the *status regni*.

To judge from a few examples of usage from the reign of Henry III, just as in the twelfth century so in the thirteenth the royal *status* was concerned in any public business that was common to king and realm; that is, a business common to king and realm touched the *status regis et status regni*. In the reissue of Magna Carta in 1216 it is stated for the young Henry that he and his *consilium* will fully take care of those things which suggest themselves for correction, all those things, that is, which pertain to the *communis omnium utilitas* and the *pax et status noster et regni nostri*.[42] In 1237 the *status noster et regni nostri* was concerned with the common business of a subsidy that was debated in a parliament held at Westminster. Obviously the *status regis* was the public right or authority which the king held for the defense of the realm and of the rights of the crown in France. The demand for extraordinary taxes could not in theory be made for any private interest of the king (although he was capable of misusing the proceeds of a subsidy), but only for a business that concerned the public interest of king and kingdom.[43] A report of a debate in Parliament in 1242 confirms this. Summoned by Henry to give him a subsidy for defending his *iura* in France, in those parts which pertained *ad regnum suum Angliae,* the prelates and barons protested, arguing that they should not give any aid unless Louis IX broke the truce (that is, unless Henry could show that he actually faced the necessity of fighting a just war of defense). They complained that the king had not respected their wishes about an earlier subsidy, which they had intended should be spent only if necessary for the utility of the king and the realm.[44] *Utilitas* in the legists was often equivalent to *status*. Clearly, the public "state" of the king, his powers or prerogative for meeting emergencies and defending the "state" of the realm, is indicated.

In 1258, according to the Burton *Annals,* the king and his son Edward submitted to the ordinances of the twenty-four on the correction of their *status* and of the *status totius Angliae*.[45] Again the sources show that the estate of the king and his heir was public. For in the

42. Stubbs, *SC*, p. 339.
43. *Op. cit.,* p. 358.
44. *Op. cit.,* pp. 360 f.; cf. Sir Maurice Powicke, *The Thirteenth Century* (Oxford, 1953), p. 78.
45. Stubbs, *SC*, pp. 330 f.

provisions of Oxford the twenty-four prescribed three Parliaments each year for treating "les communs besoingnes del reaume e del rei ensement." From the contents of the Petition of the Barons, the Provisions of Oxford, and the Provisions of the Barons, it seems evident that the business common to king and realm was largely that public authority of the king which Richard Fitzneale had related to the royal *status,* but which also pertained to the crown—for example, matters connected with the Exchequer.[46] This becomes clear also in the Award of St. Louis. After saying that the Provisions of Oxford had injured or detracted from the *ius et honor regius* (*honor,* again, often meant the public honor, dignity, or office),[47] the Award ordered that the royal castles be returned to the king, and that the king have the right freely to choose all the greater and lesser officials "regni sui ac domus suae." Most significantly, the French monarch ordered that the king of England should have *plena potestas et liberum regimen* in his realm and its pertinencies, and that he should be in *eo statu et in ea plenaria potestate* in which he had been in the past.[48]

But what was the royal *domus* mentioned in the Award? What had the provisors of 1258 thought it was when they had urged the "amendment" of the *hostel* of the king and the queen? In neither case was the term *status* used to qualify the *domus* or *hostel.* Nevertheless, did St. Louis and the framers of the Provisions have in mind the household as the more private estate of the king—which Lapsley thought was the meaning of *lestat del hostel* in the Statute of York?[49] Although it is difficult to say whether in the minds of the provisors the royal household was the private or public estate of the king, it is probable that to St. Louis it was at least an essential part and center of the public estate, which was above all the *plena (plenaria) potestas et liberum regimen* of a sovereign monarch. Perhaps the household enjoyed a similar public *status,* derived from the *status regis,* in the later thirteenth and the early fourteenth centuries. Since the king was the active head and no mere symbol of the State, the government was in some important ways centered in the household. In it the king consulted in his council with his *proceres,* counselors, and officials, and formulated policies; it was an important center of the administration of the whole realm.[50] In

46. *Op. cit.,* pp. 373–94; p. 382 for *communs bosoignes.*
47. See below, nn. 72–75, on *honor*—and above, nn. 25, 28, 33.
48. Stubbs, *SC,* pp. 395–97.
49. "Statute of York," *EHR,* LVI, 43–49.
50. On the confusion between public and private in the royal household, see

some respects, possibly, members of the royal family partook of the public estate of *hostel* and king. Certainly the heir to the throne was treated as a subject of the public law. The young Edward was deeply involved in the *negotia regis et regni* from 1258 on, and the estate of the heir along with the estate of the king was to be stressed in the Statute of York.

There was, to be sure, much that was private in the royal household. But at the same time, just as in his office the king was a *persona publica,* just as he enjoyed a public as well as private *status,* so the royal *domus, hostel,* household, shared in the public aspects of kingship. Perhaps, indeed, the very joining of *status* to *hostel, lestat del hostel,* resulted from the concept of *palatium* in the Roman and Canon law and in the legists and canonists. For the imperial palace was "sacred" and like all *sacra* was a subject of public law. Further, according to the legists, city halls, *palazzi communali,* housing the communal councils of priors and courts of justice, were called *palatia* and *domus;* and like royal *palatia* they were *sacra* and public. The *domus fiscalis,* too, was *sacra.*[51] In the *Glos. ord.* of Johannes Teutonicus on the *Decretum* we find that the bishop's *domus* was in one sense his *familia*

J. E. A. Jolliffe, *Angevin Kingship,* chap. ix; Powicke, *Thirteenth Century,* pp. 323 f., 545 f., stresses the public nature of the household in the time of Edward I; and J. C. Davies, *Baronial Opposition to Edward II* (Cambridge, 1918), on the personal and private aspects of the reign of Edward II, along with the public as well as private confusion of household activities, in that the king did not draw "any distinction between his household and the administration" (p. 63), chaps. ii and iii—indeed the whole book deals essentially with the public nature of the household as more important than the private. S. B. Chrimes, *An Introduction to the Administrative History of Medieval England* (Oxford, 1959), agrees with Davies and adds good comments, pp. 156–60. Of course T. F. Tout, *Chapters in the Administrative History of Medieval England* (Manchester and London, 1920), is invaluable—see for the twelfth and thirteenth centuries I, 18–31, 181–83, 313–17, and II, 10–59; for Edward II, Vol. II, chap. viii. Tout's emphasis is on the wardrobe, but here and there he discusses the problem of the public vs. private nature of the household.

Wilkinson, *Constitutional History,* II, 113 f., also stresses the fact that in the time of Edward II the household and royal council were at the center of the government, that even the officers of state, like the chancellor, treasurer, and justices, in carrying out the king's commands were subject to the household system.

51. For the Roman law see *D.* 1, 1, 1, 2, and *C.* 11, 77, 1; and a gloss to *C.* 11, 76 (77), 1, ad v. *excipimus*: ". . . nam cum palatia vel domus in civitatibus deputantur ad usum publicum principis, vel ad reponendas species publicas, vel ad redditionem iuris, non debent privati eas impedire nec suis usibus occupare"; Lucas de Penna says that palaces and all things which belong to the prince are *sacra,* because the power of the prince is from God (*Com.,* to *C.* 10, 6, 2, ad v. *sacris,* p. 37, No. 3). Else-

(administrative household), in another his church.[52] We must not go too far afield on a subject that needs much study. But as early as the time of Henry II, Gilbert Foliot, bishop of London after 1163, described the *palatium* as the center and place of the exercise of the authority of the king in judicial matters.[53] At the same time the con-

---

where he says that the *curia*, as the *locus* where *decuriones* assemble, is a palace, like the palaces of cities in Tuscany, "ubi morantur regimina [*regina* in the text I have used] seu priores" (to *C.* 10, 31, 41, p. 166, No. 5). He adds here his remarks about the *curia principis, curia ecclesiastica praelatorum, curia iudicum maximorum,* and the *curia* as the *fiscus.* In the *curiae* of magnates and kings, he continues, ambition and vice, informing and prying, and detraction and jealousy prevail. See Lucas also to *C.* 11, 76 (77), 1, p. 646, Nos. 4–6. The *Glos ord.,* to *C.* 4, 44, 18, had already spoken of the *palatini* as the *proceres palatii,* "quorum consilio regitur respublica"; and to *D.* 43, 6, 1, ad v. *aedes sacras:* "Id est Deo consecratas . . . ; sed et domus fiscalis dicitur sacra."

Baldus implies that the royal palace is where the king and his government are, that the king as *caput regni* is in his palace, just as the *regia civitas* is called the *caput regni* (to *D.* 1, 18, 1, No. 26; quoted by Kantorowicz, *King's Two Bodies,* p. 204 n. 35). This is related to such ideas as those of the thirteenth century which equated *corona, patria communis, caput regni,* and king and capital city; see my "Two Notes on Nationalism," *Traditio,* IX, 289–96. (See also nn. 53 and 54, below.) It is related also to the idea that where the emperor is, there is Rome (Kantorowicz, *King's Two Bodies,* pp. 204 f.). To be sure this means in one sense that the king is the realm wherever he may go. But there is also, perhaps, the meaning that the king's government and the king are present everywhere in the realm, even though the king remains in the *regia civitas* (and in his palace); see Kantorowicz, "Invocatio nominis imperatoris," *Boll. del Centro di Studi Filologici e Linguistici Siciliani,* III (1955), 1–16.

The *dignitas gloriosa* of the royal *palatium* is related to the *maximum splendor regiae potestatis* in a Frankish coronation *Ordo* of 768–816; Schramm, "*Ordines,*" *Archiv für Urkundenforschung,* XI, 369 f.—cf. below, Part III, n. 2.

On the public nature of the royal palace at Pavia in the eleventh century, see Kantorowicz, *King's Two Bodies,* p. 58 n. 34, and p. 188 n. 306. The idea of the *sacrum palatium,* so far as it concerned the legists in our period, goes back to the classical Roman law; H. Fichtenau wrongly starts it with Byzantine theologizing, whence it came, he says, to the West in the time of Charlemagne, "Byzanz und die Pfalz zu Aachen," *Mitteilungen d. Inst. f. österreichische Geschichtsforsch.,* LIX (1951), 1–54, esp. 13 f. But of course the Byzantine influence may have stimulated the revival of the classical idea in the West.

On the architectural symbolism of the *sacrum palatium* as the seat of government in the late Empire, see E. Baldwin Smith, *Architectural Symbolism of Imperial Rome and the Middle Ages* (Princeton, 1956), p. 10.

52. *Decretum,* Dist. 47, c. 8 Sicut § Necesse (Gratian), and Dist. 89 "Domui" (Gratian), and the glosses to these.

53. J. A. Giles, ed., *Gilberti Foliot Epistolae* (Oxford, 1845), I, 277: to Thomas Becket, Gilbert Foliot writes that it is the duty of bishops to serve the king, for the

cept of the *civitas regia* as the *caput regni* was anticipating the identification of the capital city and the *patria communis*—at least in France in the later thirteenth century, when Paris was, like Rome with respect to the Empire, becoming if not *urbs* and *orbis* the *caput regni* and "common fatherland" of the kingdom of France. For any city in which a king had his *sedes* became the capital, because of the *regis potentia* or the powers of the king as head of the realm.[54] Similarly the *status regis* gave the *hostel, domus,* or *palatium* its estate public. At any rate the royal *hostel* in England may have enjoyed an estate that was as public as the estate of the king. No doubt it was very different from the ancient *sacrum palatium,* but it was more the center of the public authority and government than Buckingham Palace is today.

It is thus probable that St. Louis had in mind the public nature of the *domus* of Henry III. The royal *domus* was the very core of the king's public powers of government; and surely, given the prevailing theory of kingship, Henry III should have the full right to choose the officers of his household, including the members of his council. And the old Roman term *proceres sacri palatii* (*C.* 1, 14, 2, and 8) was still in use for royal councilors, counselors, judges, and administrative offi-

---

Church thereby enjoys a greater *potestas* on earth, a *potestas* "qua magnum in palatio obtinet ecclesia principatum, cum in omnibus regni judiciis, praeterquam si de vitae periculo tractatur aut sanguine, locum habeat ipsa praecipuum: haec regi nos obligat . . . , ut ab ipso citati debeamus assistere, et singulorum causas universi discutere, et judicare."

54. So the great decretist Huguccio, *Summa,* to Dist. 96, c. 13 Sicut, ad vv. *Parva civitas praerogativam praesentis regni non minuit:* "Comparata regno, vel habens sedem regiam, nam in quacumque civitate sit sedes regia, non diminuitur regis potentia" (MS Vat. lat. 2280, fol. 87^v); also the *Summa Reginensis:* "Nam in quacumque civitate sit sedes regia, non imminuitur potentia" (Vat., MS Reg. lat. 1061, fol. 28^v). In the context the *praerogativa regni,* the *sedes regia,* and the *potentia regis* are thus closely related.

As for London as capital as early as the time of Henry II, Alexander III in 1161 called London the *regia civitas* where the king frequently sojourns, "et ibi frequentes baronum et procerum de toto regno soleant esse conventus"; and "quanto autem praedicta regia civitas inter alias regni civitates magis est nobilis et famosa," so much the more does the king want the church of London to be administered by a man who is worthy and wise in divine and human law (Giles, ed., *Gilberti Foliot Ep.,* I, 192 f.). In another letter the pope, again to Gilbert, says that Henry II had asked that Gilbert be bishop of London "ut in ea civitate quae quasi caput regni est" (II, 85 f.). But so far as I know no one in this or the following century went so far as to identify London with the *patria communis* of England, as Pierre de Belleperche did for Paris and the *patria communis* of France in the time of Philip the Fair; see my "Two Notes on Nationalism," *Traditio,* IX, 291, 293.

cers, and sometimes also for the great men of the realm who were summoned to Parliament as a greater council and court.[55] Private and personal though medieval kingship was, it was also public. If Louis XIV constantly combined and displayed his private and public persons in the palace at Versailles, and yet is treated as a modern king, it is not illogical to claim a similar treatment for Henry III and Edward I.

Altogether, then, in the Award of St. Louis the *status* of the king is virtually the same thing as the *status* of the crown; both estates are aspects of the same thing, the fullness of the king's public *potestas*. Had Bracton drafted the document for the French king, he would perhaps have spoken about the rights of jurisdiction and government, about those things which, connected with justice and peace, belonged to no one except the crown and the royal dignity. But he would have meant what the Award declared was the lawful *status* of Henry III.

The language of other sources for the reign of Henry III does not contradict the general sense of what has been said. In the Form of Peace, 1264, it was provided that the king, advised by nine counselors, should appoint greater and lesser officials to the "regimen curiae et regni" and these officers should swear to conduct themselves in office "ad utilitatem domini regis et regni."[56] The nine *consiliarii* themselves were to be chosen "ad reformationem status regni Angliae"—and here the *status regni* could as easily mean the royal government as the state of the realm. In the Confirmation of Charters of 1265, the king referred to the earlier settlement "pro regni pacis et securitate," and to the *ordinatio* "super nostro et regni nostri statu."[57] Once more, since the business treated had been the public authority of the king, the probability is that the *status regis* was again the king's lawful public rights and powers. Those who drew up the *Dictum* of Kenilworth emphasized the *honor* and *bonus et pacificus status* of the king; and the commission given delegated powers provided that the king should fully hold and freely exercise his *dominium, auctoritas,* and *regia potestas*. The *dignitas regia*, as defined by the approved *iura, leges,* and *consuetudines* of the realm, must not suffer damage. The king should pardon all who in the civil war had inflicted any injury "in ipsum vel in coronam

55. *Proceres* appears over and over again in English as well as continental royal documents; in the legists the word sometimes means the members of the government of an Italian commune. See above, n. 51, and the *Glos. ord.* to *C.* 4, 44, 18—*palatini* are *proceres* by whose *consilium* the *Respublica* is governed.

56. Stubbs, *SC,* p. 401.

57. *Op. cit.,* p. 404.

regiam"; but all places, rights, property, and other things belonging to the *corona regia* should be restored "ipsi coronae et domino regi."[58] In the *Dictum,* then, the *honor* and *status* of the king included the public powers of the royal jurisdiction (justice was a true reflection of the *regia majestas),*[59] and were equivalent to the royal *dominium, potestas,* and *dignitas.* Possibly, in fact, in this instance *status regis* signified the public office of kingship better than *corona.* But since the royal estate could not function without the rights and properties that belonged to the crown, it is likely that *corona* and *status,* along with *dignitas* and the like, were not fundamentally different in meaning.

Henry III did not have the ability to govern his realm according to the developing concepts of the public law. Edward I had the ability; and he and his advisers seem to have been intellectually and politically aware of the importance of the *status regis* and the *status regni* to each other. That the public estate royal was the king's power, which it was his duty as well as right to use, to maintain the *status Reipublicae, ratione status regis et regni,* Edward understood well enough. He realized, as Sir Maurice Powicke has so well said, "that the state of the king was in the end identical with the well-being of the community of the realm."[60] Justinian, we noted above, had long since expressed the same ideal for the imperial government, if in terms of "what profits all in common" and "the welfare of subjects is our own."[61] No matter that the terminology varied—royal policies and acts *pro re publica, pro utilitate regni, pour le profit commun* belonged to the *status regis* and the crown, and were for the maintenance or defense of the *status regni* and of the royal estate in common. A few examples will indicate, along with the well-known appeal to *quod omnes tangit,* why Edward was long ago called the English Justinian.

In 1274, Edward, ordering the great inquest, indicated that the royal rights and liberties (such as wreck of the sea), which as well as common justice and the *regia potestas* pertained to the crown, touched both his *status* and the *status* of the community of shires.[62] In 1275, Parliament granted him a subsidy—"causa suae novitatis" said some;

58. *Op. cit.,* pp. 407 f.

59. *Op. cit.,* p. 408, § 2.

60. *Thirteenth Century,* p. 37; Sir Maurice long ago observed how Edward was practicing "reason of State," "Reflections on the Medieval State," *Trans. Royal Hist. Soc.,* XIX (1936), 1–19.

61. Above, n. 14.

62. Stubbs, *SC,* pp. 421 f.

"ad relevationem status nostri," said the king. To the king and his heirs the same Parliament granted the custom on wool, woolfells, and leather.[63] These examples point, first, to the royal estate in its fiscal and judicial rights and powers; second, to extraordinary taxation for the new king as he is beginning his reign, hence for the proper maintenance of his public estate, perhaps because of the increasing costs of government and household; and third, to additional regular income for the estate of the king and his heirs, that is, probably, for Edward and his successors.

If the Statute of Gloucester, 1278, held that the "profit de office regal" (utilitas regalis officii, 1267, in the Statute of Marlborough) demanded that the king provide for the "amendment" of the realm and the fullest exhibition of justice (dreit), but did not mention the "profit" of the crown, the terms were equivalent to status regis and status coronae.[64] The business "pro re publica" for which in 1282, Edward summoned the clergy to Parliament, was a negotium (war in Wales) to be finished for the praise and honor of God, the magnificentia nostrae famae, and the peace and tranquility of the whole realm and people. And in 1294–1295 the king's war in Gascony touched king and kingdom.[65]

Disturbance of the peace, or of the common utility of the realm, was naturally another business that touched king and realm in common. In 1291, Edward appointed commissioners to investigate the private war between the Marcher earls of Gloucester and Hereford, because the matter "dominum regem et coronam et dignitatem suam tangit." The commissioners pointed out that the king by his prerogative was above the laws and customs of the realm when he was acting for the common utility.[66] Franchises, we noted in Part I, must not be

63. Op. cit., pp. 422, 443. A subsidy ad relevationem status regis reminds one of the idea expressed by Thomas Aquinas and Lucas de Penna; above, n. 18.

64. Stubbs, SC, pp. 333, 449.

65. Op. cit., pp. 430, 459, 476–80. For another emphasis on war as a business common to king and realm, see Keeney, "Military Service and the Development of Nationalism," Speculum, XXII, 534–49. For the background in legal thought, see above, nn. 16–20.

Fama, in relation to the majestas and status regis, and "illaesa" majestas, needs study; see below, Part III, nn. 7, 38.

66. On this episode see A. J. Otway-Ruthwen, "The Constitutional Position of the Great Lordships of South Wales," Trans. Roy. Hist. Soc., Ser. 5, VIII (1958), 1–20, esp. 16; also Powicke, Thirteenth Century, pp. 329 f.; and J. E. A. Jolliffe, Constitutional History of England (London, 1937), p. 305. Of course many other scholars have observed the significance of the case.

allowed to hurt the common welfare of the realm. Maintaining peace for the *status regni* certainly belonged to the king and his crown and dignity; it also belonged to his supreme authority and the public powers in his prerogative. Thus if the *status regis* was not mentioned in this case in 1291, the equivalent words implying the public *status* of the king were used. The same is true of the king's claim that the custody of the temporalities of the bishopric of Llandaff, *sede vacante*, belonged "ad nos et nostre corone dignitatem," just as in all cathedral churches of England.[67] The king could hardly claim that temporalities during vacancies of episcopal sees were his private possession as well as the possession of the *dignitas coronae*. Such rights were the king's as a "body politic," by reason of his public *status*. The implication once more is that *nos* and *dignitas coronae* could not be separated, that they meant the same thing as *status regis* and *status coronae*, two ways of describing the public office and its fiscal powers.

That the highest estate of the king was essentially the same as the estate of the crown in the thirteenth century can be shown again in sources relating to the coronation oath, or to the so-called inalienability clause.[68] According to Pope Honorius III, in the decretal *Intellecto* (*Decr. Greg. IX*, 2, 24, 33), the king of Hungary had alienated certain things to the injury of his realm and of his *honor*; but the king in his coronation oath had sworn "iura regni sui et honorem coronae illibata servare." In 1215, Innocent III had already equated the rights and honor ("ius pariter et honor") of King John of England.[69] Now, *honor* in the Roman public law was office and *administratio*; and in a legist of the late twelfth century, Johannes Bassianus, the *ratio honoris publici* was the "reason" of the public necessity of the magistracy and the *imperium* (powers of jurisdiction and coercion).[70] In the early middle

67. Otway-Ruthwen, *TRHS*, VIII, 17 f. On the great franchises and the king's public authority, see my remarks and references in *"Ratio publicae utilitatis, etc.," Welt als Gesch.*, XXI, 78 n. 73.

68. The scholarly literature has become abundant; I refer chiefly to H. G. Richardson, "English Coronation Oath," *Speculum*, XXIV, 44–75, Riesenberg, *Inalienability of Sovereignty*, chaps. iv and v; and Kantorowicz, "Inalienability," *Speculum*, XXIX, 488–502—details below, in Part III.

69. Richardson, *Speculum*, XXIV, 48 f.

70. *D.* 50, 4, 14: "Honor municipalis est administratio rei publicae cum dignitatis gradu"; for Johannes Bassianus see my *"Ratio publicae utilitatis, etc.," Welt als Gesch.*, XXI, 72. About 1228, John of Viterbo, in his *De Regimine civitatum*, identified *honor* with *regimen* or *administratio*: "Dicitur regimen administratio seu ille honor municipalis qui est administratio rei publicae cum dignitatis gradu . . .": quoted by Berges, *Fürstenspiegel*, p. 71 n. 3. Cf. above, nn. 28, 33.

ages, too, the royal *honor* could mean the public office and power of the king.[71] An Anglo-Saxon coronation *Ordo,* in a version of the late eleventh century, states that the *regalis status* was the *honoris et regni solium*—and surely the "estate royal" is already public.[72] This tradition gained strength, we noted above, among the legists of the twelfth and thirteenth centuries, and in the usage in imperial and royal chanceries.[73] *Honor* certainly refers to the king's duty and powers of public office in relation to the safety of the realm in the thought of a French legist, Bernard de Deutio (?), in the early fourteenth century. In time of war, he says in his *Quaestiones* (1318), not only vassals but all subjects are bound to follow the king "ad exercitum." For every subject, even if he is not a vassal, "iurat honori domini." But the "honor regis est regni protectio, et quod fortem et potentem habeat exercitum." Therefore not only for the *honor regis* and the *regni protectio* but also "ad utilitatem reipublice" the king's subjects can be compelled to fight in defense of the realm.[74] And Lucas de Penna stresses the *honor principis* as the supreme authority: even if a king's *rigor* seems unjust, when it is for the public welfare (*status regni*) it must be endured

71. Kantorowicz, *King's Two Bodies,* p. 58 n. 34, referring to a law of King Recceswinth in the Pseudo-Isidorean Decretals.

72. P. E. Schramm, "Die Krönung bei den Westfranken u. Angelsachsen von 878 bis um 1000," *Zeitschrift d. Savigny-Stiftung für Rechtsgeschichte, Kanon. Abt.,* XXIII (1934), 168 f.: "Sta et retine regalem statum, honoris videlicet et regni solium. . . ." Interesting also is the *Anonymous of York,* Tract. IV: ". . . quia claves regni, id est potestas et regimen regni et regnum ipsum honor est proprium regum," and the *regimen* is the *honor* or *officium regis; MGH, Libelli de lite,* III, 672 and 678.

73. Besides the glosses in the *Glos. ord.* to *D.* 1, 4, 1 (the famous *lex regia,* "Quod principi placuit, etc.," because the people "ei et in eum omne suum imperium et potestatem conferat"), earlier glosses of the twelfth century are of interest: to the word *ei* a glossator says, "ad honorem"; to *in eum,* "curam et solicitudinem" (Bamberg, Staatsbibl., MS Iur. 12, fol. 5). Another gloss, ad vv. *ei et in eum,* reads, "Scilicet, ad eius honorem" (MS Vat. lat. 1408, fol. 7). In the thirteenth century Odofredo, *Com.* on the *Dig Vetus* (Lyons, 1550), p. 17, to *D.* 1, 4, 1, says: "nam lex ortensia lata de imperio principis cavetur quod populus romanus principi omnem suam potestatem quantum ad honorem ei et in eum quantum ad onus concessit . . . Scilicet animo condendi legum: ut subditi servent . . ."; and ad v. *ei:* "Scilicet, quantum ad onus: quia sicut ipse debet habere honorem: ita onera imperii debet sustinere, scilicet, condendi legem. . . ." Thus the *imperium* and *potestas* of the prince belong to him as to his office, *honor,* along with its duties and burdens. See above, nn. 25, 28–31. See also Rassow, *Honor imperii,* pp. 78–80, 90–93, 107 n. 176; but Rassow has nothing on *honor* in the Roman law and the legists.

74. MS Vat. lat. 2642, fol. 117–117ᵛ: ". . . quia quicumque subditus iurat honori [*honorare* in the manuscript] domini, licet non sit vassallus . . . ; sed honor regis est regni protectio . . ."; no one can excuse himself from military service, because the

"propter honorem principis qui est res publica, et res publica est in eo."[75]

No doubt, then, in the letters of Innocent III and Honorius III on the inalienability clause in the coronation oath, the *honor* of a king was more than any feudal *honour*; it was the public office and powers of the king, stated also as the *honor coronae*. We must remember, therefore, when we encounter *honur* in the Statute of York, that the royal honor was sometimes either a part of or the same as the public *status regis*.

Several times we have mentioned the *dignitas regis* as comparable with the royal *status, potestas,* and *honor.*[76] Let us now see more fully what it means in sources relating to the coronation oath. *Dignitas* was often treated as office. John of Salisbury likened *publica dignitas* to *publica potestas.*[77] Azo held that the *ius publicum* itself could not be applied (for the public welfare) except by those elected or chosen "in dignitate"—that is, by magistrates who were themselves subjects of the public law. Innocent IV said that *iurisdictio* is "penes loca et dignitates, et non penes personas."[78] A decretist made the *status rei Romanae* (in *D.* 1, 1, 1, 2) virtually identical with the *dignitas* of the State and

---

royal army "vadit et ordinatur ad utilitatem rei publice. . . ." As for the author, I cannot find a Bernard de Deutio; but E. M. Meijers, *Études d'histoire de droit,* eds. R. Feenstra and H. F. W. D. Fischer (3 vols.; Leiden, 1959), III, 168, 191 f., discusses the work of an important French legist and cardinal, Bertrand de Déaux (Bertrandus de Deocio). Although Meijers mentions no *Quaestiones* among his works, nor the Vatican manuscript, it is possible that this Bertrand is the author of the gloss I have quoted.

Another gloss of the early fourteenth century closely associates *dignitas, status,* and *honor publicus* (Vat., MS Borghes. 374, fol. 262ᵛ), to *C.* 12, 1 De dignitatibus: "Aliquociens dignitas sumitur pro nobiliori et pleniori statu . . . ; aliquociens ponitur pro honore pub[lico], et ita accipitur hic, et infra e.l.ii. cunh." (No doubt *cunh.* stands for Guillaume de Cunh; Meijers, *Études,* III, 122 f.) In fact *C.* 12, 1, and 2 deals with *dignitates* as offices, occasionally as *honores.*

75. To *C.* 11, 71, 5 Praedia (*Com.,* p. 622, No. XXIIII).

76. Above, nn. 5, 6, 9, 11, 17, 18, 26, 30, 54, 63, 64, 70, 74. See also Kantorowicz, *King's Two Bodies,* p. 78 n. 34, p. 219 n. 76 (consult Index s.v. *dignitas*); and Riesenberg, *Inalienability,* pp. 98–112 (without any mention of *status*).

77. *Policraticus* IV, vii.

78. *Glos. ord.* to *C.* 8, 12, 6, ad v. *privilegiis*; Azo, *Com.* (Paris, 1577), p. 791, to *C.* 12, 1 De Dignitatibus; Inn. IV, *Com.* on *Decr. Greg. IX* (Frankfurt, 1570), to 1, 29, 14. Of course it was a commonplace that *dignitas non moritur* (as in *Glos. ord.* to *Decr. Greg. IX,* 1, 3, 36, ad v. *viveret*), which is a part of the doctrine that the king in his public body is immortal—so well developed by Kantorowicz, *King's Two Bodies.*

its government; and he covered *iudices* and kings with the mantle of the public *status-dignitas*.[79] Another decretist associated the *potestas* and *dignitas* of the pope with the *majestas* of the Roman Church; and he too defined the *ius publicum* as that law which pertains principally "ad statum, i.e., dignitatem rei romane."[80] A third decretist interpreted the *dignitas regni* and *dignitas ecclesiae* as the *constitutio* or laws (*canones* of the Church), intimating perhaps that the dignity of the monarch was also the dignity of the law and the State.[81] These decretists do not mention the *status papae*; but their use of *majestas* and *status* and *dignitas* seem to refer to the papal power and dignity, to suggest the *plenitudo potestatis,* and thus to help prepare the way for the extremists' identification of pope and Church, or of the "estate papal" and the *status Ecclesiae,* in the late thirteenth and early fourteenth centuries. *Majestas* itself, so Jacques de Révigny said, referring to the secular State, was, as it were, the *maior status* of magistrates.[82] *Dignitas,* too, in the context of the public law on the magistracy, was a higher estate. According to a French legist of the early fourteenth century, Guillaume de Cunh, "at times *dignitas* is understood for a more noble and complete *status*." Since this follows the definition of *dignitas* as a *potentia* given to man by nature, which made him the "dignicima creaturarum," and precedes the statement that sometimes *dignitas* "ponitur pro honore publico," he apparently thought that the dignity and power of public office were the same as the public *status* of a magistrate. Lucas de Penna said that the *corona* was the *insignia* of the

79. Paucapalea, *Summa,* ed. J. F. von Schulte (Giessen, 1890), p. 7: "Ius publicum est, quod ad statum i.e. dignitatem rei romanae principaliter spectat . . . Iure publico tenetur, si qui civem publicum iudicem vel regem appellantem necaverit, aut terruerit sive verberavit aut vixerit"; the same in the Brit. Mus., MS Royal 11 B. 11, fol. 2ᵛ.

80. The author of a *Summa* wrongly attributed to Rufinus (ed. Schulte [Giessen, 1892]), p. 375—see above, Part I, n. 59.

81. Above, n. 53, Huguccio was quoted on how the *potentia regis* and the *sedes regia* could not be lessened by being in a *parva civitas*—to *Decretum,* Dist. 97, c. 13 Sicut. On the same passage Simon of Bisignano says, ad vv. *Praerogativam praesentis regni . . . non minuit:* "Id est, sicut parva civitas non mutare dignitatem tocius regni, sic imperator non potest mutare dignitatem vel constitutionem ecclesie, id est, canones"; Brit. Mus., MS Royal 10 A. III; also in Rome, Bibl. Angelica, MS 1270. This has some bearing on *status, id est, magistratus.* At any rate *dignitas* is here the prerogative of king and realm.

82. Above, Part I, to nn. 58–70 (on the *status papae*); and n. 25 (Jacques de Révigny).

dignitas of the king.[83] The logical implication of these passages, therefore, is that the dignity of a king was the highest in the realm; associated with *status, honor,* and *majestas,* it was the public estate of the
supreme authority.

No wonder, then, that in papal decretals and letters on the coronation oath, and in the decretalists, the royal dignity amounted to the
same thing as the royal estate and the crown. In 1235, Pope Gregory IX,
without speaking of *honor* or *corona,* said that Henry III had sworn to
preserve the *iura, libertates,* and *dignitates regales.*[84] Honorius III in
the "Intellecto" had specified the *iura regni* and *honor coronae.* Johannes de Deo, one of the first decretalists to comment on this decretal
after it was incorporated in the *Decretales Gregorii IX,* simply speaks
of the "iura corone regni."[85] But others, Innocent IV, Hostiensis, and
Bernard of Parma, fail to mention the crown, returning to the *dignitas
regalis,* which the king must not gravely injure by alienations. They
agree, however, that moderate alienations do not hurt the royal dignity.[86] On the other hand, we observed above, the canonists were
bound to argue that alienations of a more serious kind were not injurious when they benefited the Church, for what profited the Church
profited the State and the secular authority. The public law was inter-

83. Vat., MS Borghes. 374, fol. 262ᵛ, a gloss to *C.* 12, 1: after saying that in one
sense *dignitas* is a *potencia* given to man by nature, and hence "homo est dignicima
creaturarum," he adds: "Aliquociens dignitas sumitur pro nobiliori et pleniori statu
. . . ; aliquociens ponitur pro honore pub[lico] . . . Cunh." See above, n. 73. See also
Lucas de Penna, *Com.,* p. 388, No. 2, to *C.* 11, 7, 11.

84. Richardson, "English Coronation Oath," *Speculum,* XXIV, 51; and on this
and on Honorius III's decretal "Intellecto," etc., also Riesenberg, *Inalienability,* chap.
v. See also below, Part III.

85. In his *Casus,* which I consulted in the MS Vat. lat. 2343, fol. 24.

86. *Glos. ord.* of Bernard of Parma, ad v. *regni sui;* Innocent IV, *Com.* (Venice,
1578), p. 348, c. 2: "Haec decr. intelligitur quoniam facit alienationes propter quas
graviter leditur dignitas regalis . . ."; Hostiensis, *Com.* (Venice, 1581), II, 137ᵛ, c. 2:
"Haec decr. intelligitur quando facit alienationes, per quas graviter leditur regalis
dignitas." On moderate alienations see the whole comment of Innocent IV; also
Baldus, *Margarita* to the *Com.* of Innocent IV, p. 348, c. 2: "Rex potest donare et
etiam alienare moderate, non ita immoderate ut laedatur dignitas regalis." Abbas
Antiquus (Bernard de Montmirat) was more specific: the coronation oath prohibits
the alienation of property that belongs to the royal dignity, but not the property
that is the king's own (as private property)—*Com.* to *Decr. Greg. IX* (Venice, 1588),
fol. 24, to 2, 24, 33 Intellecto. On this decretalist see Stephan Kuttner, "Wer war
der Dekretalist 'Abbas Antiquus,' " *Zeitschr. d. Sav.-Stift. f. Rechtgesch., Kan. Abt.,*
XXVI (1937), 471–87.

ested in the salvation of souls as well as the *status Reipublicae* on earth.[87] Furthermore, important alienations of royal rights in property that pertained to the crown and were not the king's private property were lawful if peace was thereby secured, the faith defended, and the *magna utilitas regni* achieved.[88] But this was no injury to the *dignitas regis,* for the maintenance of the *status regni* belonged to the king's dignity—and to his public powers or estate and to the crown. On the whole, therefore, in the decretalists the *iura coronae* and *status coronae* were understood as the *dignitas regalis*—as they had been by Gregory IX, and in the early thirteenth-century version of the laws of Edward the Confessor in the words "omnes dignitates et iura et libertates corone regni." These terms were simply other ways of speaking about the estate royal—so Pope Clement IV put it in 1265 on the injury to the *libertas, dignitas, honor,* and *status* and *iura* of Henry III and Edward and of the realm.[89] They were the source of the assertion made by Edward I that the magnates and *proceres* of the realm were bound by homage and fealty to defend "his dignity and the crown"; that nothing could be done "to the disinheritance or injury of the crown or otherwise to the king's royal dignity."[90]

As we observed earlier in another connection, the background is chiefly the terminology and theory in the Roman law and in documents of the twelfth century. In the first place, the authority of the prince and the public welfare were enhanced by privileges granted to churches. Such privileges, indeed, should be, like the *iura regni*

87. See above, n. 26.

88. Oldradus, *Consilia* (Venice, 1571), 37ᵛ–38, No. XCV, discusses the problem of how a king can give important real properties to the queen without injuring the *iura regis et regni* and also the *iura* of his heirs. A king of Leon, for example, had lawfully given *castra* to a princess of Castille when he married her, because the marriage was for the *magna utilitas regis et regni*, for securing peace for his subjects, and for the *expugnatio infidelium* (to *Decr. Greg. IX*, 4, 20, 5). Further, gifts to the queen are lawful because marriage and dowry are for the procreation of children and certainly royal children are for the public utility (cf. *D.* 24, 3, 1; and my "Ratio publicae utilitatis, etc.," *Welt als Gesch.*, XXI, 80). Hence, if such alienations violate the letter of the coronation oath, it turns out that in reality they are no violation at all, for they profit the *status regis et regni*.

89. Richardson, "Coronation Oath," *Speculum*, XXIV, 52—p. 49 on the *status coronae* in the documents of Edward I; also Riesenberg, *Inalienability*, p. 122, quoting Clement IV, from Rymer, *Foedera*, I, i, 459.

90. Trueman, "Statute of York," *Med. et Human.*, X, 70 and n. 6. Still other passages cited here by Trueman indicate that there was no real distinction between the royal dignity and the crown.

(*Angliae*) in 1235, maintained *illibata;* the patrimony of the Church must be kept *illaesum.*[91] It was the duty of the emperor, said Frederick Barbarossa (1162), as the *advocatus* and *defensor* of churches, to maintain their "iura integra et illesa." Otto of Brunswick (1198) explained to Innocent III that he wished to strengthen the *status ecclesiae,* and that he had accepted his election, consecration, and coronation "cum plenitudine regie dignitatis," and taken an oath to maintain *illibata* the possessions and *iura* of the Roman Church and other churches. The *regia dignitas,* the *status regis,* thus existed also for the protection and defense of the *status Ecclesiae.*[92]

In the second place, it was also the duty of the prince and lesser magistrates, by reason of their office—again for the public welfare of all and of the State—to protect the rights of the public fisc while at the same time protecting the rights of all subjects. All judges, said Justinian, should take the oath of office that they would practice equity, protect the fisc, be impartial, and keep "subditos . . . illaesos undique." If the emperor wanted to aid private persons who suffered injustice, he also wished the "publicum (fiscum) illaesum manere."[93] Let us repeat how Frederick Barbarossa put it: it behooved the imperial *sollertia* so to govern the Republic and investigate the *commoda* of subjects, that the *regni utilitas* persist *incorrupta* and the "singulorum status iugiter servetur illaesus." Hence the *status principis* included the powers necessary for taking care of the *status* of all subjects and the *status regni.*[94] The officers of the fisc or Exchequer in the kingdom of England, said Richard Fitzneale (obviously reflecting the Roman law if not the words of Frederick), exercised a *sollertia* by which "totius regni status indemnis servatur." Naturally the *ratio status regis,* about which he had spoken earlier, included the *sollertia* of the royal officers—*ad statum conservandum,* as the glossators put it.[95] In 1231 the Constitutions of Frederick II prescribed that the royal *bajuli* and *camerarii* should swear to maintain *illaesa* the *demania* and *iura* of the *curia regis.*[96]

These passages indicate, in the full context of ideas about kingship,

---

91. *C.* 1, 2, 12, and 1, 2, 14, 2; above, nn. 26–31; see below, Part III, in general.

92. Frederick, *MGH, Legum S. IV, Const.* I, No. 217; Otto, *Const.* II, No. 18. On *iura illibata,* see below, Part III, in general.

93. See below, Part III, pp. 3 f.

94. *MGH, Legum S. IV, Const.* I, No. 148; *Libri Feudorum,* pp. 2, 55; above, n. 30, and Part I, n. 77.

95. Stubbs, *SC,* p. 205; above, n. 9, and Part I, n. 77.

96. Huillard-Bréholles, *Hist. Dipl. Frid. II,* IV, i, 41 f., Tit. LXII.

justice, and the *status regni,* that the majesty, office, dignity, *honor, sollertia,* duty, and powers of the king were the *status regis et coronae.* This royal estate was in substance the powers of the king or rights of the crown; and it was based on the king's *iura* and *libertates,* and on the royal demesne and on customary revenues that came into the fisc. It was the king's public *status,* his fullness of power; and it existed for maintaining unharmed the *status* of churches and of all subjects, that is, the public welfare or *status* of the whole body of the realm. In other words, in the twelfth and thirteenth centuries, whatever the actual history of the clause in the coronation oath on the preservation of the rights of the crown, the main purpose and *ratio* of the public *status regis,* in terms of the royal honor, dignity, skill, and the like, was the preservation or maintenance of the *status Reipublicae*—"ne pereat." Therefore the king had no right to give away, except by way of delegation, either the powers of kingship or the essential revenues and rights on which his public estate or authority was based. If alienation was permitted with respect to property rights (but then not to the extent of weakening seriously the king's capacity to govern for the *status regni*), no alienation of the substance of the *status regis* or *status coronae* was lawful. The public law of the State forbade any fundamental change of the accepted constitutional *ordo magistratus regis.*

In the twelfth and thirteenth centuries, therefore, in England and on the Continent, the estate of the king was his public office and powers, and it was the same as the estate of the crown. Was the *status regis* substantially different from the *status coronae* in the reign of Edward II? Edward II himself, or those who framed the wording of a writ of 1312 to the sheriffs, used a terminology that reflected the older idea of the public authority embodied in the royal *dignitas, regimen,* and *majestas,* without indicating any real distinction between these and the *corona.* All rights of the crown, he said, the royal dignity, the *regimen* of the people, the peace and tranquility of the Church, and in sum the royal majesty, must be maintained *integra et illaesa.*[97] In 1314, Edward used the expression, "ad iura nostra regia . . . manutenda," as equivalent to rights of the crown and the royal dignity.[98] At other times, we find, the "state" of the king implied the meaning of *dignitas* as well as the *status regis* in the sense of royal rights and powers. Judicial processes should not prejudice the "state of the king and of his crown." Piers Gaveston was accused of damaging "the state of the king and his

97. For the whole passage, Richardson, *Speculum,* XXIV, 62.
98. Richardson, *Speculum,* XXIV, 62.

crown" by alienating lands and tenures of the crown. The royal estate in Gascony was certainly the king's rights in revenues and in jurisdiction. The king's state and right of the crown included his rights in a church; and the state of the king and kingdom was concerned in the war against Scotland.[99]

No doubt occasionally the estate or state of the king was related to the household, e.g., in 1309–1310.[100] At times, probably, it might refer chiefly to the material or financial support of the king and household. But was this estate in revenues and in the household kept distinct from the estate of king and crown? The *Dialogue of the Exchequer,* we must constantly remember, had measured the *status regis* or royal *potestas* by the wealth of the king that came not only from the demesne, but also from all kinds of rights of patronage, from his feudal empire overseas, and from extraordinary taxation. The fisc or Exchequer was public. In taking care of the revenues of the king it provided him with the normal income of his public office (the Exchequer and the wardrobe in the household remained closely connected in the reign of Edward II).[101] Quite properly, then, Richard Fitzneale had held that by its work "totius regni status indemnis servatur." The financial estate of the king, apart from purely private property, was evidently the main support of his public estate, dignity, honor, powers, or authority. It supported but was not the same as the public *status regis.* The *utilitas* or *status regis* was surely the public welfare of the royal magistracy, and it was at the same time the *potestas* or *dignitas* or *majestas* of the king; it was the *status coronae.*

Against Lapsley and Trueman, then, I must argue that still in the time of Edward II the estate or *bene esse* of the king looked to the rights of the crown as well as the household administration. His rights of public jurisdiction in his realm and in his feudal Empire could hardly as yet be fully separated from the household and the financial and military resources which it held at his disposal.[102] It seems strange, at any rate, that the *status regis* in 1322 should be quite different from

99. These examples are given by Trueman, "Statute of York," *Med. et Human.,* X, 72 f. Trueman admits that the king's estate might on occasion mean powers of jurisdiction, or the "well-being of the government." On Piers Gaveston and the general situation in 1311–22, see May McKisack, *The Fourteenth Century* (Oxford, 1959), pp. 21 ff.

100. Trueman, "Statute of York," *Med. et Human.,* X, 71 f.

101. See above, n. 9; on the wardrobe and the finances, Davies, *Baronial Opposition,* pp. 178–99, 181.

102. Lapsley, "Interpretation," *EHR,* LVI, 43.

what it was in the twelfth and thirteenth centuries and in the sixteenth century—or in the fourteenth century after the death of Edward II.[103] At times, we have seen, the *ratio status regis* not only existed for but sometimes was the same as the *ratio status regni*. Further, quite often the *status*, whether of king or communal magistracy, was defined as government.[104] So, too, at least for the French legist, Jacques de Révigny, the crown was not only the king's jurisdiction over the whole realm but was also the *corona regni* and *communis patria*.[105] For the crown was the *caput regni*. The *bonus status regis* was the healthy strength, dignity, and power of the king in his public office, and surely meant the same thing as the *bonus status coronae*.[106]

So often did the king say that the business of war and justice, not to mention revenues for himself and his government, touched himself, his *honor, profit, utilitas*, and *dignitas*, as well as the crown, that evidently he was speaking of his own public *status* as the head (*caput*) of the community of the realm. We have noted that King John held that the members of the realm should aid the *caput* in his war in France. In 1321 the canon of Bridlington was astonished that the magnates or *membra* in Parliament were acting without the assent of the king and were thus separating themselves from the *caput*.[107] This kind of thinking reappeared in the words which Henry VIII addressed to Parliament. If it was present only occasionally in English legal thought on the king and the realm, it reflected the abundantly expressed doctrine in corporate theories applied to the State by canonists and legists and by political theorists.[108] It therefore has its importance for the meaning of the *status regis*. Above all the king as head of the realm had a public estate, an estate that to be sure was based on the normal revenues of the fisc and on the household, but an estate which was the ensemble of

103. Trueman gives examples from the later fourteenth century, "Statute of York," *Med. et Human.*, X, 80 f. Also for the late fourteenth century Jean Gerson is interesting: the king's "second life," his *vita civilis et politica*, is the *status regalis aut dignitas*; Kantorowicz, *King's Two Bodies*, pp. 219 n. 76, 402 n. 299—Kantorowicz supports my identification of *dignitas* with *status*; also pp. 383–450.

104. Above, Part I, in general.

105. Above, Part I, nn. 26, 27.

106. Kantorowicz, *op. cit.*, pp. 368 f., tends to draw some distinction between *status regis* and *status coronae* for 1322.

107. Quoted by B. Wilkinson, "The Coronation Oath of Edward II and the Statute of York," *Speculum*, XIX (1944), 460.

108. See my "Statute of York," *Speculum*, XXIX, 421 f., 425 f., for general remarks. Of course, Gierke, *Political Theories*, devotes himself largely to the corporateness (or degree of corporateness) of the State. There is a great deal on the subject in Lagarde,

his powers as the supreme authority. His real public *status,* again, was also the *status coronae.* As head of the State, by reason of his "state," the prince enjoyed the fullness of public power to use right reason for all reasons of the public welfare (*status regni*). His dignity, public office, *honor, potestas, majestas,* and rights of the crown were the estate royal.

The conclusions reached can now be applied to the interpretation of the Statute of York with respect to the terms *lestat del hostel, lestat du roi,* and *lestat de la coronne.*[109]

Lestat del hostel.—In § 1 the Statute refers to the Ordinances of 1311 and the committee chosen by the magnates and prelates to "ordener et establir lestat del hostel nostre dit seignur le roi et de son roialme," and to do so "al honur de Dieu et al honur et profit de saint eglise et al honur du dit roi et a son profit et au profit de son poeple." Here the estates of the royal household and of the realm are as closely related as the old *status regis* and *status regni.* Like the *status regis* the *estat del hostel* exists for the *honur* of God, Church, and king, and for the *profit* of king and people. Except for the insertion of the "honor of God" the language used is simply a French version of the traditional ideas about the *status regis* (including his officers and counselors) that was necessary for the maintenance of the royal office (*honor*) and powers (*profit* or *status regis*), the *status Ecclesiae* and the *status regni* (common welfare or *profit* of people and realm). Even if the *estat del hostel* is not quite the same as the *status regis,* it logically implies the same thing, since the baronial ordainers were chiefly interested in controlling the king's choice of advisers, who were members of his "body politic." At any rate, the estate of the household was essential to the public office of the king and to his *status,* as it was to the *status regni.*

In other words, the magnates wished to regulate and control *lestat del hostel* precisely because it was public.[110] The accusations leveled at

---

Naissance, II[2], in every chapter on the scholastic philosophers, and in the conclusion, chap. xi, p. iii. Kantorowicz, *King's Two Bodies,* p. 208 n. 42, and chap. v, shows how important the concept was that the king or prince was *caput* both of the magistracy and of the *Respublica.* Cf. above, Part I, to nn. 29–38, 71–75, 91.

109. For the text of the Statute I have used *Statutes of the Realm,* I, 189—the division from Lapsley *EHR,* LVI, 50 f. Davies, *Baronial Opposition,* pp. 1–48, offers a good introduction to the Statute, especially to § 1, in his discussion of the royal prerogative. Wilkinson, too, presents a good general statement of the problem; *Constitutional History,* II, 113 f. Cf. above, n. 2.

110. I assume, of course, that the household of Edward II as an institution was not very different from that of his father; see Powicke, *Thirteenth Century,* pp. 323 f.; and above, nn. 49–53.

Piers Gaveston were a criticism of one aspect of the king's public power, his right to choose his counselors, who were members of the household. Essentially the Ordainers claimed that the king was getting the wrong advice from his favorite; he should appoint to his council men who were under baronial control. Whether they understood the legal theory of counsel I do not know. But according to the theory every prince must consult with counselors or experts on important matters of public policy and law and justice. The royal advisers were legally obliged to give good, wise counsel that was for the public welfare. The problem was: Did subjects have the right to determine whether the counsel given to the king was good or bad? This cannot be treated here. The point is that royal counselors, members of the household, were members of the government too.[111] It is likely, then, that the household was an essential part of the public estate of the king—so in the intention of the Statute. Hence there was no need of repeating "lestat del hostel" in the clauses that followed.

§ 2. *Le poair real* and *lestat de la coronne.*—In fact, it is significant that in § 2 there is no mention of the estate either of household or of king in the criticism of the ordinances. It is stated that examination of the ordinances by king and Parliament showed that they limited the *poair real* and thus blemished the royal *seigneurie* and the estate of the crown. The weakening of the royal power had in the past resulted in troubles and wars by which "la terre ad este en peril." Since the king's *potestas* was the *status regis* or its substance in earlier legal thought, and since its weakness brought on peril to the realm, this language reminds one again that the glossators had said that the public law, above all in dealing with the magistracy, pertained to conserving the *status* of the Republic, "ne pereat." An attack on the *status regis* was a danger to the *status regni*—at least in the standard theory of monarchy. Hence again there is a suggestion that the public *status* or power of the prince is necessary for the *status regni*. And again the royal power, the royal *seigneurie* (*majestas, dignitas,* or prerogative; not feudal *dominium,* although it too is involved), and the estate of the crown are equivalents of *status regis*.

§ 3. Here we have the declaration that the king and the whole community of the realm in Parliament (a suggestion of the idea that the king as head and the members—magnates and sometimes also the representatives or commons—were the community of the realm) have

111. On the king's council as a part of household and government, see Davies, *Baronial Opposition,* chap. xi.

annulled the ordinances, and that the royal statutes made before 1311 shall remain in force. This clause is not important for this study, but its meaning is surely that the old *status regis,* which included the right of the king to make statutes, *ratione utilitatis communis,* with the counsel and consent of his advisers and of the magnates, and, if need be, of all who were touched by a statute, was herewith restored. King and Parliament, not Parliament or any group of subjects without the authority of the king, should legislate.[112]

Now we come to § 4. This provision is negative: no subjects of the king or of his heirs shall make any ordinances "on the royal power of our lord the king or of his heirs, or [*ou*] against the estate of our said lord the king or of his heirs, or against the estate of the crown." The fact that *lestat del hostel* is not mentioned is no indication that "lestat nostre dit seignur le roi ou de ses heirs" has taken its place to mean the private aspect of kingship—indeed, the estate of the king is probably the same as, and as public as, the estate of the household. In any case, I think, the intention of the drafters was to make it clear that unlawful ordinances made by unauthorized persons *on* the *poair real* of king and heirs were also contrary or injurious *to* the royal estate, or to the estate of the crown. *Ou, or,* does not have to mean that the *poair real* was different from the estate of the king and his heirs; nor that the royal estate was not the same as the estate of the crown. The drafters wanted to make it clear to all that the royal power was the essence of the public *status* or office of the king, whether called *status regis* or *status coronae.* If they were guilty of a tautology, which is not strange for men trained in legal thought, it was a useful tautology, reflecting different ways of looking at the substance of kingship as the highest public office responsible for maintaining the state of the realm. Any ordinance made by subjects by themselves on the *poair real* was an illegal limitation of and injury to the royal estate and the estate of the crown. Nor does the inclusion of the king's heirs seem to imply a private estate. The heirs were probably mentioned in order to stress the continuity of the public power or *status regis* in a monarchy that had become hereditary. We have seen that Edward I, even before coming to the throne, shared in the public estate of Henry III in 1258–1266.

This interpretation is strengthened, in my judgment, by § 5, which is affirmative and thereby makes more effective the preceding negative provisions. The subjects of the king could not by themselves regulate

112. I have given my views on this in my "Statute of York," *Speculum,* XXIX, 429–32.

the power or estate of king and crown. Indeed it was a negation of kingship and the royal prerogative for them to do so. Therefore, in this clause, the authors, who of course were champions of the traditional doctrine of kingship, declared that only the king and his subjects in Parliament could provide for the estate of the king and his heirs and for the estate of the realm and the people. But there is no mention of the estate of the crown, nor of the *poair real!* A strange omission, on the face of it. But is it strange, after all? For the words "pur lestat de nostre seignur le roi et de ses heirs" meant that all provisions for the royal estate included those which maintained the royal dignity and power and the rights of the crown. In the following discussion of § 5, therefore, I shall use these terms as equivalent to each other: estate royal, estate of the crown, royal dignity, royal power, and prerogative.

Now, no medieval political or legal theory admitted that in a monarchy (or in the Church) subjects by themselves could legislate, "leges novas condere"; they surely could not pass a law declaring that the king's authority was henceforth subordinate to the great men of the realm. The king was the ultimate authority in making new laws for new situations.[113] He needed counsel and consent; he could not be arbitrary in making new laws. But he must have the final right to make a statute valid. It would therefore be absurd to think that he could, except momentarily under compulsion, consent to an ordinance initiated by subjects which limited his power or rights of the crown in legislating, judging, and interpreting the law. Therefore no proposal of a law that restricted or weakened or limited the royal power, the royal *status,* was, shall we say, constitutional (§ 4). Yet the barons or magnates had tried to set up their own committees to give the "right" advice to the king, and had limited the king's right to choose his own counselors. In a way, they had lawfully appealed from the king poorly informed to the king better informed. But they had gone beyond the public law in forcing the king to accept as normal their advice and their control of his council, and thus in damaging his own powers of magistracy. Apart from having, in the legal thought of the time, the right to be consulted about any business that touched them, they had no right to cripple the right of the king to make the final decision. If the king must in great matters touching the realm consult with them, they had to consult with the king and get his willing or free approval

113. I am referring to the legists' theory of legislation, which cannot be treated here; but see the *Glos. ord.* to *D.* 1, 4, 2; *C.* 1, 17, 2, 18; and *Auth.* 6, 13 (*Nov.* 84).

in a business that touched the royal authority. In both cases the *status regis* was superior to their *status*. If the *status* of the king was limited by his duty to maintain the *status regni*, it was enhanced by his right to interpret the *status* or *commun profit* of realm and people. This right, which was a part of his right and duty to maintain the *status regni*, increased his powers and public *status*. It was the essence of the royal prerogative in the estate royal. Since his *status* existed for the *status regni*, it was not subject to the power of any group of magnates acting by themselves.[114]

If this is true, it follows that any business that was for, or improved or strengthened, the just powers of the king was the business of the king as head and of the members of the realm in Parliament. It was a business that profited both the public authority and the welfare of the people, even when it primarily interested the king. And any important act of the king that improved the functioning of the royal jurisdiction and ability to defend the realm was the business of the *universitas* or *communitas regni*. For in the prevailing ideas of public law and efficient enforcement of the law in the courts, the maintenance of peace within, and the successful defense of the State were for the *commun profit*, the *utilitas communis et publica*. What therefore profited the public office of the king profited the people and the realm as a whole— so in theory.

Statutes and extraordinary taxes touched the *status* of the king with respect to his powers and duties. For example, in the reign of Edward I statutes strengthened his jurisdiction by developing or interpreting the feudal law. A grant of the customs on wool improved the financial basis of the royal government. Extraordinary taxes for the defense of the king and the rights of the crown were equally for the *status regni*. Magnates might object to going on a campaign when the king did not lead in person, or they might argue that a war was unjustified because there was no aggression or emergency. But they did not say that when the king's rights were in actual danger in Gascony that this touched neither their feudal obligations nor the safety of the realm of England. When the king could present a good case of necessity, his plea—based on a long tradition of public law in England as well as on the Continent—that both his dignity and rights of the crown and the *status regni* were concerned, met no serious opposition. The king was *caput* and the

114. Cf. Davies, *Baronial Opposition*, pp. 1–48, for a like conclusion in different terms and with a great richness of detail.

members of the realm were all in varying degrees involved in the common business of facing the threat of an aggressor in order to assure the *status regis et regni.*

What, then, were the matters which the king should establish in Parliament with the assent of the prelates, magnates, and community (*communalte*—which does not mean, but could include, the "commons") of the realm? They were, in the first place, any public business that was "for the Estate of our Lord the King and of his heirs, and for the Estate of the Realm and of the People."[115] To be sure the business could be the grant of revenues for the estate of the king; and in such a case, it has been argued, the royal estate was the material wealth or financial rights of the king—indeed, estate meant property.[116] But again one must consider the traditional idea that the income of a king was not his estate in the highest, public sense, but the means of supporting his *dignitas* and *status,* the means of carrying on his public *potestas.* If such revenues were sometimes for the maintenance of *lestat del hostel,* again this estate was either the same as or part of the public estate of the king's dignity and authority, of the estate of the crown.

In the second place, a business treated and settled by king and Parliament was often that of the royal jurisdiction, of legislation, or of war. Traditionally, I have shown, such a business definitely touched both the public *status* of the king's duties, rights, and powers, or the *status coronae,* and the *status* of people and kingdom. In § 5 of the Statute of York, then, establishments for the estate of the king and his

115. I quote from the translation by G. L. Haskins, *Statute of York,* pp. 95 f. As for the community of the realm, I cannot understand why *communalte* is still sometimes translated as the *commons*—as May McKisack interprets the word, *Fourteenth Century,* pp. 71 f. *Communalte* is simply, of course, the French for *communitas,* which at times included the *communitates* or *commons* especially in cases of extraordinary taxation in Parliament and occasionally in legislation. I agree with Strayer, "Statute of York and the Community of the Realm," *AHR,* XLVII, 1–22, that the *universitas regni* or *communitas regni* was chiefly the king as head and the magnates as members; but I hold that by the end of the thirteenth century it included the commons in Parliament when a proposed tax or law affected their interests—hence the rise of representation of the *communitates.*

116. Haskins, *Statute of York,* pp. 100–103. His argument is based in part on the belief that the *status Ecclesiae* was the properties of churches and ecclesiastics. But as I am trying to demonstrate in a special study, the *status* of the Church was the public welfare and safety of the Church and the faith, but included the instruments necessary for maintaining the faith, namely, the hierarchic *ordo* and government and the property rights and liberties that were deemed necessary for the existence of clergy and Church and its doctrines, all for the salvation of souls.

heirs were not limited to provisions for the property rights of the household and the royal family. They surely at times were statutes and extraordinary taxes that pertained to and strengthened the public office of the king, that supported the *ratio iurisdictionis et gubernationis* and at the same time the *ratio publicae utilitatis.* If for Henry of Ghent (*ca.* 1280) *ratio status* was the king's use of "right reason" in his power of making statutes for the "evident utility" of the State,[117] how can it be said with confidence that the estate of the king in the Statute of York was his *bene essere* only in relation to that part of his administration which looked to his person more than to his crown and was ordinarily carried on through the household organization? How can it be said that the estate of the crown was "the *bene essere* of the king in relation to that part of his administration which looked to his crown and realm rather than his person," as if the estate of the king were different from the estate of the crown?[118]

On the whole, in the light of the prevailing legal theories of public law, kingship, and the State, in the context of coronation oaths and the inalienability of anything necessary for the proper exercise of the royal authority, one must not distinguish sharply, if at all, between *status regis* and *status coronae.* The king, of course, had his private estate in property. But why should it be stressed in Parliament, where normally, as in the time of Edward I, the far more important joint or common businesses of the king's government and the *status regni* had to be treated or debated and settled? The Statute, in § 5, dealt positively with public, "national" affairs of king and people, and only indirectly with the private aspects of kingship. It is not literally said, but it is implied, that the king in Parliament was, as *caput* of the body of the realm, in his highest *status regalis.* The crown was the symbol of those public powers of governing which belonged to the king *ratione status sui,* and included rights and revenues necessary to the end. The public estate of the king was the royal dignity and power which were also the estate of the crown. Both belonged to and existed for the estate of the realm, as the care of the estate of the realm belonged to the estate of king and crown.

I conclude, therefore, that the royal estate in § 5 of the Statute of York is the traditional public *status* of the king with respect to his supreme authority. Deriving in large part from the Roman law and

117. In my *"Ratio publicae utilitatis, etc.," Welt als Gesch.,* XXI, 88–93.
118. Lapsley, *EHR,* LVI, 43.

the glossators, it was that *status magistratus* which was public and existed for the necessity of conserving the *utilitas communis et publica,* the *status Reipublicae,* the *status Regni.* It was that royal estate which Professor George Sayles has said was virtually the same as the prerogative and the crown, which made it lawful for the king in 1290–1291 to enforce peace on the great lords for the common utility of the realm.[119] What injured the public authority of the king, the royal estate, and crown, injured the *status regni.* It was at least similar, this estate of the king, to that *plenitudo imperii* for which, Lucas de Penna thought, the *corona regis* or *diadema* stood as a *signum:* the diadem or crown is the symbol of the king, but does not make the king; the *corona regis* designates the *plenitudo imperii* and is its symbol, but it does not give him the *imperium.*[120] It was that royal estate which Professor S. B. Chrimes, for the fifteenth century, has found in the kings' prerogative, power, authority, sovereignty, and duties: "His realm was bound to provide him with the means of maintaining his estate, and hence it was not clear that Parliament had the right to refuse him a grant."[121] In a word, the supreme powers of the king were the highest estate royal.

Finally, my conclusions in part confirm Chrimes's opinion, that the "estate of the king meant the mass of rights, duties, and attributes which constituted the kingship." Perhaps the royal estate was the prerogative, although Chrimes may put it better in holding that the prerogative was only one element in the king's estate. But if the *status regis* was, above all, the *potestas, honor, dignitas, majestas, corona,* and all the king's public duties and rights in governing in order to maintain and preserve the *status regni,* "lest it perish," it was at times virtually the same as the state of the realm. To repeat the words of Sir Maurice Powicke, Edward I realized "that the state of the king was in the end identical with the well-being of the community of the realm."[122] Edward II probably did not appreciate the true meaning of the "estate royal"; but it can hardly be doubted that his advisers who were the authors of the Statute of York fully understood it, and deliberately asserted it.

119. *Select Cases in the Court of King's Bench,* III, xlviii (Selden Society, LVIII; London, 1939).

120. To *C.* 10, 58, 1 Reos (p. 298, c. 1, No. 5). In another place Lucas emphasizes the *potestas* and *dignitas regis:* it is treason to seize or usurp the "maiorem potestatem et dignitatem regis . . . , quia quantum in se est totum reipublicae perturbat ordinem" (to *C.* 11, 53, 1 Si quis; p. 537, No. 39).

121. *English Constitutional Ideas of the Fifteenth Century,* pp. 38–43, 39, 91 f.

122. *Thirteenth Century,* p. 37; above, n. 59.

Naturally in the twelfth, thirteenth, and fourteenth centuries the English monarchy was still in many ways highly feudal and personal, sometimes more a subject of private law than of public. Nonetheless, when Henry II was with "ira et malevolentia" indulging in personal *vis et voluntas,* he and his counselors were also aware of the public *iura* that belonged to the *status regis*.[123] And when kings in the thirteenth and early fourteenth centuries were learning to deal with a business that was common to the *status regis* and the *status regni,* they and their *proceres,* counselors, and judges in some measure arrived at an appreciation of the public character of the royal majesty, dignity, honor, crown, and estate. Involved in the business of maintaining the state of the realm, the State itself, the "estate royal" was necessarily public, existing *ratione iurisdictionis et gubernationis* and *ratione publicae et communis utilitatis.* The *status regis et regni,* the estates of the head and of the realm as a whole, belonged to each other and each was indispensable to the other.

John of Salisbury and Richard Fitzneale had long since understood the spirit and even, to some degree, the letter of the revived Roman theory of public law and the State, and applied it to the kingship of Henry II. If John could not anticipate how Parliament would represent the community or *universitas* of the realm in *ardua negotia* which affected the *status regni,* he eloquently described the *status regis* as it essentially persisted in the following centuries and was so understood in the royal government in 1322. Let him, therefore, in his Christian–Stoic, Roman way, tell us how the *potestas regis* was public and, sanctioned by God and Nature, was exercised by the king as head for the public and common welfare of people and realm; and how the necessity, health, welfare, and strength of head and members belonged chiefly to the king:

Unde merito in eum omnium subditorum potestas confertur, ut in utilitate singulorum et omnium exquirenda et facienda sibi ipse sufficiat, et humanae rei publicae status optime disponatur, dum sunt alter alterius membra. In quo quidem optimam uiuendi ducem naturam sequimur, quae microcosmi sui, id est, mundi minoris, hominis scilicet, sensus uniuersos in capite collocauit, et ei sic membra subiecit, ut omnia recte moueantur, dum sani capitis sequuntur arbitrium. Tot ergo et tantis priuilegiis apex principalis

123. See J. E. A. Jolliffe, *Angevin Kingship,* esp. chap. iv. I think that Jolliffe has neglected the understanding of public law in the time of Henry II. Cf. below, Part III, nn. 7, 27, 35, and in general; also above, nn. 35–41, 50.

extollitur et splendescit, quot et quanta sibi ipse necessaria cre-
didit. Recte quidem, quia populo nichil utilius est quam ut principis necessitas expleatur; quippe cum nec uoluntas eius iustitiae
inueniatur aduersa. Est ergo, ut eum plerique diffiniunt, princeps
potestas publica et in terris quaedam diuinae maiestatis imago. . . .

Cum enim potestas publica sit . . . omnium uires exhaurit et,
ne in se deficiat, incolumitatem omnium debet procurare membrorum. Quot autem in administratione principatus extant officia, tot
sunt principalis corporis quasi membra . . . Nec diu subsistit in-
columitas capitis, ubi languor membrorum inualescit.[124]

124. *Policraticus* IV, i, xii (ed. Webb, I, 235, 278 f.). And on John's appreciation
of "reason of State" see my *"Ratio publicae utilitatis, etc.," Welt als Gesch.*, XXI,
20–22.

III. THE ROMAN LAW AND THE "INALIENABILITY" CLAUSE IN THE ENGLISH CORONATION OATH—AND THE *STATUS REGIS*

IN THE preceding part of this study I called attention to the terminology of the so-called inalienability clause of the coronation oath in relation to the *honor, dignitas,* and *status* of king and crown. Now I wish to treat in some detail the origins of the terms, and offer a few reflections about their constitutional significance.

In recent years Mr. H. G. Richardson has been ably studying the history of that part of the medieval English coronation oath in which the king promised or swore to maintain *illaesa* or *illibata* the *iura* (or *consuetudines, libertates, dignitates,* or *honor*—the terms vary) of king, realm, crown, and churches. He believes now that an inalienability clause phrased in some of this terminology appeared first in the coronation oath of Henry II in 1154, perhaps because of the influence of Nigel, bishop of Ely, and that the papal chancery, from the time of Pope Alexander III on, used the terminology in reference to kings' promises and oaths.[1]

In this small study I do not intend to deal primarily with the history of coronation promises and oaths, nor with the ceremonials or *Ordines* for the coronation of medieval kings. I want simply to indicate that in all probability the principle terms of the clause (whether it was actually added to the oath or not) came from the legislation of Roman emperors of the fifth and sixth centuries, and that the usage of the terms, from the mid-twelfth century on, resulted from the revival of the Roman law in the *Corpus Iuris Civilis* of Justinian. Mr. Richardson and other historians of the *Ordines,* the coronation oath, and the inalienability clause, have apparently failed to observe the importance of the Roman law.[2]

1. "The Coronation Oath in Medieval England: The Evolution of the Office and the Oath," *Traditio,* XVI (1960), 111–202, esp. 151–69, 174–80. In his earlier study, "The English Coronation Oath," *Speculum,* XXIV (1949), 44–75, he held that the inalienability clause appeared in the time of Henry III.

2. The works of Professor P. E. Schramm are fundamental: "Die Ordines der mittelalterlichen Kaiserkrönung," *Archiv für Urkundenforschung,* XI (1930), 285–390; "Die Krönung bei den Westfranken und Angelsachsen von 878 bis um 1000," *Zeitschr. d. Savigny-Stiftung f. Rechtsgeschichte, Kanon. Abt.,* XXIII (1934), 117–

Now, one precedent has been found, and greatly emphasized, for the king's coronation promise or oath that he would alienate no rights belonging to crown and realm, and that he would preserve these rights whole and uninjured. This precedent is the oath of office taken by bishops who were immediately subject to the pope. By the beginning of the twelfth century the bishops swore fealty to the papacy; and bishops in general promised not to alienate the estates of their churches.[3] No doubt such oaths, along with the whole early tradition of oath-taking, played a role. But a serious difficulty weakens the bishop's oath as a precedent: it was not phrased in such terms as *iura illibata* or *illaesa*.[4]

Nor do the terms in question appear in the early coronation *Ordines*, whether Frankish, Carolingian, German, or Anglo-Saxon.[5] What, then, is the origin?

The logical place to look for them is in the *Corpus Iuris Civilis*. For the laws of late Roman emperors prohibited the alienation of the properties and privileges of churches. And in fact it is first in these laws that one finds our terminology on inalienability. Here are the principal texts (the italics are mine):

(*C.* 1, 2, 12; Valentinian and Marcian, *an.* 451) *Privilegia,* quae generalibus constitutionibus universis sacrosanctis ecclesiis . . .

242; "Die Krönung in Deutschland bis zum Beginn des Salischen Hauses," *Zeitschr. . . . f. Rechtsgesch., Kanon. Abt.,* Vol. XXIV (1935); *A History of the English Coronation* (Oxford, 1937); *Der König von Frankreich* (2 vols.; Weimer, 1939). The following studies are also important: Eduard Eichmann, "Die römischen Eide der deutschen Könige," *Zeitschr. . . . f. Rechstgesch., Kanon. Abt.,* VI (1916), 140–205; Fritz Hartung, "Die Krone als Symbol der monarchischen Herrschaft im ausgehenden Mittelalter," *Abhandlungen d. Preus. Akad. d. Wissenschaften, Philos.-Histor. Kl.,* No. 13 (1940), pp. 3–46; Ernst Kantorowicz, "Inalienability: A Note on Canonical Practice and the English Coronation Oath in the Thirteenth Century," *Speculum,* XXIX (1954), 488–502; Kantorowicz, *The King's Two Bodies* (Princeton, 1957), pp. 346–58; R. S. Hoyt, "The Coronation Oath of 1308," *Traditio,* XI (1955), 235–57; Peter N. Riesenberg, *Inalienability of Sovereignty in Medieval Political Thought* (New York, 1956), chaps. iv and v; and B. Wilkinson, "The Coronation Oath of Edward II and the Statute of York," *Speculum,* XIX (1944), 445–69, and *Constitutional History of England,* III (London, etc., 1958), 73–83.

3. Kantorowicz, *King's Two Bodies,* pp. 348–50; Richardson, "Coronation Oath," *Traditio,* XVI, 151–53.

4. Richardson, "Coronation Oath," *Traditio,* XVI, 151–53, offers no sources containing the terms, nor does Kantorowicz, *King's Two Bodies,* pp. 348–50.

5. See in particular Schramm's studies referred to in n. 2; and Richardson, "Coronation Oath," *Traditio,* XVI, 162 f., 174–80.

retro principes praestiterunt, *firma at illibata im perpetuum decernimus custodiri.*

(C. 1, 2, 14, 2; Leo and Anthemius, *an.* 470; after decreeing that the real properties of the Church of Constantinople should not be alienated) *Ea enim quae ad beatissimae ecclesiae iura pertinent* vel posthac forte pervenerint, tamquam ipsam sacrosanctam et religiosam ecclesiam *intacta convenit venerabiliter custodiri, ut, sicut ipsa religionis et fidei mater perpetua est, ita eius patrimonium iugiter servetur illaesum.*

Justinian extended this legislation to the Church of Rome (*Nov.* 9; *Auth.,* Coll. 2, t. 4 Ut ecclesia Romana centum annorum gaudeat praescriptione). In this law he referred to the earlier laws without repeating the words quoted above. But he did use other words that are closely related and were to be repeated centuries later: the Roman Church, and churches subject to it, should enjoy the *praescriptio* of a hundred years, "*ut maneant* per totum supradictum tempus [that is, in perpetuity] *integra iura ecclesiastica.*"

Still more important, perhaps, was the influence of similar terms in laws of Justinian on the duties of imperial judges or magistrates, and on their oaths of office. In the famous *Praefatio* to *Nov.* 8 (*Auth.,* Coll. 2, t. 2), the great emperor spoke of working day and night for the *quies* and *utilitas* of his subjects in order to relieve them of every burden and "omni damno extrinsecus illato." In § 1 Cogitatio, he stated that if his subjects were kept *indempnes* and prosperous by the magistrates, both the *imperium* and the *fiscus* would flourish—the fisc was weakened (*imminuitur*) by the abuses of magistrates. Repeatedly he expressed the pious ideal that all subjects be kept *illaesi*: "Semper cum dei auxilio omnem facimus providentiam, *ut subiecti* ab eius clementia traditi nobis *illaesi serventur*" (*Nov.* 80, Praef.; *Auth.,* Coll. 6, t. 7[8]); "Magnum Deum . . . semper invocantes, studemus *omnes subiectos nostros* . . . *illaesos* et sine calumnia custodire" (*Nov.* 85[86]; *Auth.,* Coll. 6, t. 13 Praef.).[6] But if the emperor and his judges should protect subjects from injury, the public rights of the fisc (and of the emperor, of course) must also be kept unharmed. So Justinian declared (*Nov.* 17, c. 1; *Auth.,* Coll. 3, t. 4, c. 1 Oportet) that all magistrates should "undique servare ius," keep the *fiscus* unharmed, and vigilantly collect all *fiscalia tributa,* "ne forte fiscus minuatur." For "sicut enim privatos iniustitiam

6. These two passages are quoted by Antonio Rota, "Le fonti del diritto civile e la loro autorità alla metà del XII secolo," in *Studi Sassaresi,* XXIV (1952), 17 n. 5. Rota does not take up the problem of the coronation oath.

passos adiuvamus, sic et *publicum illaesum* manere volumus." (One can add the possible influence of the Roman law on treason. If *majestas laesa,* in the *lex Iulia majestatis* [*D.* 48, 4; *C.* 9, 8] was treason, surely the *majestas* of the prince must be kept *illaesa!* Yet I have found no specific evidence of the influence of the *lex laesae majestatis* on the concept that the *iura regis et regni* should be maintained *illaesa* and *illibata.* But perhaps it is significant, as will be seen, that Henry II of England was to make use of the idea that princes should "famam suam conservare illaesam." Since Henry was accusing Thomas Becket of treason, the implication is that the royal *majestas* must be kept *illaesa.* In fact, the English chronicler, Ralph de Diceto, associated injury to *fiscalia* and *laesa majestatis principis* [*an.* 1179]: "fiscalia supprimentes, et quae principis laederent majestatem, regiam indignationem incurrerent."[7] In any case, if the *fiscus* should remain *illaesus,* all the more should the royal *majestas* and the *iura regis* be kept *illaesa.*)

The twofold ideal of maintaining undiminished and unharmed not only the subjects of the emperor but also the rights of the public treasury (prosperous subjects and a prosperous treasury were both necessary for the public and common welfare of the Empire and of the emperor, the fisc, and the people)[8] was particularly emphasized in the oath which Justinian prescribed for all magistrates. This oath is given in *Nov.* 8, Iusiurandum, "Iuro ego" (*Auth.,* Coll. 2., t. 3, Iuro ego). Every imperial *administrator* must swear by God, etc., that he will serve the Emperor Justinian and the Empress Theodora by doing good work in his office; that he will be zealous and vigilant in looking after all fiscal business; that, insofar as possible, he will everywhere keep subjects unharmed by being *aequus* in all cases, just and fair to both parties; and that he will everywhere preserve the innocent unharmed. These are, for our purpose, the important terms:

> Et primum omne habebo studium *ut fiscalia vigilanter inspiciam,* . . . et *subiectos . . . illaesos* undique, quantum possibiliter habeo, *custodiabo . . .* et eos quidem, qui innoxii sunt, undique *innoxios illaesosque conservabo.*

Such are the imperial laws and the terminology. Do the terms appear in medieval sources before the twelfth century? Apparently

---

7. See below, n. 38; Stubbs, *SC,* p. 155.

8. *C.* 6, 51, 1, 14a, where Justinian states that the welfare (*commodum*) of his subjects belonged to him and was to his profit—and this law is on the rights of the *fiscus* to properties left by men who had no heirs and died intestate.

they do not. Although early councils and popes condemned alienations of church rights and properties, whether by bishops or by laymen, they did not repeat *privilegia illibata, patrimonium illaesum,* and *integra iura ecclesiastica.*[9] Nor were oaths of bishops and of German kings to the papacy drawn up in these terms.[10] Moreover, one does not find them either in the early coronation *Ordines*[11] or in feudal oaths of

9. Richardson, "Coronation Oath," *Tradito,* XVI, 151 n. 3, refers to the early Canon law as given in Ivo of Chartres and in the *Decretum* of Gratian, C. 12, q. 2, esp. cc. 19, 22. Not until the late twelfth and early thirteenth centuries do any decretists, so far as I have found, use the terms in commenting on the inalienability of the privileges and properties of churches. One decretist connects them not with a king's oath but with the duty of the Church to demand that a king preserve the *iura ecclesiae* unharmed, to C. 12, q. 2, c. 66, ad v. *poposcit:* "Poscere debet ecclesia regem, ut ecclesie iura servet illesa, ut xcvii di. ecclesie"; in the Paris, BN, MS lat. 15393, fol. 145ᵛ. Strangely, the reference is not to the Roman law but to the *Decretum,* Dist. 97, c. 1 Ecclesiae, which is a letter of Pope Boniface I asking the Emperor Honorius to protect the Roman Church and clergy and have care for the *status Ecclesiae.* Apparently the decretist did not think of the Roman laws from which his terms were derived; but the terminology was current and he used it.

Perhaps the author of the gloss just given is Alanus Anglicus—see Stephan Kuttner, *Repertorium der Kanonistik* (Vatican City, 1937), pp. 67–74; and Alfons M. Stickler, "Alanus Anglicus als Verteidiger des monarchischen Papsttums," *Salesianum,* XXI (1959), 348–50, 371–78. Alanus is certainly the author of another gloss that is interesting in connection with the coronation clause on inalienability. He offers the argument that the pope can depose a secular prince if the situation clearly justifies it and if the "status ecclesie nichilominus illesus permaneret"—to *Decretum,* C. 15, q. 6, c. 3 Alius item, ad v. *deposuit;* quoted by Stickler, "Alanus Anglicus," *Salesianum,* XXI, p. 367, col. 2.

Just as in the laws of Justinian the *status* (or *iura*) of the fisc and of the emperor and the *status subiectorum* should be kept *illaesus,* so the "state" of the Church must be *illaesus.*

But the fact that Alanus was English is no indication that he had any knowledge of the inalienability of the *iura regni,* etc., in an English coronation oath. As suggested above, he probably got the terms from the currency of them among canonists who studied the Roman law. Of course other decretists of this period may have used the terms and thus given them to Alanus.

10. Eichmann, "Römischen Eide," *Zeitschr. . . . f. Rechtsgesch., Kanon. Abt.,* VI, 140–205, reveals no such terminology until the late twelfth century. But then the terms appear only in Roger Howden's own words on the oath of fealty of the Emperor Henry VI to the pope, "quod ipse ecclesiam Dei et iura ecclesiastica fideliter servaret illibata, etc." (p. 176). See also Schramm, "Ordines," *Archiv für Urkundenforschung,* XI 295 n. 5, for the oath to the Roman people: "se in omnibus leges et dignitates Romana servaturum illesas"—"illibatas" in another version. The point is that these terms did not remain in this oath, which returned to the older form.

vassals—and lords do not promise to maintain the *iura* of vassals *illibata*, or to keep vassals *illaesos*.[12] Finally, I know of no oaths of the ancient Roman emperors that could have survived in these terms and influenced the formulation of oaths of medieval kings. It is remotely possible that some tradition of oaths of Roman soldiers and magistrates lingered on, but again I have found no evidence of it.

Since, probably, the imperial laws given above largely created the terminology, and Justinian developed a new form of the oaths of magistrates and judges of the Empire, no doubt the main reason for the silence of early medieval sources is the fact that the *Codex* and *Novellae* were not the subject of scientific study before the late eleventh and early twelfth centuries. While it is possible that our terms came into use in the eleventh century, I have not observed them in the polemical literature in the time of Gregory VII, or in the *Anonymous of York*. It was no doubt the teaching of Irnerius and his disciples that caused the Roman terminology to become current as early as the second quarter of the twelfth century. But if Irnerius and the Four Doctors of Bologna do not stress the terms, their teaching acquainted their students, some of whom served Frederick Barbarossa and Henry II and other princes (and also the Church and churches), with the twofold concept that the *iura regis et regni* and the *iura ecclesiastica* should be preserved *illibata* and *illaesa*. Vacarius does not mention the terms in his *Liber pauperum*, and perhaps did not directly introduce them into England; but Anglo-Norman bishops, we shall see, were students of the Roman as well as the Canon law in Italy, and may have brought them into English usage. One must remember, too, that the court of Archbishop Theobald of Canterbury was important.

The few public documents and letters that I have consulted point to the use of the Roman terminology well before 1154 (the year of the coronation of Henry II) both in Germany and in England. Almost as soon as Frederick Barbarossa was crowned at Aachen in 1152, the royal chancery began to formulate his letters in more terms from the Roman law than had appeared in the reigns of preceding kings and emperors. But did Frederick at his coronation promise or swear to maintain *illibata* or *illaesa* the rights and privileges of churches and of his realm

11. That is, in the *Ordines* studied by Schramm and Richardson—above, nn. 1-5.

12. See *Decr. Greg.* IX, 2, 24, 4 Ego N. (oath of bishop to the pope); *Decretum*, C. 22, q. 5, c. 18 De forma fidelitatis, and the *Glos. ord.* of Johannes Teutonicus thereto; and the *Libri Feudorum*, Book 2, chaps. 5-7.

and subjects? I find no evidence that he did so. His *professio* was apparently made in the traditional terms—as the exchange of letters with Pope Eugenius III indicates. He promised to honor the pope and to defend and do justice to the Roman Church and all ecclesiastical persons; and "viduis ac pupillis et universo populo nobis commisso legem et pacem faciamus et conservemus."[13] Not yet, therefore, was the king of the Romans promising to keep the *iura ecclesiastica illibata* and the *iura regis et regni illibata* or *illaesa*, and his subjects *illaesos*, although the substance of the *professio* bears essentially the same meaning. (As emperor he haughtily told Arnold of Brescia and the Roman citizens that he was not obligated to take oaths to confirm old laws and customs or to defend the *patria*—above, Part I, n. 76. Perhaps this reflects the idea of the "imperialists" that the emperor was above oath-taking— that kings, however, were lesser magistrates of "provinces" in the Empire, and therefore should take an oath of office.

But in 1153, Frederick condemned the alienation of the properties of the archbishop and church of Cologne, declaring that the emperor should "inviolabiliter conservare" the *iura* of the clergy and churches, and that the *iura* of the church of Cologne should remain "perpetuo robore illibata et inconvulsa"—cf. *C.* 1, 2, 12. The ecclesiastical *iura* so protected, however, were those which were recognized in the imperial courts![14] More significant is the famous *constitutio* of 1154 against the alienation of fiefs. Already in 1136 the Emperor Lothair III had prohibited any future alienations of fiefs, and he had said that it was the duty of the emperor "commoda subiectorum investigare, et eorum calamitatibus diligenti cura mederi: similiter reipublicae bonum statum ac dignitatem imperii omnibus privatis commodis praeponere."[15] The influence of Justinian in *C.* 6, 51, 1, 14a is evident.[16] But Frederick Barbarossa's law reflects also the legislation of Justinian on the duties and oaths of magistrates. Like Justinian he balanced the public utility (*regni utilitas*) and the common welfare (*status singulorum*) of his subjects:

13. A full account, with abundant citation of sources, in H. Simonsfeld, *Jahrbücher des deutschen Reiches unter Friedrich I*, I (Leipzig, 1908), 39–43, 122 n. 395. See also *MGH, Legum Sectio IV, Const.* I, 193 f., Nos. 137 and 139.

14. *MGH, Legum S. IV, Const.* I, 204 f., No. 146. (As usual in this study the italics are mine.) Note that the king emphasizes the superiority of his *iura* in his courts—implying the theory that the *iura regni et regis (et coronae)* are superior in public law to the *iura ecclesiastica* within the kingdom. See also below, n. 23.

15. *Libri Feudorum*, Book 2, chap. 52; *MGH, Legum Sectio IV, Const.* I, No. 120.

16. See above, n. 8.

> Imperialem decet sollertiam ita reipublicae curam gerere, et subiectorum commoda investigare, ut regni utilitas incorrupta persistat, et singuloum status iugiter servetur illaesus.[17]

Let us note also that the words "singulorum status iugiter servetur illaesus" represent the transfer of the Roman law on the inalienability of ecclesiastical property (*C.* 1, 2, 14, 2: "ita eius [ecclesiae] patrimonium iugiter servetur illaesum") to the inalienability of the welfare and rights of people and realm. Moreover, in 1167, Frederick declared that both the *status Romani Imperii* and the *status* of the illustrious princes (including bishops) who maintained the glory of the Empire should be "preserved unharmed."[18] And in 1162 he said that he was the *defensor ecclesiarum Dei,* "ut eas et earum iura integra et illesa sub nostro imperiali protectione defendamus."[19]

On the basis of these documents one might argue that in 1152, Frederick at his coronation had added the new inalienability clause to the traditional *professio.* As remarked above, however, there is no direct evidence that he did so; and no evidence, therefore, that he furnished a precedent for Henry II's adding an inalienability clause in 1154. Nonetheless it is interesting that the Roman terminology of the inalienability clause was appearing by 1153 in Germany. It is still more interesting that Frederick and his advisers were putting to use these Roman concepts of public law: it was not only the duty but the public right of the emperor of the Holy Roman Empire to preserve *illaesa* and *illibata* the public welfare, *status,* of the Empire itself along with the rights and welfare, *status* again, of all subjects, including the clergy and the churches. His *iura* as king and emperor existed chiefly for the defense and maintenance of the public and common welfare—therefore also for the defense of the Church within the State, since the public law was concerned with the magistracy, *sacra,* and priests (cf. *D.* 1, 1, 1, 2 and the *Glos. ord.* thereto). If the supreme authority of the prince included these duties and rights, it included also the right to preserve and strengthen the *status principis,* else he could not keep unharmed the rights of subjects and of the State. Implied, accordingly, of not stated in an inalienability clause, was the principle that the emperor could not alienate what belonged to his necessary authority. *Ratione gubernationis et protectionis, ratione status imperii,* it was the

---

17. *Libri Feudorum,* Book 2, chap. 55; *MGH, Legum S. IV, Const.* I, No. 148.

18. *MGH, Legum S. IV, Const.* I, No. 231: "...utriusque status servatur incolumis. ..."

19. *Op. cit.,* I, No. 217.

public right of the prince to keep *illibata* and *illaesa* the *iura regni, regis, et coronae.*[20] In a word, the laws of Frederick Barbarossa show that there was already the assumption that if it was the duty and right of the king and emperor to keep unharmed the Empire and its subjects, he could not alienate any of that sovereignty which was necessary for the end of maintaining the *status Imperii,* which included the *status ecclesiarum.* His *majestas* must remain *illaesa*—so I venture to put it.[21]

Naturally the papacy could hardly interpret the German king's rights in this fashion. As Pope Eugenius III said in a letter of 1152, the German bishops should resist any attacks on the Church, "ut . . . et aecclesiae Dei ac regni status in suo decore incolumnis conservetur."[22] The power of the prince was limited by his duty to preserve the *status Ecclesiae,* which in the pope's mind as in the Canon law was superior to the *status regni.* Frederick, however, was expressing the late Roman imperialist doctrine, that it was the emperor's *right* to defend and preserve the *iura* of State and Church, and that the secular prince was the supreme judge with respect to the rights in property of clergy and churches. He intended to enhance the public *iura* or powers of the imperial government, and in some matters, chiefly on the side of property rights, to subject the German churches and clergy to his authority. This intention is expressed in the decision of 1153 concerning the *iura* recognized by the royal court as lawfully belonging to the church of Cologne—only these *iura* were to be kept *illibata* and *inconvulsa.*[23] Above the *iura* of churches were the *iura* of the authority of the prince. Thus Frederick was in reality, if not always in these words, asserting his right to maintain *illaesa* and *illibata* the *iura regis et regni.*

We must now turn to England and Henry II. Did the Roman

20. See my study, *"Ratio publicae utilitatis,* etc.," *Welt als Gesch.,* XXI, 8–28, 71–99; also Part II of these studies on the *status regis* as the public authority and powers of the prince, including his right and duty to do all that is necessary for the preservation of the *status regni.*

In 1231, Frederick II reflected the laws of Justinian on magistrates' oaths and on the inalienability of fiscal *iura*—"curie nostre demania et jura quelibet illesa servabunt"; Huillard-Bréholles, *Hist. Dipl. Frid.* II, IV, i (Tit. LXII), pp. 41 f.; cf. below, n. 48.

21. A separate study of *status ecclesiarum* and *status Ecclesiae* is in preparation. On *laesa* and *illaesa majestas* see above, n. 7; also Part I, n. 76.

22. Simonsfeld, *Jahrbücher,* I, 122.

23. *Op. cit.,* 1, 188 n. 138, quoting *MGH, Legum S. IV, Const.* I, 205, No. 146; "ea, que ad nostram cognicionem . . . illibata et inconvulsa permaneant." Cf. above, n. 14.

terms come from the documents of Frederick Barbarossa? Probably the example set by Frederick and the Roman concept of the authority of the prince offered some encouragement to Henry and his counselors to assert his rights of justice at the expense of ecclesiastical courts. But the principle that a king and others should keep the properties and *iura* of churches *illibata* had long since been stated firmly and explicitly by Popes Innocent II and Eugenius III. Perhaps popes still earlier had used the standard formulas, that the *possessiones* and *bona* of churches and monasteries "firma in perpetuum et illibata permaneant," and "omnia integra conserventur." But from 1137 to 1153 Innocent II and Eugenius III repeatedly stated them in confirming the rights of churches in England and elsewhere—*illibata,* therefore, did not originate in the chancery of Frederick Barbarossa.[24] It is interesting (but of no importance for arguing that at his coronation Henry added an inalienability clause for the sake of English churches) that the famous bull of Hadrian IV, 1155–1156, the *Laudabiliter,* which approved Henry's plan for the invasion of Ireland, states that Henry should "jura Ecclesiarum illius terrae illibata et integra conservare."[25] Nor does a decretal of Innocent III, 1202, have any bearing on a coronation oath, although the pope does say that a monastic *ordo* should be kept *illaesus.*[26]

The style used in the papal chancery, then, was one source of the revived Roman terminology. Another source, the letters of Anglo-Norman prelates, resulted from the study of Roman as well as Canon law in Italy, in the court of Archbishop Theobald of Canterbury, and perhaps in the school of Vacarius at Oxford. (But the teaching of Vacarius may not have included an emphasis on the Roman law on the inalienability of church properties; at least I have not found that he

24. There are many examples of the usage. See, for a few, from the letters of Innocent II, Jaffe-Löwenfeld, Nos. 7945, 7868, 7877, and 8005 (in *MPL* 179, cols. 401, 343, 349, and 449 f.); also Rymer, *Foedera,* I, i, 3. For Eugenius III see *MPL* 180, cols. 1017, 1037, and 1513, Nos. 4, 23, and 496; and Rymer, *Foedera,* I, i, 4.

25. Rymer, *Foedera,* I, i, 5 f. On the authenticity of the bull see Raymonde Foreville, *L'Église et la royauté en Angleterre sous Henri II Plantagenet* (Paris, 1942), pp. 83–85, 494–99. For another example in a letter of Hadrian IV see E. Friedberg, *Quinque Compilationes Antiquae* (Leipzig, 1882), *Compilatione I,* 3, 26, 15: (*an.* 1154–59) the pope betrayed his succession to St. Peter "si cunctarum iura ecclesiarum integra non debeant illibata servari." This decretal was not included in *Decr. Greg. IX.*

26. Friedberg, *Quinque Comp. Ant., Comp. III,* 3, 24, 5—again this decretal was not included in the *Decr. Greg. IX.*

used our terms in his *Liber pauperum,* either to *C.* 1, 2, 12, and 14, or elsewhere.) Mr. Richardson, assuming that the inalienability clause was added to the coronation oath in 1154, offers the conjecture that Nigel, bishop of Ely, was the author.[27] I have not examined the correspondence of Nigel, and cannot say whether he was familiar with the terms. But no doubt he did know them, if only from letters of Archbishop Theobald, Gilbert Foliot of Hereford, and other bishops.

Long before 1154, indeed, Theobald's chancery used *illibata*: the *bona* and *iura* of churches, and gifts to them, should remain *illibata* (several examples 1139–1151).[28] And perhaps also before 1154, but at any rate between 1150 and 1161, *illaesa* seems to have been preferred: bad *consuetudines* must be rooted out "et utiles et antiquitus habitas libertates illesas perpetuo conservare"; the *patrimonium* of the Church "illesum debet perpetuo conservari"; and the archbishop should keep the *libertates* and *dignitates* of the church of Canterbury "integras at illesas."[29] Since Theobald participated in the coronation of Henry II, he could have been the author of the inalienability clause—if it was actually added.

Gilbert Foliot, bishop of Hereford, 1148–1163 (of London after 1163), in a letter to Pope Eugenius III, therefore not later than 1153, hints at the influence of the *lex Iulia majestatis* in expressing the wish that the papal *majestas* be preserved *illaesa* and *inoffensa*.[30] In a letter

27. "Coronation Oath," *Traditio,* XVI, 151–69. I am not sure, as I will indicate more fully below, nn. 31–36, that Henry took an oath instead of the traditional *professio* or promise. Nor is it certain, I think, that Professor M. David is right about the change from *professio* to *iuramentum* at this time, although he does hold that Henry II made the traditional *professio; La souveraineté et les limites juridiques du pouvoir monarchique du IXe au XVe siècles* (Paris, 1954), p. 168 nn. 9 f. Mr. Richardson argues that Henry II took an oath to which the inalienability clause was added in terms of *iura* or *consuetudines illibatae* or *illaesae.* My argument is that whether there was a traditional *professio* or an oath, it is doubtful that the inalienability clause was used at the coronation. See below, nn. 35 and 47.

We have seen that Bishop Nigel's son, Richard, in the *Dialogue of the Exchequer,* had some acquaintance with terms and concepts from the Roman public law, such as *status regis* and *ratio publicae utilitatis;* above, Part II, nn. 9 and 10, and my *"Ratio publicae utilitatis,* etc.," *Welt als Gesch.,* XXI, 71 f.

28. In charters published by Avrom Saltman, *Theobald Archbishop of Canterbury* (London, 1956), pp. 280 f., 284, 298, 350, 366 (Nos. 54, 55, 58, 73, 128, 144).

29. Saltman, *Theobald,* pp. 250 f., 297, 277 (Nos. 23, 72, 50).

30. Giles, ed., *Gilberti Foliot Ep.,* I, 114, No. 87. Gilbert probably had studied the *Digest*—there was a copy at Hereford about 1160 (Saltman, *Theobald,* p. 175 n. 6). No doubt his copy had been obtained in Italy, or sent to him from there. Did he know the *Codex*?

addressed to Bishop Nigel and dated 1148–1160 (hence not necessarily before 1154), he asked for the protection of the rights of Robert de Clare in a church, "ut ecclesiam, quam sibi tuitione vestra possidet, sibi, illaesam impurtabatamque patrocinio conservetis."[31] In still another letter he rejoiced that God had kept Joannes de Dinan *illaesum*, and that Joannes had maintained God "illaesum in membris suis" by defending the rights of the clergy of a church.[32] One notes that Gilbert liked *illaesus* better than *illibatus*.

Important, too, is a letter to Pope Alexander III, written of course some ten years after the coronation of Henry III, since it relates to the affair of Thomas Becket. Gilbert says that Henry had declared that Thomas could return to England and receive satisfaction from the king, "dum tamen in satisfaciendo sibi super his, unde conqueritur, regias sibi, et in quam ipse juratus est, velit dignitates integre conservari."[33] In another letter connected with the controversy Gilbert explains that the royal authority had asserted that it belonged "ad summam regni sui dignitatem," that no prelate should use the weapon of excommunication against any baron engaged in a suit in a royal court, and that the king held that all the bishops of the realm had sworn not to diminish or injure the *privilegia* of the realm.[34] These letters, of course, refer to the famous "promise" of the prelates of the realm in connection with the Constitutions of Clarendon, the "promise" or oath (which Thomas Becket retracted when the Constitutions were promulgated) to respect the *consuetudines, libertates,* and *dignitates* of king and realm.[35] It is thus possible that not only the tradi-

31. Giles, I, 103, No. 80.
32. *Op cit.*, p. 111, No. 85.
33. *Op. cit.*, p. 240, No. 174.
34. *Op. cit.*, pp. 244 f., No. 176.
35. Stubbs, *SC*, pp. 163 f., and chaps. 1 and 7, pp. 164 f. On the events of 1163–64 and Henry's obtaining a promise from the prelates, see also Frank Barlow, *The Feudal Kingdom of England 1042–1216* (London, 1955), pp. 292–94; Foreville, *L'Église et la royauté en Angleterre*, pp. 107–30; 145–53, 249; and Foreville and J. Rousset de Pina, *Du premier Concile du Latran à l' avènement d'Innocent III* (Part 2; Paris, 1953), pp. 99 f. Mlle. Foreville pays insufficient attention to elements of Roman public law that influenced the policy of Henry II—Henry is always *arbitraire*, while Becket rightly represents the Canon law. But it is doubtful that a king, inspired by principles of public law, and claiming the right to exercise his authority both for the *status regis* and for the *status regni*, was any more *arbitraire* than the pope, who could use his powers of dispensation in order to maintain the *status Ecclesiae*. Of course the danger of absolutism was present in State and Church alike. But in both cases the theory was that the supreme authority should

tional feudal oath of fealty but the Roman's magistrate's oath ordered by Justinian is in the background of Henry's policy in 1263–1264.

Whether Henry II's counselors and his chancery got the Roman terms from the letters of popes and prelates or from a more direct contact with the Roman law, I cannot say, but his letters do contain the terms. Indeed, in 1151 at Rouen, as duke of Normandy he ordered that those things which the pope had confirmed to the monks of Mortemer should be conserved "integra et illibata."[36] How soon after his coronation the royal chancery employed the terms can be decided only after a study of all his documents. But the quarrel with Thomas Becket probably caused an increasing use of them. For, against the argument of Thomas that the king was not keeping the *iura ecclesiastica illibata,* Henry replied that the pope and the Roman court in supporting Thomas, who he said was a *proditor* and *infamis,* were injuring the royal *honor* and *dignitas,* as they were injuring the realm and its *iura* and *consuetudines.*[37] He accused the pope of violating his own teaching, that it should be the care of princes "famam suam conservare illesam." He said that he would gladly persevere in his regard for the pope "si nobis et regno nostro eundem honorem et honoris et dignitatis conservationem observaverit." But if anyone attempted to violate the *iura* and *consuetudines* of the realm, the king would reckon him a "publicum hostem et manifestum nominis nostri et honoris et regni . . . inimicum."[38] Henry even spoke of demanding that the pope take public oath that he and his successors would preserve *inconcussae* and *inviolatae* the *regiae consuetudines* of Henry I![39]

Clearly, the king and his advisers were virtually saying that the prince in keeping his *fama illaesa* must also preserve *illibata, illaesa, inconvulsa,* or *inconcussa* those *iura* of the royal honor and dignity, and of the realm, which were sanctioned by the *consuetudines* of the

rule in accordance with the law, but was above the law in cases of emergency and necessity.

36. L. Delisle and É. Berger, *Recueil des actes de Henri II,* I (Paris, 1916), 43 f., No. 37.

37. *Recueil,* I, 385, 392, 407 (Nos. 237, 246, and 261).

38. *Recueil,* I, 392, f., No. 246, *an.* 1165. See above, n. 7, for *laesa* and *illaesa majestas.*

39. *Recueil,* I, 407 f., *an.* 1166. The idea of this perhaps came from the promise made by cardinal-legates to Frederick I in 1158, that the pope would "in nullo regiae dignitati derogare, sed honorem ac iusticiam imperii semper illibatam conservare"; Rahewin, *Gesta,* III, 24—quoted by Rassow, *Honor imperii,* pp. 79, 107 n. 176; also by Simonsfeld, *Jahrbücher,* I, 644 n. 173.

realm in the time of Henry I. There is a suggestion, moreover, of the concept that the *majestas regis* should be *illaesa*, since a traitor and those who protected him, even if it was the pope himself who abetted the *proditor*, were guilty of *laesa fama regis* if not precisely of *laesa majestas*.

The sources, therefore, show that the Roman terms in the inalienability clause were in circulation, and were used in the proper contexts, well before 1154 as well as thereafter. But a serious problem remains: Was an inalienability clause added to the coronation *professio* (or oath, if it was such) of Henry II? Did the new king swear to maintain *illibata* or *illaesa* the *iura* (or *libertates, consuetudines,* etc.) of king and realm, and also the *iura* and *privilegia* of churches? Mr. H. G. Richardson, we remarked at the outset, thinks that he did, that the inalienability clause first appeared in 1154. As evidence Richardson offers the Third Recension of the *Leges Edwardi Confessoris* (and dates it 1154–1161),[40] and a letter of Alexander III, 1170.[41] Roger of Howden's statement, that in 1199, John swore to preserve "sanctam ecclesiam et dignitates illius . . . illaesas," could be added.[42] And the sources I have given both for the period before 1154 and for the following years seem to support Mr. Richardson's contention.[43] Certainly the revival of the Roman law had reinforced the doctrine of inalienability and had furnished the terminology well before the coronation of Henry II.

Yet I am not convinced that the new inalienability clause was actually added to the coronation *professio*[44] or oath in 1154. Despite the

40. Richardson, "Coronation Oath," *Traditio,* XVI, 167 f.: "Debet rex omnes terras et honores, omnes dignitates et iura et libertates corone regni huius in integrum . . . obseruare et defendere. . . ."

41. *Traditio,* XVI, 163; the argument, probably of Thomas Becket himself, that the king at his coronation promised "ut consuetudines quas auitas dicunt . . . illibatas omni tempore conseruare."

42. Quoted by Hoyt, "Coronation Oath," *Traditio,* XI, 249 n. 53. For another indication that King John thought in terms of keeping the *libertas* and *dignitas* of the crown *illesa,* see Richardson, *Speculum,* XXIV, 53 n. 54.

43. Two more sources can now be added: a letter of Alexander III to his legates, that they should effect a reconciliation of Becket and the king, "ita quod sibi et ecclesiae suae intiqua jura et libertates integra et illibata servetis" (in Giles, *Gilberti Foliot Ep.,* II, 55, No. 331); in 1160, Archbishop Theobald urged the king to preserve *indempnis* the church of Canterbury, for it was the *caput regni* and its *honor* was the *honor regis* (in *Letters of John of Salisbury,* eds. W. J. Millor and H. E. Butler, I [London, 1955], 190 f., No. 116).

44. See above, n. 27.

fact that Henry II and Nigel of Ely actively reclaimed the *iura fiscalia* which Stephen had alienated, and that prelates and others had long since been talking about *iura illibata* and the like, no specific statement has come to my attention that Henry and his counselors and judges were putting into effect what had been sworn to as a principle. The coronation charter itself indicates a traditional promise, not one in the new terminology.[45] Nor does the increasing use of the Roman terms in 1163–1170 prove more than the fact that partisans of the king and of Becket found them useful in arguing about the rights of the king and realm and the rights of the Church. Similarly, there is no certainty that John swore to keep the *libertas* and *dignitas coronae illaesa* even though one source attributes the words to him.[46] Even Pope Honorius III's decretal, *Intellecto* (*Decr. Greg. IX*, 2, 24, 33), containing the statement that the king of Hungary took a coronation oath that he would maintain unharmed the rights of the crown, is again no positive evidence that the oath was taken in the same terms.

Nonetheless I do not fully agree with Professors Wilkinson and Hoyt, who have taken the position that there is no evidence of an inalienability clause added to the English coronation oath before the late thirteenth or early fourteenth centuries.[47] It is possible that Mr. Richardson is right. It is possible, given the currency of the Roman terminology in the mid-twelfth century, that Henry II—or John or Henry III—added the clause to the oath. But it is not certain. I therefore leave the problem to be settled by others.

In one sense it is not important to settle the date of the first use of the inalienability clause. It is important, however, to note that the idea of the inalienability of the *iura regis et regni* was asserted by Henry II and his counselors and supporters. Whether stated in the older terms of defending the *dignitates* and *consuetudines* and *iura* and *libertates* of the crown or of the king and realm, or in the newer Roman terms of keeping these *iura illibata* or *illaesa*, the idea was that of a consti-

45. Barlow, *Feudal Kingdom of England*, p. 284.
46. See above, n. 42.
47. Wilkinson, "The Coronation Oath of Edward II and the Statute of York," *Speculum*, XIX, 445–69, and *Constitutional History*, III, 73–83; and Hoyt, "Coronation Oath of 1308," *Traditio*, XI, 235–57. But I agree with them to this extent, that one must treat with caution any use of the terms, outside the coronation oath itself, as evidence of an added inalienability clause. Yet because of references to an oath couched in the Roman terminology it is possible that the clause was added to the oath in the thirteenth century, even as early as 1154.

tutional principle. The public rights of kingship, that *status regis*, which was necessary for the *status regni*, must be preserved, "ne pereat." Henry II went too fast, and without tact, in trying to re-establish the old superiority that William the Conqueror and Henry I enjoyed over the English church and clergy, and to strengthen it in accordance with the concepts of the *status regis et regni*. The Church at the moment was too strong for a king to succeed in "nationalizing" the clergy and their churches.

Frederick Barbarossa's policy probably encouraged Henry II. But the revival of the Roman law was of great importance to both. In the legislation of late Roman emperors the great secular princes of the twelfth century and their learned advisers began to find new support in striving to consolidate their States. Even more than lesser magistrates or judges, kings should maintain *illaesa* and *illibata* the *iura* of their public authority in order to keep their subjects *illaesos*. Since the public *iura* of the king included his *iura fiscalia*, Richard Fitzneale could say that by the work of the Exchequer "totius regni status indemnis servatur."[48] But the maintenance of the "state of the realm" gave to the king the right (as well as duty) to defend and keep unharmed the *iura* and *privilegia* of ecclesiastical as well as lay subjects; for all, clergy and laity alike, were members of the body of the realm of which the king was the head. The difficulty was, that if ecclesiastics were subjects of the king they were also members of the Church and subjects of the pope. Naturally the pope as head of the Church held that the clergy, in matters that pertained to the faith and the *status Ecclesiae*, were not members of the secular State and were not subjects of the king. The pope, not the king, should be the final interpreter of the public law in all matters that touched the Church and its *libertates* and *privilegia*. According to the Canon law, therefore, the king must submit to the pope's interpretation of that public law which dealt with *sacra* and *sacerdotes*: the *iura ecclesiastica* first, thereafter the *iura regis et regni*, must be kept *illibata*. For if the Church was impeded in its work of saving souls the "state" of king and realm had no value.

But this short study is not intended as a contribution to the history of the relations of the Church and State. I have simply wanted to emphasize the origins in Roman law of the terminology, and of the concepts, in the "inalienability" clause. If Justinian ordered magis-

---

48. Stubbs, *SC*, p. 205 (I, iv). There is here a similarity to a law of Frederick II, *an.* 1231, that the "curie nostre demania et jura quelibet illesa servabunt"; Huillard-Bréholles, IV, i, *Constitutiones*, p. 42.

trates of the Empire to keep the public *iura* of the emperor *illaesa,* and *subiectos illaesos,* kings and their advisers in the twelfth century understood very well that it was the right of the prince to keep *illibata* and *illaesa* the *iura* of his public authority, and thereby to keep *illaesos* his subjects and the *status regni.* In other words, the rights and powers belonging to the public *status regis* must not be alienated lest the *status regni* suffer injury.

CONCLUSION

In the three parts of this study I have presented so many variations on the theme of *status regis* and *status regni* that a general conclusion is not needed. But a few reflections may help to indicate what I have tried to do by means of repetition and of concentration on public at the expense of private law—and at the expense of what actually happened.

Given the human element in statesmen, the public and private aspects of government can never be so sharply distinguished as theorists dealing with the modern State like to believe. Henry VIII, Louis XIV, and Napoleon, not to mention many other great princes, were not above letting their private, personal pleasures and *ira et voluntas* influence actions alleged to be for the public interest. Indeed, displays of private emotion have often been instruments of public policy. It is not necessary to assume that personal wrath and arbitrariness were a practice only of feudal monarchs. The private as well as public "body" of the ruler has been of great public importance whether at Versailles or in the Kremlin. Even in the United States the private estate of president and household is not always kept separate from the public estate of the presidency. The White House is more than a residence: it is a public, "sacred," palace. How often, moreover, have presidents and senators and their wives spent public money, and used transportation paid for by public taxation, in pursuit of private relaxation! Naturally the personal well-being of higher magistrates and their families may be necessary for "right reasoning" in the practice of the art of statesmanship in the public interest. For better or worse the private estate of the head can still affect the exercise of his public powers and be related to maintaining the "state" of the Nation.

In the feudal monarchy of the twelfth and thirteenth centuries there was, of course, far more of the personal and private, far more of the feudal proprietary, in kingship than in governments of States in the twentieth century. In this study, however, I have assumed that the private elements are so well known that it was permissible for me to stress the rise of important ideas belonging to the realm of public law. For the State and its public law were in fact developing, and they should receive at least as much attention as the admixture of things private in the history of politics and of the public law of the United States. I have therefore tried to present, not a story of the confusion

100

of private and public in a medieval "government at work," but an interpretation of the history of a few of the ideas that played a significant role in the gradual formation of the medieval and early modern State. For this purpose I have concentrated on one part only of the public law, the part that deals primarily with the magistracy and its *status*. In passing I have also indicated that the public law dealt still more with the *status* of the community governed; but the public authority has been my chief preoccupation.

Some concept of the *status* of the king and his powers that should be used for the maintenance of the *status* or public welfare of the kingdom persisted from the end of the Roman Empire in the West to the twelfth century. Even in regions that succumbed to feudalism the idea found occasional expression that it was the right and duty of the king to assure the *status Reipublicae*. And in strong feudal principalities like Normandy and Flanders dukes and counts were achieving success in applying principles of public law in their fiefs while obstructing their application by the king of France for the higher *status regni*. The revival of Roman law and the development of legal science undoubtedly gave them, but above all gave to kings of the twelfth century, an intelligent *rationale*, and greatly stimulated and strengthened what they were trying to do, in the work or art of making States. By 1150, and more and more from that time on, royal counselors, judges, and heads of "departments of State," such as chancellors and treasurers, were studying or were influenced by those who did study the Roman and Canon law. Increasingly the Roman terms and the ideas stated in them influenced these men and the kings whom they served. The frequency of *ius publicum, respublica, utilitas publica,* and *status regis et regni* meant that there was far more than a mere copying or rhetorical usage of terms that sounded impressive but had no meaning for the users. It meant that those jurists and magistrates who found a place in royal councils and government were becoming intelligently aware of problems of public law and the State. It is probable, moreover, that a few able monarchs, such as Roger II of Sicily, Frederick Barbarossa, and Henry II, not to mention popes and kings of the thirteenth century, learned from their counselors and were consciously—and conscientiously—trying to enhance their public "estates royal" and, at the expense of the feudal rights of their vassals, to govern in the public interest. They were intelligent men, not simply charming or picturesque and childlike feudal personalities engaged in the game of "playing castle." Nor did religious piety always stand in the way of a steady policy of making principles of public law effective. The government of St. Louis, *rege sciente et volente*, steadily asserted the public authority of the king.

In sum, if the public law was the "constitutional" law dealing with the public welfare or *status* of the realm as a whole, and with the royal magistracy that had its *raison d'être* in the *ratio jurisdictionis* and the *ratio publicae utilitatis* or *ratio status regni*, it gave to king and crown their public estate, that is, the public rights and powers of governing in order that the public and common welfare of realm and people be maintained lest the *status* of king and realm together suffer harm. By the public law it was the right and duty of the king to keep *illibata* or *illaesa* both the *iura* and *status regis* and *coronae*, and the *iura subiectorum* and *regni*. The "estate royal" like the estate of the crown was essentially the *potestas publica* of the head of the State. But the *status* was also becoming the government or constitutional order as well as the public authority vested in it. It was at times the equivalent of *lo stato* in the Italian renaissance. In principle, of course, the *status* of king or prince was always subordinate to the all-embracing *status* of the corporate realm or State. Yet the "estate royal," meaning also in the context of public law the *majestas, honor,* and *dignitas regis,* and the *status coronae,* was not the State. It was the ensemble of those rights of the supreme authority that existed for the welfare and safety of the head and members of the body of the State, indeed, for the State itself considered apart from head and members. Because of the concentration of attention on the public authority in the State, however, legists and scholastic philosophers were viewing the supreme magistracy and the "body politic" as that *status* which was indispensable to the existence of the State. In consequence the idea was at hand, if not openly expressed, that in cases of "national" emergency or necessity involving the very safety of people and community, the "estate royal," *lo stato,* was above not only the positive or human law but also the natural law. The safety of the State was beginning to "know no law"; for if it was by this time approved by God and the law of nature it enjoyed a higher moral right than individual members with respect to their souls. Rather, it was no longer a mortal but venial sin if a man violated the Ten Commandments in order to preserve that higher moral entity, the State. A king who was confident that his power came from God and was for the public welfare might well feel that he was not merely *lo stato*: he was the State. At least one finds the anticipation of the extreme modern concept, *l'État, c'est moi,* in the legal thought of the thirteenth, perhaps even in the twelfth, century.

The word *status,* then, as a subject of public law, was as much a symbol as the crown was of the medieval creation of the early modern State. Not even England, in its imagined isolation from continental influences, was free of its impact.

PETER CHELČICKÝ: TREATISES ON CHRISTIANITY AND THE SOCIAL ORDER

by Howard Kaminsky

University of Washington

PRINCIPLES OF TRANSLATION

1. I have made consistent use of F. Šimek's *Slovníček staré češtiny* (Prague, 1947) as a guide to the translation of Chelčický's Old Czech; other glossaries have also been used. There is no adequate, full dictionary of Old Czech, however, and some conjecture has been inevitable.

2. Chelčický's biblical quotations represent translations from the Vulgate, which they follow very closely. I have tried in all cases to follow the King James version, except for its more obtrusive archaisms; when the King James translation does not give the sense of Chelčický's text, I have made my own translations.

3. Chelčický did not read Latin fluently and his Czech is notably different from that of John Hus, Jakoubek of Stříbro, and other Hussites, whose ordinary language of religious and theoretical discourse was Latin. Chelčický uses a very concrete, rough style, which is sometimes too simple for his thought. At the cost of some sacrifice of smoothness and congruity in the English text, I have tried to avoid paraphrase or even transpositions of sequence, wherever possible. The resulting peculiarity of the English should therefore be understood as—in principle—indicative of Chelčický's own peculiarity in his own time, rather than as striving for archaic atmosphere.

4. A few particular points may be mentioned. Chelčický did not use the second person plural as a conventional singular, and I have been careful to preserve the distinction between singular and plural in the English, usually by using "you people" or "your party" for the plural; "you" by itself should be understood as singular. The Czech word "obec" meant "community" or "commons," but also, sometimes, "laity"; as always in such cases, it is impossible to disjoin these meanings in translation. The same may be said about the word "milost," which meant "love," "grace," and "mercy"; I have used one or another of these as the context seemed to require, but the reader will be well advised to try to understand each of the three, when he encounters them, in the light of the other two. Finally, "arms" and "hands" both translate the Czech "ruky," "legs" and "feet" the Czech "nohy."

Peter Chelčický: Treatises on Christianity and the Social Order

I. PETER CHELČICKÝ'S PLACE
ON THE HUSSITE LEFT[1]

IN THE hands of its more radical protagonists, the Hussite program of reform developed very quickly from a conventional moral critique of abuses to a theory that attacked the Roman system as a whole. Inspired by the eschatological scheme of total war between Christ and Antichrist, the reformers came increasingly to see all of the things they objected to as aspects of a single organism, the Mystical Body of Antichrist, the Synagogue of Satan, the "ecclesia malignancium"—all designating the papal institution. It was the vicious corruption of that institution's clergy and the externalized forms of its religious observance that threatened to kill the spirit of true faith, which in turn could be preserved only by the kind of resistance to evil that would regenerate the pure church of Christ himself, his Mystical Body. The Hussites followed Wyclif in defining this body as the collectivity of those predestined to salvation, but this theory, true by definition, had its main value merely in undermining the claims to authority of the pope and prelates—who perhaps were not predestined, hence not members of the true church, hence unfit to lead the Church. For more positive purposes the Hussites tacitly turned away from predestinarian ecclesiology—as in fact Wyclif had also done—and took as the model of the true church the body that Jesus himself had founded on earth, the Primitive Church portrayed in the New Testament. The idea of this church became the great common principle of Hussite reform, and was used both as a slogan and as a functional ideal.

But in practice, below the level of explicit theory, the model of the Primitive Church frequently gave way to something that can be defined *ex post* as a calque off the Roman system, a positively valued

1. When I began these translations a number of years ago I enjoyed the invaluable help of Dr. Dagmar Perman, who made sure that I did not ignore the complexities of Chelčický's Old Czech. If I have still not produced a perfect translation she is not to blame. I should also like to express my gratitude to Professor S. Harrison Thomson of the University of Colorado, who encouraged me to persist in my belief that the project was worthwhile. Finally I wish to thank the Acquisitions staff of the University of Washington Library, especially Mr. Kenneth S. Allen, now Associate Director, for energetic help in acquiring necessary books.

counterpart to all of the evil features of the Synagogue of Satan. These features had come into being after the age of the Primitive Church; they could be totally negated according to the slogan of the Primitive Church, but they could not be practically reformed except in the light of a model that did justice to contemporary realities. In fact the basis of both Romanist and Hussite ideology was the consciousness of a situation that had not existed in apostolic times, when the Christians were a minority living within a pagan state; in the middle ages the secular powers were Christian and society itself was presumed to be a Christian community, a presumption expressed in the ideal of Christian society. It was self-evident to both Romanists and Hussites that the social order was an organism animated by the principles of the Christian faith, with each social group or estate legitimized in terms of a functionalist Christian sociology. "The Church" could designate the whole social order as such, not merely as the community of the baptized or of the faithful, and it could also designate the ecclesiastical institution proper, which figured as one estate of the whole. Within the framework of these common assumptions the chief sociological difference between the Romanists and the Hussites was that the latter rejected the European system of organization in favor of a national one, and in consequence were prepared to allow the secular powers a much more active role in Church government, as replacements for the papacy. The property of the Church, justified by the Romanists as indispensable to the Church's *libertas,* could be freely secularized, since there was no reason for the spiritual part of Bohemian society to maintain a privileged freedom against that society. But in other respects the position of the Church in the social order was not fundamentally different, in theory, from what it had been before the reform. The leaders of Prague, of Tabor, and of the other Hussite groups that carried through a reformation, were all products of the Hildebrandine order that they sought to change, and while they did change it, with varying degrees of thoroughness, in strictly religious matters—liturgy, doctrine, morality—they could not bring about the basic change that would have in fact revived the Primitive Church. They were not prepared to destroy the Christian character of society itself.

It is at this point that we can define the significance of Peter Chelčický and his followers. Sharing some of the religious ideas of Prague, but still more those of Tabor, they nevertheless refused to follow the major parties in accepting the elements of social reality as Christian. They sought a genuine revival of the Primitive Church, at all costs and with no compromises. Since this position was nothing more or less than one of absolute fidelity to Hussite ideals, it provided a magnificently solid theoretical foundation for Chelčický's critique of other Hussite groups; in fact his is the only body of Hussite theory that may qualify as genuinely original, and most moderns find that he is the only Hussite whose ideas still seem absolutely, not just historically, interesting. At the same time, of course, his concept of radical disengagement from the world had the practical defects of its theoretical virtue, and the consequences of these defects make his position on the Hussite Left all the more interesting to the historian.

If we follow the recent hypotheses of Professor F. M. Bartoš,[2] we may trace Chelčický back to a Peter Záhorka, the son of Svatomír, a squire who held the fortress and estate of Záhorčí, very close to Chelčice in South Bohemia. In 1378, Svatomír married Betty, the daughter of Zdislav of Bílsko, and their son Peter was probably born in 1379 or 1380. The family was neither wealthy nor powerful, but its connections were good: a cousin of Peter's, Aleš of Březí, was named bishop of Olomouc in 1416, and a maternal uncle, Hostislav, was parish priest in Krumlov, one of the better cures of the region, in the gift of the greatest baron of South Bohemia, Lord Henry of Rožmberk. If in fact the Peter Chelčický who appears in later years was identical with Peter Záhorka, we can account for his evidently fine intellectual training by supposing that he received it from his uncle, with the help perhaps of the good library known to have existed in Krumlov.[3] Peter remained a layman, with little Latin,[4] but he was very well versed in the abundant Czech literature of the Bohemian reform movement that had its origins in the previous century and its contemporary representatives in the movement led by John Hus. His works show a special familiarity

---

2. F. M. Bartoš, "Kdo byl Petr Chelčický?" *Jihočeský sborník historický,* XV (1946), 1–8; cf. V. Mostecký, "Je Petr Záhorka P. Chelčickým?" *JSH,* XXV (1956), 97–100, and Bartoš, *Petr Chelčický* (Prague: Kalich, 1958). Certain reservations about Bartoš's thesis were expressed by V. Chaloupecký, *Český časopis* historický, XLVIII/XLIX (1947–48), 482 f.; cf. Bartoš's reply, *JSH,* XIX (1950), 112 f.

3. Bartoš, *Petr Chelčický,* pp. 8 f.

4. He is not known to have used any Latin works, and his own are all in Czech. In his "Reply to Biskupec" (see below), discussing Wyclif's eucharistic doctrine contained "in many Latin words," Peter says, "But I can offer only light and insignificant testimony about Latin." ("Replika protiv Biskupca," eds. J. Annenkov and V. Jagič, *Sborník otdělenija russkago Jazyka . . . ,* LXVI [St. Petersburg, 1893], 479).

with the writings of Thomas Štítný (*d.* 1400), another member of the South Bohemian gentry, whose orthodox piety went hand in hand with a sharply critical attitude to abuses in society and Church.[5] But precisely in the decade after Štítný's death the continued development of the reform tradition in the hands of the Czech masters of Prague's university involved walking the path of disobedience and heresy, a path that these masters sought to illuminate by taking over, virtually *en bloc,* the doctrines of John Wyclif.[6] Peter followed this movement, perhaps in Prague, perhaps from South Bohemia, and he discussed Wyclif's eucharistic doctrine with John Hus himself, as well as Jakoubek of Stříbro, the leading radical among the Czech masters.[7] The latest date when this would have been possible was 1414, the year that Hus left Bohemia for Constance, and we may confidently suppose that for some years before this date, Peter had become actively committed to the movement of reform.

With the institution of the lay chalice in the autumn of 1414, the rapid spread of this practice to the provinces—especially to South Bohemia—and the martyrdom of John Hus in July, 1415, the Czechs' involvement, both in Prague and in the provinces, in militant anti-Romanism was immensely accelerated; and although many of the Prague masters continued to think of their reform movement as one taking place *within* the Roman Church, the logic of reality favored the more extreme radicals who saw that reform could only mean the replacement of the Roman system by their own.[8] The sharpness of the break even elicited acts of physical violence; thus in 1416 a group of

5. See V. Chalopecký, "Štítný a Chelčický," *Časopis matice moravské,* XXXVIII (1914), 72 ff.; R. Urbánek, *Věk poděbradský,* III (Prague: Laichter, 1930), 890 f. For Štítný see J. Macek *Tábor v husitském revolučním hnutí,* I (2d ed.; Prague: Czechoslovakian Academy, 1956), 136 and *passim.*

6. The indebtedness of Hus and his associates to Wyclif was shown by J. Loserth, *Hus und Wyclif* (1884); there is a large Czech literature on the subject, some of it extending Loserth's documentation, some of it reacting against his inferences. See the sound discussion by K. Krofta, "John Hus," *Cambridge Medieval History,* VIII (1936), 45 ff. Cf. also S. Harrison Thomson, ed., *Magistri Johannis Hus, Tractatus de ecclesia* (Boulder, Colo., 1956), pp. xxxii–xxxiv, and *passim.*

7. Urbánek, *op. cit.,* p. 893, conjectures that Chelčický met Hus in Prague; most other scholars incline to the conjecture that the meeting took place during Hus's "exile" from Prague, 1412–14, a period which Hus spent for the most part in South Bohemia. In his "Reply to Biskupec," p. 472, Chelčický writes: "I have spoken about them [*scil.,* Wyclif's works on the eucharist] with faithful Czechs . . . such as Master John Hus, of good and holy memory, and Master Jakoubek."

8. See my "Hussite Radicalism and the Origins of Tabor 1415–1418," *Medievalia et Humanistica,* X (1956), 102 ff.

Hussite priests and laymen allegedly plundered the parish house in Heřmann, laid violent hands on the vicar's servant, and, according to the accusation, held services in the Czech language, outside of consecrated churches, and proclaimed their veneration of John Hus and Jerome of Prague. Among these radicals was Vojtěch, parish priest in Chelčice,[9] and we may reasonably suppose that this was not his only act of Hussite militancy—that, very likely, he functioned as a leader and organizer of radical Hussitism in his region. If so, he may well have been one of the influences working on Peter.

Eventually, out of this matrix of South Bohemian radicalism, there emerged the Taborite movement of 1419: when King Wenceslas IV ordered the restoration of parish churches to the Romanist clergy, the radical priests reacted by organizing great open-air congregations on the hilltops of South Bohemia in the spring and summer of that year. Renaming one such hill Mt. Tabor, after the supposed scene of Christ's transfiguration, they acquired the name of Taborites.[10] The leaders of the movement developed the congregations into regularly organized mass meetings, and sought first to reverse King Wenceslas IV's reactionary policy, then after the king's death in August, to win Prague and the nation for the radical program. Twice in the autumn the great congregations set their meetings in Prague itself; and both on the way to the capital and in it, they engaged in battles with the royalist forces—the elements of the feudality, both Catholic and Hussite, that sought to insure the reception of Wenceslas's brother, the Emperor Sigismund, as king of Bohemia. In mid-November the leaders of Prague Hussitism—the university masters and the bourgeoisie—adhered to the royalist party, and the Taborites had to return to the provinces, politically isolated, and face the challenge of a royalist campaign aimed at their physical extermination. It is reasonable to imagine that Peter, perhaps under Vojtěch's leadership, took part in the Taborite movement from the first, and that the events just outlined were episodes of his life. In any case, although Peter Záhorka again appeared on the public scene, as witness to a document in 1424,[11] he had probably long ceased to live the life of a member of the gentry, and we may begin to think of him as Peter of Chelčice, or Chelčický.

9. Bartoš, *Petr Chelčický*, p. 12 n. 14, draws attention to this circumstance; the source is published by J. Macek, "K počátkům táborství v Písku," *JSH*, XXII (1953), 119 ff.

10. For this whole development in 1419 see my "Chiliasm and the Hussite Revolution," *Church History*, XXVI (1957), 43 ff.

11. Bartoš, *Petr Chelčický*, p. 9.

His position as leader of the Chelčice brethren may well have dated from Vojtěch's martyrdom in 1420.[12]

Very early in the development of radical Hussitism in the provinces it had become clear that the ideology of this movement went substantially beyond that of even the most radical Prague masters of Jakoubek's party. Many of the features of the Roman religion that Jakoubek wished to diminish—the cult of saints, the use of holy images, prayers for the dead, the elaborate liturgy, the exclusive use of Latin in the mass—the provincial radicals wished to eliminate entirely; moreover the latter rejected the doctrine of purgatory and the use of force, while Jakoubek did not.[13] All points considered, the extreme radicals of the provinces must be described as adhering to a type of religion virtually identical with Waldensianism, and quite possibly derived from it;[14] their general concept of reform, moreover, was obviously of a sectarian sort. While all of the Prague masters, from left to right, stood for a national reformation, carried through with the use of secular power and aiming at the establishment of a reformed social organism, the Waldensianists who made up or dominated the Taborite movement began by forming secessionary communities, congregations that embraced the faith of the New Testament and renounced Caesar's sphere of action. Ample evidence attests to the prevalence of this point of view up to and including the first period of the Taborite congregations in the spring of 1419.[15] In this year, however, we can trace the rise of two other currents, one seeking to make Tabor's sectarian religion the faith of a reformed society, the other, coming to the fore

12. The point is made by Bartoš, *Petr Chelčický*, p. 13, and analysis of the sources bolsters the hypothesis. Master Laurence of Březová's "Hussite Chronicle," ed. J. Goll, *Fontes rerum Bohemicarum*, V (Prague, 1893), 386, tells us that about July, 1420, Vojtěch was taken prisoner, brought to the German Catholic town of Budějovice (Budweis), imprisoned, and burnt, solely because of his adherence to the lay chalice. Laurence goes out of his way to insist that Vojtěch "consented to no excesses beyond the chalice and was revolted by the Taborites' burnings and homicides"; since we can be fairly sure that Vojtěch was in fact a radical, going well beyond mere utraquism in his doctrine (see the text cited above, n. 9), we may interpret Laurence's testimony as an indication that Vojtěch broke with the Taborites when the latter went beyond religious radicalism to chiliasm, total war, and, in general, the use of power. But this was also the background of Peter Chelčický's break with Tabor (see below), and we may reasonably assume that Peter's leadership of the Chelčický Hussites was in succession to Vojtěch's.

13. See my "Hussite Radicalism . . . ," pp. 105–12.

14. *Ibid.*, pp. 113–16.

15. See my "Chiliasm . . . ," pp. 44 ff., and Peter Brock, *The Political and Social Doctrines of the Unity of Czech Brethren* (The Hague: Mouton, 1957), pp. 29 f.

when this project failed, proclaiming the imminent advent of Christ and the necessity for total physical war between the elect—the Taborites—and the minions of Antichrist—the Hussite-Catholic coalition composing the royalist party. Associated with this latter movement of thought, and perhaps at its root, was a complex of doctrines evidently stemming from the heresy of the Brethren of the Free Spirit, the heretical Beghards, known in Hussite Bohemia as "Pikarts."[16] In the view of this sect, the advent of Christ and the great battle with Antichrist were preludes, not to the end of the world and a Last Judgment, but to a new secular age, in which a regenerated mankind, fully possessed of the Holy Spirit, would live in perfect happiness, free of sin, pain, and death.

Such a vision had at first a great deal to offer the desperate Taborite movement—there was no doubt who the elect would be—but the situation soon changed. In February to March, 1420, the Taborites founded their own city, Tabor; the logic of a movement began to give way to the logic of a stable society; and the Pikarts lost ground to a party of order that sought to combine the radical *religious* doctrines of Waldensianist sectarianism with the political and social doctrines appropriate to a societal reformation. Tabor's collaboration with Prague in resisting the anti-Hussite crusade, during the spring and summer of 1420, further strengthened the party of order. Pikartism survived as the sectarian faith of groups organized around the celebration of love feasts, with an ethos based on their own putative regeneration—they were the elect of the New Age.[17] Those who pushed their doctrine of sinlessness to the point of liberating their sexual desires—so-called Adamitism[18]— merely pushed the Free-Spirit ideology to its inevitable conclusion. The Pikart-Adamites were expelled from Tabor and many of them were slaughtered by the Taborite armies; within Tabor, however, despite the ascendancy of the party of order, the Pikart message of hope and rebirth to a happy life died hard. Deep into the 1420's there were still those who held that "a good age was coming in which there would be no evil-doers, and that they would not suffer at all but would be filled with ineffable joy."[19]

Peter Chelčický was intimately concerned with this rapid and com-

16. See my "Chiliasm . . . ," *passim,* and my article, "The Free Spirit in the Hussite Revolution," *Millennial Dreams in Action,* Supplement II to *Comparative Studies in Society and History* (1962), pp. 166–86.

17. See my "The Free Spirit . . . ." pp. 173–81.

18. *Ibid., passim.*

19. See my "Chiliasm . . . ," p. 63.

plex sequence of events, not primarily as a participant but as an observer whose judgments were valued by all sides. When the Taborites began themselves to take up the sword against their persecutors, and when Tabor joined Prague and the other Hussites in defending the capital against the Crusade, Chelčický went along with the rest but preserved his Waldensianist doubts about such use of secular power.[20] While in Prague during the siege he asked Master Jakoubek of Stříbro how it was possible to justify the use of force by Christians; Jakoubek admitted that he could find no justification in the New Testament, only in the Fathers.[21] Later, after the Crusade had been defeated, Peter asked Jakoubek how he could justify the killing that had taken place, and the latter said, according to Chelčický's account, that he could not condemn those who had killed others in the battles, because such condemnation would dishonor the knightly estate.[22] We may guess that what the Prague master actually said was that the knightly estate was a part of Christian society, with the function of ruling over and defending the law of God. In fact a great deal of Jakoubek's effort in 1420, from the beginning of the year on, was devoted to justifying Christian warfare; he did so by trying, characteristically, to ride both horses at once: the *real* Christian would prefer the safe path of suffering, even unto death, but the insecure path of armed resistance was also justifiable, according to the standard scholastic conditions—an upright intention, a valid authorization, a just cause, and combat in a caritative spirit.[23] But although Chelčický kept his respect for those reformers—Jakoubek, and before him, John Hus and Matthew of Janov—who adhered to this way of thought, he nevertheless felt obliged to condemn their doctrine:[24]

> . . . and I say this of them, not abusing their good works that they have done in the name of God, by zealous preaching and other good things, but still I say this of them, that they too have drunk of the wine of the Great Whore, with which she has besotted all the nations and peoples. . . . Therefore I cannot regard as true what

20. Nothing suggests that Chelčický ever gave up his commitment to evangelical pacifism, nor is it likely, but if he had been as absolutely clear on the subject in early 1420 as he later became, he would hardly have gone to Prague at all during the Crusade.

21. See the account in N. Jastrebov, *Etjudy o Petre Chelčickom i jego vremeni* (St. Petersburg, 1908), pp. 116 f., 142; cf. Brock, *op. cit.*, pp. 31 f.

22. Jastrebov, *op. cit.*, p. 117.

23. *Ibid.*, pp. 33 ff., 92 ff.

24. In his "Reply to Rokycana," quoted by Urbánek, *op. cit.*, p. 894 n. 1.

those masters have passed on of an offensive nature, to the scandal-
izing of many. . . . Many have so confirmed themselves in murder
that it would seem that if an angel taught them otherwise, they still
would not believe anyone but Master Hus.

But the Taborites were no better. Returning from Prague in
August, 1420, they began to develop the organizational and doctrinal
aspects of their polity; it was no doubt in this period that a meeting
took place, reported by Peter, of Taborite priests in the city of Písek,
in order to determine just how far Tabor might go in justifying her
secular power by means of the orthodox scholastic theory—actually
derived through Wyclif—that defined the three Estates of priests, secular powers, and workers as the three functions of Christian society, the
triple division of Christ's body. Peter was there, and it was perhaps
before this debate that he composed what was probably his first treatise,
"On Spiritual Warfare."[25] Subsequently he addressed himself to the
social theory itself, in "On the Holy Church" and "On the Triple Division of Society." All three show their author as a man who remained
true to original Taboritism, who refused to follow the majority in
their work of societal reformation, but who also refused to follow the
chiliasts, Pikarts, and Adamites in their notions of Christian liberty, so
different from the disciplinary orientation of Waldensianist evangelical
sectarianism.

In this way, standing aloof from the work of reformation, Chelčický
carved out a unique position for himself and the Chelčice brethren who
looked to his leadership. While all the others were trying to remake
the Christian order of society—drinking "the wine of the Great Whore"
—he and his group preserved in their purity the ideals of Hussitism's
childhood. At one time or another, leaders of every major Hussite
party sought his opinion on matters of doctrine or ideology; but since
hardly anyone ever followed his advice we must suppose that these
contacts were valued as sources of refreshment rather than as opportunities for instruction. For the historian, however, their value is beyond
price: Chelčický has done much of our work for us, setting all specific
points of issue within their proper sociological context, infallibly revealing the basic spiritual and moral implications of secular programs,
and serving himself as a kind of yardstick against which everything else
can be measured. His early works—those mentioned above and the
"Reply" to Nicholas of Pelhřimov, bishop of Tabor—are thus indis-

25. See the Appendix, below.

pensable guides to an understanding of what was really going on in the period of Tabor's establishment and consolidation, from 1420 to 1425; at the same time, Chelčický's own place in this development reveals itself to us in these works precisely as it was in fact defined, by discussions and arguments with the leaders of Tabor's various parties. After about 1425 these discussions seem to have ended, and Chelčický was able to devote himself to elaborating his own religious program; still later, however, from about 1435 on, he began to exchange ideas with the leader of Prague Hussitism, John Rokycana, and although the exchange produced no immediate effect, it led to the most important contacts of all, those between Chelčický and the founders of the Unity of the Brethren. Here at last were men who listened and learned; the Unity indeed took over and preserved the basic elements of Chelčický's idealism, which thus turned out to be the most realistic of all Hussite programs.[26]

The following discussion will deal only with the first period of Chelčický's activity, from about 1420 to 1425, and will focus on three main aspects of his relationship to the Taborites: (1) the problem of defending the true faith by warfare or other forms of secular action; (2) the problem of whether an evangelical Christian religion can extend its scope to include a "Christian" social order; (3) Chelčický's attitude to the Pikarts and to the "Pikart" eucharistic doctrines taken over by Tabor.

§ 1. THE TREATISE, "ON SPIRITUAL WARFARE"

In the winter and spring of 1419–1420, when first the Taborites, then all the Hussites, were faced with the threat of extermination, the problem of Christian warfare became the subject of many disquisitions, all of which somehow found their way, usually by circuitous routes, to the conclusion that it was after all legitimate to fight for self-preservation and defense of the Truth.[27] Since the Prague masters could fall back on the traditional scholastic justification of the role of the established powers—including the feudality as well as the crown—in the medieval order, their task was not too difficult and their literature *de bello* seems rather trite. But for the Taborites the question of warfare had a more fundamental meaning; existing as new communi-

---

26. Brock, *op. cit.*, pp. 73 f., *passim.*

27. The best review of the literature *de bello* is in Jastrebov, *op. cit.*, pp. 33–115; cf. J. Goll, *Quellen und Untersuchungen zur Geschichte der Böhmischen Brüder*, II (Prague, 1882), 47–57.

ties, without any legitimacy save that provided by urgent need, they could solve the problem of Christian warfare only by defining their whole position vis-à-vis the world, and in consequence stating exactly how their particular brand of reformation corresponded to the Truth. As a rootless, dynamic movement, the product of a profoundly sectarian religious faith, Tabor inevitably developed an ideology of total war,[28] and in Free-Spirit chiliasm found the ideas of self-deification that could make such warfare reasonable. Eventually, as noted above, the consolidation of Taborite society made this ideology less appropriate than the basically scholastic style of thought developed for Tabor by the party of order, but in the second half of 1420 all currents existed side by side and were in fact still contending for mastery. The meeting at Písek in the autumn of 1420 must have been an important step in the supplanting of chiliasm; at the same time, we may be sure that Peter Chelčický's presence at the meeting meant that the pure doctrine of the gospels, nonresistance to evil, was also represented. It seems likely that the treatise he wrote, "On Spiritual Warfare," may be referred to this period,[29] perhaps as a cause of the meeting itself, and it is in this context that we can best understand its line of attack. Warfare is not considered as an abstract problem, nor is it approached via the easy rationalizations of scholasticism; it is the Taborites that Peter is talking to, and it is nothing less than the soul of Tabor that is at stake. Hence the extraordinary depth of penetration and breadth of interest in the work, which continually passes from the question of Christian warfare to questions of Christian ethos and way of life, questions of the meaning of the reform that gave Tabor its reason for being. The treatise is cast in the form of a commentary on Eph. 6:10–20:

Finally, my brethren, be strong in the Lord, and in the power of his might. Put on the whole armour of God, that ye may be able to stand against the wiles of the devil. For we wrestle not against flesh and blood, but against principalities, against powers, against the rulers of the darkness of this world, against spiritual wickedness in high places. Wherefore take unto you the whole armour of God, that ye may be able to withstand in the evil day, and having done all, to stand . . . , your loins girt about with truth . . . and your feet shod with the preparation of the gospel of peace. . . . Take . . . the sword of the Spirit, which is the word of God: Praying always with all prayer and supplication in the Spirit. . . .

28. See my "Chiliasm . . . ," p. 17.
29. See the Appendix, below.

The text itself, its language and imagery evocative of the mood of holy war against a totally evil and vastly powerful enemy, was ideally suited to Chelčický's message; it evoked this mood but at the same time showed that the war in question was one of the spirit. In a similar sense Chelčický could define the method of his holy war as one reminiscent of Tabor's military code; in II Tim. 2:5, Paul had written, "He too who fights in battle will not be crowned unless he fights rightly,"[30] and Chelčický commented (pp. 79 f.):[31]

> That is, he will not be recompensed unless he is brave and wise in battle, striking his blows energetically and not running away, nor spreading fear and confusion to others in the battle. Similarly with spiritual battle, and incomparably more so, he must cast out physical fear and kill everything that comes to his hand. Otherwise the battle against spiritual enemies will not be fought rightly, and the warrior will be unwilling to kill any of them, but will prefer to have peace with them.

Just as Taborite Písek had prepared for a siege by laying waste its suburbs, so the true Christian could withstand the siege of the Devil only by disengaging himself from worldly interests (p. 76)—again the practice of total physical war became an *exemplum* for the war of the spirit. Moreover, Jesus had said, "If any man come to me and hate not his father, and mother, and wife, and children, and brethren, and sisters, he cannot be my disciple" (Luke 14:26); this "terrible word" remained as true as ever, no matter what people might say in favor of their natural loves, and the Christian who refused to listen to it was lost (pp. 81 f.). "Therefore," Chelčický wrote, "let us not follow desire, or custom, or law, or man, and let us not come to terms with this world" (p. 114). In fact the Taborite movement had originated in flight from "this world," a flight that sometimes involved the abandonment not only of property but of family,[32] and Chelčický was merely reminding his former brethren that the very ideals that had inspired their new community required a permanent posture of separation from worldly interests.

30. In Latin, "Nam et qui certat in agone non coronatur nisi legitime certaverit." Peter's Czech translation understandably missed the point of the original, that athletic games should be played according to the rules; my English preserves the sense of the Czech.

31. The page numbers in parentheses refer to K. Krofta's edition: *Petr Chelčický: O boji duchovním* . . . (Prague: J. Otto, 1911).

32. See my "Chiliasm . . . ," pp. 51, 55.

The opposite view, dominant at Tabor, was that the evil world and the world of anti-Hussite•or anti-Taborite powers were identical, and that, in consequence, God's elect, the Taborites, had not only a right but a duty to take up the sword of secular power for defence of the Law of God—hence for self-defence or even for attack against the enemy. Power indeed existed at Tabor, in the form of governing officials, military captains, and armed forces, and it was defended, in a general sense, by the priests who could cite the classic scriptural text, Rom. 13:1–7, with its clear dictum, "the powers that be are ordained of God," and its recognition of the state's role in enforcing justice— "for he beareth not the sword in vain." Chelčický, profoundly alienated from the style of thought that used the Scriptures to justify its own purposes, and in any case untrained in the scholastic system of abstracting texts for use as authorities, cut through this defense of the state by a kind of sociological interpretation of the text in question. Paul, he noted, was talking not about Christian power but about pagan, Roman power, and although it was true that God used the secular sword to punish His enemies, still the "word of life" was not "he beareth not the sword in vain" but "take the sword of the spirit." And if anyone doubted this, let him remember that it was the very sword of Roman secular power that put St. Paul to death (pp. 128 f.). Chelčický's social theory indeed consists precisely in this refusal to use scriptural texts composed at a time when the state was pagan to justify the same sort of state among Christians as a Christian state.

But the argument does not rest here. Chelčický's first treatise is not a work of schematic social theory, it is a study of the evangelical Christian ethos, which involved social questions only as aspects of moral issues. The Taborites thought that they could fight the Devil by fighting the enemies of the Law of God. Chelčický replied (pp. 17 f.):

Those people now who think this think so in vain, when they arm themselves with the power of this world and with weapons, hoping to destroy the Devil. For when they march up [to a fortress] with their war-machines, seeking to smash down the walls within which the Devil dwells among the evil people who have shut themselves up there, the Devil doesn't care. When the attackers smash the walls and mercilessly destroy the evil people, the Devil goes out from those walls and into *them,* and he will dwell in their cruel and loveless hearts. Nor will it be easy for them to besiege their hearts with machines, for they don't even see that the Devil is there. And so no physical power or strength will destroy him, for with his cleverness he can easily bring it about that all those who wish or think to destroy his dominion by the power and strength of this world, that they *fight on his side,* serve him thus, and exalt him higher than ever.

The armament of this world can help to defeat and kill human enemies, but not the Devil, who is too powerful (pp. 16 ff.); Žižka is a clever warrior but Satan is cleverer (pp. 96 f.). The tragedy is that the people have been so corrupted that they do not even see that it is a sin to kill a human being (p. 26), and the source of this corruption is precisely the self-righteous pride of those who observe evangelical commandments and think that they are thereby entitled to execute divine judgment on others (p. 27 f.):

> . . . to our great shame and sorrow, we must acknowledge how our brethren have been cleverly seduced by Satan, and how they have departed from Holy Scriptures in strange and unheard-of ideas and acts. When Satan first came to them it was not with an open face, as the Devil, but in the shining garb of voluntary poverty, which Christ commanded priests to hold to, and in the zealous work of preaching to and serving the people and in giving them the Body and Holy Blood of God. And all of this flourished to the point that a great many people flocked to them. Then the Devil came to them clothed in other garb, in the prophets and the Old Testament, and from these they sought to confect an imminent Day of Judgement, saying that they were angels who had to eliminate all scandals from Christ's Kingdom, and that they were to judge the world. And so they committed many killings and impoverished many people, but they did not judge the world according to their words, for the predicted time has elapsed with which they terrified the people, telling them strange things which they collected from many prophets.

The reference here is obviously to the chiliasts, who had preached that the Day of Wrath would come between February 10 and 14, 1420, and who had indeed declared themselves to be God's angels, sent to destroy the evil,[33] but Peter sees deep enough to understand that chiliasm was no accident, that it had its roots in the peculiar dangers attending a movement that set the masses into motion under the slogan of evangelical perfection.

But if Peter Chelčický could thus cast a cold eye on the ideals of even Waldensianist Taboritism, he did not thereby signify his rejection of those ideals. He insisted only that neither they nor any other

33. *Ibid.,* pp. 54 n. 36, 57.

objective virtues carried their strength within themselves, as good works; if they *were* viewed as good in themselves, they became so many pathways for the Devil to enter, chinks in the armor of the faithful. The other Hussites saw things more superficially: reform meant a renewal of the evangelical virtues, and when Hussite reality failed to measure up to Hussite idealism, the preachers fed their patients new doses of the same medicine. Only Chelčický saw, or admitted seeing, that since the virtuous actions of humanity, no less than its evident sins, were products of man's tainted soul, even the most ardent evangelical reform would carry a burden of potential evil. Good remained better than bad, but the struggle to achieve the good brought ever greater dangers of destruction. He who newly acquired virtuous habits could be easily seduced by the admiration of others (pp. 39 f.) and, more profoundly, as soon as one of the Devil's disguises was torn off, "he assumed other clothing, still more respectable; thus he has poured much heresy into Bohemia, taking on the guise of blameless lives, virtuous acts, many scriptural texts—both in their lofty meanings and in the simple meanings of the letters alone" (p. 29). Good works, however important as sources of strength and consolation, and as witnesses to one's inner condition, do not earn eternal life: "it is the great richness of God alone that suffices to save us, along with those works, and we can have the richness even without the works" (pp. 118 f.). The armament of good works is not strong enough to stand up to the Devil, nor is it a protection that lasts by itself (p. 129); only God does the work of salvation, and only by constant prayer to God, utter reliance on Him (p. 22), can a man avoid both the obvious dangers of the vices and the hidden snares of virtue. "There is no man on earth whose goodness is so great and strong that it cannot be lost if unguarded" (p. 22); it is for this reason that God allows the Devil to be so powerful, so that "great and small will be careful and entrust their defense to God alone" (p. 22).

Peter thus marked out the way to salvation as the path of evangelical virtue, cultivated in a spirit of humility that relied on God alone; in practice, it was necessarily a path of harsh discipline and suffering. A hard-minded connoisseur of human nature, Peter saw that no one would walk this path unless he was bolstered by faith in the rewards of the next world, in regeneration to eternal life. Some, to be sure, asked why man "could not serve God without expecting something from Him, serve Him for His goodness alone," but Chelčický observed: "these are fine words, but foggy ones, for they do not correspond to the truth about people" (pp. 116 f.). On the other hand, it was equally fatuous to suppose, as the Free-Spirit—Pikart-Adamites did, that the elect, in the age of the Holy Spirit, enjoyed sinlessness here on earth, and that for them "it was not necessary to fight against the flesh, but only to live freely, enjoying one's own body in its desires" (pp. 8 f.). "But no man's evil passes away," Chelčický wrote, "and even though he thinks something of the sort about himself or others, he will not thereby make it so" (p. 10). The chiliast idea, that "this world will shine with praise, honor, happiness, peace, and wealth," had "intoxicated many with its success and brilliance," and it was "hard to set oneself against something that was so widespread and seemed so magnificent," but Chelčický here as always spoke the words of disenchanted common sense (p. 67). Moreover, as he observed, the net effect of Free-Spirit fantasy was to cast doubt on the all-important tension between this world and the next, to destroy the people's faith in the bliss of the next world by preaching that this bliss would come to pass here on earth (p. 10); when the preaching turned out false, it must have left the old faith weaker.

Since Peter saw the essence of reform in the moral conversion of the individual, whose sole reliance was in God, he naturally set the theater of spiritual warfare in the individual person. Like the other Hussites, he condemned the Roman system, often abusively, for its externalization of religion: "holy masses, beautiful singing, lofty churches" and "many other honorable things in which the service of God was performed" were disguises of the Devil that had to be ripped off (pp. 25 f.), and the "honorable" covering of the pope merely concealed Antichrist (pp. 23–25). Nor were the monks any better, for all of their good works: "hell is shut up in those cloister walls" (p. 26). But the Hussite preachers who, having attacked these same things, were currently trying to define the nature of a reformation of the Christian order, also came in for Chelčický's criticism. It was the Devil who stirred up men's hearts "to take on what was above their power and . . . impose laws on all things, without setting themselves under the Law of Truth" (pp. 42 f.). "A great evil and danger has come to Bohemia because there are so many blind teachers" (pp. 133 f.) who do not have the gifts of the Holy Spirit and consequently can do no more than give the literal sense of the Scriptures, or else develop false expositions according to their carnal spirits and their own inventions (pp. 42 f.). Both the Prague masters and the leading theologians of Tabor's party of order held to the traditional Romanist principle, that a theo-

logical education was at least one of the qualifications for understanding the truth of Scripture, but Chelčický observed that the learned
were among those most easily deceived by the Devil (pp. 40 f.). In any
case, he argued, learned men "work for a single end, that of accumu-
lating many books of various doctors"; whenever something new comes
on the book market, they buy it or rent it, and their libraries are their
pride—"as though they knew a lot just by having the books" (pp.
134 f.). But the books were useless: their owners had so many that they
could not read and understand them all, and their authors frequently
disagreed with each other in interpreting the evangelical commands,
some holding to a strict line, others willing to compromise with reality
(p. 135). Only the gift of the Holy Spirit could qualify a man to preach
the Scriptures truly, but few had the gift or even prayed for it (pp.
133 f.); there were plenty of preachers who knew the Bible, but "dam-
agingly, without God's Spirit" (p. 122). The "spiritual sword" that the
Christian had to take up to fight the Devil was nothing but the word
of God (p. 122), but if this word was preached falsely, it became the
Devil's own weapon: "And we see this evil now before our eyes, how
the Devil has cut down many people more powerfully with this sword
than by dumbness" (p. 122). Chelčický's advice was simple: "Godfear-
ing people should humbly use and listen to the Word of God expounded by faithful teachers . . . and especially should they listen to
what is expounded about the contempt of the world and of physical
life, about the vanity of this world's praise" (p. 123). It was in fact the
humility, suffering, love, and faith of the New Testament that constituted the most effective spiritual weapons against the Devil (p. 125)—
this must be understood as an attack on the currently popular practice
of using the Old Testament for direct support of Tabor's use of force.[34]
Nor is Peter unwilling to push his ideas to their logical conclusion:
since the canons of true understanding of Scripture are so simple, and
since the preachers as a class are so unqualified for their work, the
layman himself must study the sacred pages. Again the imagery is
drawn from battle: just as in physical warfare it is not enough for

34. The Taborite clergy acknowledged the "excesses" of some of their priests in
citing the Old Testament in a spirit contrary to the life and doctrine of Christ and
the Apostles, so that occasion was given for tyranny and cruelty. They also condemned the use of the "particular judicial provisions" of the Old Testament in
judging current cases, including questions of killing ("The Chronicle of the Priests
of Tabor," by Nicholas of Pelhřimov, ed. K. Höfler, *Geschichtschreiber der husi-
tischen Bewegung in Böhmen*, II, *Fontes rerum austriacarum*, Erste Abteilung, VI
[Vienna, 1865], 482 ff.).

someone that his friend have a sword—he must have one himself, so "in this hard battle it is not enough for the layman that some learned pastor or prelate know Scriptures—he himself must know and understand them" (pp. 121 f.). But few do, and they prudently keep their peace (p. 106):

> Now that the Devil has sown so many different kinds of spirits, who will take up the shield of faith for Christ, to confess something truthful about him? For he will be counted as in error when he says that he follows Christ and truly stands for Christ's faith. And so he to whom the pure faith now is given from heaven above, he will preserve it, not indeed speaking out very much about it, but suffering with it.

In this way, defining Christian warfare as spiritual battle against the Devil, Chelčický refutes all varieties of the attempt to work out the scheme of the Christian faith in terms of current societal realities, and he comes to rest, inevitably, with the individual who follows the true way in exclusive reliance on God, and who in consequence stands apart from the world of Hussite affairs. Even the most basic external functional distinction that can create a social body, the distinction between priest and layman, falls away in the extremely important matter of preaching—it survives, to be sure, in the sphere of the sacraments, particularly the Eucharist—and the other prime distinction, that between ruler and ruled, is recognized only as part of the order of secular justice. The secular officials "who rule in a pagan manner over the subjects" are "proud, greedy, carnal, and blind men who do not fear God and care nothing for the people"; they regard the people not as a flock entrusted to their care, but as a "pasture for the rich" (pp. 55–57). Like the Taborites who, in August, 1420, demanded that the law of God replace "pagan and German laws" in governing society,[35] Chelčický believes that "the laws of the land are opposed to God's commandments" (p. 56). But he does *not* go on to indulge in the fantasy of supposing that the law of God can be made the law of the land: it makes very little if any difference to him whether government is good or bad, just or unjust—in the best of cases it can do nothing more than settle disputes according to *its* mode of justice (p. 56), and thus distract the people from exclusive obedience to the one law that contains true justice, the law of God—the New Testament, which of course makes no provision for magistrates, courts, and executioners. Thus the ideal of

---

35. Laurence of Březová, p. 398.

evangelical reform cannot be sociologically creative. In coming years Tabor would know both glory and disaster, but Peter and the Chelčice brethren who followed him would share in neither, except insofar as the Taborite power that they condemned provided the security that they needed for continued life in this world. In exchange, Peter continued for several years to serve as a kind of unofficial conscience for the Taborite leaders, whose highly creditable inner uncertainties would be revealed in their discussions with their neighbor.

§ 2. CHRISTIANITY AND THE SOCIAL ORDER

At the beginning of his treatise, "On the Triple Division of Society," written in the mid-1420's, Chelčický states that he will once again not speak of his doubts on the matter; he will write something only because he has been asked, presumably by one of the priests of Tabor.[36] Later on in the same work he mentions the encounter between himself and a group of the Taborite priests at Písek, in the first year of the war—i.e., 1420: the Taborites, trying to prove the Christian legitimacy of their use of power, opposed Chelčický by citing the Wyclifite doctrine that secular power was a function of the Church, with the duty of defending the law of God by the sword.[37] Putting these items together, and remembering that surviving sources must represent only a small fraction of what once existed, and that in any case only a very few important conversations were memorialized in writing, we may suppose that for some time after the Taborites had begun to take up the sword and build a social order, their leaders were bedeviled by the same doubts that had attended the very beginnings of the enterprise. At first it had been a question of Christian warfare—was it a possibility, or was it a contradiction in terms?—but this soon turned into the more general question of whether there could be such a thing as a Christian society. The Bible, recognized by the Taborites as the sole source of truth, was naturally mute on this point, except insofar as the New Testament presupposed a *non*-Christian society, and while the Fathers and scholastics made good the lack, the Taborites could hardly follow medieval tradition on this point when they explicitly rejected it on all others.[38] Moreover, according to the historical scheme based on the Donation of Constantine, the secular order had become Christian precisely when Constantine entered the Church and endowed

36. See the translated text, below.
37. See the Appendix, below.
38. Laurence of Březová, pp. 403 f., 412 f.

it with the wealth and power that, in the Hussite view, were the prime sources of the corruption that made their reformation necessary. There was one way out: John Wyclif, the "Doctor Evangelicus," who had won the enthusiastic approval of the Hussites by his savage, revolutionary attacks on the Roman system, had recognized the legitimacy of secular government and had assigned it the role of carrying through the reform.[39] The English state and society were never far from Wyclif's mind, even when his theory purported to be universal, and he seems never to have given due consideration to the thought that evangelical Christianity excluded *any* coercive power *within* the faith. "The main duty of kings and temporal lords is to defend the evangelical law with their power"; "the secular lords . . . must compel those travelling the broad way of the Devil . . . to enter the narrow path that leads to heaven."[40] Society should be ruled by Christ's law, the law of God, but human laws could be regarded as branches of God's law insofar as they were useful to it.[41] Accepting his own society as fundamentally sound, Wyclif had no trouble assigning functions to each of its estates, according to the tripartite scheme: the commons worked, the secular powers ruled and defended, the clerics prayed and preached.[42] University Hussitism, which followed Wyclif in so many points, followed him here too, without evident difficulty, and when the priests of Tabor found themselves operating within a reformed social order—their own—they could find no better guide than the Evangelical Doctor. But unlike Wyclif, who never had a chance to direct a reform, and unlike the

39. H. Workman, *John Wyclif*, II (Oxford, 1926), 20–30; H. Fürstenau, *Johann von Wiclifs Lehren von der Einteilung der Kirche und von der Stellung der weltlichen Gewalt* (Berlin, 1900), pp. 115, *passim*. And see my "Wyclifism as Ideology of Revolution," *Church History*, XXXII (1963), 57–74.

40. Cited by Fürstenau, *op. cit.*, pp. 74 n. 104, 86 n. 139.

41. *Ibid.*, pp. 37 f., 78 n. 117. Wyclif's concept of the "Law of God," the "Evangelical Law," was not very concrete; he asserted that "it would be best *simpliciter* if the whole church were ruled purely according to evangelical Law," and that "the best polity would be if the people were ruled purely according to the divine Law, by judges," but what he had in mind was just the usual medieval concept of the state of innocence as best—in man's present condition, kings were necessary, and a government suitable to the state of innocence could serve only as an ideal to be approached, but not reached.

42. *Ibid.*, *passim*. Wyclif also used the idea, derived from Augustine, that the king had the image of God, the bishop the image of Christ, or in other terms, the king had Christ's godhood, the priest Christ's humanity (*ibid.*, p. 93). Here as often elsewhere in Wyclif's work, the anti-Romanism of the later middle ages shows its kinship with the anti-Hildebrandinism of the eleventh century, when the York tractates used similar imagery (*MGH, Libelli de lite*, iii, 666).

Prague masters, who simply operated with existing social and theoretical elements, the Taborites had to assume direct and continuous responsibility for the entire structure of reality that was guided by their theory. When they adopted the theory of a triple division of society, they were associating themselves with the bloodbaths perpetrated by Žižka's armies and the exploitation of the peasantry by the Taborite magistrates, who collected the usual seigneurial rents in the areas they controlled. No wonder then that at least the more conscientious of the priests of Tabor felt the need for repeated debate about what they were doing; inevitably such priests were drawn to Peter Chelčický.

His position in the debates had the strength of absolute simplicity. All Hussites agreed that the "Holy Church" was the congregation of those predestined to salvation, that no one could be sure of anyone's predestination, and that no visible community in this world could be taken as constituting the Holy Church proper. But most Hussites went on to modify this rigid doctrine to suit practical needs: virtue was taken as a generally valid indication of predestination, and the whole social order was thought of as the Church, in an equivocal but significant sense.[43] All that Chelčický did was to insist that there could be no equivocations. The Church was the congregation of the predestined, who enjoyed the gifts of the Holy Spirit; it was a spiritual community that had nothing whatsoever in common with any social community. It was therefore absolutely meaningless to call any social community Christian, to justify it in terms of the Christian faith, or to suppose that it could be of value to the faith. This is the essence of his argu-

43. Predestination remained the theoretical principle of the true church, and no one ever suggested that virtue was its infallible sign, but *in fact* the distinction between good and bad in the Hussites' anti-Roman polemic perforce turned on external indications, and the model of the true church among men—i.e., the Church Militant—was the Primitive Church, its doctrines and institutions. At the same time, the secular powers were called on to fulfill their function *within* the church, of promoting reform. Thus to cite only one case from very many, Jakoubek of Stříbro, writing *ca.* 1417 to guide his followers who were ejecting Catholic priests and forming their own congregational communities, defined the basis of the latter as union in Christ, "consisting in observance of his evangelical law" (*De quibusdam punctis*, Prague University Library, MS VIII E 7, fol. 105). There could be no talk here of predestination. And he went on to say that such a union was to be formed by the priests, whose preaching should "destroy all mortal sins," and what they could not effect by their words, the magistrates (*scabini*) should effect by the sword (*loc. cit.*). The principle itself is derived from Isidore of Seville (*Decretum*, XXIII, q.v, c. 20); it was used repeatedly by the Hussites to define the coordinate roles of the spiritual and secular powers in Christian society—cf. Chelčický's refutation of it in "On the Triple Division of Society," below.

ment in the treatise "On the Holy Church," written sometime in the early 1420's; in the treatise "On the Triple Division of Society," written about 1424/1425, he works out the point with special reference to social theory. The "secular order through power" and "Christ's order through love" cannot stand together within one Christian faith. To the obvious objection, that power could be used for a good end, to impose justice, Chelčický replied that the truly Christian people were held together by mutual love, neither injuring others nor seeking vengeance nor even remedy for injuries done to them; they did not need the regime of power that enforced external justice. The faithless did need such a regime, and power was therefore necessary and according to the will of God, but only to promote temporal good; this sort of good was identical among Christians and pagans—that is, it was not a *Christian* good and could not, therefore, be integrated into a scale of values proper to the Christian faith. On this basis, Chelčický can easily dispose of the theory of a triple division of society: nothing in Christian doctrine justifies such a division, and in point of fact the harsh exploitation of the working people by the two upper estates, nobility and clergy, is opposed to the spirit of love that holds the real Christian body together.

These brief formulations convey Chelčický's main ideas, without of course doing justice to their complexity or profundity; the treatises themselves, here offered in English translation, may stand as proofs. But something may still be said about the significance of their style of thought, as momentous for the future as it was impotent in its own time. If Peter stood for the utter separation of the "secular order through power" and "Christ's order through love," he also, by the same token, stood for the rejection of any order of civilization within the framework of the Western Christian tradition. From the eleventh century on, the medieval order had taken shape as a conscious fusion of the temporal and the spiritual, the spheres of nature and of grace; the world was in theory directed toward moral goals derived from or at least harmonious with the Christian religion, the values of that religion were made to penetrate the order of secular society, and the religious sphere proper was penetrated by reason, from the bottom almost to the top. Such at least was the ideal, and the effort to achieve it imparted a distinctive stamp to the West that remains with us today and is undoubtedly at the heart of what we legitimately regard as our success. By the fifteenth century, however, the Christianization of secular society had hardly done more than begin to establish a merely external order among essentially non-Christian realities, and it needed only a disenchanted and alienated spirit to see the gulf between the orders of power and love, to be revolted by the hypocrisy and downright falsehood required by the ideal of Christian society, and, finally, to speak the truth, that the emperor had no clothes: for power does exactly the same thing in Christian nations as it does among the pagans, and to call this power Christian is not to make it so.[44] Nor was there hope of improvement: the world "has never acknowledged the Lord . . . nor ever will." A man who thinks in this way will see very little significant difference between good government and bad; while Chelčický was able to recognize the value of external order, and slightly softened his harsh view of the state as Bohemia became more and more thoroughly Hussite,[45] he never—to use his vocabulary—drank the wine of the Great Whore and put power under the faith of Jesus Christ. Similarly he never accepted the practical consequences of orthodox Christian sociology, which required the masses of the poor to hold still while their secular and spiritual lords squeezed them dry, lived off them, and treated them with heartless brutality. Setting the fighters and rulers outside the faith, Chelčický also refused to allow the preachers and prayers to justify their economic parasitism on the basis of a New Testament that recognized no priestly claim to idleness. The function of economic exploitation in making a higher civilization possible was not, in his view, worth very much, if anything: Peter rejected both the carnal and cultural delights of this world under the same title of worldliness.

Some scholars have compared Chelčický to Karl Marx on the basis of their common utopian rejection of their respective societies, and in other ways too Chelčický has been seen as a radical social theorist.[46]

44. "On the Triple Division of Society," below, p. 146. Jakoubek of Stříbro made a similar point in his *De prediis et potestate coactiva* (ed. Bartoš, "Z dějin chiliasmu r. 1420," *Do čtyř pražských artykulů* [Prague, 1925], p. 100): "hec potestas coactiva mundana est eadem in specie in paganis, iudeis sive christianis, licet gradualiter secundum magis et minus in individuo sive singulari differant. . . ." But Jakoubek went on to argue that since power was justified in the Old Testament it could therefore be used by Christians.

45. V. Chaloupecký, *Selská otázka v husitství* (Bratislava, 1926), p. 59; cf. Jastrebov, *op. cit.*, pp. 148 f.

46. Matthew Spinka, "Peter Chelčický, the Spiritual Father of the Unitas Fratrum," *Church History*, XII (1943), 283: "Peter . . . long antedates Karl Marx in voicing a demand for an utopian classless society." More recently Dr. Radim Foustka, a Communist, has sought to define the social character of Chelčický's ideas by associating them with the class position of the propertied peasants, who were

Enough has been said in the present essay to show both the truth and falsity of such an approach. Chelčický does in fact condemn the world, but he does not wish to improve it; the society of his day is not in his view a theater of struggle for something better, but is a bleak wasteland in which the Christians live as aliens. The light of the true faith illuminates only the path of withdrawal and suffering, the narrow path that only a few will travel; outside it there stretches the dark landscape of violence, brutality, sin, and seduction. Above all, the world had no place for the spirit of love. People killed, plundered, and stole, they hated their fellows or treated them like beasts, without pity. The social intercourse of the market place was, to be sure, relatively free of the worst features of seigneurial oppression but it had its own variety of lovelessness that was perhaps even colder:[47]

> Others who are against this edict and law of Christ [i.e., the Golden Rule] are those who forestall it by not taking any kindness from others, so that they themselves need not show love to anyone. . . . For it is their custom in all things to deal with people according to the ruthlessness of this world, and according to the intentions of greedy people, and according to the obligations of the market and of debts. When they get someone in their power by hiring him or paying him wages, they do not pity him in his troubles, but rather squeeze all they can from him, trying to work him so hard in his day or year of hire that he does more than enough to earn their money. And in the work they do not consider his strength or life, but their own profit. Thus it is against the words of Lord Jesus that these people do not accept love because they do not want to give themselves to others in love, or that they buy a man for themselves with wages and, without love, threaten his life by loading great

---

opposed to the feudality but shrank from an all-out war of liberation—"the typical petty-bourgeois position." Thus we can explain both Chelčický's critique of feudal oppression and his renunciation of war. (*Petra Chelčického: Názory na stát a právo*, Acta universitatis Carolinae, I. Iuridica [1955], 65). Peter Brock, *op. cit.*, is rather less heavyhanded, but his formulation (p. 63), "Chelčický saw in a society founded on class inequalities the antithesis of a Christian social order," itself points to a misunderstanding; for in Chelčický's view, there was no such thing as a Christian social order. Elsewhere, too, Brock tries to build up Chelčický's social theory by associating his point of view with that of the peasantry (p. 66), although he does not press the point. What he misses is the point made by Chelčický at the end of his "On the Holy Church": the exploitation of the faithful is not such a terrible thing— it is indeed sanctioned by Paul; "the worst thing is that this paganism is accepted into the faith and is joined with it. . . ."

47. *O boji duchovním*, ed. Krofta, pp. 92 f.

labors on him. For it does not seem to such people that they ought to show love in their dealings, when they hire someone, or transact business for money and make payments. . . .

Peter did not have to wait until the nineteenth century to catch the odor of the bourgeoisie in his nostrils. At the same time, in his ideas about power he resembled not Marx but Hobbes. Power cannot be mitigated by love without being weakened, nor can it be distributed without being disintegrated;[48] its function is nothing but the preservation of external peace, and its justice consists not in the justness of its laws but in the uniformity and effectiveness of its system of courts.[49] And there is no hope of a social development that will make absolute, monolithic power unnecessary. By treating power in so abstract a fashion, Peter rejects even the more hopeful realities of his own day, and makes impossible any *principled* relation between the worldly majority and the Christian minority. But the world goes on, and the net effect of a style of thought that devalues it is to bring into being precisely the schema of bourgeois liberalism, which denies the values of the whole and composes society from the free association of freely valuing individuals. That Chelčický would not have liked the world of bourgeois liberalism is not to the point; he must be ranked as one of its fathers. In this sense we may attach sociological meaning to Peter's religious doctrine; his social criticism itself is merely an aspect of his evangelical morality, but his concept of the relation between Christianity and the world presents the true religious form of the principle that, masked by secularization, has animated the postmedieval world. In his own world of Hussite Bohemia, Peter's uniquely merciless critique of the established order was balanced by his renunciation of social struggle, and Communist historians have thus classed him as "objectively" a reactionary,[50] but if we see the revolution against the medieval order as a centuries-long process, involving all aspects of societal reality, then we must see Chelčický as the first genuine revolutionary ideologist. For he alone separated the secular from the sacred, and set each adrift, to find its own future.

§ 3. THE PROBLEM OF THE EUCHARIST

The last of what may be called Peter Chelčický's early works—those composed in intimate relationship to the development of Taboritism—

48. See "On the Triple Division of Society," below, pp. 140, 141.
49. *Ibid.*, pp. 141 f.
50. See J. Macek, *Tábor* . . . , II, 174.

was his "Reply to Nicholas Biskupec," directed against Nicholas of Pelhřimov, bishop of Tabor, and probably composed about 1425.[51] It deals with the question of how to define the presence of Christ in the eucharist, but since, in the absence of any evidence for any kind of presence at all, each Hussite group defined the presence in the light of its own concept of religious community, the question involved most of the basic problems of Taborite society. The more radical Prague masters held to Wyclif's doctrine of remanence—the bread and wine are not annihilated, as in transubstantiation, but remain, and Christ's body and blood are added to them—and this was the doctrine of the priests of Tabor at first,[52] but the Free-Spirit sectarians at Tabor brought a new point of view to the whole question, which thus came to the fore as a subject of polemic. These "Pikarts" rejected the so-to-speak mechanical aspect of the eucharist, and converted the sacrament from a formalized, liturgical action to a love feast, in which the bread and wine, along with other foods, served as occasions for the reception of the Holy Spirit by the participants. Joy and love animated such a gathering, which in this real sense actually enjoyed the Spirit, even through the foods that they ate contained no divine presence in themselves. This was the positive aspect of Pikartism; its negative aspect consisted in a contemptuous, often violent attack on the sacrament as taken by the other Hussites—the consecrated bread and wine were declared to be empty of any real presence, the reverence shown them was thus denounced as idolatry, and the elements themselves were sometimes seized and thrown to the ground.[53] Combined as it was with a whole corpus of Free-Spirit doctrine that was entirely incompatible with the theological requirements of Taborite society, Pikart eucharistic doctrine could only be rejected along with the Pikarts themselves, who were expelled from Tabor in 1421; Nicholas of Pelhřimov played an important role in this action, and defended the Hussite orthodox doctrine of a real presence.[54] But after the Pikarts had been driven out and destroyed as a group, their eucharistic doctrine proved very attractive to the Taborite leaders: the love feast was of course rejected, but the idea of communion as essentially a congregational action, with grace coming through the action rather than in the excessively objec-

51. For the dating see F. M. Bartoš, "K počátkům Petra Chelčického," *ČČM*, LXXXVIII (1914), 149–60.

52. On this whole subject, see J. Sedlák, *Táborské traktáty eucharistické* (Brno, 1918), *passim*.

53. See my "The Free Spirit in the Hussite Revolution," pp. 173 ff.

54. *Ibid.*, p. 179.

tified form of bits of bread and sips of wine, resonated with the other aspects of Taborite religion. The Roman mass had been abolished, and the whole concept of a liturgy existing apart from congregational worship had been overcome; communion, moreover, was not an incidental part of the service—everyone was supposed to take it, at every service.[55] Hence from perhaps 1422 on, if not even earlier, the leading Taborite theologians, including Nicholas of Pelhřimov, worked out a definition of the presence in the eucharist that was close to that of the Pikarts: Christ was present in the consecrated bread and wine in three modes, sacramentally (i.e., figuratively), through his power, and spiritually, but *not* substantially or corporeally.[56]

The leader of the Pikarts, Martin Húska, came to Chelčický in the first part of 1421 (Martin was martyred on August 21, 1421), and explained both his eucharistic doctrine and its nourishing matrix of Free-Spirit hopes and ideals—there would be a new kingdom of the saints on earth, and the good Christians would no longer suffer. Apart from this hope, Martin said, there was no reason to serve God.[57] Not long after, Nicholas of Pelhřimov asked Chelčický to meet him in Vodňany, a Taborite town, for a discussion of eucharistic questions; Nicholas asked what Peter had heard about his doctrine, and when Peter replied that some people said it was good, others bad, Nicholas assured him that he held only the true faith of the Bible. Some time later, Nicholas again sent for Peter, for the same purpose; since we know that in the years after early 1421, Nicholas was changing his eucharistic doctrine from remanence to the modified Pikartism described above, we may suppose that the second meeting was made necessary by this development; again Peter heard what seemed to be sound views, but this time he asked to have them in writing. And when he received Nicholas's treatises—delivered to him in Chelčice by Nicholas

---

55. The fullest treatment of Taborite liturgy is that by Z. Nejedlý, *Dějiny husitského zpěvu* (new edition), IV (Prague, 1955), 179 ff. Just before communion the congregation sang the hymn, "Časy svými jistými," which included the verses: "We ridicule him who dares not take communion" (*ibid.*, pp. 289 f.; cf. pp. 202 ff.).

56. The distinctions are fully worked out by the Taborite theologian John Němec of Žatec, in his treatise, *Cum spiritus veritatis summe odiens mendacium*, ed. J. Sedlák, *op. cit.*, pp. 9 ff. He regarded his formulation as "the middle view" between heretical Pikartism, which denied any divine presence that would make the consecrated bread different from ordinary food, and the "gross" view, that "the material flesh of Christ" is in the sacrament (pp. 19 f.). As Chelčický observed in his "Reply to Biskupec" (p. 421) John Němec's ideas were all held by Nicholas of Pelhřimov too.

57. Chelčický, "Reply to Biskupec," pp. 464 f.

and other Taborite priests, he found that the doctrine they contained differed from what Nicholas had explained orally; there followed another meeting between the two, but by this time—*ca.* 1424—the gulf was evident and unbridgeable. Chelčický's "Reply" is a defense against Nicholas's charge that Peter had defamed him like another Judas; as far as we know it ended both the series of discussions between the two and the other contacts between Chelčický and the priests of Tabor. The turbulence of societal and doctrinal creativity gave way at Tabor to relative stability, and there was probably no reason for further conversations with Chelčický.[58]

This story is summarized here partly as a striking indication of Chelčický's importance to early Tabor, partly as evidence of the kind of religion cultivated by the Chelčice brethren. It is not hard to understand why Peter should have been horrified by Martin Húska: the harsh, disciplinary orientation of Waldensianist sectarianism stood confronted by doctrines of liberation, seeking happiness in this world. Moreover, by the time Peter came to write down his ideas about the Pikarts, they had given ample evidence, in their Adamite phases, of the sensual license that followed upon their ideas of liberty and joy. Indeed, some of the best evidence we have for the Adamites comes from Chelčický's "Reply." What he did not see was that Tabor could combine a denial of the real presence with all of the moral restraints of traditional Christian religion, and that, in the context of the same sort of evangelical congregationalism that he himself espoused, an objectively real presence was less satisfactory than a spiritual presence. Without for a moment suggesting that varying eucharistic doctrines should be understood as conscious contrivances for social goals, we may observe that doctrines on this subject did vary, and that Chelčický, who went down the line with the most radical sort of Waldensianist heresy, could not have been motivated by any reckless lust for

58. The discussions with Chelčický should probably be understood as part of the Taborite theologians' efforts to explore and define their doctrine—Chelčický obviously functioned as a prime representative of a contrary view *within* the area subject to Taborite power and sharing Tabor's basic religious doctrines. But on November 11, 1424, a Taborite synod at Klatovy made the doctrine espoused by Nicholas of Pelhřimov binding on all Taborite priests (for the text of the synod's decrees see F. M. Bartoš, "Klatovská synoda táborských kněží z II. listopadu r. 1424," *JSH*, VIII [1935], 6 f.), and it then became necessary to defend this official Taborite doctrine against the official doctrine of Prague. Thus for twenty years after 1424, Nicholas and his associates were involved in formal disputations with the Prague masters on this question (as well as others).

orthodoxy in just the single matter of the eucharist. Nor on the other side, could the Taborites have espoused semi-Pikart doctrine for the sheer joy of innovating: there is ample evidence that the people at Tabor felt uncomfortable with the new doctrine, which indeed was presented in deliberately ambiguous language for just this reason,[59] while the party of order's concern for at least the appearance of harmony with Prague was frustrated in the years after 1424, chiefly by Tabor's denial of a real presence.[60] But while the theologians of Tabor evidently felt obliged to develop a body of religious thought and practice that would be both intellectually and emotionally self-consistent, and which could thereby serve as the ideology of a definite form of social organism, Chelčický, rejecting any such involvement of religion and society, was free to embrace inconsistencies. Since he believed that denial of an objectively real presence paved the way to Adamite licentiousness, by absorbing the central sacrament of the faith into the actual, human life of the congregation,[61] and since he had a keen

59. John Němec of Žatec, in his eucharistic treatise referred to in n. 56 above, wrote (p. 7): "Et sic fidelis potest indifferenter sacramentum appellare nunc corpus Christi nunc vero panem. . . . Et sic fidelis potest dicere infidelibus quandoque uno modo quandoque alio modo, secundum quod viderit ex hoc profectum. . . ." And the Klatovy decrees of 1424 (above, n. 58) similarly show concern for the right way to present the doctrine to the laity (especially No. 4). Peter Chelčický strongly criticized what he regarded as the hypocrisy of the Taborites' approach ("Reply to Biskupec," p. 496): ". . . you priests have one understanding of this sacrament and the lay people have another. . . . And this is an unheard-of thing, that the people seek salvation in one interpretation but the priest ministers to the people in another, and dares not tell the people frankly what he thinks of that which he ministers to them" (cf. also pp. 433 f., 441). In justice to the Taborites, however, it should be observed that they were engaged in a very difficult enterprise, that of educating a large mass of religiously awakened people toward a more spiritual and immensely more demanding conception of the relationship between man and God. Thus John Němec justified his counsel of prudent discourse by the need to make the laity understand that while on the one hand Christ does have "many bodies in many places"—that is, each sacrament in each church is, figuratively, the body of Christ, on the other hand none of them is the "corpus Christi, quod naturaliter et personaliter actuatur per animam suam in celo"; by calling the sacrament bread, the people will be led away from the "idolatry of thinking that the sacrament is identical to its God."

60. The many disputations on this subject between the Taborite and Prague theologians are summarized and documented in Nicholas of Pelhřimov's "Chronicle of the Priests of Tabor," Höfler, II, 589 ff.

61. There are several passages in the "Reply to Biskupec" in which Adamite sensuality is linked to the Pikart eucharistic heresy, and it will be useful to quote some of them at length: ". . . these blasphemers, having turned away from that 'dead sign' [*scil.*, the eucharist] as from an idol, have turned to foul and unbridled

appreciation of the illogicality of Tabor's doctrine—if the bread and wine merely symbolized God's presence, then why could not any substance or action serve equally well?[62]—he preferred to stick to the definitions of Wyclif and the Prague masters. Here we see the limits of his value to the reformation; it was only much later, after the societal embodiment of Hussitism had exhausted its capacity for development, and when the need was felt to liberate the values of the reformation from the reformed society, that Chelčický again came into his own as a source of inspiration—as the "spiritual father" of the Unity of the Brethren.

fornication [smilství]" (p. 435). ". . . These people, having committed murders and having blasphemed against the sacrament, have turned to foul fornication in the woods and hidden places. . . . And some have based their fornication on the eating of Christ's body, and they have agreed to use the words 'white bread' as a sign: when they want to speak of fornication, they just say 'white bread', and thus understand each other" (p. 439). [Nicholas of Pelhřimov tried to get the people to turn away from the bread of the sacrament to the living bread that descended from heaven, communion in which involved the doing of Christ's deeds. But] "Many who hold your doctrine . . . are not observed to have the deeds of Christ in themselves and united to them, as they should according to your doctrine, but rather they are seen to lead carnal and profligate lives, with excessive eating and drinking, and—some of them—in unbridled fornication. And this will be the net result of your doctrine for such people, that they will abandon the consecrated bread, but will also not have the living bread that you praise to them in good deeds, and will thus soon begin to lead the lives of animals" (p. 461). "But those fornicating blasphemers, who hold your doctrines about the sacrament and speak your good words, which rejoice them . . . —those people call their perversion the imitation of the deeds of Christ, the love of God, the communion of the saints, the Lord's Supper—when they encourage each other in gluttony and copious drinking, in fondling each other and in other lascivious incitements . . . , and such foulness and lascivious acts they call, in front of others, the eating of Christ's body" (p. 498). Cf. also pp. 438, 459. We may infer from these passages that Adamitism still survived into the mid-1420's, although the main body of the sect had been liquidated in 1421; the survivors evidently made good use of the quasi-Pikart eucharistic doctrine that had become Taborite orthodoxy, and Chelčický certainly implies that the doctrine led to Adamite practice, but there is no evidence that it actually did so among the main body of Taborites.

62. "Reply to Biskupec," p. 460.

II. "ON THE TRIPLE DIVISION OF SOCIETY"[1]

THIS TIME again I shall avoid speaking to you of my doubts about the justification of the division of the people into three parts, considered by some to be part of Christ's faith. But I will write something about it because you[2] ask me to, although I must say at the outset that I cannot do so briefly, as you do. Although you are capable of briefly understanding things more difficult than my tractate, still, the way I understand these matters forces me to devote a lot of hard thinking to them. For me to try to write about them briefly would be like trying to build a great town with five stones, which would not even be enough for laying the foundations. Of course I well know that, as far as the teachings of Christ's faith about the clergy and laity are concerned, you have enough understanding of the matter even without my work, and I shall not, therefore, write much about that. But as to the status of secular power: I have considered your reasoning and scriptural authorities, and I have diligently collected the writings of all the priests of Tabor and of the Prague masters from the beginning of the war,[3] and I have pondered on what they have said and are still saying about that power. But I do not want to write you something that would just add to that long series of writings and theories about secular power, for everyone who has written has his own theory about it, and where is the limit, where is the end? I shall rather touch on just a few things among many points concerning it.

1. Literally: "Statement about the triple division of the people, and about the clergy and laity."

2. That Chelčický's addressee was a Taborite priest is clear from the treatise itself. Some scholars guess that he was Markolt of Zbraslavice, who is known to have come close to holding that evil priests did not possess sacramental powers (see Höfler, II, 589 ff.): Chelčický mentions (below, p. 161) that his addressee had criticized the Roman clergy. (Cf. R. Urbánek, *Věk Poděbradský*, III (Prague, 1930), 916; N. Jastrebov, *Etjudy*, pp. 157 f.). But F. M. Bartoš points out that all the Taborite priests had criticized unworthy priests, and suggests that the addressee was more probably Nicholas of Pelhřimov: for his arguments see his "K počátkům Petra Chelčického, "*Časopis českého musea*, LXXXVIII (1914), 306 f. On this point there can at present be no certainty; I agree with Bartoš that the arguments in favor of Markolt are not cogent enough, and I also agree that Nicholas of Pelhřimov seems more likely, although I do not accept all of Bartoš's arguments.

3. That is, from early 1420 on: see the Appendix, below; cf. also n. 27 to the Introduction.

First of all, the attributes of power must be understood, and we must understand that it breeds fear, for power makes it possible for cruelty to rule, threaten, abuse, do violence, imprison, beat, and kill. Furthermore, it was God himself who established this secular power from the beginning among all peoples, for his order, which the world needs and which he wishes to have in all things. And I say that God establishes power as the external secular order among those nations that he has not established under his Law, as it is written: "In all nations the Lord established a prince or ruler, but Israel was the evident portion of God" [Ecclus. 17:14–15]. For Israel God established neither lord nor king on earth, because he himself wished to rule over them, and it is shown in Holy Scripture that from the time they came into the Promised Land until the time of Saul, no king was established for them by God. But when they themselves scorned God and desired a king, then God said to the prophet Samuel: "Listen to the voice of the people; they have not only scorned you by asking for a king, but they have also rejected me as their ruler, according to their acts, which they did from the day that I led them out of Egypt" [I Kings 8:7–8; but cf. the Vulgate]. And when the prophet Samuel had spoken at length to the people and had shown them that they were bringing misfortune upon themselves, opposing God by demanding to have a king to rule over them, then they took fright at his words and said: "Today we have added this sin to all our others, demanding to have a king over us" [I Kings 12:18–19]. Thus we have it from Scripture that over those nations not under God's yoke, he established the dreadful power of the sword, so that the disobedient and unwise people in them would be kept in line by the dreadful sword. However he chose the nation of Jacob for himself, as a special people, and ruled it in peace and plenty until the people scorned him and asked to have a king.

It should further be realized that when King David or another Jewish king was established as ruler, he was established according to the Law, so that through the power of the sword he might do what the Law commanded, using the royal power by virtue of the Law. Moreover, the Law of the Jews commanded physical battle against their enemies, and prescribed death for various kinds of sinners, as well as many punishments short of death, such as an eye for an eye, a tooth for a tooth, a blow for a blow, and so forth; and it also provided for law courts. All these prescriptions of the Law were to be executed by the royal power, and because the commands of the Law had to be carried out by power, the king could be legitimately established for this purpose. And if Christ also establishes and orders some things—many, all, or some in particular—in his Law that have to be carried out by power, then his Law too will find its execution and success through royal power. In that case there will be no doubt but that the king will stand in justice and holiness on the effects of Christ's Law. But if the Law has been commuted, and if we are liberated from the Law of death through the love of our Lord Jesus Christ, and subjected to the Law of love,[4] then let us see on what foundation power can be placed in Christ's faith!

And I should like you diligently to judge, from everything that I am going to write, whether the Law of Christ follows in the way of the Old Law in the matter of shedding blood. If it does, then securely and fearlessly set king, prince, and lord on the path of Christ's Law, and they, carrying out this Law, will be holy people. Likewise, no matter whether you take your Scripture from the Old Law or the New, which seem to establish princes and lords securely in Christ's faith, you may be sure that you are rightly guiding them in their offices through those Scriptures, when by the Law of Christ you show them the proper acts of their offices. For since you hold that the triply divided society mentioned above constitutes the Body of Christ, then hold too that this Body has to be ruled by his Law! And if he has composed his Body of such people, then the founder of the Law certainly did not leave out the secular power as the arms of the Body, or neglect to give the sword to those arms, so that they might serve the other limbs of the Body with it. This matter cannot be questioned further; for either the secular powers are to be assured of salvation under the Law of Christ, and their path is to be shown them through the Law, or they have to be confirmed through something else, apart from the Law, as they are now falsely secured in Christ's faith by many of the clergy, in their writings. But these writings never have in them the fundamental sense of the scriptural passages on this subject that the Holy Spirit has inspired, although the clergy interpret them thus, to the deception of the princes and lords. For if power were supposed to be administered through Christ's faith by means of battles and punishments, and try to benefit Christ's faith with those battles and punishments, then why would Christ have abolished the Jewish Law and established a different, spiritual one? If he had wanted people to cut each other up, to

4. The reader is reminded that the Czech "milost," here translated "love," also means "grace" and "mercy"; cf. R. Holinka, *Traktáty Petra Chelčického* (Prague, 1940), p. 96.

hang, drown, and burn each other, and otherwise pour out human blood for his Law, then that Old Law could also have stood unchanged, with the same bloody deeds as before.

Therefore take from this what seems right to you, and reflect seriously on what basis you wish to give power, with its battles, punishments, and such cruelties, a path in Christ's faith. For there can be no power without cruelty. If power forgives, it prepares its own destruction, because none will fear it when they see that it uses love and not the force before which one trembles. Therefore the sweet fig, the fat olive, the grapevine, which gladden men, are none of them fit to wield power as is the cruel thorn, which has no qualms about grieving a man, striking him, flaying him as though stripping bark from a linden tree, throwing him into prison, and killing him. [Cf. Judges 9:8–15.] Power will better prosper and endure by these means than by feeding the hungry, clothing the naked, healing the sick, without ever being able to wound and grieve, as would be the case if power stood according to love. There is thus a great difference between power and love.

We must therefore understand, in regard to the order of public power, who is to be kept in order by it and what sort of order can be established through it. It is a different order that God brings about among some people through his son; this order must be diligently and thoroughly understood, as well as that the order based on power exists among unwise people, who do not know God and are not under his yoke. For all lands need some sort of justice and peace, and without them people could not survive on earth. Because there are many nations in the world who do not have in themselves any virtue or knowledge of God, and who preserve no justice toward others, God, desiring that these many peoples continue to exist in the world, establishes kings and princes over them, so that they may be kept in peace by the latters' power, and so that every sort of injustice may find remedy, every complaint have recourse, through power. And that thanks to this power no one may wrong another nor deprive him by violence of his possessions, nor steal from him, nor disturb the boundaries. For since all power seeks to rule peacefully over many people and thus multiply its honor and wealth, it therefore has to avenge such injustices and forcibly introduce peace and justice. The more peacefully it seeks to rule, the crueler it must show itself in its punishments, so that the people should fear it all the more and so be content, each with his own, through dread of power. And when all injustices are bridled by power, then order will prevail among all, and they will be at peace with each other, enjoying their possessions without hindrance. Indeed, such order must prevail in each nation, for otherwise some would do injury to others, one band would rise against another, the strong would suppress the weak, dragging them out of their cottages and taking over their villages, their houses, their lands, and even their women; but through power such violence is stopped. Therefore power is called secular, because it administers the course and welfare of this world in order that external order and welfare may be maintained in it.

Power is thus the foundation of a country and preserves its stability against disruption. But the things of power are used only by the worst people, who are without faith or any virtue; through cruel punishments, power forcibly imposes such justice on evil people in external matters that those inclined to harm others do not undertake such action, or, having begun, stop. Power does all this for its own benefit, so that over no man will its dominion be negated through injuries done by some to others. Because power wishes to profit from all, it zealously avenges every injustice, even that happening to the most insignificant of people, and thus zealously defends the peace of all. On the other hand, of course, the unwise people who are without God neither know, love, nor do justice at all; therefore they are subjected merely by fear to the powers in the things that are enjoined on them. And so on neither side do they have righteousness at the basis of their intentions, although external righteousness does find a place thereby. The one side seeks its profit by punishing; the other side by obeying seeks to avoid harm. Neither sort of behavior is virtue in itself; nevertheless good has its place thereby. But the justice and peace enforced by power are far removed from Christ's faith; people are safeguarded through the success of secular power only in their temporal good.

And I also say this: This temporal good is secured and administered in peace through power by that land which provides a recourse and remedy for any complaint or injustice through one unified power. Many powers, opposed to each other, will ruin even this temporal good, and the land will have neither righteousness nor peace, nor will there be any order among the people. For whoever possesses anything will have many people snatching it out of his hand. Whoever has been great will fall into poverty, while the poor will gain honor for themselves, and nothing orderly will remain.

But we must now speak more attentively about the order which Christ introduced as his own true one, according to the virtue and love of the Holy Spirit. For God, through a prophet, said of Christ that

"He will rule my people of Israel" [II Kings 5:2]. And Christ established his people under the Law of love and gave them a Law under
which there are no complaints, in order that real spiritual order, similar to that of the angels in heaven, might exist in the people, as well
as the peace of undivided union, like that of many limbs in one body,
and also perfect justice, superior by far to that which stands on earth
through the power of princes and to that which was brought about
through the Old Law. For Christ rejected the justice of the Old Law,
saying: "If your justice be not more abundant than that of the Jews,
you will not enter the Kingdom of Heaven" [Mat. 5:20; cf. the Vul-
gate]. When therefore we are established under mercy and without
complaints, we have in ourselves and in our hearts the foundation of
the higher justice that has love for all. Where that love prevails, it
wishes good to all from its heart, and it not only wishes but does good
to all, as it is able according to its strength, goods, and understanding.
Nor does it wish, ask, or do evil to anybody; nor does it deprive, hin-
der, or torture anyone, or harm anyone, but rather consoles and helps
everyone according to its power and the other's need. [Cf. I Cor. 13:
4–7.] Even more, that love suffers the injustice done by others, and in
return loves, prays for, and benefits those who scorn or harm it.

Thus those who belong under that Law do not lodge complaints
because, observing the kind of conduct described above, they abolish
complaint on both sides: they do not harm anybody, so that no one
can justly complain of them, and when they are wronged they suffer
it. Turbulent complaints and quarrels do not therefore find any place
among them, and with them secular courts are a shame and a sin,
according to the words of the Apostle, who said: "And if there are
courts among you, then already there is certainly sin among you" [I
Cor. 6:7; q.v.]. The justice of such people is perfect, because they truly
love God and their fellows, and seek peace with all in what is good.
This sort of order, which prevails and should prevail among God's
people, cannot be taught by any wisdom of this world, nor can it be
enforced by any secular power, but it is born from the heart of good
will, a heart not in servitude as a slave but under love as a son. These
people are taught by the Law of Truth written down in the Scriptures,
and are led into this order by the Holy Spirit, according to the words
of the Apostle, that those who are sons of God are governed by the
Holy Spirit [Rom. 8:14]. The power of the world, on the other hand,
can dispose of cases only on the basis of what can be established in
them through witnesses, and it uses power to settle matters, all of

which is far removed from the heart of good will. For he [who is outside of the order of love] has to be just toward others in spite of his own will, and he will not tell the truth against himself in a dispute until he is confronted with witnesses. Such a person is not just in his heart, but in the end he must be summoned by power against his will concerning the external injustice between him and his neighbor. It is for such unjust people that the secular power is established, because they have neither the knowledge nor the fear of God in them, and because only the terrible power of the sword can become a law to their unjust and unfair wills.

This division in two parts, the secular order through power and Christ's order through love, sets them far apart, and it must be understood that these two orders cannot stand together so that both would be included under the name of one Christian faith. The order of Christ and the secular order cannot exist together, nor can Christ's order become the secular order. That which is done through power and under compulsion is one thing, while that which is done through love and good will is another, which stands on the words of Truth. It is thus clear that as far as secular power is from Christ's Truth written in his Law, so far is Christ's faith from the requirements of secular power. Power is not regulated by faith, and faith does not need power—as though faith were to have its fulfillment and preservation through power. As much as many goods, large bodies of soldiers, strong castles and towns, constitute the fullness of power, so God's wisdom and the strength of the Holy Spirit constitute the fullness and welfare of faith. Therefore faith, having spiritual power, prospers without the power that induces fear and drives people to do its bidding through terror and against their will; for the Apostle says, "You have not received the Spirit once more in fear, but you have received the Spirit of election as sons of God, in which Spirit we call out, 'Father, Father'" [Rom. 8:15; *q.v.*]. Therefore I consider those who belong under this order to be the spiritual Body of Christ.

But you perhaps say: "It would be good if all were like that, but since they are not, power is necessary to coerce the evil ones into justice." Certainly it is necessary in respect to that which pertains to the justice of princes. But I say this: Of what concern is secular power to the priest, whom Christ has sent out to preach with the Scriptures, in order to bring people under Christ's rule and to accept as Christ's faithful those who comply with the Scriptures, but not to rule those not complying through secular power within Christ's faith? For he who will not be truly set in Christ's faith through the teaching of the Scriptures will certainly not be set in it through power, just as a person cannot be taught Czech through the German language. Weak is the preaching of Christ's priest who, unable to bring some people into Christ's justice through Scripture, calls upon power and announces their adultery, drunkenness, and other sins in the church, forces power to punish them, and believes that in so doing he is successful in his preaching, although even with the help of power he hardly measures up to the pagans. For pagan princes, without any priestly preaching, suppress adultery, murder, theft, and all disturbances, so that they may have peace and so that their people may not be harmed by evildoers, and they do this much more effectively than many priests through power, because the latter believe that their power is some kind of Christian power, very beneficial to the faith, and which had not yet attained justice with the pagans. Thus while pagan princes will not neglect to stop evil things, simply as a function of their office, the priest, appearing to be a servant of Christ's faith even if he really is not, will therefore barely manage to put someone into the stocks. Yet even if a more perfect justice is found among the pagans in such actions, all of this is still far removed from Christ. And a priest who does not observe that many or some people have benefited from his preaching of the Scriptures, does a small thing by his preaching when he brings a drunkard into the stocks through power.

And if you wish to understand truly what power does or can do in Christ's faith, you may know it through the analysis of the theories that admit power as being just. For although many glorify secular power in Christ's faith, as though power were its strength and fullness, still no one of the many can demonstrate any greater benefit to Christ's faith through power than the benefit resulting when priests espouse the cause of power and give it the function in Christ's faith of fighting battles and inflicting punishments, which they define according to the Jewish Law or their own will. And when they are obeyed in the carrying out of those punishments, they exalt themselves as most zealous in Christ's faith. But if that power cannot contribute anything more zealous to the faith, its benefit is nothing. And I say in general: If they did not mix power into the faith by this pretext, the faith would be better off, because it has its fullness in all things without secular power; faith directs a man perfectly in his conscience and in all his life, but physical power orders the world in temporal matters. It is thus as small a thing that power does in comparison with what faith does, as that which the yeast does in comparison with the clear wine; the yeast only holds the dregs on the bottom, while the clear wine that the master will drink is separated out through faith.

Furthermore, although I hold that the apostles and other holy men after them may have accepted many powerful people into the Christian faith in order to set them on Christ's path by teaching them, I have not been able to discover from any place in the Scriptures, or from any sermon that I have heard, or from anybody, whether any Christian people had established a king or prince for itself as its master under Christ's faith, before the time that Silvester accepted the Roman emperor into the faith, where he remained with all the characteristics and properties of all pagan power.[5] From then on the power of the Roman Empire stood under the faith, and from that beginning the powers came in under the faith in other countries too. It is indeed known to us that Antichrist found all his strength in the Christian faith through the secular power, and that it was through this power that the Great Whore who sits on the Roman throne[6] spread all her poison. For when power was accepted into the faith while still enjoying the pagan honors, goods, and rights that it had previously enjoyed in paganism, it in return endowed the priests with goods; so it falsely entered the faith itself, and it took away the priests' faith with its property. But I think that if Silvester had truly offered Christ's faith to the emperor, the latter would not have accepted it from him in its true form, but would have persecuted him instead! Secular power and the clergy having thus falsely merged at the beginning, the fleshly clergy have further flourished since then in the goods and honors of this world, deriving property from the secular powers and from the other estate too, until now they have reached their peak, and with their benedictions and sweet talk have poured all the poisons of the Devil's heart out on the world. Furthermore, when that decked-out Whore had obtained all her power and fullness from secular power, she then in return, as was fitting to her shameless obscenity, began to kiss, love, and fondle that power. She blessed, flattered, forgave everything, made all the kings of the earth participants of all her pieties, and thus she fornicated with them all, tempted them, and always exalted power, until she should no longer

5. A reference to the Donation of Constantine, which both Romanists and anti-Romanists regarded as marking the formal association of the Christian Church with the power and wealth of the world.

6. Cf. Apoc. 17:1–6, which the Hussites and other heretics customarily applied to the papacy.

call it "part of the Holy Church and the vicar of divinity,"[7] but, more justly, "a third part of hell and the vicar of proud Lucifer, which will not humble itself before God or man."

And through the most evil union of these two estates in Christ's faith, the poor and painful life of our Lord Jesus Christ and his straight path are stamped down by the evil people who are the greatest enemies of his Cross. Moreover, the acceptance of pagan power into the faith meant that the whole world came in under the faith, for if those powerful and proud people could come under the faith, whom of all the people in the world would they not admit into it? Usurers and merchants? But they were best of all in the faith, for having got their money without any trouble by usury and swindle, they endowed the most churches and gave precious vestments and incomes to the clergy, while the priests blessed everything because they thus kept their stomachs filled to satiety. Therefore, having received the whole world into the faith, they then had to twist the Scripture thoroughly to show everyone his function in Christ's faith and establish him on the path of salvation. But thereby all Scripture and faith fell into great confusion; seeking to give the whole world a function in Christ's faith through the Scriptures, so that the whole world, by their accounting, could be called the Holy Church and the Bride of Christ—a world that has never acknowledged the Lord of the whole world nor ever will [cf. John 14:17]—these false, peace-loving priests admitted the world to his faith so that they themselves would not fall into the world's disfavor but would remain at peace with it.

From what has been said, those who care to can see that for Christ, God, to establish and ordain by law that a king should be set up as lord over Christ's church so that it may stand truly in the faith through royal power—that this is a very different thing from a deceived priest's admitting the emperor under the Christian faith, through a hole and not through the door, and making him lord of Christ's people. These two things are very far apart from each other.

It will thus be seen that there is a grave confusion in the faith when the fullness of Christ's faith is ascribed to power—so that what power does, in ordinary nations that are outside the faith and the Law of God—so that this originally pagan affair becomes Christ's affair. So that power, now existing under the faith, should shed much blood in

7. See below, pp. 150 f.

battles, inflict many punishments, according to the doctrine drawn by the priests from the Jewish Law, and, according to pagan laws, inflict many deaths, by hanging, drowning, burning, beheading, breaking on the wheel, letting people die in prisons, strangling them, plundering and otherwise tormenting them, and grinding the people down with violence. And because this power has been admitted under the faith, the things it does are things of Christ's faith. And so Christ, who shed his blood for the sinning people, has had his faith enriched with the secular power by the priest Silvester, so that this power might, in the name of Christ, drain much blood from the people in battles and other acts of killing, and so that everything thus done by power should count as the richness of the Christian faith. But since we believe that Christ won us from the Devil's power through the weakness and humbleness of his Cross, we cannot agree that he causes our perfection in the faith through the secular power, as though power were more beneficial to us than faith. Nor can we believe that everything done by power in the ways we have described belongs to Christ's faith or is its fullness, unless all these acts be founded in Christ's Law; for only his Law is man's life, and only if all the works of power are commensurate with his Law can power be our life.

But perhaps you will reject these ideas of mine and argue against me: "But St. Paul, Christ's Apostle, had a better knowledge of Christ's faith than you, and he orders Christians to be subject to the higher powers, of whom he truly says that they cannot be except of God; and those things that are of God are ordained, and whoever opposes power is opposing the divine ordinance. [Rom. 13:1–2.] And since power has been introduced by God's ordinance, or for the fulfillment of it, how can the way of life not be in it? And in these words the Apostle orders power in Christ's faith, with the sword, and he commands the faithful to be subject to power, to pay tribute, and to fear its sword." To this I say that the Apostle's words are true, but we must understand how and to whom he is writing. In the epistle he offers many instructions to the faithful in Rome, many of the Roman people, both Jews and pagans, having come to believe in God through the preaching of the apostles. The epistle is therefore not to be understood as though he were writing to the state power and directing it to defend God's faith, nor as though he were teaching the faithful to set up a power for themselves under the guidance of Christ's Law. Rather was he in this letter admonishing the faithful to be subject to the pagan power of the Roman emperor, because for a long time afterward the Roman Empire remained without the faith, and the Roman emperors, before they were brought into the faith through a hole, spilled much blood of the saints.

In regard to the words of the Apostle, therefore, there is a great difference between on the one hand teaching power or teaching the community to establish power over itself for the faith, and on the other hand teaching the holy people to be subject to the power of a pagan emperor, for the time being and for various reasons that are useful both to the faithful and to the state power. For if the faithful have been liberated from the power of the Devil and the burden of the Old Law by the love of our Lord Jesus Christ, should they not also be liberated from the burden of power? But since, for the time being, power differs in its properties from the Devil and the Old Law, the Apostle does not exempt the faithful from the burden of power, but rather orders them to be subject to it.[8] Still, the Apostle does not thereby establish power with its sword over the faithful, under the Law of Christ, as though setting a bogyman and the power of his sword on the necks of the faithful, through Christ's Law. For since Christ redeemed the faithful from the Law of fear, it is not likely that, through the Apostle, he would reimpose the fear of the sword on them by his Law. It is for those who are outside the Law of God that power exists, and it includes all of them; only for them is the sword alone a law, before which they tremble, not daring to overstep the bounds that the sword sets for them. But when the faithful are associated with these people in the lands and domains of the pagan powers, it is the command of the Apostle that the faithful be subject to these powers in suitable matters. This is partly by reason of humility, as befits the servants of Christ, and partly because this power has been introduced by God's ordinance so that it may bring about his order, which can exist in people who are without the Divine Law, when power does justice and keeps the peace among these people. Therefore the Apostle says to the faithful: "Be subject to them not only for wrath, but also for conscience sake" [Rom. 13:5]. He says, "not only for wrath," so that the faithful not arouse the sword of power's wrath against themselves by refusing obedience, "but also for conscience sake," because when power commands that peace be kept, that injustice not be done to others, or any

8. The original reads: "A že moc mezi tím jiné zvláštnosti má nežli d'ábel a Zákon Starý. . . ." The theory implicit in the thought is, as often with Chelčický, archaic: secular power is a remedy for sin and belongs by nature to the sinful condition of unredeemed humanity; it is a necessary evil, for the time being.

other proper things, then God also commands such things to be done. If a Christian were to scorn commands that were in the interests of justice and peace, and not want to obey them because they were commanded by power, he would also be scorning God and flouting his commandments. Certainly such a man, by opposing himself to God in this, would lose his good conscience. Therefore, even though it is power that commands such proper things, the faithful man will fulfill them and thereby please God too.

However it must be understood here that when these public powers outside the Law issue any good command, making for justice and peace, they do not thereby and at the same time issue these just commands for the sake of God. It is for their own advantage that the princes drive unwise people to hold to justice and not injure others, whereas God moves people thus because he is himself just and loves truth, and he enjoins every virtue on man, every truth, both great and small. What a far cry it is from the princes' intention, in commanding this external justice, to the divine intention! Nevertheless, as far as injury to one's neighbor is concerned, it is all the same thing: both the prince and God are angered by the one who does injury to his neighbor, even though in each case the reasons are different. Therefore he who violates the prince's command in such matters also violates that of God, and he who does the justice that the prince commands ought to do it primarily in consideration of the divine intention and for the sake of God's commandment. So he will keep a good conscience and at the same time win favor from the prince.

The Apostle, moreover, especially commands the faithful to obey the pagan powers in good things on account of the wrath of these powers, in order that they may not take offense at the faith, as they would if the faithful refused them obedience. For then the pagan powers would suppose that the Christian faith was a kind of knavery that refused to be subject, and thus the faithful would so incite the powers against themselves in a little thing that the powers would take action against the faith. Therefore the apostles, having so many of their faithful among the pagans and under the pagan powers, admonish these faithful to behave as good members of pagan society and to be subject to the pagan kings, in order not to give offense to them by bad example and not to arouse the powers against themselves, so that the powers should not take action against the faith on account of the improper acts of the faithful. But if the faithful people had not been living on the domains of those powers, among evil pagans, the apostles would not have given the faithful these teachings, for they would not have established the secular powers over them with the sword. For God put the people of the Old Law in freedom and without a lord, intending himself to rule over them, as he would have done if they themselves had not scorned him, and he certainly did this even more for the people whom he redeemed with his own blood, and himself he remains king in the House of Jacob forever; for, as he says, he is the King of Truth [cf. Joh. 18:37]. These people hear his words, and whoever listens to this king will not only live properly but will also have life. From all of this it may be understood that the Apostle does not, by his words, bring the sword of power under Christ's Law or make it lord over the faithful, but rather, for reasons of necessity, admonishes the faithful to be obedient to the pagan powers in whose domains they had their homes, here and there in the various lands and kingdoms.

But I have read a work of Master Jakoubek's, translated from the books of Wyclif "On the Endowment of the Clergy," which deals with the ideas now held by many about the secular powers—namely that they are under Christ's faith.[9] In the beginning of this work he divides the Christian people into three parts, and tells each part its special functions; he calls the secular power a third part of the Holy Church and the vicar of divinity; this power has to defend the Law of God and the other two parts, the clergy and the common people, with its sword. The clergy, he explains, are the vicars of Christ's human nature, and they must follow him in poverty, toil, and patience, and teach the other two parts. As for what he says about power: if it is a just idea according to Christ's faith that power should defend the Law of God with the sword, then you people and the masters were truly in accord with the faith in this matter, when you began to fight for the Law of God.[10] For in the first year that the war had begun, some of your

9. N. V. Jastrebov, *Etjudy*, p. 118 n. 4, demonstrates that Chelčický here refers to Jakoubek of Stříbro's translation of Wyclif's *Dialogus* (the original Latin text has been edited by A. W. Pollard [London: Wyclif Society, 1886]). The translation has been edited by M. Svoboda, *Mistra Jakoubka ze Stříbra Překlad Viklefova Dialogu* (Prague, 1909).

10. It is interesting that Nicholas of Pelhřimov, bishop of Tabor, put the matter similarly in his "Chronicle" (Höfler, II, 481): "totus . . . populus, . . . nolens . . . a bono resilire et a fide cessare catholica una voluntate et unanimi asensu et consilio magistrorum Pragensium et aliorum sacerdotum pro tunc populum dictum gubernantium bellum ex necessitate, non voluntate erexerunt et hoc solum in dictarum veritatum defensionem, . . . ut . . . promoveatur fides Christi, ordo, justitia et veritas per viam et media debita secundum legem Dei. . . ."

party's priests in your party's town of Písek argued against me with these and other ideas, seeking thereby to confirm power to themselves. as it were through faith.[11] Indeed, since a great deal of work has already been erected on these theoretical foundations, it should not be torn down if it was based truly on them; and if the structure has been so well set on that foundation, then there is no need to look for another, nor should one shrink from it, but rather hold to it as sure faith and look forward to God with hope.

I will carry the argument even further. If the secular power is the vicar of divinity, and follows in the way of God's power, and defends the Law of God and the other two parts with the sword, then it cannot defend the Law of God more directly than by defending the priest, who has to go all over the world and preach it. Power should therefore be zealous with its sword so as not to let anything injure the priest, in order that, being secure, he may spread the Law of God everywhere. But if it is a true opinion that the priest is the vicar of Christ's human nature and has to follow him in toil and patient suffering, and if evil people, when he preaches, want to beat him, seize him, or hurt him, and if the vicar of divinity, its sword in readiness, does not let anything happen to him, then how will he be following Christ in patient suffering? If power will not allow anything to be done against him, and hence frustrates his following of Christ, will not the vicar of divinity be blocking Christ's human nature in its functions? And the same holds for every man in the community, for it is Christ's injunction to him that he turn his other cheek to the one who strikes him in the face [Matt. 5:39; Luke 6:29], and the Apostle's injunction that he not defend himself against wrong [cf. Rom. 12:19; I Cor. 6:7]. But if power's official duty is to help the man in this situation by defending him so that no wrong be done him, then again he will not be able to fulfill Christ's words in the manner of his defense. Moreover, it is a bigger thing to be defended by power than for the individual to defend himself, for alone he can barely defend himself against someone equal to him or weaker, but if he has power to defend him as its official duty, when wrong is done him, he can thereby defend himself against many people and thus remain far from any suffering. But this is the pagan way and the way of this world, which will not come under the yoke of Christ; always unwilling to suffer anything, they defend themselves against every wrong, organizing themselves to have greater strength

11. See the Appendix, below.

against it, and they therefore look to secular power and desire to be defended by it. But the Christian is obliged by Christ's command not to defend himself, and who has ordered him to have power come to aid in his defense and thereby enable him to break Christ's command on an even larger scale than he could manage by himself?

And here I ask you, since these matters concern you, to pass over my unimportant words and think the thing out yourself: just what is this division of Christ's Body into separate parts or special limbs, when some limbs, merely by performing their functions and serving the others, prevent the latter from doing what they should according to Christ's commandments? And this cannot be otherwise. For if the division of Christ's Body truly stands thus, then power will not let anyone suffer wrong on account of Christ's faith, but will punish all such injustice; and yet, by Christ's command the limbs ought to suffer affliction. Again, since the priest is one part of that Body, with the office of teaching the two others, he will teach power that its duty is diligently to stand up for the other two parts and not let them suffer violence or harm from evil people; and he will teach other Christians of the community to follow in Christ's footsteps, imitating him in patient suffering. But what is the priest doing, teaching the one group to suppress injurious actions and not to torment [the faithful], and teaching the other group to suffer injury? He is behaving like one who forbids bakers to bake bread and commands others to eat bread. When the priest thus says things that contradict each other, what good does he do by teaching the limbs of the body so imperfectly?

Moreover, since the priest is to stand in the place of the apostles, he has to take unto himself the words of the Apostle: "Indeed God was in Christ, reconciling the world, not imputing their sins to them, and he put the word of reconciliation in us" [II Cor. 5:19]. Just as God himself in his son reconciled the people with himself, not imputing their sins to them, so he placed the word of grace in the apostles, that they might summon the people, proclaiming the forgiveness of sins in the blood of the son of God—to those who would turn to God and do penance. And this is the priest's office. But the vicar of divinity, who does not bear the sword in vain, but rather for the punishment of the evil, as the avenger of wrath [Rom. 13:4]—if his only official duty is to avenge God's wrath against the evil with the sword, then he cannot, as his official duty, do anything else against the evil but harass them with the sword. But the priest's official duty is to direct sinners to penance and grace, and to receive them. And if the priest receives the evil ones unto grace, then on whom will vengeance be taken by the one who bears the sword against the evil ones? And if this one comes forward with the sword and strikes down the evil ones, then how can the priest direct them to penance and receive them in love? And so the very thing which the one does well in his office frustrates the other in his, or else the function of the latter's office vanishes. What then are the limbs doing in that body when some obstruct others? And in truth it is impossible for it to be otherwise, except if we do not examine the matter thoroughly and perhaps disregard something. If the one who holds the sword kills many people, we do not feel sorrowful about it; and if the priest never turns anyone to penance, we do not ask too many questions about it. Therefore this sort of foolishness can be spoken among us.

When we consider these contradictions, we see that it is a strange Body of Christ that is arranged in this way. And, distrusting it, I say that these are creatures of this world, who stand up under an accusation without humility or patience. Refusing to suffer abuse, injustice, or any offense, using power as a matter of course, always lodging a complaint about every wrong, desiring that power either punish one's enemies for some reason or help out the right in case of some sort of damage—this sort of thing is useful for the world. And therefore God set up princes with the sword for such a paganized people, since they do not have justice otherwise, but rather harass and despoil each other; so at least under the threat of power, which stands over them with its sword like a bogyman, they may fear God and not dare to harm others. Then too if anything evil should occur, it can be dealt with and disposed of by power, so that the evil may not spread further. But Christ has established his people without [the lodging of] accusations, in peace and perfect justice, not only not doing evil to others, but peacefully suffering when others do evil to them; not only not stealing the property of others, but lovingly giving their own to the needy. Therefore even without this power, they are well enough able to act so as to benefit others and win a reward for themselves.

You say, moreover, that: "The secular power has a place in Christendom, with an office attributed and assigned to it by Christ and his apostles, just as a place was given to the official of the Roman emperor who had a hundred knights under him, but whose faith led Christ to heal his servant" [cf. Luke 7:1–10]. This is all well and good. If that power, along with its duties, has a foundation with Christ and his apostles, then he is secure who labors for it or who has to direct it—he has before him the Law of Christ and the apostles. And if the secular power has its foundation in the centurion, then Christ did establish it and issued proper commands for it which belong to its office. And, finding this in the Law of Christ, you can say: Christ, the leader of Christianity, spoke thus, and thus you should suffer, or thus you should strike; and so there will be peace for priests and for the powers, when the latter perform their official functions determined by the Law.

But I do not allow this to be a true way of founding something in the Law of Christ—to milk it violently out of various passages in the Scriptures, and to put something into the foundation just because the Scriptures mention it or name it. It is a false sort of foundation, hiding under beautiful language like a robber who sneaks into a home at night and takes what is in it. So now when it sets the secular power into Christ's faith in the person of that official of the Roman emperor, because Christ praised him for his great faith. And yet Christ did not praise him because he used secular power in battles on the basis of his faith, but because he believed that Christ could cure his servant even though not with him in the house. The Bible does not go on to say that Christ spoke with the centurion about power or the office of power.

There may be many such passages in the Scriptures, and anyone can prove what he will with them, but what is truly founded in the Scriptures can be recognized by what is constructed on that foundation. From the milking of the Scriptures there have sprouted many exalted spiritual discoures, as well as despicable things, very offensive to God. It is proper for a man to cite a case in the Bible in aid of his own ideas only when it seems that the scriptural text may itself have the idea that is in his mind. But the Bible says that Lord Jesus did not go into the home of the centurion; when Lord Jesus was still a distance away, the centurion sent his friends to meet him and said through them: "I am not worthy to have you come under my roof, but only say the word while you are here, and my servant will be healthy." Thus there is no certainty that Lord Jesus actually spoke with him. How then could he have summoned the centurion to rule his church through power? If only because he praised a man of the knightly estate, then we can easily see that he did not praise him because he was of that estate, but for his faith. And because Jesus praised him for his faith alone, it is impossible to give princes a foundation in Christ's faith thereby, although they can be told of the centurion's great faith as an example, that they may also believe as he did. Indeed, Cornelius, a man of the same estate, can be praised more, for he manifestly received the Holy Spirit, having believed in the preaching of St. Peter [cf. Acts 10]. It is one thing to be praised for faith, and another to be called to a certain position with a doctrine pertaining to that office; and the difference is still greater between secular power's having an equal place in Christ's faith with the faithful centurion, and its having equal praise with him in the faith.

And to the assertion that this [attempt at scriptural] foundation is supported or confirmed by the words of St. Paul about the spiritual Body of Christ and the limbs of that Body, to this I say: If it be right to base secular power under Christ's faith on the centurion, or on any other text of the New Testament, and hence to say that this power is a third part of Christ's Body, then the words of St. Paul about this Body will in fact confirm that foundation and truly demonstrate it— according to what has been said above.

But when the Apostle wishes to speak of this Body, he first names the spiritual things, and wanting the faithful to know about them, he enumerates them in these words: "There are diversities of grace but the same Spirit; there are divisions of service but the same Lord; there are diversities of operations but the same God who works all in all. But the manifestation of the Spirit is given to every man, for benefit. Thus to one is given by the Spirit the word of wisdom; to another the word of knowledge according to the same Spirit; to another, faith, in the same Spirit; to another the grace of healing, in one and the same Spirit; to another the working of wonders; to another, prophecy; to another, discerning of spirits; to another divers kinds of tongues; to another the interpretation of speech. But all of these are the works of one and the same Spirit, dividing among all as it wills; for the body is one and has many members, but all the members of the body, although they are many, are still one body" [I Cor. 12:4–12]. Thus the Apostle enumerates the parts of Christ's Body entirely according to spiritual things, with not the least reference to an internal complication of this body into three parts according to physical offices, as though the people thus divided into three parts were the Body of Christ. On the contrary, he lists many graces and gifts of the Holy Spirit, which it is wont to distribute variously to holy people, that together they may serve each other, each according to his special gift, as the natural limbs of a body together serve each other. But the triple division of the Christian people according to physical actions and according to secular power and other physical offices cannot truly be called the Body of Christ because

among people divided thus there is room for this world, and all the
children of Hell,[12] the great enemies of God who do not in any way
belong in the Body of Christ, can come under such a triple division.
The true limbs of Christ's Body are rather those who have the afore-
mentioned gifts of the Holy Spirit, and together they form the one
Body of Christ.

Nor do I see that these words of St. Paul tend to support or confirm
anything about the secular power or about the triple division of society, called the Body of Christ, for neither the words themselves nor
their meaning says anything of the sort according to the distinction of
three classes of people. What he names are many limbs of that body
and their functions, all spiritual, which are accomplished through the
gifts of the Holy Spirit, differently in the case of each particular limb.
As in a natural body many limbs are united and very eager to serve
each other, each according to its function, so the life of the Holy Spirit,
which is in many holy people through the gifts respectively assigned to
each, brings a single understanding together with a single will, so that
the functions of many may be to the advantage of each, and likewise
the functions of each for the benefit of all, according to the gift given
him. What alone makes this possible is the inner life of the Holy Spirit
which dwells in them; flesh and blood cannot establish that unanimity
and readiness for beneficial service between two men or even in one
household, when they follow a physical spirit, each going according to
his own will and his proud heart. The triply divided Christian people,
carnal and full of dissension, neither can nor ever will have that unity
and love of one another; it is the world, and it has in itself only worldly
desires. Therefore it cannot rightly be said that the Body of Christ is
composed in that triple form, for even among the pagans there is such
a division of the people into three parts. Indeed, among them the
princely estate is a glorious one, which seeks to enforce external temporal justice among the people much more diligently than our slug-
gards under the faith, for the pagan princes keep the people in greater
terror, and so no one dares to injure another. Therefore temporal peace
and justice are better secured by the pagan princes than by these
incompetents under the faith, who still neglect to enforce justice among
their people—until they are bribed, *then* they prosecute stubbornly.

12. In Czech, "pekelníci," sing., "pekelník"—literally someone who comes from or
belongs to hell ("peklo"). But John Hus used the word to translate the Latin "eth-
nici" (cf. K. Novák, *Slovník k českým spisům Husovým* [Prague, 1934], p. 101), and
perhaps Chelčický too means only "pagans."

And among the pagans also there are working people, who plow and work at other things, and there are priests among them, who seduce them, through many gods, away from the one God, the creator of all things, just as among us there are great seducers who draw the people away from God. They do so not only with wooden gods, but with the genuine words of God, and with the whole faith, and with hell, heaven, and the saints in heaven. Even more, they seduce the people from God with God himself, showing him deceitfully in one aspect in order to destroy him among the people in that aspect in which the people ought really to find him.

Since among the pagans, who do not know God, there is such a threefold division of the people for their mutual advantage in certain things, and yet they are not thereby the Body of Christ, then among us too they are not the Body of Christ on the basis of these material things, if they have not been made into limbs of Christ by the gifts of the Holy Spirit in such a way that each have in himself the life of grace, for the benefit of the other limbs. The sword of the lords does not join the peasants into a unity of mind, although it can bring them under a yoke like bond-slaves. And the voluptuous table of the lord delights the foolish priest, so that he considers the lord's favor a benefit to the faith, because his belly has prospered at the lord's table. None of this is part of Christ's Body, but rather the merriment of the impious and the coercion of the poor.

And St. Paul continues his discussion of the limbs of Christ's Body, saying: "The eye cannot say to the hand, I have no need of your works; nor again the head to the feet, You are not necessary to me. Nay, much more, those members of the body which seem to be more feeble are the more necessary. And those members of the body which we think to be less honorable, these we cover with honor; and our uncomely parts have more abundant comeliness. For our comely parts have no need: but God has tempered the body together, having given more abundant honor to that part which lacked, that there should be no schism in the body, but that the members should have the same care one for another. And so if one member suffer, all the members suffer with it; and if one member rejoice, all the members rejoice with it" [I Cor. 12:21–26]. In these words St. Paul speaks of a natural body, telling how it consists of many members and how there is among them no scorn of disparate rank, but rather care of one for all, and zealous helpfulness. He says this as an example, and to this body he compares the spiritual Body of Christ, for in fact by faith and grace many can be as one body, each having special gifts of the Holy Spirit so that he may help the other limbs with them. And the Apostle particularly emphasizes in this passage that there is no loathing or scorn on the part of the greater toward the lesser and more ignominious members, as if the greater ones did not need their service; on the contrary, the lesser limbs are protected from the greater ones by greater honor. And the Apostle also emphasizes that they all care for each other, and that all the limbs together feel sorrow for any one limb and suffer with it; likewise they all rejoice over the prosperity of one.

And because these words of the Apostle are used to justify the triple division of the Christian people into lords, priests, and working people, as the Body of Christ, it is in order to apply these words to this Body, to see if the one fits the other. And we must see if the Apostle, in his discussion of this Body, says anything about how the secular power has to defend the other two parts with its sword, how the priests have to teach the other two parts, and how the working people have to feed the lords and the priests and provide them with food, drink, and incomes by their labor. The scheme must go according to the scriptural justification, so that when one limb suffers all the limbs suffer with it; but how then does it happen that the crooked limbs that hold the sword oppress the other, lesser limbs, afflicting them, beating them, putting them into prison, weighing them down with forced labor, rents, and other contrivances, so they go about wan and pale, while the others, satiated and idle like well-fed horses, give them the horselaugh [cf. Jer. 5:8]? And the priests, like the eyes of the body, watch sharply over both other parts, looking for a way to strip them of their property and take it for themselves. Both together, the lords and priests, ride the working people as they will. Oh how far they are from the words of St. Paul, that all the limbs should suffer for the distress of each! The working people weep, and the others plunder them, imprison them, and extort money from them, all the while laughing at their great misery.

And since those who hold the sword are the hands of the body and the common people are the feet, let us see what the hands do for the feet according to the Apostle's true doctrine. How pleasant it is to think about the deeds that hands perform for the feet! They always put shoes on them so they should not get hurt, freeze, or get muddy; and if they do get muddy the hands at once wash them; and if the feet do get hurt the hands at once bind up the wound and heal it and perform beneficial services in every way. But these hands with the sword, when the feet get food for themselves, they take it from them by force, nor do these hands know of anything else to do for the feet except to plunder them. And these hands bear the sword. What medicine do they apply to the feet, except to shed their blood, torment them in all sorts of ways, and flog them like repulsive beasts that mean nothing to them?

But perhaps you will say: "That is because they are ignorant; if they were instructed, they could be merciful to the others." I would answer: Only consider that it is through power that their office must succeed, power which carries terror and cruelty. If it is to be moved toward mercy, only difficult intercessions and gifts can influence it to be merciful and abandon its wrath—or else the thing that it wants and for which it threatens. But if it intentionally inclines itself to be compassionate and does not torment the unwise people who do not understand mercy, and if it abandons what it ought to do by virtue of its office, it will multiply future complaints to itself and about itself. For love does not succeed with those who are not under love but under fear; if the fear be taken away, then there will be many injuries done and complaints will multiply. Power thus ruins itself with mercy, and it will not be esteemed if it does not use force. Power is for those who are without God's yoke and who do not belong under love, so that they may intimidate the unwise people with cruel power. Therefore Scripture must be fulfilled for those powers: the fig, the grapevine, and the olive will not rule, but the thorn boldly says, "If I am king over you, let fire go out from me and burn all of you" [Cf. Judges 9:15].

Again, if the lords and the priests are the honorable limbs of that body, its [arms and] head,[13] and if the common people, as the feet, are considered more ignominious, how remote is the [Apostle's] rule, that the less noble limbs should have more abundant honor from the other limbs, which are to protect them! For if this triple division of society is truly Christ's Body, then the peasants, shepherds, and beggars should have the greatest honor as the least of men in the community. But this is far from the case. For the common, scorned people are like dogs in the eyes of the powerful, who can hardly even think up new ways of insulting them. Some say "peasant blister," some say "peasant," some say "screech-owl," some say "hornet," some say "lout"—insult is more abundant than honor from the more honorable limbs.

Nor is it the case, as it is written, that there is no dissension in the

13. The Czech text here seems to require emendation, to preserve the figurative construction, although neither Krofta nor Holinka signals the passage as corrupt.

body, but that the limbs take care of each other. Far from the priests is the care that Paul had for all: "Who is sick, and I am not sick, and who is offended, and I burn not with shame?" [II Cor. 11:29]. Such eyes [scil., of Christ's Body] are not on earth now. And the common people detest both the others. The lords and the priests have already tortured them so much, that when the common people have to give them something or obey them in some matter, it is always with rancor and grumbling; and all of this is far from mutual benevolence. Those people are supposed to be limbs of Christ's Body, but we cannot recognize them or consider them as such because of those inequities, and they cannot come under the rule that there should be no disparity in the Body but rather equality, without some ruling over others. For such is Christ's command to those who are limbs of his Body. When "strife arose among them [scil., the disciples], which of them should be accounted the greatest," Jesus said to them: "The kings of the pagans exercise lordship over them, and those who have power over them are called officials; but you shall not be so. He that is greatest among you, let him be the servant of the others" [Luke 22:24–26, q.v.]. Here the Son of God clearly showed that this [domination] belongs to this world and the pagans, for they do not know God and some, out of pride, desire to rule over the others. But to his own people he says: You are not to be like the pagans, seeking to exalt yourselves the one over the other; but rather set yourselves humbly under others, in equality and through service, in the manner shown by the limbs of our Body, among whom there is no exaltation of rank. Certainly there is no place for the exaltation and domination of this world among those who are guided by the Spirit of Truth as spiritual members of Christ's Body.

Therefore the words of St. Paul about the spiritual Body of Christ cannot apply to the physical disposition of those three classes of people, for these words are entirely spiritual and can apply only to holy people, who have the gifts of the Holy Spirit and who can join in a true union through love, so that each spontaneously looks out for the other, grieves with the other in his distress, prefers the other over himself, and is ready zealously to do all sorts of service for others. And when there are many such people, with the various gifts of the Holy Spirit, they are the Body of Christ. At the same time it will also be true that if anyone of them is able to perform some physical function or work, in that respect too he will not fail to serve the others. But setting up a physical lord over themselves with the sword, to chop off all the dead limbs and to drive others against their will, to put others in prison, to torment people and enslave them, just as he likes—this is as far from the words of St. Paul as the throne of Lucifer is from that of Christ. Indeed, this is all the disposition and division of the Lady who sits on the Beast and has fornicated with the kings of the earth. She has invoked the "Body of Christ" especially for her own benefit and has got herself a place in that body, sitting in luxury and riding around on the people as though on an animal, whom she calls the feet of the body; she sits together with the kings of the earth—the head and the hands together, as the most honorable limbs of the body. [Cf. Apoc. 17.] We trust ultimately in God, that he will uncover that blood-stained body, and it will not smell sweet like the Body of Christ but it will stink with a disgusting stench, like the body of that Great Whore who has taken all the world to mate and has sucked out its fatness through the bleeding side of Christ. And she has spread the pleasures of her fornication in the sign of his painful wounds; she has made it her joy to walk in delightful coolness in the shadow of his dolorous suffering; she has used Christ's cross and Christ's faith to prepare an eternal slumber and sleep in hell for the world, soothing the world in her poisons. May God not prolong your days on earth, who scorn to bear Christ's cross but rather use it to put food in your belly![14]

As for the clergy, I do not know what I can write to you that would be moderate, for you yourself have long been providing testimony that their works among you people are unseemly; they have already been sifted out as through a sieve—by Scripture, by the doctors, and by you people.[15] A vial filled with God's wrath has been emptied on their heads, and their roots will perhaps not be regenerated because of you people! Do not grow, cursed sons of Canaan [cf. Gen. 9:25], not of Judah! They have destroyed the divine heritage, may their stock perish! As they have done to Christ and his agony, so may it happen to

14. The text continues with "Such are the words of that other passage, etc."—Krofta suggests: "Such is the meaning of the other passage from St. Paul"; but he conjectures that the text is corrupt.

15. The reference would seem to be to Taborite literature that exposed the corrupt estate of the Roman clergy by using texts from Scripture and the Fathers. The next sentence seems to refer to the actual eradication of the Romanists. If Chelčický was in fact writing to Markolt (n. 2, above), it would seem reasonable to refer the ensuing discussion of "good and bad priests" to the dispute over Markolt's alleged Donatism. Indeed, the reference may be made even on the supposition that Chelčický was writing to Nicholas of Pelhřimov, who incorporated Markolt's position in his Chronicle, and who, as bishop of Tabor, would have been concerned with the problem of just what standing was to be assigned to evil priests.

their lives here! But I will say this: When many voices call out together they cannot be properly considered, for the sense of each voice is lost because of the large amount of general clamor. The same thing holds true in discussion of the clergy—too much detailed theorizing interferes with judgment of the truth, so that it will not be easy to accept any theory in this matter.

Therefore I always confess this, that Christ, the Son of God, is the true and supreme priest of the New Law, holding an eternal priesthood by right of his pledge, and thus also able to offer salvation eternally. He is the bishop of the future good state and stands before the face of God, and is ever alive to intercede for us. When he was here in the flesh he consecrated twelve and seventy-two priests [cf. Luke 10:1], and entrusted them with his flock which he had won with his blood; and he sent them to preach his Bible over the whole world. They filled the earth with their preaching, carried on arduously, in travel on foot, in hunger, imprisonment, lack of clothing, fasting, prayers, the hostility of men, jails, wounds, and much affliction; they were poor people, walkers not riders, without secular power, seeking no protection from the world but setting their hope in God alone. When princes and kings gathered against them, instead of using shields and guns they prayed to God, until the people were with them, and, filled with the Holy Spirit, they trustfully preached the Word of God. Nor even with the help of the pagans could the priestly princes do anything to them, for they had put their hope directly in God himself, and had faithfully carried on the leadership of his flock. Like good shepherds of Christ's sheep, they laid down their lives. These I consider true priests of Christ, and all those after them who followed in their footsteps and who still follow in them, and will do so to the end. Such people help others and gather benefits for eternal life.

But the clergy to whom the Whore who sits on the Roman throne has given birth, freely and without pain, sitting on silken cushions, and whose lives she has established in soft effeminacy—these are accursed sons, who have dishonored God before his enemies and before the eyes of all, who have mocked him and who blaspheme his holy name with their numerous wicked follies. They have poured out all their mother's poisons and are now prospering, straying into ever worse errors and drawing innumerable multitudes into error after them. Careless of God's flock, the evil hirelings have fled from it in time of trial and have shut themselves up in castles and towns, organizing war and shedding the people's blood. These base sons are filled with every iniquity, and in all their acts they show themselves to be whoresons, who have no shame or honor. They will not remain in the house of God forever, nor will they always be able to plunder God's flock, whom they have given as prey to all the beasts of the earth. But since you know all this that I have said, I have set forth my ideas briefly; you will have enough of them for your needs. I do not know what else I can write on this subject to help you, and have only written the above to make my thinking known to you. This is what I hold to be true, from faith, in regard to the question of good and bad priests.

But as for what the common people—the third part of that Body of Christ about which we have spoken previously—are supposed to do as members of the Body for the benefit of the other limbs: I say that if you guide yourself by this particular distribution of the Christian people into three parts, you will easily distinguish the subdivisions of the part that includes the working people: plowmen, artisans of various kinds, merchants, shopkeepers, and various kinds of wageworkers; and their duty is to work and earn, thereby providing for the physical needs of the lords and the clergy. And if this is a true disposition of the Body of Christ, you can easily teach the commons to work diligently, you priests to be zealous, and the soldiers of the towns to defend the Law of God. These last ride out from the towns in the evening, visit the chests and cattle of the peasants, or whatever they meet up with—ardent lovers of God's Law, they cannot leave even so much as a cheese where they find it! But I, trusting in God, will not concede as long as I live that this meaning of the Body of Christ is a true one. Nor will I grant such a large estate to the two upper parts by putting them over the common people so that they can ride the latter at their own pleasure, and even consider themselves thereby better members of the Body of Christ than the common people whom they ride, and whom they subject to themselves not as limbs of their own body but as beasts whom they think nothing of tearing apart.

It is indeed evident that because of this situation too great a number of various kinds of clergy and rulers have proliferated, for all want to be lords, squires, soldiers. For it is easy to ride on stout horses, to threaten and to speak haughtily, to call the simple people oafs and screech-owls, to flay them like linden trees and smash their heads; it is easy always to eat and drink abundantly of the best things, to be idle, to wander about from place to place, to speak vainly and profitlessly, and to commit all sorts of sins without shame. There are far too many such good-for-nothing gluttons proliferated everywhere in castles and towns; they use their power to treat the common people violently or to take money from them and so enjoy a good life at home, carousing and living in idleness. To make all of this an article of faith for Christians, to divide them up into three classes of people and to consider this inequitable division as the Body of Christ, to make some people lords over others so that they can oppress the others and do violence to them, but still be considered members of one body along with those whom they trample down—let us concede all of this to the pagans, but it can never become part of Christ's faith and of his spiritual Body. Similarly the monks of various colors have multiplied: canons, Knights of the Cross, the regulars, and all the other priests; for they eat and drink delightfully well, like the lords, they dress themselves in many and expensive garments, they make themselves lofty houses and clean chambers, and they are idle. And they do all of this with the blood of the common working people, from whom they get these things with the many lies they think up—not as though from limbs of one common body, but as though from contemptible dogs.

I therefore have no intention of lending more support to such confusion about the Body of Christ. For St. Paul does not reckon the Body of Christ according to these physical properties, but according to the gifts of the Holy Spirit, which, various in form, make for the common obedience of the many limbs of the Body. And the limbs know their God and fear him; they preserve justice to God and to their neighbors in both material and spiritual matters, and whatever such people do of a physical nature is done for the benefit of all. Enjoying as they all do the separate gifts of a single Holy Spirit, many are of course able to participate in one physical action. But when St. Paul speaks about physical actions he does not command that spiritual priests set themselves on top of the common working people, or that the lords rest on the workers like useless drones among the bees, eating and drinking the fruits of their toil. Therefore, although he does not prohibit worthy preachers from taking necessary things, he offers himself as an example to others, saying: "In order not to do hurt to Christ's gospel by taking, we have not used our power in this matter" [I Cor. 9:12]. Again in another place he says to the faithful: "We behaved not ourselves disorderly among you, neither did we eat any man's bread among you for nought, but worked with labor and travail night and day, that we might not be a burden to any of you, but rather make ourselves an example unto you to follow us" [II Thess. 3:7–9]. Thus although the Apostle says that those who preach the gospel should live from the gospel, he does not consider it best to take material things in exchange for preaching from those to whom the gospel is preached. But stipulating three considerations, he says, "worked night and day." First that preachers should not do hurt to Christ's gospel by taking things, so that no one may say that they preach the gospel for bodily food, and thus belittle the preaching of Christ's gospel. Second that they should not be a burden to anyone by taking bodily necessities from him. Third that they should set a good example to those to whom they have preached the gospel, by diligent labor night and day, so that their example may lead the others to work all the harder and thus be able to give to those who do not and cannot have anything. In what he says here the Apostle is being prudent, looking out on all sides for what is best for the gospel and for those to whom he has preached it. He considered a reward in heaven for preaching the gospel to be better than bodily necessities, and he was very afraid of doing hurt to the gospel by taking necessities, for he prized the gospel more than his bodily life. But if his belly were to call him to preach, not esteeming the gospel, he would try not to hurt his belly, and he would say: "Ask God for the lord's favor, that he may always offer an invitation to dinner."

From these passages it can be seen that the apostles did not establish the common people as such as a part of Christ's Body. Indeed, the apostles themselves performed services for others with the physical things that they earned; but they did not require such services of the whole community, although they might sometimes use the services of one man, given from love and without obligation. Thus they did not call the common people the feet, as though these should carry them with service, but they themselves were the feet for others in this way, as though they were lesser. And the Apostle, teaching workers that they should work with their hands, also says: "For even when we were with you, this we proclaimed to you, that if any would not work, neither should he eat. For we have heard that there are some which walk among you disorderly, working not at all, but acting haughtily"[16] [II Thess. 3:10–11]. He teaches those who were the Body of Christ to work, and then, if they are unwilling to work, that they not eat. He does not wish there to be among them idle people, like courtiers, people who have no work to do but only to loaf and roam about. To such people

---

16. The Vulgate has, "sed curiose agentes"; Chelčický's Czech text has, "ale dvorsky činíce"—a literal translation, with "dvorsky" (from "dvůr" or "dvór," "court") a *calque* off "curiose." Chelčický's subsequent remark about "idle people, like courtiers" ("dvořáci") must be understood in reference to this passage.

he would not say: "You should seek knightly things and defend the Truth!" Rather does he teach them too what they ought to do, saying: "Let him that stole steal no more; but rather let him labor, [working] with his hand the thing which is good, that he may have to give to him that needeth" [Eph. 4:28].

And we believe this doctrine is right. Thus those who are true limbs of Christ's Body, confirmed through the gifts of the Holy Spirit and through the evident justice expounded in the Law of Christ, should be taught physical occupations, which are good not just because the people may thereby provide bodily necessities especially for the idle parts, but that they may do this from love for all those in need, like true limbs of the Body who all suffer along with the limb that is hungry or naked. And still more important, that they may thus "work the thing which is good"; for, as limbs of the Body, they should preserve true love and justice toward the other limbs; as each seeks what is good for himself, just so should he do for others. Thus he should "work the thing which is good," in order truly to benefit each one with his work and not cheat him in any respect.

If this doctrine be followed, then no limb of Christ will do any vain, evil, or harmful works to the damage or deception of his neighbors. Nor will he sell or buy anything like an avaricious man who has evil desires in business, who thinks up many words of great praise to heap on what he sells, swearing oaths by the faith in order to persuade the one buying from him, and who vilifies what he himself is buying from the other. Rather will he esteem his brother more than material profit and love him always, even in business, like a true limb of Christ. He will not smell out earthly things, but will seek heavenly ones, and will always choose what hurts him, before that which hurts others. But that body which is divided up into three parts, two riding on the third —in it are allowed commerce, shopkeeping, and other kinds of moneymaking that are evident avarice and concealed usury, as well as various harmful trades serving only to manifest vanity to the eye, in colors, costumes, and adornments for the deception of foolish eyes. And what various evils and frauds there are in that body with the selling of drinks in taverns!

For when the triply divided body shuts itself up in Prague, with no villages or hamlets for three miles out of Prague, and the third part has come from the pagans to defend the Truth with many armed men, and there are many priests and masters, and above all many of the commons: then that great body needs much food and drink, and the

commons must feed everyone.[17] But there is nothing to be taken any-
where, only from each other, with the sword; thus they work, with
fraudulent buying, retailing, and selling of drink—anything to gain
something from others so that the community might feed all. For
Prague has too many greedy mouths, now that they are waging war for
God's Truth. Other places too are full of this unrighteousness, for
everywhere they are waging war and are in difficulties. To attempt,
therefore, to use the teachings of Scripture to order the Body of Christ
in this way is to order the world under the cover of Christ's faith, to
disguise the course of secular affairs as the service of Christian Law.
For he who sets up such a threefold division of the people in a certain
place has to provide for that place in such a way that some will have
the function of defending it, others of digging the trenches and building the walls, and others of keeping watch at night. And the priest has
to teach all this so that it should go properly, for if they are all limbs
of one body, the priest's function is to teach how the other limbs should
all help each other with one will in everything that pertains to the
defense of the Truth.

But I say that to act thus is to cultivate the world under cover of
the faith, to call the world the faith, and, ultimately, so to confuse the
faith by mixing the world into it as thereby to make it impossible to
recognize what is the world and what the faith. For whatever unanimity is achieved in this respect is for physical defense, and it is more
perfect among the pagans than among these benighted Christians. And
nothing among the pagans is called the Body of Christ because of that
unanimity.

17. R. Urbánek, *op. cit.*, p. 916 n. 1, explains this passage as a reference to the
siege of Prague by the Taborites, led by John Žižka, in August, 1424, at a time when
the city was under the control of the Lithuanian prince Sigmund Korybut, whose
retinue was drawn from his still-pagan people—Lithuania had only recently been
converted, in the usual formal sense. Holinka (p. 104) accepts this interpretation, and
Krofta mentions it as possible. But Krofta observes that the reference may be to the
siege of Prague by the Emperor Sigismund in 1420. I believe Urbánek's conjecture
to be the more probable, but it seems strange that Chelčický should not, in that
case, have mentioned the fact that it was the Taborites who were besieging the
capital.

III. "ON THE HOLY CHURCH"[1]

WE SHALL now consider the definition that is given to the Holy Church: the congregation of those elected to salvation.

First, it is only so—as the congregation of those elected to salvation—that the Holy Church can be defined without adding or taking away anything.

Second, there are certain things unmistakably belonging to that Holy Church: the gifts of the Holy Spirit, with which gifts it is endowed, so that through them it can be composed of limbs diversely fitted to perform services for the benefit of the whole body or Church.

Third are the various deeds and services, which are true and certain attributes of that Church. These deeds and services have been set by God as works for the just, who by doing them have earned eternal life.

But it cannot at once be determined, when many or a few people are found to exhibit such deeds, that they certainly constitute a part of the Holy Church, or a limb of it. For the unjust can also come in under the cover of such deeds, and these people may temporarily or perhaps even permanently persist in them, even though they are not truly sincere in them. For hypocrites can possess all the attributes of virtue, excepting divine love alone. And this can best be seen in a man in the forgiveness of injustice done by others, and in the love of enemies, and in the abandonment of beloved things or the forgiveness of offenders for the sake of God's commandment. These are the most demonstrable attributes of true divine love in man, nor can an insincere man readily have them; hence while other good attributes can truly subsist only on these, still it cannot be demonstrated on the basis of those others that they who possess them are therefore members of the Holy Church.

Fourth are the estates or offices of the Holy Church, and in these least of all is there certain evidence of membership in it. Such is the priestly estate with its office, which is known to be an estate of the Holy Church; but it is far from true that all those entering or existing in this estate with its office are limbs of the Holy Church,

1. Translated from the text edited by R. Holinka, *Traktáty Petra Chelčického* (Prague, 1940), pp. 79–86.

for evil people can belong to this estate, people who are limbs of the Devil and serve only to drive souls to the Devil, for his profit, through their deceptions. But when faithful people are in this estate, serving the Holy Church in it through Scriptures, then it can be called an estate of the Holy Church, serving it and increasing it in the good. Thus it has the worthy attribute of an estate of the Holy Church when it has worthy servants in itself.

Furthermore there are such other estates of the Holy Church as virginity, widowhood, and marriage, which are the least certain signs of membership in it. It is chiefly on account of fornication that these are reckoned as estates of the Holy Church, in order that their sequence may exclude fornication: virginity must entirely exclude it, and widowhood after marriage . . . ;[2] and of course there must be a state of mind opposed to fornication, or marriage would be only adultery and sinful fornication within the marriage-bond. Otherwise, however, these estates are not impugned, and certainly whatever lies outside them must be considered either the irregularity of open sinners, or adultery, or other kinds of sinful fornication. Hence the Holy Church ought to reckon such estates as a palliative of many evils.

But otherwise, for these estates to be more truly included in the Holy Church, they must have the virtues appropriate to them, like true faith, unfailing love, and indeed even more, according to what one can attain by virtue of the gifts given him. Thus these estates have in themselves room for goodness to justify the Holy Church's containing them; but merely by themselves, without the gifts, they cannot be included in the Holy Church. For such estates can exist among the pagans or the Jews; for a Jewish or pagan woman can be a virgin or a widow, in the physical sense, and among Christians a heretic can be a virgin, as can those in mortal sin. And all of this is far removed from the Holy Church. And so married couples are generally called, as such, estates of the Holy Church, but this can never be truly said of them if they do not have the true virtue of the estate. For they may most of all be reckoned estates of the Holy Church if they possess election to salvation or the justice that inheres in or follows election. For although election may sometimes fall on someone without mani-

---

2. The editor notes that this passage ("virginity . . . marriage") is written on the margin of the manuscript, with an indication that it belongs in the text. Trimming has destroyed part of it, and the requirements of translation have caused me to abridge it further by leaving out two words that cannot be satisfactorily joined to the rest in English.

festing itself in righteousness, still usually the justice commanded by God inheres most of all in the saints along with election. And when one of the elect in these estates holds to the justice commanded by God, then he is a limb of the Holy Church; and if there is a large number of such, together they form a part of the Holy Church. Thus the Holy Church cannot be determined by physical ends or bases, as though it were composed of these or those classes of people, on the basis of physical deeds which can or do exist without virtue and without faith. It is not a matter of estate but of whether election be combined with estate.

It is necessary to know these things because of the excessive confusion arising from the fact that this world, which has wandered so far from God, is called the Holy Church on account of such classes. And priests no longer seek in their service to distinguish the pure from the impure, but rather guide themselves by the idea that here there must be a mixture of the evil with the good. Moreover, to set up these estates: the priestly estate, the knightly, and the laboring; the virgin, the widowed, and the married—this is to chop up the Holy Church. And to this Holy Church is applied all the doctrine ordained by the Roman doctor and whatever doctors he has accepted as holy— all this is accepted as doctrinal law.

And priests, caught up in this confusion as though in a net, creep about through the world spreading its errors by their service. They always say that the world is the Holy Church, that they can always see and sense the estates of the Holy Church—those who roam about with swords are the knightly estate; those who give children to be baptized are the married estate; the peasants who plow are the laboring estate. And all together they are the Holy Church. But in truth it can be said that these offices, which after all the pagans and the world also have need of, cannot be attributed to the Holy Church, as though to provide her with an administration or to satisfy her needs, even though the Holy Church or her members may on occasion derive some benefit from the service of these offices. But they are necessary only to the pagans or to the world, and God does not ordain them as the parts composing his Church.

For God did not, through his apostles, ordain a king for the Holy Church, to bear her tribulations on his sword, to fight for her against her enemies, and through force to make that Church serve him. Nor did he give her judges or magistrates, so that the Holy Church might come before them and litigate over the goods of this world. Nor did he give her bailiffs and hangmen, so that some members of the Holy Church could hang others, or torture others on the rack, for the sake of material things—this is for the pagans and for this world. Therefore when St. Paul speaks of the limbs of the Holy Church he defines nine divisions and says of them [cf. I Cor. 12:8–10]: "God has indeed set various people in the Church: first apostles, then others as prophets, others as teachers, others who perform miracles, others who heal the sick, others as helpers, others as administrators, others who speak in various tongues, and others who interpret." Such is what he says about the offices of the Church. But he never puts those officials together with secular power, not even those that he defines as rendering physical services, but rather associates them with the various gifts of the Holy Spirit in them; for only those officials are necessary to the Holy Church. For the Holy Church is spiritual and needs spiritual officials for her establishment; her sufficiency consists wholly in her spiritual regimen, and even though she has physical tasks, she does them always according to the spiritual sense.

Nor can it be truly argued that the apostles divided the Holy Church into three parts and commanded one part to work, so that the two others might be maintained by its labor, and rest on it as though on a bed, in idleness. St. Paul speaks of this, talking about himself and other priests [II Thess. 3:7–11]: "You know yourselves, brethren, how you must follow us. For we were not turbulent when we were among you, nor did we eat another's bread for nothing, but we worked and strove, night and day, laboring with our hands, so that we should not be a burden to any of you. For when we were still with you we made it known to you that if anyone should not want to work, neither should he eat, for we heard of some among you who were turbulent, not working but acting haughtily." Here, in this text of the Apostle, try to find that principle of a church divided in three, as though here he established lords and priests and ordered them to be idle and gave them peasants and other workers to support them and hold them up, as though forming a bed beneath them! But in fact he says of the clergy that "night and day they labored with their hands." Why does he say, "so that we should not be a burden to any of you," that is, by letting ourselves be supported by you others? For this reason: "so that we ourselves should thereby be an example to you, that you may follow us in this and work with your hands; and whoever will not work, then let him not eat; for we heard of some among you who were turbulent, not working but acting haughtily."

Thus Paul evidently condemns the doctrine about priests and lords that makes them the two first parts of the Holy Church. And they twist the truth so that it lies for them when they say that peasants and other workers have to toil to maintain the lords and priests, so that these may be supported. Or perhaps indeed priests have no other means of support in the Holy Church than to stuff their bellies with the fruits of the workers' toil? But against them is the example of the Apostle and his assistants, who worked day and night so that they would not be a burden to the workers, and rebuked those among them who did not work but went around doing nothing, like courtiers. And since he rebuked idle and haughty [dvorský] actions, how would he have established such courtiers [dvořáky] in that community, when, as he says, they refused to correct that haughty [dvorského] idleness, to see it for what it was and put it away from them? And since he does not allow fellowship and peace in faith with those haughty idlers, how could he be supposed to have set up such lords over them in the faith, and to have called them a third part of the Holy Church, to devour what is earned with such hardship?

Therefore he teaches that equality is to be preserved among those who compose the Holy Church, equality of the kind that the limbs of a natural body have, and he says [I Cor. 12:25–26]: "There should be no division in the body, but let each limb take care of the others, and if one limb suffers let all the others suffer with it, and if one limb rejoices, let all the others rejoice with it." Let some wise man consider this passage and try to derive pagan lordship from it, and to shove that lordship into Christ's Church, and call it a third part of that Church, on the analogy of the nature of the limbs of a body! And the truth is grander than the example; it requires undivided equality among the limbs of the body, so that without envy they serve each other, take care of each other, share everything with each other—if the good, they rejoice together; if the bad, they suffer together. The more honorable do not scorn the more lowly, but rather guard them with greater honor.

And since the limbs of the Holy Church have this relation to each other, one will not make others pay excessive rent or devise all sorts of forced labor for others to do, so that he can sit in the cool shade and ridicule the "louts" and "boors" [chlapóm a výróm] roasting in the heat, or drive them out into the bitter cold in their smocks to trap hares, and himself sit in the warm indoors. Nor will one impose on others any involuntary servitude that he would not want for himself.

Therefore this sort of paganism is very far from the Holy Church, according to the Apostle's definition. If then such people appear to be the Holy Church, that appearance can come from nothing but the fact that the world seems to be the Holy Church, and the world's errors seem to be Christian faith. But it is a false appearance and will continue to cause bitterness.

And I say this: If God does not provide priests who can separate all of this from the faith and show those people up as manifest pagans, then Scripture will not after all be truly preached. For as long as they the priests do not turn their backs on the world, and as long as they bless that paganism by the faith, with their violent cruelty, with their pride and multifarious excesses and lives of pleasure and ever-multiplied offenses against all the virtues: how can they really preach Christ? For all of this is the body of this world, and as long as it is blessed by the faith and made a part of Christ, to whom in the world can the priests deny participation in Christ, since the priests themselves are as evidently worldly as all the others. Therefore when the obvious paganism of these men is blessed in the faith, and when this paganism is even called advantageous to the faith, then every worldly man will rightly seek participation in the faith.

My reason for speaking of these matters has not been that I consider it the greatest disaster, that the faithful are subject to those powers and bear their burden. This is not the case. The Apostle set the faithful under the manifest pagans for worthy reasons, but he did not join the two together in the faith. The worst thing is that this paganism is accepted into the faith and is joined with it, and it has already corrupted the faith, even while it now poses as beneficial to the faith—this is what repels me.

And if these words are to remain valid, namely that heresy is erroneous doctrine, contrary to Holy Scriptures, then this many-sided heresy should be shown up as such. But if all these heresies are advantageous to the faith, then they will bear down on me, because I am spoiling something very beneficial to the Holy Church, while power gives her, so to speak, cool shade against the sultry heat and benefits her in all the things that she attempts through the power of this world; but without power she would exist as a forlorn widow.

APPENDIX

The Discussion of Christian Social Theory at Písek in 1420

IN HIS treatise "On the Triple Division of Society" Peter Chelčický writes (above, pp. 150–51):

> But I have read a work of Master Jakoubek's, translated from the books of Wyclif "On the Endowment of the Clergy," which deals with the ideas now held by many about the secular powers—namely that they are under Christ's faith. In the beginning of this work he divides the Christian people into three parts, and tells each part its special functions; he calls the secular power a third part of the Holy Church and the representative of divinity; this power has to defend the Law of God and the other two parts, the clergy and the common people, with its sword. The clergy, he explains, are the representatives of Christ's human nature, and they must follow him in poverty, work, and patience, and teach the other two parts. With regard to what he says about power—if it is a just idea according to the Christian faith that power should defend the Law of God with the sword, then you and the masters were truly in accord with the faith in this matter, when you began to fight for the Law of God. For in the first year that the war had begun, some of your party's priests in your party's town of Písek cited these and other reasons against me, seeking thereby to confirm power to themselves, as it were through faith [Neb když první léto boj se počel, tehdy proti mně ty i jiné rozumy u vás na Písku mluvili jsú kněží někteři z vašich, chtíce tím moc jako skrze víru sobě ujistiti].

This passage has been more or less neglected by most scholars, except Jastrebov, who however interprets it as a loosely dated reference to the Taborite synod of Písek, in 1422 (*op cit.*, p. 118 n. 1). Holinka, *op. cit.*, p. 100, dates the synod "perhaps at the end of 1420," but does not fix the date closely enough to bring out the full import of the passage. Precisely dated, however, in accordance with its own words, the text yields extremely valuable information about a subject whose importance is matched only by its obscurity: the process by which Tabor passed from societal dynamism to societal stability, from fanaticism to rationalism.

The dating is actually rather easy, since we know "the first year that the war had begun." On November 4, 1419, royalist forces intercepted the contingents of South Bohemian Taborites who were on their way to a mass congregation in Prague, and forced them to fight the bloody battle of Živhošt'; as the Old Czech Annalists remark, "It was from this that the great wars began" ("a skrze to se veliké války počely"), (*Staři letopisové čeští*, ed. F. Palacký, *Scriptores rerum Bohemicarum*, III [Prague, 1829], 29 f.). After the Prague-Royalist truce of November 13, 1419, the Taborites in South Bohemia were subject to constant royalist attack, and those in Plzeň were actually besieged by royalist armies. Finally, on March 17, 1420, the Crusade was proclaimed, and the armies of the Emperor Sigismund entered Bohemia at the beginning of May; Prague was besieged in the summer. Thus it would seem clear enough that Chelčický's reference must have been to 1420; conversely, if we ask how a writer in his position, looking back from *ca.* 1425, would have referred to 1420 in the context under discussion, we can hardly imagine a better way than by the phrase, "the first year that the war had begun." All of this is fairly obvious, but the point is that we have not the slightest reason to suppose that there is any room for a loose interpretation of the key phrase.

We may now proceed to a more difficult question: *when* in 1420 did this meeting at Písek take place? It is clear that at the meeting a group of Taborite priests, arguing with Chelčický, asserted that Tabor had the right to use arms in defense of the Law of God and of the community, and they based this assertion on the traditional medieval doctrine that defined the functions of the estates of Christian society, a doctrine that they had probably picked up from Wyclif. The work mentioned by Chelčický was Wyclif's *Dialogus* (Jastrebov, *op. cit.*, p. 118 n. 4), which had been translated into Czech by Jakoubek, about 1415 (F. M. Bartoš, *Literární činnost M. Jakoubka ze Stříbra* [Prague, 1925], No. 103); the Taborites could have in any case used the work in Latin, or they might have derived the theory from other works by Wyclif. But when would they have been most likely to have used it? Not at the beginning of 1420, when the Taborite movement was fighting for its very life and was dominated by chiliast doctrines and an ideology of total war based on them (see my "Chiliasm...," pp. 50 ff.). Perhaps in May, when the Taborites were preparing to heed the summons of Prague, and march to the capital to help repel the Crusade; but although we can imagine Chelčický trying to dissuade the brethren from this step, we can hardly imagine a significant number of Taborite priests using scholastic arguments against him—the spring of 1420 was a period of great militancy and aggressiveness, with chiliast influence still strong, if not predominant. But later in the year, after the Crusade had been defeated and after the Taborites had left Prague, toward the end of August, things were very different. Back in South Bohemia, the leaders of the movement had to cope with the permanent problems of social organization and regulation; in September they elected a bishop, Nicholas Biskupec of Pelhřimov, to regulate preaching, supervise the clergy, and administer the common funds according to need. We know that Nicholas made his seat in Písek rather than Tabor. Shortly after, when the customary day for the collection of peasant rents came around (St. Gall's day, October 14), Tabor collected the rents from the peasants under her control, even though in the summer her priests had preached that such exactions were to be discontinued—they would have no place in the millennium (Laurence of Březová, p. 438). In fact we know from these and other facts that the autumn of 1420 was a period of antichiliast reaction, in which a party of order, led by Nicholas of Pelhřimov, sought to overcome Free-Spirit influence and provide the new society with a regular ecclesiastical order. It is hard to imagine a better period for a discussion of Christian social theory—at Písek, not at Tabor, which was probably still dominated or at least strongly influenced by the chiliasts. Thus Peter's information fits in perfectly with the evidence of other sources, and supplements them in the most valuable way: we may now be fairly sure that one aspect of the rise to power of the party of order was a shift from earlier sectarian ideas about secular power to a theory that was identical with that of the Prague masters and indeed of the medieval tradition. We are not therefore surprised to find that by the end of the year Nicholas of Pelhřimov was busily engaged in discussing the new simplified Taborite liturgy with the Prague masters, and that at the beginning of 1421 he called upon these masters for help in overcoming the Free-Spirit party. (For all of this see my "The Free Spirit in the Hussite Revolution," pp. 171 ff.)

But if the Písek meeting was part of a process of reaction against Free-Spirit sectarianism, it also dealt with the Waldensianist sectarianism represented by Chelčický. The general question was whether an evangelical community, no longer able to solve all problems in absolute terms by reference to an imminent Day of Wrath and millennium, could solve its societal problems at all. Could it, in short, use power— could it *be* a society? Chelčický, as we know, stood for a flat negative, and it was this position that he worked out in his treatise "On the

Triple Division of Society," about four or five years after the Písek meeting. Now it is interesting in this connection that his earliest work, "On Spiritual Warfare," says nothing about the theory of a triple division of society; it discusses social problems only obliquely and scantily, its main subject is the question of Christian warfare. But, as we have seen, Chelčický discussed this subject so profoundly as to raise the most basic questions about the validity of any social institutionalization of the Christian faith. The problem presented itself primarily as one of warfare, but it was really a problem of power. And we know, from the work, what the opposing positions were: one was that of the chiliasts, who based their justification of warfare on their prophecy of a Day of Wrath soon to come, and the other was that of the more evangelically minded priests, who cited Rom. 13. We may suppose that the latter position was taken by those priests who became the party of order in the second half of 1420, and we may guess that Chelčický's arguments were perhaps successful in refuting the use of Rom. 13, or indeed any New Testament text, as justification for Christian power. Here we are on very thin ice, for there is no evidence that could confirm or disprove our hypothesis, but if we refer the "On Spiritual Warfare" to the period before the Písek meeting—i.e., before the autumn of 1420 (cf. J. Macek, *Tábor v husitském revolučním hnutí,* II [Prague, 1955], 170 n. 109), and if we assume that Peter's presence at the meeting was part of the same involvement attested by the treatise, then we can also assume that the meeting brought the argument to a new level. Realizing that the New Testament could not serve to guide either warfare or the ordinary social use of power, the Taborite leaders used the theory of the triple division of society, that is, the scholastic ideology of medieval Christian society, and they included this theory in their arguments against Chelčický's position. We do not know who won the debate, or if anyone did; we may carry our guesswork further, however, and suppose that the scholastic argumentation was new to Chelčický, that he studied it in the subsequent period, and continued to discuss the matter with the Taborites. The treatise "On the Triple Division of Society", which begins by informing us of this history of exchanges of opinion, was his final answer to the problem. And in the light of what has been said, we can perhaps agree with F. M. Bartoš ("K počátkům Petra Chelčického," *Časopis českého musea,* LXXXVIII [1914], 306 f.), that the treatise was most probably addressed to Nicholas of Pelhřimov.

BIBLIOGRAPHY

The following list includes the editions of Peter Chelčický's early works and some of the more valuable literature about him in languages other than Czech. Those who read Czech are referred to the practically complete bibliography compiled by Eduard Petrů, *Soupis díla Petra Chelčického a literatury o něm* (Prague: Státní pedagogické nakladatelství, 1957).

I. Peter Chelčický's Early Works

Annenkov, J. S., and Jagić, V. (eds.), *Sočinenija Petra Chel'čickago . . . 2. Replika protiv Biskupca*, Sbornik otdělenija russkago jazyka i slovesnosti Imperatorskoj akademij nauk, LXVI. St. Petersburg, 1893.

Holinka, Rudolf (ed.), *Traktáty Petra Chelčického. O trojím lidu— O církvi svaté*. Prague: Melantrich, 1940.

Jastrebov, N. V. (ed.), *Petra Chel'čickago O trogiem lidu rzec—o duchovných a o swietských*, Sbornik otdělenija russkago jazyka i slovesnosti Imperatorskoj akademij nauk, LXXVII. St. Petersburg, 1903.

Krofta, Kamil (ed.), *Petr Chelčický: O boji duchovním a O trojím lidu*. Prague: J. Otto, 1911.

Both Krofta and Holinka base their editions of *O trojím lidu* on that of Jastrebov; they modernize the spelling, but not the language itself; I have used Krofta's text, but consulted the others. The edition of *O církvi svaté* by Holinka is original, as is that of *O boji duchovním* by Krofta.

II. Modern Works

Brock, Peter. "Peter Chelčický, Forerunner of the Unity," in Brock's *The Social and Political Doctrines of the Unity of Czech Brethren in the Fifteenth and Early Sixteenth Centuries*, Slavistic Printings and Reprintings, XI. The Hague: Mouton & Co., 1957. Pp. 25–69.

Goll, J. *Quellen and Undersuchungen zur Geschichte der Böhmischen Brüder*, II. *Peter Chelčický und seine Lehre*. Prague: J. Otto, 1882.

Jastrebov, N. V. *Etjudy o Petre Chel'čickom i jego vremeni*, I, *Zapiski istoriko-filologičeskago fakuľteta imperatorskago S. -Peter-*

178

burgskago Universiteta, **LXXXIX.** St. Petersburg, 1908. (All published.)

Spinka, Matthew. "Peter Chelčický, the Spiritual Father of the Unitas Fratrum," *Church History,* XII (1943), 271–91.

Vogl, Carl. *Peter Cheltschizki. Ein Prophet an der Wende der Zeiten.* Zűrich and Leipzig, 1926.

There are also treatments of Chelčický in F. Palacký's *Geschichte von Böhmen,* IV, i (Prague, 1857); E. Denis, *Fin de l'indépendance Boheme,* I. *Georges de Podiébrad. Les Jagellons* (Paris, 1890), 303–23; J. T. Müller, *Geschichte der böhmischen Brüder,* I (Herrnhut, 1922).

The above titles represent only a fraction of even the non-Czech literature.

FRENCH REPRESENTATIVE ASSEMBLIES: RESEARCH OPPORTUNITIES AND RESEARCH PUBLISHED

by J. Russell Major

Emory University

French Representative Assemblies: Research Opportunities and Research Published[1]

THE STUDY of representative institutions has always held an honored position in the English-speaking world. Bishop Stubbs was by no means the first to see in Parliament the basic ingredient for the constitutional history of England and during the last few decades Sir Lewis Namier and Sir John Neale have demonstrated how parliamentary history can be used as a means of studying the social and political structure of a nation. The work of Namier has already led to a reinterpretation of eighteenth-century England and that of Neale may in the long run have almost as much revolutionary significance for the Elizabethan age.[2] Little wonder that a group of English historians are now working on a monumental parliamentary history of their country.

Continental representative institutions have been less thoroughly studied in spite of the activity of the International Commission for the History of Representative and Parliamentary Institutions. This situation may result from the belief that the continental assemblies were less important than their English counterpart either because they often became inactive during the seventeenth century or because they functioned at the provincial rather than the national level. This situation is to be regretted because during the middle ages and the renaissance representative assemblies frequently played as important a role in continental countries as in England and they often provide valuable bases for studies on social and political structure. France is no exception to this rule and it is the purpose of this article to survey the existing studies of its local and provincial representative assemblies and to indicate source materials that provide the bases for further studies.[3]

1. The research for this article was done in 1961–62 by virtue of a Fellowship of the Social Science Research Council and a leave of absence from Emory University. I would also like to express my appreciation to the numerous French archivists whose unrivaled knowledge and unfailing courtesy made this article possible. To them it is gratefully dedicated.

2. Lewis Namier, *The Structure of Politics at the Accession of George III* (2 vols.; London, 1929) ; and *England in the Age of the American Revolution* (London, 1930) ; John E. Neale, *The Elizabethan House of Commons* (London, 1949) ; *Elizabeth and Her Parliaments, 1559–1581* (London, 1953) ; and *Elizabeth and Her Parliaments, 1584–1601* (London, 1957) .

3. I have omitted the Estates-General and other comparable assemblies from

It is true that the techniques developed by the English parlimen-
tary historians cannot be applied directly to the French provincial and
local estates. The election of the deputies which Namier and Neale
have studied to so much advantage in England is of little value because the clergy and nobility usually attended the French estates by
right and the town councils generally named one or two of their number without argument.

On the other hand, the quantity of surviving documents on some
of the individual provincial estates during the renaissance is far greater
than for the English Parliament during the same period in spite of
a dearth of diaries. The official nature of the French documents does

---

this survey because I am engaged in writing their history from 1421. For a
summary chapter and references to the more important works on the earlier
period see Ferdinand Lot and Robert Fawtier, *Histoire des institutions françaises
au moyen âge* (Paris, 1958), II, 545–77. Attention should also be called to the
various articles published in the *Studies Presented to the International Commission
for the History of Representative and Parliamentary Institutions* and to P. S. Lewis,
"The Failure of the French Medieval Estates," *Past and Present*, XXIII (1962),
3–24. I also plan to write a one-volume history of the provincial estates from the
Wars of Religion to the reign of Louis XIV, but this study will not be of sufficient
depth to remove the need for detailed studies of the individual institutions.
References in this article to the archives and printed works are more complete for
the renaissance than for the fourteenth and eighteenth centuries where I have
neither done nor intend to do any research, but I have included some comments
on these centuries in the hope of making the article more useful. There have
already been several general studies of the provincial estates, but although those
of F. Laferrière, "Mémoires sur l'histoire et l'organisation comparée des États
provinciaux aux divers époques de la monarchie jusqu'à 1789," *Mém. de l'ac. des
sciences morales et politiques de l'Institut de France*, XI (1862), 341–576; and
Lucien Lachaze, *Les États provinciaux de l'ancienne France et la question des États
provinciaux aux XVIIᵉ et XVIIIᵉ siècles. L'Assemblée provinciale du Berri sous
Louis XVI* (Paris, 1909), are of sufficient length to be of value, they are not based
on an adequate amount of research and were written before many of the studies
on the individual provincial estates were published. Too brief, but more up to
date and penetrating are H. Prentout, "Les États provinciaux en France," *Bul. of
the International Committee of Historical Sciences*, (July, 1928); G. Dupont-
Ferrier, "De quelques problèmes historiques relatifs aux États provinciaux," *Journal
des Savants* (Aug.–Oct., 1928); Étienne Delcambre, *Les États du Velay des origines
à 1642* (Saint-Étienne, 1938), pp. 5–10, 449–82; Émile Appolis, "Les États de
Languedoc au XVIII siècle. Comparaison avec les États de Bretagne," *L'Organisation corporative du moyen âge à la fin de l'ancien régime*, II (1937), 129–48; and
R. Doucet, *Les Institutions de la France au XVIᵉ siècle* (Paris, 1948), I, 337–59.
There are also accounts of the provincial estates in the various histories of
French law.

make it difficult to discover the web of family alliances and personal enmities so characteristic of the age, but other types of sources can in part fill this gap. The official documents do, however, provide excellent opportunities to study the relations between the various social classes and between the estates and the *parlements*, financial courts, and above all the local royal officials. Most of the estates had syndics or other officials who looked after local administrative matters when they were not in session. From their activities much can be learned about how provinces were actually governed. In their debates and through their officials the estates dealt with every aspect of life from the building of roads and the support of postal services to the financing of educational institutions and the army. Studies conducted by the provincial and local estates to determine the basis for the division of taxes could be most effectively used by economic historians. The *cahiers* or petitions of grievances submitted to the crown after each session of the estates provide unrivaled sources for the study of public opinion and, if carefully used, insights into the actual conditions and problems of the locality in question. Statements of the poverty of a province, for example, should not be taken too literally when accompanied by requests for a reduction in taxes, but complaints about local royal officials and about the nobles purchasing nonnoble land suggest at least the growing importance of these classes.

The actions of deputies of the estates to the king in council can also be used to considerable advantage. These deputies often resided at court for months and their correspondence with local officials in their respective provinces and their reports after returning from their missions provide not only opportunities to study the relations between central and local government, but also insights into the policies and intentions of the royal councilors themselves. Ranke and many others have based their histories of the various European states largely on the reports of the Venetian ambassadors who had no direct contact with the internal affairs of the country to which they were accredited and often had little knowledge of its society, institutions, and culture. How much better it would have been if these historians had also used the letters and reports of the deputies of the estates, towns, and other corporate bodies who dealt directly with the royal councilors, financial officials, and judges of the sovereign courts. Most of their correspondence has been lost, but enough remains to be a major source for the history of France. Sometimes these deputies to court wrote of their contact with royal officials in general terms; a few, however, had no hesitation in naming those officials who were friends of provincial liberties and those who were exponents of an increase in royal power. Through their correspondence we can glean valuable insights into how and why the more absolutist and more centralized monarchy of Louis XIV replaced that of the consultative, decentralized renaissance.

There are those who scorn local history or at least relegate it to the local antiquarian who spends his evenings and holidays studying the past of his native town. Such an attitude is never justifiable, and least of all for France, a country that has never systematically published the records of its past, and one too large and diversified to be approached from the vantage point of Paris. Henry IV is the only French king after Charles VIII whose letters have been almost entirely published, and for his reign alone do we have an inventory of the acts of the king's council. It is true that the editions of the letters of Catherine de Medici, Cardinal Richelieu, and others are of help and that a summarized edition of the letters of Henry III[4] are now being published, but useful as these collections are they do not solve all the historian's problems even in the realm of political history.

Policy was frequently made at the local level in France especially before the reign of Louis XIV, and even when made at court, it was based largely on reports that came from local officials and other persons in the provinces. Thus the letters and reports a king and his council received are as important as those that they sent, but they have rarely been published, and then usually in relatively obscure provincial journals where they have all too often been neglected. Thus the absence of adequate published collections of documents severely limits the number of significant research topics that can be undertaken at the national level. One is left with a choice of summarizing the work of others or of choosing topics in local history based largely on archival material. The last will remain the most fruitful course until new local studies have provided a more adequate basis for synthesis or until calendars of state papers on the English model are published. Of the areas of local history that need to be exploited few provide as many and as important opportunities as the provincial and local estates.

There were representative assemblies in all parts of France, but in the northern and central provinces they rarely met after the reign

4. Michel François *Lettres de Henri III, roi de France. Soc. de l'histoire de France* (Paris, 1959), Vol. I.

of Charles VII except to ratify treaties, redact customs, or to elect deputies to the Estates-General.[5] As a result there seems to be little need for research on the individual estates of this region except for brief studies on the medieval period.[6] It is to the remainder of France where the surviving documents are more numerous that one must turn to find the best opportunities to study the provincial estates. But before beginning this survey, it would be best to make some general comments on the sources for the history of the estates.

Nearly all the provincial and local estates established archives during the late middle ages or the renaissance that were kept by competent clerks. Where these archives survive there is a superabundance of material for historical research. In general they are to be found in the departmental archives in the capital town of the province catalogued under series C. In addition, copies of the *procès-verbaux* of the assemblies and other documents were often prepared for the deputies to take back to their constituents. These documents have found their way into the other departmental archives in the province where they too are catalogued under series C, into the communal archives where they have generally been placed under series AA or CC, into the various collections of the Bibliothèque Nationale, and less often into the Archives Nationales where they have usually been placed in series K, KK, or H.

Another valuable source for the history of the estates may be found in the registers of the meetings of the town councils. Here the deputies of the third estate were chosen to the provincial estates and here they made their reports on the assemblies upon their return. These registers are in the communal archives under series BB. Additional documents may sometimes be found in other series and in special collections in the departmental and communal archives. Published or manuscript inventories are generally available[7] and the local archivists are

5. For a survey of the composition and procedures of the estates in this region and for bibliographical references on both the medieval and renaissance assemblies see my *The Deputies of the Estates General of Renaissance France* (Madison, 1960) .

6. The only study of one of the provincial estates of this region from its origins until its demise based on an adequate amount of archival research is Joseph M. Tyrrell, "A History of the Estates of Poitou" (unpublished dissertation, Emory University, 1961). Another fruitful approach would be to study these estates collectively by reign as Antoine Thomas did for the assemblies in central France. See his *Les États provinciaux de la France centrale sous Charles VII* (2 vols.; Paris, 1879) .

7. A list of the inventories has been published in *État des inventaires des*

both anxious and able to provide valuable advice. A few documents, especially those related to the nobility, are still in private hands, but they can sometimes be located and permission obtained for their use.

Other types of documents are also available for the study of the provincial estates. The acts and decrees of the king's council are essential and collections may be found in the Bibliothèque Nationale and Archives Nationales.[8] There, and in the Archives du Ministère des Affaires Etrangères are also located the correspondence and papers of many of the leading royal ministers including the reports they received from the provinces.[9] Other sources include the papers relating to the sovereign courts, the *trésorier généraux* of France, and other tax officials. They are located in the departmental archives in the former provincial capitals under series B and C. In the Archives Nationales, the *Trésor des chartes,* series J and JJ, are valuable for the medieval period and series G (especially G[7]) on financial matters should be consulted by those who study the estates of the old regime. Much has been lost, but in most instances enough remains to form the basis for excellent histories of provincial estates.

Because of the valuable insights that could be obtained from the study of the provincial estates, there is need for many more histories of these institutions. Some provincial estates, such as those of Languedoc and Burgundy, seem to have been neglected in the postmedieval period because their archives are so rich; others because they are scarcely known to exist. Even when histories of provincial estates do exist, there are often opportunities for further research.

Archives Nationales, départementales, communales et hospitalières au 1ᵉʳ janvier 1937 (Paris, 1938) ; and *Supplément, 1937–1954* (Paris, 1955). In several instances I have relied on these inventories and have not yet visited the archives cited in this article. I have used the following abbreviations: AN = Archives Nationales, BN = Bibliothèque Nationale, AD = Archives Départmentales, AC = Archives Communales, *IAD = Inventaire sommaire des archives départmentales antérieures à 1789,* and *IAC = Inventaire sommaire des archives communales antérieures à 1789.*

8. See Noël Valois, *Inventaire des arrêts du Conseil d'État. Règne de Henri IV* (2 vols.; Paris, 1886–93).

9. See for example in the BN, Bellièvre Papers, MSS. fr. 15,890–15,911, and the Séguier Papers, MSS. fr. 17,367–17,412; in the AN, series H[1] on provincial administration, an important source for the estates during the old regime, and in the *Archives du Ministère des Affaires Étrangères,* the Richelieu and Mazarin Papers. Printed documents and secondary works on the provincial estates may be found at the BN under call numbers LK[14] 1-.

Most of the studies on the estates have been theses at the *École des Chartes* or in law. The former are often published only in abstracts and the latter are generally organized on a topical basis and are devoted to describing the composition, procedures, and duties of the provincial estates during a given period, usually several centuries in length. This approach has its merits, but little sense of a chronological development emerges. Indeed, constitutional history in the English sense, that is, the day-by-day evolution of an institution as a result of the interaction between the crown and the people in an ever-changing political, social, economic, and intellectual milieu, can scarcely be said to exist in France in studies of the prerevolutionary period. There are, therefore, instances when there is a need to complement an excellent history of a representative institution written with the French topical-institutional approach with an English type chronological-constitutional study. The research opportunities in the field of the French provincial and local estates are therefore almost unlimited. Let us consider some specific examples.

Burgundy.—The estates of Burgundy usually met only once every three years, but when not in session its affairs were looked after by a *Chambre des Élus généraux* and a host of minor officials. The archives of the estates which are among the richest in France offer opportunities to study nearly every type of history from the renaissance until the Revolution.[10] Their great wealth has perhaps been a factor in causing historians to seek less time-consuming subjects and Billioud not unnaturally halted his excellent history of the relatively poorly documented medieval period in 1477.[11] Weill has investigated the estates during the reign of Henry III, but he based his work too narrowly on the *procès-verbaux* of the estates and his conclusion that the estates lost ground to the crown during the reign is open

10. Jean Rigault has recently published Joseph Garnier's introduction to the inventory of the archives of the estates located in AD, Côte-d'Or with an up-to-date bibliography. See *AD, Côte-d'Or, ser. C., introduction aux tomes III et IV* (Dijon, 1959). This introduction based on the classification of the archives of the estates suggests many of the topics that could be investigated using this material. Other departmental and communal archives in the province also contain material on the estates and AN, H¹ 98–217 should be consulted on the post-1670 period.

11. Joseph Billioud, *Les États de Bourgogne aux XIV⁰ and XV⁰ siècles* (Dijon, 1922). On the medieval period see also H. Prost, "Les États du Comté de Bourgogne des origines à 1477," *Positions des thèses de l'École des Chartes* (1905), pp. 115–22; and R. de Chevanne, "Les États de Bourgogne et la réunion du duché à la France en 1477," *Mém. de la soc. d'archéologie de Beaune,* XLIII (1929–30), 195–245.

to suspicion.[12] Drouot has written a brief account of the estates during the League in his monumental study of Mayenne.[13] Thomas' treatment of the estates during the reign of Louis XIV is useful in spite of its great age, and Dumont has published an excellent book-length article on the session of the estates in 1718.[14] Outside these works little has been done, although many historians have touched on the estates in their investigation of other subjects.[15]

There were five counties known as the *pays adjacents du duché de Bourgogne*. In two of them, Auxerrois and Bar-sur-Seine, taxes were collected by royal officials and there was no need for regular meetings of the estates, but in the remaining three the estates met at least every third year as in Burgundy. The most important of these estates, Mâconnais, was both *pays d'états* and a *pays d'élection*. Such a combination did not become unusual until the seventeenth century when the crown generally ceased to convoke the estates in those provinces where *bureaux d'élections* had been established to collect taxes. The survival of the estates of Mâconnais is probably to be attributed to the special privileges its officials had obtained in regard to the local royal tax officials and to its close association with the estates of Burgundy to whose meetings it sent a deputation. The estates of Mâconnais have been the subject of an unpublished thesis on the medieval period by Verdat[16] and of an administrative history of the seventeenth and eighteenth centuries by Roussot.[17] The archives of the estates[18] offer sufficient resources for a study of the estates during

12. G. Weill, "Les États de Bourgogne sous Henri III," *Mém. de la soc. bourguignonne de géographie et d'histoire*, IX (1893), 121–48.

13. Henri Drouot, *Mayenne et la Bourgogne, 1587–1596* (Paris, 1937), esp. I, 94–102. See also his *Notes sur la Bourgogne et son esprit public au début du règne de Henri III, 1574–1579* (Dijon, 1937); and with the collaboration of L. Gros his "Recherches sur la Ligue en Bourgogne, II. Matériaux pour servir à l'histoire des États royalistes," *Revue bourguignonne*, XXIV (1914), 47–239.

14. Alexandre Thomas, *Une Province sous Louis XIV. Situation politique et administrative de la Bourgogne de 1661 à 1715* (Paris and Dijon, 1844). F. Dumont, "Une Session des États de Bourgogne; la tenue de 1718," *Annales de Bourgogne*, V (1933)–VII (1935).

15. For some additional works see Rigault's, *Introduction*.

16. M. Verdat, "Les États du Mâconnais aux XIVe et XVe siècles," *Positions des thèses de l'École des Chartes* (1926).

17. Jean Roussot, *Un Comté adjacent à la Bourgogne aux XVIIe et XVIIIe siècles; Le Mâconnais, pays d'États et d'élection* (Mâcon, 1937).

18. The archives are at AD, Saône-et-Loire, C 462–C 772. See Roussot for other sources.

the intervening period and for a more chronological history of the estates during the old regime, but on the whole Roussot's study comes close to fulfilling these needs and there are other representative institutions that offer greater opportunities.

The three estates of Auxonne and Charolais met periodically and through their officials collected taxes, for in neither were there *élections*. The archives of the estates of Auxonne are rich enough to make possible a short study;[19] those of Charolais have already been exploited.[20]

There was a marked tendency for the duchy of Burgundy to absorb the *pays adjacents* during the seventeenth and eighteenth centuries. Auxonne lost its independent status in 1639, Auxerre in 1668, Bar-sur-Seine in 1721, and Charolais in 1751. The estates, where they existed, disappeared at the time of the union and the inhabitants were given representation in the estates of Burgundy. It was only with difficulty that the estates of Mâconnais maintained its independence until the Revolution. Apparently this centralizing movement originated among the officials of the Burgundian estates at Dijon and not from the royal officials at Paris, but it would be interesting to know more about the administrative problems and general climate of opinion that led to these changes.[21]

In 1601, France acquired Bresse, Bugey, and Gex from Savoy. These territories were incorporated into the government and the *généralité* of Burgundy, but their estates continued to meet until the Revolution in spite of some centralizing tendencies and the establishment of *élections* shortly after their conquest. The early history of these estates has been studied, but there is need for research of their activities after their final union with France.[22] Documents in the departmental and

19. The archives are located in AD, Côte-d'Or, C 7482—C 7513.

20. L. Laroche, "Les États particuliers du Charolais," *Mém. de la soc. pour l'histoire du droit et des institutions des anciens pays bourguignons, comtois et romands*, VI (1939), 145–94. The principal sources for the estates are at AD, Côte-d'Or, C 7519—C 7534; and AD, Saône-et-Loire, C 452—C 461.

21. F. Moreau, "La Suppression des États du comté d'Auxonne et leur réunion aux États du duché de Bourgogne," *Mém. de la soc. pour l'histoire du droit et des institutions des anciens pays bourguignons, comtois et romands*, II (1935), 189–94.

22. A. Tallone, "Les États de Bresse," *Annales de la soc. d'émulation et d'agriculture . . . de l'Ain*, LV (1927–28), 272–344, is a good study and includes a good bibliography. See also R. Pic, "Les anciennes assemblées provinciales de la Savoie et du Bugey aux XIIIᵉ et XIVᵉ siècles," *Le Bugey* II (1911–12), 627–35; and "Les États de Savoie, 1400–1601," *Le Bugey*, VI (1923–26), 387–407. On the post-1601

communal archives are adequate to support such a project.[23]

Dauphiné.—The representative assemblies of Dauphiné offer several opportunities for further research. Here there were a wide variety of representative institutions, none of which has been completely studied and some of which are virtually unknown except to a few specialists.[24] The most important of these institutions was the estates of Dauphiné. A. Dussert planned a three-volume history of this institution from its origins, but he died before completing the third volume. As a result there is still no chronological history of the estates for the post-1559 period and no description of its procedures and duties except for the middle ages.[25] To complete Dussert's work would be both a challenging and rewarding task.

period see "Observations au sujet des listes électorales de la noblesse du Bugey en 1651 et 1789," *Revue de la soc. littéraire, historique et archéologique du département de l'Ain,* X (1881–82), 218–21; R. Pic, "Les États du Bugey, les trois ordres, l'hôtel de Province 1761–1790," *Le Bugey,* I (1909), 113–18, 329–37; A. Vayssière "Les Archives de l'Ain. Assemblées du clergé de Bresse et de Bugey," *Annales de la soc. d'émulation et d'agriculture . . . de l'Ain,* IX (1876), 82–91, 329–37; and Louis Ricard, *Les Institutions judiciaires et administratives de l'ancienne France et spécialement du bailliage de Gex* (Paris, 1886).

23. The archives for the estates are at AD, Ain, C 886—C 990 for Bresse; C 991—C 998 for Bugey; and C 999—C 1025 for Gex. The archives of the *Intendance de Bourgogne* in AD, Ain, and in AD, Côte-d'Or also should be consulted. Some documents on the estates of this region have been published. Armando Tallone, *Atti delle assemblee costituzionali italiane dal medioevo al 1831. Serie prima, Stati generali e provinciali. Sezione quinta. Parlamenti piemontesi. Parlamento Sabaudo* (3 vols.; Bologna, 1928–29). Jules Baux, *Nobiliaire du département de l'Ain* (2 vols.; Bourg-en-Bresse, 1862–64); and *Mémoires historiques de la ville de Bourg, extraits des registres municipaux de l'hôtel de ville, de 1536 à 1789* (5 vols.; Bourg-en-Bresse, 1868–88), contain some documents.

24. André-Alexandre Fauché-Prunelle, *Essai sur les anciennes institutions autonomes ou populaires des Alpes-Cottiennes-Briançonnaises* (Grenoble, 1857), Vol. II, contains an account of the various representative institutions in Dauphiné, but it is not based on extensive archival research and is not of sufficient length to remove the need for further studies.

25. A. Dussert, "Les États du Dauphiné aux XIVe et XVe siècles," and "Les États du Dauphiné de la guerre de cent ans aux guerres de religion," *Bul. de l'académie Delphinale,* ser. 5, Vol. VIII (1914); and ser. 5, Vol. XIII (1922). Fortunately Dussert did publish several articles on the post-1559 period. They are: "Le Baron des Adrets et les États du Dauphiné (novembre, 1562—février, 1563). Essai d'organisation protestante durant la première guerre de religion," *Bul. de l'académie Delphinale,* ser. 5, XX (1929), 93–136; and "Catherine de Médicis et les États du Dauphiné. Préludes du procès des tailles et arbitrage de la reine-mère en 1579," *Bul. de l'académie Delphinale,* ser. 6, II (1931), 123–89.

It would be a challenging task because few relevant documents have been published and the archives of the estates became scattered before the Revolution. However, enough material may be found in the depositories at Paris, in the departmental archives of Isère, Hautes-Alpes, and Drôme, and in the various communal archives and libraries in Dauphiné to provide the sources for an excellent study.[26]

It would be a rewarding task primarily because there was an unusual social alignment in Dauphiné probably brought about by a famous dispute concerning the *taille*. In some parts of France the *taille* was *réelle*, that is, both noble and commoner paid the *taille* on the nonnoble land they held. In other parts of France the *taille* was *personnelle*, that is, the commoner paid the *taille* and the noble did not, regardless of the legal status of his holdings. In Dauphiné the matter was in dispute and for several generations there was a bitter quarrel between the three estates. At first the privileged were victorious, but as the nobility bought more and more land, up to one-half or even three-fourths in some localities, there was less taxable land upon which to base the *taille*.[27] At the same time the size of the royal demands grew rapidly. The inevitable result was a sharp increase in the *taille* assessed upon nonnobles. Led by their gallant syndic, Claude Brosse, the villages protested again and again to the king in council.[28] Failure followed failure until 1634, when the *taille* in Dauphiné was finally declared to be *réelle*, but already the three orders had become so divided that they had been able to offer no effective opposition when in 1628 the crown had suppressed the estates.

During the long struggle between the three orders, each had begun to meet in separate assemblies. The nobility had sought to strengthen its position by welcoming the *anoblis* and the royal officials of the

26. Dussert discusses the sources for the history of the estates in the introduction of each of his volumes. Since he wrote, the holdings of AD, Isère, have been greatly enriched. See Fonds Chaper, J 524^1–J 524^2; IJ 669, IJ 176, and IJ 177. At Paris attention should be called to the Richelieu Papers in the Archives du Ministère des Affaires Etrangères, MSS. 1546 and 1548, and to the pamphlets in the BN, esp. LK^2 661–LK^2 671 and LK^{14} 61–LK^{14} 65.

27. Pierre Cavard, *La Réforme et les guerres de religion à Vienne* (Vienne, 1950), p. 398. This excellent book will prove very useful to anyone studying representative assemblies in Dauphiné during the Wars of Religion.

28. A. Lacroix, "Claude Brosse et les tailles," *Bul. de la soc. départementale archéologie et de statistique de la Drôme*, Vol. XXXI (1897)–Vol. XXXIII (1899). This is a good study, but it is too narrowly based on the sources available at AD, Drôme, to be definitive.

sovereign courts into its ranks.[29] The third estate, on the other hand, was divided against itself because of the divergent interests of the towns and villages. It could not hope to hold its own against the nobility, and some individuals within the order probably welcomed two edicts of 1628 which substituted royal tax collectors (*élus*) for those of the estates and suppressed the estates.

The above facts are not too well established and the motivation behind the actions of the crown and the individual estates is largely a matter for conjecture. Still less well known is the *assemblée du pays* consisting of a handful of members from each estate that the crown turned to after the demise of the estates and that was still meeting as late as 1664 under the presidency of the bishop of Grenoble, or of the assembly of the ten principal towns of Dauphiné whose life extended at least until 1670.[30] The nobles proved to be the strongest defenders of provincial liberty and their efforts to thwart the royal will led to several decrees of the council forbidding them to meet and probably to a somewhat earlier death of their assembly.[31]

The *assemblée du pays* and the individual assemblies of the nobility and third estate should be treated in any history of the estates of Dauphiné because their activities were so interrelated, and the same is true with the assemblies of the individual *bailliages* of Dauphiné which seem to have met rather frequently. An exception to this statement should be made in regard to the assemblies of the Alpine *bailliages* of Embrun, Briançon, and Gap where there was an interesting hierarchy of representative institutions. At the bottom were the assemblies of the *escartons*. There were five *escartons* in the *bailliage* of Briançon prior to the treaty of Utrecht in 1713 when three were ceded to Piedmont, and three *escartons* in the *bailliage* of Embrun each with its separate assembly. The *bailliage* of Gap does not seem to have had any. The *escartons* were small, those in the *bailliage* of Briançon con-

29. One does not have to rely on circumstantial evidence for this statement. The idea was specifically voiced in a joint meeting of the nobility and clergy in 1627. AD, Isère, IJ 669.

30. Heavy reliance would have to be placed on the communal archives for these assemblies. For last-known meetings see AC, Grenoble, BB 111 and BB 112.

31. AD, Isère, has recently acquired the register of the deliberations of the nobility from May, 1602, to July, 1622; IJ 175. Additional material may be found in AD, Isère in l'Hôpital de Grenoble, H 357. For the quarrel between the crown and the nobility the archives of the Conseil des finances should be consulted. See for example, AN, E 24^A, fol. 360–360v; E 129^c, fol. 1–2; and E 134^c, fol. 197–198v.

taining only from four to twenty-one communities apiece. Each community sent deputies to the assembly of the *escarton*. Above the *escarton* there were assemblies of each *bailliage* and above the *bailliage* assemblies there was the assembly of the *trois bailliages des montagnes*. The assemblies of the *trois bailliages des montagnes* and of the *bailliage* of Gap appear to have ceased in the 1650's, but those of the other two *bailliages* and their *escartons* survived until the Revolution.[32] They provide an excellent opportunity to study the small Alpine towns and villages.

The Provincial Estates in Central France.—There were active provincial estates in all of the provinces of central France during the first half of the fifteenth century and these institutions have been the subject of an excellent study by Thomas.[33] Thomas, however, overemphasized the decline of the representative institutions in the region that took place during the reign of Charles VII. In Basse-Auvergne, Haute-Auvergne, and Forez there were estates that were active enough during the sixteenth and sevententh centuries to merit special studies. By this time, however, the three orders had ceased to meet together except on rare occasions, and assemblies of the towns had assumed many of the duties formerly exercised by the three estates.

The archives in Forez are not rich, but there is one collection of documents that includes many *procès-verbaux*.[34] From this collection and from other sources Galley was able to compile an incomplete list of the assemblies of the nobility, the towns, and the three estates. His

32. There are some documents on the assemblies of the *bailliage* and of the *escarton* of Briançon in AC, Briançon, which have been exploited by Fauché-Prunelle II, 311–39, and others. The deliberations of Vallée du Queyras provide an excellent source for the assemblies of the *escarton* of Queyras and of the *bailliage* of Briançon during the seventeenth and eighteenth centuries. The assemblies of the *bailliage* of Embrun and of the *escarton* of Guillestre can be investigated during the same period through the rich archives of Guillestre. Especially valuable is BB 18, the deliberations of the *escarton* of Guillestre, 1591–1626. Paul Guillaume has written a brief account of the *escarton* in *IAC, Guillestre* (Gap, 1906), lviii–xci. The archives of the town of Gap provide the best source for the assemblies of the *bailliage* of Gap. All of the above sources contain material on the assemblies of the *trois bailliages des Montagnes* and all but AC, Briançon, are conveniently located in AD, Hautes-Alpes. Together they provide enough material for a doctoral dissertation if it were extended from the origins of the assemblies to the Revolution.

33. Antoine Thomas, *op. cit.* The text of this book, but not the documents, was also printed in the *Revue historique*, Vols. X and XI (1879).

34. AD, Loire, C 32. See also series B for references to the estates.

account of the assemblies themselves, however, is too brief and inadequate to remove the need for a new short study.[35]

In 1788, Bergier published a history of the estates of Auvergne and some documents collected by Dom Verdier-Latour.[36] His work was not devoid of merit, but it was hastily prepared, based on incomplete sources, and dedicated to supporting the pretensions of the town of Clermont-Ferrand at the expense of those of Riom. Rivière did not go much beyond Bergier and Verdier-Latour in his account of the estates in his history of the institutions of Auvergne.[37] Since that time Rouchon has written a penetrating article on the quarrel between the thirteen "good towns" of Basse-Auvergne and the *plat pays,* and Henry has pointed to the research opportunities provided by the estates.[38] Opportunities there are indeed for the departmental archives of Puy-de-Dôme and some of the communal archives contain rich resources.[39] Perhaps they could throw some light on why the "good towns" began to meet without the clergy and nobility, on the quarrel involving the town officials of Clermont, the royal officials of Riom, and the inhabitants of the *plat pays,* and on why meetings of the "good towns" became less frequent in the middle third of the seventeenth century and ceased altogether after 1680. On the last, the adverse comments made by the intendant Mesgrigny should be taken into account.[40]

Almost no work has ever been done on the estates of Haute-Auvergne.[41] As in Basse-Auvergne the clergy and the nobility ceased

35. Jean-B. Galley, *Les États de Forez et les treize villes* (Saint-Étienne, 1914).

36. Antoine Bergier and Dom Verdier-Latour, *Recherches historiques sur les États généraux et plus particulièrement sur l'origine, l'organisation et la durée des anciens États provinciaux d'Auvergne* (Clermont-Ferrand, 1788).

37. Hippolyte-F. Rivière, *Histoire des institutions de l'Auvergne* (2 vols.; Paris, 1874).

38. G. Rouchon, "Le tiers état aux États provinciaux de Basse-Auvergne aux XVIe et XVIIe siècles," *Bul. philologique et historique de comité des travaux historiques et scientifiques* (1930–31), pp. 165–89. P. Henry, "Note sur les États provinciaux de Basse-Auvergne," *Revue d'Auvergne,* LVIII (1944), 57–66.

39. AC, Clermont-Ferrand, Fonds Clermont and Fonds Montferrand are both exceptionally rich. Other communal achives such as those of Aigueperse, Riom, and Thiers should be consulted. In AD, Puy-de-Dôme, ser. C, are the records of the intendance of Auvergne in which there is some important material.

40. Mesgrigny's comments have been published by J.-B. Bouillet, *Tablettes historiques de l'Auvergne* (Clermont-Ferrand, 1842), III, 145–94. See esp. pp. 147–50.

41. Bergier's few comments are based entirely on the handful of documents

to meet with the third estate and the composition of the third estate itself underwent some changes during the sixteenth century. Meetings of the nobility were probably rare, but the third estate was active until about 1625 and met occasionally thereafter until 1693.[42]

Provence.—Provence had the usual wealth of representative institutions, the most important of which was the provincial estates, an aristocratic assembly in which the nobles without fiefs, the chapters, and the lower clergy were excluded and the urban patricians dominated the representation of the third estate. The participants in this assembly were among the most independent minded in France. They did not hesitate to negotiate with foreign powers or to reduce sharply the amount of the grants requested by their king. In 1630 they were threatened by an edict creating *élections* in their province, but it was only when the Prince of Condé was sent with a royal army that order was restored and they purchased the revocation of this and several other edicts at a price considerably lower than that asked by the crown. This very independent spirit, indeed, seems to have led to the demise of the estates, for the crown learned that the general assembly of the communities, an institution that consisted only of the *procureurs* of the clergy and nobility and the representatives of the communities that attended the estates, was much more pliable. After 1639 the estates were no longer convoked and the general assembly of the communities was used until the Revolution to consent to taxes that fell primarily on the third estate. Separate assemblies for the nobility and clergy of Provence also continued to meet, but the former, at least, were infrequently convoked and neither was especially important. In addition to the above institutions there were the usual diocesan assemblies of the clergy and assemblies in the twenty-three *vigueries* and *bailliages* into which Provence was divided.

This motley array of institutions has been studied by Busquet.[43] His work is excellent in most respects, but of necessity his account of

Verdier-Latour found for him in Clermont-Ferrand, and Rivière's brief statements come mostly from Bergier. However, see P.-F. Fournier, "Le Cahier de la noblesse de Haute-Auvergne aux États-généraux de 1614," *Revue de la Haute-Auvergne,* XXXII (1947–49), 117–21, and R. de Ribier, "L'Assemblée des États particuliers de la Haute-Auvergne en 1649," *Revue de la Haute-Auvergne,* VI (1904), 125–72.

42. AD, Cantal, contains very little, but there are a few documents on the estates in AD. Puy-de-Dôme ser. C. More valuable are AC, Aurillac, and AC, Saint-Flour.

43. R. Busquet, "Histoire des institutions," *Les Bouches-du-Rhône, Encyclopédie, Départementale* (Marseille, 1921), Vols. II and III.

each institution is too brief to remove the need for further research and he failed to use the rich resources of the Paris depositories. In addition, there is a description written near the end of the eighteenth century of how the estates functioned,[44] a study of the estates in the medieval period that has been published only in an abstract,[45] a volume on the general assembly of the communities that employs the institutional approach almost entirely for the period after the demise of the estates,[46] and a study of the *viguerie* assemblies that for the seventeenth and eighteenth centuries is admittedly only a description of the *viguerie* of Aix.[47] The rest remains to be done. The archives of the estates and of the general assemblies of the communities are rich as are some of the communal archives.[48] Research in this region would be of especial interest because here as in northern Italy noble and commoner often lived side by side in the towns and enjoyed frequent and friendly relations until social stratification became more pronounced after the middle of the seventeenth century.

Languedoc.—Languedoc was one of the largest provinces in France and it possessed one of the strongest and most aristocratic of the provincial estates. Attendance became more and more restricted during the late middle ages and in the eighteenth century only the twenty-three archbishops and bishops, twenty-three barons, and sixty-eight deputies from towns or dioceses could attend the estates where they deliberated together in a single house. The only serious attempt to write a complete history of this institution was published in 1818,[49]

44. Gaspard H. de Coriolis, *Dissertation sur les États de Provence* (Aix, 1867).

45. J. Denizet, "Les États de Provence depuis l'origine jusqu'à la réunion de la Provence à la France, 1481," *Positions des thèses de l'École des Chartes* (1920), pp. 5–17.

46. Bernard Hildesheimer, *Les Assemblées des communautés de Provence* (Paris, 1935).

47. M.-J. Bry, *Les Vigueries de Provence* (Paris, 1910).

48. The archives of the estates of Provence and of the general assemblies of the communities are at AD, Bouches-du-Rhône, Marseille. They are especially rich from about the middle of the sixteenth century. In the seventeenth century the estates and the general assemblies of the communities usually voted to publish their decisions. The largest collections of those of the general assemblies may be found in the BN and in the Bibliothèque Municipale at Aix. These *Abregé des délibérations* are very useful, but do not replace the need to consult the more detailed unpublished *procès-verbaux*. AN, H^I 1182–1362, is valuable for the eighteenth-century assemblies.

49. Baron Trouvé, *Essai historique sur les États généraux de la province de Languedoc* (Paris, 1818), Vol. I.

but since that time there have been two studies of the medieval period that explain how its organization and procedures developed,[50] one of an unusually high quality on the period around 1630 when the estates were threatened by the establishment of *élections* in the province,[51] and several articles.[52] Most of the archives of the estates, one of the richest in France, remain to be exploited. They provide a splendid source for nearly every type of history.[53]

There were also estates of the *sénéchaussées* and of the dioceses in Languedoc, but the former were so closely connected with the provincial estates that they ought to be studied together. The diocesan estates, on the other hand, must be treated separately, for while they were closely connected with the provincial estates, they often acted in local affairs and have separate archives. Some of these diocesan institutions were genuine assemblies of two or three estates; others permitted little or no participation by the clergy or nobility, but rather consisted of only the local bishop or his representative and the deputies of the communities. Of the former there have been studies of the estates of Vivarais, [54] Velay,[55] and Albi,[56] but they all end before or

50. Paul Dognon, *Les Institutions politiques et administratives du pays de Languedoc du XIIIe siècle aux guerres de religion* (Toulouse, 1895) ; and Henri Gilles, "Les États de Languedoc au XVe siècles," *Positions des thèses de l'École des Chartes* (1952), pp. 51–54.

51. Paul Gachon, *Les États de Languedoc et l'édict de Béziers, 1632* (Paris, 1887).

52. See for example É. Appolis, "La représentation des villes aux États généraux du Languedoc," *Fédération historique du Languedoc méditerranéen et du Rouissilon, congrès de Rodez, 1958*, pp. 305–10; also in *Album Helen Maud Cam* (Louvain, 1960), I, 219–27; and "Les États de Languedoc et les routes royales au XVIIIe siècle," *Studies Presented to the International Commission for the History of Representatives and Parliamentary Institutions*, XVIII (1958), 215–36.

53. The archives of the estates are at AD, Hérault, but there are many copies of the *procès-verbaux* and other documents both in Paris and in the various archives of the province. Particular attention should be called to AN, H¹ 748¹⁰–H¹ 1101, which contains some valuable documents such as the acts of the syndics of Languedoc. Documents have been published in Jean Albisson, *Lois municipales et économiques de Languedoc* (7 vols.; Montpellier, 1780–87) ; Cl. de Vic and J. Vaissete, *Histoire générale de Languedoc* (15 vols; Toulouse, 1872–92) ; and many other less important places.

54. Auguste le Sourd, *Essai sur les États de Vivarais depuis leur origines* (Paris, 1926) ; and *Le Personnel des États de Vivarais, 1601–1789, répertoire alphabétique* (Lyon, 1923). The archives of the estates are at AD, Ardèche.

55. Étienne Delcambre, *Contribution à l'histoire des États provinciaux. Les États du Velay des origines à 1642* (Saint-Étienne, 1938). The archives of the

just after the reign of Louis XIII. Companion volumes are needed to carry their stories up to the Revolution. In each case there is ample documentation to support the study. Two historians have written on the three estates of Gévaudan and a number of documents have been published.[57]

The remaining diocesan assemblies in Languedoc were of the latter type. There are studies of the estates of Alais[58] and Lodève[59] in the eighteenth century, of Castres[60] and Lavour[61] during the medieval-renaissance period, of Toulouse[62] during the seventeenth and eighteenth centuries, and of Rieux[63] throughout its history, but the remaining assemblies await their historian.[64]

---

estates are in AD, Haute-Loire. Some documents in these archives have been published in Antoine Jacotin, *Preuves de la maison de Polignac* (5 vols.; Paris, 1898–1906).

56. Elié A. Rossignol, *Petits États d'Albigeois* (Paris, 1875). The archives of the estates are at AD, Tarn.

57. J. Deniau, "Les États particuliers du pays de Gévaudan," *Soc. des lettres, sciences et arts de la Lozère. Chroniques et mélanges*, V (1930), 1–67. Atgar, *Les États du Gévaudan* (thèse de droit, Montpellier, 1957). I have not seen this last work and do not know whether it removes need for further study. The archives of the estates are at AD, Lozère. Numerous documents have been published. See especially F. André, "Procès-verbaux des délibérations des États du Gévaudan," *Bul. de la soc. d'agriculture, industrie, sciences et arts du département de la Lozère*, Vols. XXVI–XXXIII (1875–82); and Gustave de Burdin, *Documents historiques sur la province de Gévaudan* (2 vols.; Toulouse, 1846–47).

58. Jean Mazel, *Histoire administrative du diocèse civil d'Alais, 1694–1789* (Montpellier, 1936). Since Alais was not erected into a diocese with estates until 1694, there is no need for further research.

59. Appolis, *Un Pays languedocien au milieu du XVIIIe siècle, le diocèse civil de Lodève* (Albi, 1951); and "Une assiette diocésaine en Languedoc à la fin de l'ancien régime," *Comité des travaux historiques et scientifiques, section d'histoire moderne et d'histoire contemporaine. Notices, inventaires et documents*, XXII (1936), 5–58. These are the best studies of the diocesan estates.

60. Rossignol, *Assemblées du diocese de Castres* (Toulouse, 1878). The archives are at AD, Tarn, and would support an excellent study on the later period.

61. Rossignol, *Assemblées du diocèse de Lavour* (Paris, 1881). The archives are at AD, Tarn.

62. Thomas Puntous, "Les Assemblées de l'assiette dans le diocèse de Toulouse aux 17e and 18e siècles," *Rec. de législation de Toulouse*, V (1909), 185–225; and *Un Diocèse Civil de Languedoc: Les États particuliers du diocèse de Toulouse aux XVIIe et XVIIIe siècles* (Paris, 1909).

63. Jean Contrasty, *Histoire de la cité de Rieux-Volvestre et ses évêques* (Toulouse, 1936).

64. The archives of most of the remaining diocesan estates are in AD, Hérault,

Guyenne.—The representative institutions in the duchy, government, and *généralité* of Guyenne are the least known in France. Here there was an infinite variety of assemblies, but there is not a complete study of a single one of them. At the top of the hierarchy of representative assemblies was the provincial estates. These estates were rarely assembled during the middle ages and early renaissance. By 1556, however, the leading inhabitants of the region had become conscious enough of a community of interest to point out to Henry II that there were assemblies of the estates in each jurisdiction of the region to levy and collect taxes and to regulate other affairs, but that there was no assembly in which the estates of the entire region could meet together to deal with their common problems. Henry II recognized their grievance and on October 24, 1556, wrote the king of Navarre, his lieutenant-general in Guyenne, telling him to have the estates of every diocese and province of his government name one deputy from each order to attend an assembly to be held at a time and place of his choosing.[65] Thus a renaissance monarch authorized the creation of a representative institution whose deputies were drawn from a larger territory than any other in France with the possible exception of Languedoc.

The estates of Guyenne assembled at Bordeaux in September, 1557, but meetings do not seem to have become periodic until 1561 when the deputies began to play a major role in taxation. Between 1561 and 1605 there were over sixty meetings of the estates, but during the last years of the reign of Henry IV its activities declined considerably because that monarch, unlike most of his predecessors, had a profound dislike for representative institutions and did all he could to weaken their power. In 1603 he struck a blow at the smaller estates of the region by creating eight *bureaux d'élections* to assume their tax collecting duties. Whether Henry IV chose Guyenne as the place to begin his attack on representative institutions because he believed that they

---

AD, Gard, and AD, Aude, but those of Mirepoix are in AD, Ariège, those of Bas-Montauban are in AD, Tarn-et-Garonne, and those of Petit-Comminges are in AD, Haute-Garonne. Appolis has written several brief articles on the diocesan estates. See "Les compoix diocésains en Languedoc," *Cahiers d'histoire et d'archéologie* (1946), pp. 81–93; and "Les Assiettes diocésaines en Languedoc au XVIII⁰ siècle. Essai de synthèse," *Fédération historique du Languedoc méditerranéen et du Rouissilon, XXVII⁰ et XXVIII⁰ congrès, 1953–54*, pp. 115–24; also in *Anciens pays et assemblées d' états*, IX (1955), 53–65.

65. AD, Haute-Garonne, C 3796, No. 3.

were weaker (due to the failure of the clergy and nobility to participate fully in the provincial or in many of the local estates) cannot be
said. His death in 1610 was followed by a return to the popular consultative traditions of the renaissance monarchy. The new *élections*
were suppressed and the estates of Guyenne met about nine times
during the following decade.

Soon after Louis XIII began his personal government, but well
before Cardinal Richelieu became chief minister, the attack on representative institutions was renewed. *Bureaux d'élections* were once more
created in Guyenne in 1621, meetings of the estates of Guyenne became exceptional, and apparently ceased altogether after 1635.[66] The
local estates, stripped of their tax-collecting duties in the mid-1620's
when the *élus* actually began to function, slowly waned until by 1680
there were no representative institutions in the entire area except for
the diocesan assemblies of the clergy.

The estates of Guyenne is certainly worthy of a study because of
the great area over which it operated, because it was the first to suffer
from the more authoritarian character of the seventeenth century
monarchy, and because it is the least known of all the large representative institutions in France. Unfortunately, only a few related
documents have been published[67] and there are no archives for the
estates. The historian who undertakes this task will have to search the
various depositories at Paris and the departmental and communal
archives of the region.[68] Enough could be found to provide the basis
for an excellent book.

66. The meeting which the prince of Condé addressed at Bordeaux in November, 1638, was composed of the lieutenant-generals of the local *sénéchaussées* and not elected deputies. BN, MS. Dupuy, 869, fols. 87–91.

67. Most of the published documents are to be found in *Archives historiques
du département de la Gironde;* see especially XXVIII (1893), 44–108, and
XXXV (1900), 72–75, 192–208. See also Henri Stein, *Charles de France* (Paris,
1919), pp. 714–19; The assemblies of the clergy of the archdiocese of Auch have
been studied; see A. Degert, "Les Assemblées provinciales du clergé gascon,"
Révue de Gascogne, Vol. LV (1914) –Vol. LXII (1926).

68. AD, Gironde, ser. C, contains the financial records of the *généralité* and provides a valuable source for the local and provincial estates from the late sixteenth
century. For an account of the complicated changes of territory in this *généralité* see L. Desgraves, "La Formation territoriale de la généralité de Guyenne,"
Annales du Midi, LXII (1950), 239–48. Nearly all the departmental and important communal archives contain material, the most important being AD,
Haute-Garonne, archives of the estates of Comminges, and AC, Agen.

At the time the *généralité* of Guyenne was created in 1523, Haut-and Bas Limousin, Périgord, and Lannes were *pays d'élections* and the *sénéchaussée* of Guyenne (Bordeaux and the surrounding territory) became one soon thereafter. Here the absence of tax-collecting duties led the estates to be less active than elsewhere and, except for the estates of Périgord, an article on each would suffice to relate their history.[69]

The estates of Périgord would be worthy of a short book although the efforts of Cardenal have made its last years fairly well known.[70] It was probably the first representative institution to feel the full displeasure of Henry IV, and after 1595 he did not permit it to meet again during his reign. The estates had an executive committee consisting of six members from each order that continued to meet at least until 1605[71] when its mandate expired. Henry IV refused to permit the three estates to assemble again to renew it or to elect new syndics. Thereafter, the three estates met only to elect deputies to the Estates-General. The surviving documents on the estates are not numerous, but enough remains to form the basis for an interesting study.[72]

The three estates of Quercy met regularly under the presidency of the bishop-count of Cahors until the mid-1620's when the *élections* were established. Deprived of its tax-collecting duties, the assemblies

69. On Haut- and Bas-Limousin see Thomas, *Les Etats provinciaux de la France centrale sous Charles VII;* and *IAC, Haute-Vienne,* ed. Alfred Leroux (Limoges, 1891), ser. C, pp. xxxii–xxxvi. For Lannes see Leon Cadier, *La Sénéchaussée des Lannes sous Charles VII, administration royale et États provinciaux* (Paris, 1885), extract from *Revue de Béarn, Navarre et Lannes,* Vol. III; and AC, Bayonne, Dax, and Saint-Sever. AC, Bordeaux, Bourg-sur-Gironde, Saint-Émilion, and Libourne, contain information on the assemblies of the three estates and of the towns of the *sénéchaussée* of Guyenne. AD, Haute-Garonne, should be consulted. A few documents have been published in *Archives historiques . . . de la Gironde* and other places.

70. L. de Cardenal, "Catalogue des assemblées des États de Périgord de 1376 à 1651," *Bul. philologique et historique du comité des travaux historiques et scientifiques,* XLIX (1938–39), 243–66; "Les États de Périgord sous Henri IV," and "Les dernières réunions des trois ordres de Périgord avant la Révolution," *L'Organisation corporative du moyen âge à la fin de l'ancien régime* (Louvain, 1937 and 1939), Vols. II and III.

71. AD, Dordogne, 5 C 29.

72. What remains of the archives of the estates is at AD, Dordogne, 5 C 1–5 C 29. See L. de Cardenal, "Note sur les archives des États de Périgord," *Bul. de la soc. historique et archéologique du Périgord,* XXXIX (1912), 145–52. AC, Périgueux, Bergerac, etc., contain material as do the Périgord MSS. in the BN.

became infrequent, the last-known one being in 1673. The archives of
the estates are not rich, but Baudel's study is so mediocre that a short
one-volume history is needed.[73]

Nestled between Quercy and Limousin lay the Viscounty of Turenne with its eighty-eight parishes and its two assemblies of the
estates, both summoned by the viscount as feudal lord. Occasionally
the two assemblies met together especially in the eighteenth century,
but the more common practice was to meet separately to vote gifts for
the viscounts. Only with the reunion to the crown in 1738 did these
assemblies cease to meet. This interesting feudal survival has been the
subject of two studies.[74] There is little need for further research.

The rich archives in Agenais, however, remain to be exploited.
Here in the middle ages there were assemblies of the three estates,
but during the course of the sixteenth century the more common
practice came to be for the *consuls* or deputies of the towns and communities to meet alone to deal with taxation and other matters. Often
the initiative in convoking the estates was taken by the *consuls* of
Agen and they generally headed deputations to Paris and served as
syndics of the *sénéchaussée*. The estates met several times annually until the early seventeenth century when both Henry IV and Louis
XIII sought to limit the number of assemblies to about one a year.
Even the edict creating an *élection* in Agenais did not bring the activities of the estates to an immediate end. There was, however, a
notable decline in the late 1620's. Assemblies of the twelve principal
towns came more and more to be substituted for the assemblies of
the estates and even these appear to have ceased altogether after 1679.
The archives of the estates of Agenais[75] are the richest in southwestern France and provide an admirable opportunity to study the
activities of the bourgeois patricians of Agen in regard to the crown,
the local royal officials, and the inhabitants of the smaller towns

73. M. J. Baudel, *Notes pour servir à l'histoire des États provinciaux du
Quercy* (Cahors, 1881). There are a few documents at AD, Lot, especially in ser.
F; and in the manuscript collection of the Bibl. Mun. de Cahors. AC, Cahors,
Gourdan, Moissac, Figeac, etc., contain a little as do the BN and AD, Gironde,
ser. C. A few documents have been published in Edmond Cabié, *Guerres de reli-
gion dans le sud-ouest de la France et principalement dans le Quercy* (Paris, 1906).

74. René Fage, *Les États de la vicomté de Turenne* (2 vols.; Paris, 1894). Jean
Bressac, *Privilèges, libertés et franchises de la vicomité de Turenne* (Toulouse,
1922).

75. The archives are a part of AC, Agen, and are located in AD, Lot-et-
Garonne. Additional material may be found in the communal archives in the
area, some of which have also been transferred to AD, Lot-et-Garonne.

and communities. Tholin's writings suggest rather than fully exploit the possibilities.[76]

The clergy rarely attended the estates of Armagnac, but the other two orders met frequently until the mid-1620's when the *élus* assumed their tax-collecting functions. Meetings thereafter were exceptional. The *sénéchaussée* was divided into seven *collectes* and each *collecte* had its assembly that was usually attended by a few nobles and the deputies of the towns and communities. A least one of these little estates continued to function until the end of the seventeenth century. For Vic-Fezensac there are a large number of *procès-verbaux*[77] and for Bas-Armagnac there are several for the period 1632–1634.[78] The assemblies of the *collecte* of Auch could be studied through the registers of the deliberations of that town and for the seventeenth century the registers of Isle-Jourdain provide some information on the *collecte* of that name.[79] The estates of the viscounty of Bruilhois with its capital of La Plume, a hilltop community that was taxed on the basis of having only sixteen hearths, provides an opportunity to study the small rural communities. No *procès-verbaux* have been found, but the registers of the deliberations of the councils of La Plume and several other localities are rich enough to justify research from the late sixteenth century.[80] Both Isle-Jourdain and Bruilhois were part of the *aides* of Agenais and

76. G. Tholin, "La Ville d'Agen pendant les guerres de religion du XVIe siècle," *Revue de l'Agenais*, Vol. XIV (1887) —Vol. XX (1893); "Des Tailles et des impositions au pays d'Agenais durant le XVIe siècle jusqu'aux réformes de Sully," *Recueil des travaux de la soc. d'agriculture, sciences, et arts d'Agen*, Vol. XIII (1875); "Les Cahiers du pays d'Agenais au États généraux," *Revue de l'Agenais*, Vol. X (1883) —Vol. XII (1885); "Documents relatifs aux guerres de religion tirés des archives municipales d'Agen," *Archives historiques du département de la Gironde*, XXIX (1894), 1–282. For the earlier period, see T. N. Bisson, "An Early Provincial Assembly: The General Court of Agenais in the Thirteenth Century," *Speculum*, XXXVI (1961), 254–81.

77. They are in AC, Vic-Fezensac, now located in AD, Gers. See E suppl. 23, 985–23,987, for scattered *procès-verbaux* of the sixteenth and seventeenth centuries and above all E suppl. 23,936, which contains the *procès-verbaux* of the estates between 1598 and 1671. They are bound in a register, but are not in chronological order. Z. Baqué, "Vic-Fezensac au temps de la Fronde," *Bul. de la soc. archéologique du Gers*, XXXVI (1935), 40–53, has made limited use of this valuable document.

78. AC, Nogaro, AA 11. These archives in AD, Gers.

79. AC, Auch and AC, Isle-Jourdain, are now in AD, Gers.

80. AC, Layrac and AC, Fals, are in AD, Lot-et-Garonne, but AC, La Plume, is still in the commune.

also deputed to the estates of that *sénéchaussée*. Very little survives on the estates of Armagnac beyond what is in the *procès-verbaux* of the estates of the *collectes* and the deliberations of the councils of the towns, but there is probably enough on its assemblies and those of its *collectes* for a good book.[81]

The estates of Condomois, Bazadais, and Astarac should also be studied together because they were in the same financial jurisdiction. Very little is known about these assemblies, but it seems probable that the estates of Condomois divided the tax between the three localities in an assembly attended by the deputies of the towns of Condomois and the syndics of Bazadais and Astarac. The estates of Bazadais and Astarac then met separately to divide the tax between the parishes of their respective jurisdictions and to discuss other matters. Almost no *procès-verbaux* have been found concerning these meetings, but it is known that both the nobility and the third estate participated in Astarac. There were also estates in Albret that named deputies to the Estates-General, but in tax matters the individual towns deputed to the estates of Condomois or of Bazadais, depending on their location. As elsewhere the estates ceased to meet regularly soon after the edict was issued in 1621 turning the area into a *pays d'élection*.[82]

The estates of Rivière-Verdun consisted of deputies from twelve towns. Its archives have been lost and Contrasty has extracted what

81. In addition to the above sources a little material may be found in AC, Lectoure, ser. BB and CC. Published works are Paul Parfouru and J. de Carsalade du Pont, "Comptes consulaires de la ville de Riscle de 1441 à 1507," *Archives Historiques de la Gascogne*, XII (1892), esp. I, xvii–xxvi; A. Branet, "Les États d'Armagnac en 1631–32," *Bul. de la soc. archéologique du Gers*, XIV (1913), 168–83, 214–29; J. Duffour, "Députés de l'Armagnac aux États généraux d'Orléans en 1649," *Revue de Gascogne*, LX (1924), 31–33.

82. For Condomois, See AC, Condom, now located in AD, Gers. AA 16, containing twenty-two documents on the estates, could not be found when I was there. However, the deliberations of the municipal council are very detailed from 1588. The deliberations of the councils of Mézin, Astaffort, and Francescas located in AD, Lot-et-Garonne, are valuable from about the same time. For Bazadais the deliberations of the councils in AC, Réole, AC, Monségur, and to a lesser extent AC, Couthures (in AD, Lot-et-Garonne), contain material. For Albret the deliberations of the councils of Casteljaloux, Meilhan, Monheurt, Fieux, Moncrabeau, for the most part in AD, Lot-et-Garonne, contain material as do the deliberations of the council of Tartas located in AD, Lannes. For Astarac see Duffour, "Les États d'Astarac de 1582," *Revue de Gascogne*, ser. 2, VI (1906), 19–30.

there is of value from a variety of sources. Once more meetings ceased to be regular after the creation of the *élection,* the last-known one taking place in 1654.[83]

Mlle Darbin has just completed a thesis for the *École des Chartes* on the estates of Comminges. Her work, when published, will undoubtedly supplant previous studies, but the rich archives of these estates and the published documents drawn from them are of use to historians of the estates of Guyenne and of the neighboring smaller estates. As elsewhere the establishment of an *élection* in the 1620's reduced the role of the estates; assemblies became infrequent, the last-known one being in 1673.[84]

It is surprising that the estates of Rouergue has never found a historian.[85] All three orders participated actively in its proud history. In between the annual sessions the bishop of Rodez presided over numerous meetings of an executive committee of twelve elected by the estates to administer the affairs of the *sénéchaussée.* Regular meetings of the estates ceased with the establishment of the *élus* in the mid-1620's, the last-known assembly being in 1674. There were also estates in the Haute-Marche, the Basse-Marche, and the county of Rodez including four *châtellenies.* Sufficient documents may be

83. Contrasty, *Histoire de Sainte-Foy-de-Peyrolières* (Toulouse, 1917), pp. 198–210. See also Abbè Galabert, "Note sur les États de Rivière-Verdun," *Bul. de lo soc. archéologique du midi de la France,* X (1897), 105–10.

84. The archives of the estates are in AD, Haute-Garonne, C 3401–C 3807. Published documents on the estates include Jean Lestrade, "Les Huguenots en Comminges," *Archives historiques de la Gascogne,* ser. II, Vols. XIV, XV (1910–11); and "Cahiers des remonstrances des États de Comminges aux rois de France ou à leurs lieutenants généraux en Guyenne, 1537–1627," *Soc. des études du Comminges,* Vol. II (1943). See also B. de Gorsse, "Cahier documental concernant le pais et les États de Comminges," *Revue de Comminges,* XLVI (1932), 5–28; V. Fons, "Les États de Comminges," *Mém. de la soc. archéologique du midi de la France,* VIII (1861–65), 161–206; and L. Sahuqué de Goty, "Deux documents sur les États de Comminges et de Nébouzan ou rôle des assemblées provinciales sous l'ancien régime," *Revue de Comminges,* XIX (1904), 177–84.

85. Marc-A. de Gaujal, *Études historiques sur le Rouergue* (4 vols.; Paris, 1858–59); L. Guirondet, "Mémoire sur les États du Rouergue," *Mém. de la soc. des lettres, sciences et arts de l'Aveyron,* Vol. IX (1859–67); and L.-C.-P. Bosc, *Mémoires pour servir à l'histoire du Rouergue* (3 vols.; Rodez, 1797), are of very little value. H. Affre, *Dictionnaire des institutions, moeurs et coutumes du Rouergue,* (Rodez, 1903); and Jacques Bousquet, *En Rouergue à travers le temps* (Rodez, 1961), pp. 89–91, are helpful but much too brief.

found to support a study of these estates in the middle ages as well as the later period.[86]

The Estates in the Pyrénées.—The Pyrénées boasted a large number of representative institutions that survived until the Revolution. There is a certain unity to their history, for during the middle ages and renaissance most of the region belonged to the house of Foix-Navarre. The various estates came directly under the authority of the crown between 1589 and 1620 and were seriously threatened by the creation of *élections* in 1632. The following year they won a reprieve although limits were placed on many of their activities at the same time. The geographical similarity of the region and the historical parallels in the development of the estates offer an ideal situation for a comparative study. The value of such a work is enhanced by the fact that the composition of the various estates and their procedures varied greatly. In a microcosm one can study nearly every type of European representative institution. There were one-, two-, and three-house legislatures; there were some that were dominated by the nobility and others by the third estate. Some were very aristocratic with the lower clergy and the inhabitants of the villages being excluded and the lesser nobility being relegated to a secondary status. Other assemblies practiced an almost pure form of democracy. Two excellent comparative studies exist for the eighteenth century.[87] Sim-

86. The archives of the estates of Rouergue are in AD, Aveyron, ser. C. In view of the prominent role played by the bishop of Rodez, ser. G is of unusual value. AC, Millau, and AC, Rodez (cité), are especially valuable and AC, Rodez (Bourg), AC, Conques (in AD, Aveyron), AC, Saint-Affrique, and AC, Ville-franche-de-Rouergue, contain material. Published documents include C. Couderc, "Notes sur les fastes consulaires de B. Arribat et documents sur l'histoire de Villefranche," *Mém. de la soc. des lettres, sciences et arts de l'Aveyron,* XIV (1893), 119–294; J Artières, "Documents sur la ville de Millau," *Archives historiques du Rouergue,* Vol. VII (1930); "Mémoire sur la tenue des États de Rouergue, écrit vers 1623, par Durieux, député du pays de Rouergue," *Bul. philologique et historique du comité des travaux historiques et scientifiques* (1885), pp. 23–27; and C. Valade, "Réunion des États de la province de Rouergue à Ville-franche en 1649," *Mém. de la soc. des lettres, sciences et arts de l'Aveyron,* XVII (1906–11), 438–44.

87. Maurice Bordes, *D'Étigny et l'administration de l'intendance d'Auch, 1751–1767* (Auch, 1957), I, 254–303; and H. Jolly and H. Courteault, "Essai sur le régime financier des petits pays d'états du midi de la France au XVIIIe siècle," *Bul. de la soc. des sciences, lettres et arts de Pau,* ser. 2, LIV (1931)–LVI (1933). There are unpublished eighteenth-century documents for most of these estates in the AN, ser. H¹.

ilar works on the earlier, formative period of the estates would be of even greater interest.

There are also opportunities to study several of the estates individually. Other estates have already found their historian or cannot be studied because of a scarcity of documents.

The *bilçar* or estates of Labourd was one of the most democratic institutions in Europe. When the syndic thought it advisable, he directed, with the approval of a local royal official, the forty parishes in the jurisdiction to send a *jurat* to the estates at Ustaritz. Here the syndic presented propositions that required a solution, the *jurat* returned to his parish, assembled every head of a house to discuss the syndic's propositions, and then returned to Ustaritz to a second assembly to report the decision of his parish. The will of the majority of the parishes ruled. Unfortunately, few documents concerning this bizarre institution survive for the period prior to the eighteenth century and its historian has not been able to offer a satisfactory explanation of why the nobility and clergy did not participate or why the refer-back system was used in lieu of giving proxies to the *jurats*.[88]

The assembly of the third estate of Soule operated in a somewhat similar manner, but here the nobility and clergy seated together in a separate chamber were able to dominate proceedings. In 1730–1731 the third estate abandoned the refer-back system and the towns began to give their representatives proxies. The estates have been studied only for the eighteenth century, but there is insufficient documentation to support research on the earlier period.[89]

The dismemberment of the kingdom of Navarre as a result of the Spanish conquest left the small portion of that little country on the northern side of the Pyrénées without any estates. As a result a new institution, the Estates-General of Basse-Navarre, was created about 1523. It was divided into two chambers, one for the clergy and nobility and one for the third estate. The three orders often deliberated together, but they voted separately. Two estates could give the law to the third except in matters of finance when the third estate had the final say. Only the upper clergy was admitted, even the chapters

88. Étienne Dravasa, *Les privilèges des Basques du Labourd dans l'ancien régime* (Saint-Sabastien, 1952), contains a good study of the *bilçar*.

89. M. Etcheverry, "À travers l'histoire anecdotique de Bayonne et des pays voisins," *Bul. de la soc. des sciences, lettres et arts de Bayonne*, No. 22 (1937), pp. 107–18. N. Saint-Saëns, "Contribution à un essai sur la coutume de Soule," *Bul. de la soc des sciences, lettres et arts de Bayonne*, No. 34 (1940), pp. 85–97.

having no representation; but all owners of noble houses could enter. No distinction was drawn between the nobles because land in Navarre was alodial and a feudal hierarchy was almost nonexistent. Five towns named deputies directly to the third estate, but the remaining communities sent deputies to assemblies in seven *pays* or valleys where, in turn, deputies were chosen to attend the Estates-General. As these assemblies of the *pays* or valleys met frequently for purposes other than to elect deputies to the Estates-General, there were a goodly number of representative institutions in the tiny kingdom. These assemblies used the refer-back system and other procedures similar to the *bilçar* of Labourd except that the nobility was permitted to participate.

The archives of the Estates-General of Navarre are not especially rich for the period before the personal reign of Louis XIV, but Daranatz has been able to find enough material for a study of estates during the sixteenth century and Destrée has published one on the following period. Both accounts are good, but both rely almost entirely on the institutional approach and the reader emerges with little sense of the chronological development of the estates, a disappointing fact in view of the special relation between the little kingdom and the crown of France. Destrée describes the assemblies of the *pays* and valleys insofar as documentation permits.[90]

There were in a sense four orders in the viscounty of Béarn, some distinction being drawn between the barons and the lesser nobility. The estates, however, was divided into two chambers, one for the clergy, barons, and lesser nobles, and one for the third estate. Voting was done by head in the *Grand Corps,* or upper house, and by community in the lower, each individual vote being carefully recorded in the *procès-verbaux* of the estates. Thus for Béarn, almost alone among the provincial estates of France or for that matter of Europe, the historian can ascertain how each individual or community stood on each issue that was presented to the estates. A unique opportunity is thereby presented for a Namier-like study in which family, religious, and regional alignments are sure to play an important role. A

90. J. B. Daranatz, "Les États de Basse-Navarre au XVIe siècle," *Gure Herria,* Vol. III (1923), and Vol. IV (1924). Alain Destrée, *La Basse-Navarre et ses institutions de 1620 à la révolution* (Zaragoza, n.d.). To the above should be added F. Olivier-Martin, "La Réunion de la Basse-Navarre à la couronne de France," *Anuario de historia del derecho español,* IX (1932), 249–89. For specific data on the archives which are located in AD, Basses-Pyrénées, and for other published works see Destrée, pp. 447–63.

study of the relation between the estates, the house of Foix-Navarre, and finally the crown of France would also be of great interest because of the claims of Béarn to be a sovereign state and because of the powerful position the Protestants achieved there during the late sixteenth century.

The archives of the estates of Béarn are very rich for the renaissance and old regime, but this very fact has probably caused historians to be hesitant to study this period.[91] The continued use of Béarnais well into the seventeenth century and the unusually difficult handwriting in the *procès-verbaux* may have added to their reluctance. Cadier has written a good study of the medieval estates and he and Courteault have published some documents. Rogé has made additional contributions to this period.[92] Dartigue-Peyrou has published two volumes on Béarn between 1517 and 1572, but almost nothing has been done on the later period.[93]

The viscounty of Marsan was a part of the estates of Béarn until 1607 when a separate assembly consisting only of the third estate was established. In the eighteenth century it was further divided with one assembly for Mont-de-Marsan and the thirty-two neighboring parishes and one for the twenty-two or twenty-three remaining communities known as the estates of the *bastilles*. There is insufficient documentation to study these assemblies prior to the middle of the eighteenth century.[94]

91. The archives of the estates of Béarn are in AD, Basses-Pyrénées, C 679–C 1525. The *établissements* or complaints of the estates begin in 1436, the series of financial documents in 1487, and the *procès-verbaux* in 1558.

92. Cadier, *Les États de Béarn depuis leurs origines jusqu'au commencement du XVIᵉ siècle* (Paris, 1888); and "Le Livre des syndics des États de Béarn," *Archives historiques de la Gascogne*, Vol. XVIII (1889). Paul Courteault, "Le Livre des syndics des États de Béarn," *ibid.*, ser. 2, Vol. X (1906). P. Rogé, *Les Anciens fors de Béarn* (Paris, 1908).

93. Charles Dartigue-Peyrou, *La Vicomté de Béarn sous le règne d'Henri II d'Albret, 1517–1555* (Paris, 1934), is an excellent general history of Béarn in the period indicated, but the estates is only incidentally treated. His *Jeanne d'Albret et le Béarn d'après les delibérations des États et les registres du Conseil souverain, 1555–1572* (Mont-de-Marsan, 1934), contains a brief description of the estates and many documents. See also Paul Raymond's introduction to *IAC, Basses-Pyrénées*, ser. C and D, (Paris, 1865), III, 58–138; and J. de Bertier, "Les Réceptions aux États de Béarn dans l'ordre de la noblesse," *Actes XIIIᵉ congrès fédération des soc. académiques et savantes Languedoc-Pyrénées-Gascogne, Tarbes, 1957* (1959), pp. 157–61.

94. Henri Tartière, *IAC, Landes*, ser. A-F (Paris, 1868), Introduction, pp. 15–16.

The estates of Bigorre consisted of three chambers, one for each estate. Most of the clergy, including the chapters, were excluded. A distinction was drawn between the barons and lesser nobility, but the third estate was more democratic. Some towns and communities named deputies directly to the estates, others deputed to one of the assemblies held in five valleys where in turn deputies were named to the estates. The archives of the estates of Bigorre[95] contain little for the medieval-renaissance historians, but there was enough here and in other depositories to provide the basis for a good institutional study of the later period.[96] A chronological history would be of some value.

The estates of Quatre-Vallées had a single chamber that was composed of deputies of the third estate. In addition, there were active assemblies in each of the four valleys. The nobility sometimes sought, but with little success, to be included. The archives of the estates contain sufficient material for a history from the late seventeenth century, but it has very little for the earlier period except for some of the estates of the individual valleys, especially between 1622 and 1637.[97] To date almost no research has been done on these institutions.[98]

All three orders participated in the estates of Nébouzan, where they often sat in one chamber but voted apart. Not many documents

---

In AD, Landes, see esp. C 154. Abbé-Bessellère, "Étude sur la ville communale d'une petite ville dans le Marsan au commencement du XVIIIe siècle," *Bul. de la soc. de Borda*, XIII (1888), 304–6.

95. The archives are in AD, Hautes-Pyrénées.

96. Gilbert Pene, *Les Attributions financières des États du pays et comté de Bigorre aux XVIIe et XVIIIe siècles* (thèse, doctorat de droit, U. de Bordeaux, 1959). A copy of this thesis is at AD, Hautes-Pyrénées. It completely replaces Gustave Bascle de Legrèze, *Histoire du droit dans les Pyrénées* (Paris, 1867), pp. 70–92, and may be consulted for archival and bibliographical material on the estates.

97. The archives are at AD, Hautes-Pyrénées, C 279—C 349 bis. See C 284—C 288 for the assemblies of the individual valleys, 1622–37.

98. See Armand Sarramon, *Les Quatre-Vallées: Aure, Barousse, Neste, Magnoac* (Albi, 1954), pp. 282–86; F. Marsan, "Réglement des États du pays des Quatre-Vallées au XVIIIe siècle," *Bul. de la soc. archéologique du Midi de la France*, No. 19 (1896–97), pp. 136–42; Marsan, "La Déclaration du dixième et le pays des Quatre-Vallées en 1741," *Bul. de la soc. académique des Hautes-Pyrénées* (1927), pp. 89–93; and L. Ricaud, "Un Régime qui finit," *Soc. académique des Hautes-Pyrénées. Bul. local*, V (1901–4), 269–358, 367–448.

concerning this institution have been found and no one has attempted to write its history.[99]

All three orders also participated in the estates of Foix, but here they sat in one chamber and voted together. Not many documents on the estates have been found before the reign of Louis XIV, but there were enough to permit Arnaud to prepare an institutional study.[100] There were no provincial estates in Roussillon, but the estates of the valley of Andorra, so like those of the French Pyrénées before the Revolution, is still functioning today.[101]

Brittany.—There is still a need for further research on the estates of Brittany. The study of Carné[102] has some merit, but it was not based on an exhaustive use of the archives and is too brief and too outdated to answer many questions. Sée has published a long article on the estates in the sixteenth century, but he relied almost entirely on the institutional approach.[103] Only from 1661 is there a completely satisfactory history thanks to the efforts of Rebillon.[104] The archives of the estates of Brittany are very rich from about 1567 when the *procès-verbal* begins, and an excellent history could be written from the Wars of Religion until the personal reign of Louis XIV where Rebillon begins his work.[105] One would especially like

99. Most documents on the estates of Nébouzan are in AD, *Haute-Garonne*, C 3113—C 3117, and C 3253—C 3260. See also AD, Basses-Pyrénées, B 1391—B 1404. Published is a seventeeth-century account of the estates by Louis de Froidour, "Mémoire du pays et États de Nébouzan," *Revue de Pyrénées,* III (1891), 94–104, 387–428; J. Lestrade, "Documents inédits sur les États de Nébouzan," *Revue de Comminges,* XX (1905), 18–30, 57–70; Alphonse Couget, *Les États du Nébouzan tenus à Saint-Gaudens en 1743 et 1789* (Saint-Gaudens, 1880); and Ricaud, *Soc. académique des Hautes-Pyrénées. Bul. local,* V (1901–4), 269–358, 367–448.

100. The archives of the estates of Foix are at AD, Ariège, IC 50—IC 52, IC 189—IC 238. See also C. de La Hitte, "Lettres inédites de Henri IV à M. de Pailhès, gouverneur du comté de Foix, et aux consuls de la ville de Foix," *Archives historiques de la Gascogne,* Vol. X (1886); and G. Arnaud, *Mémoire sur les États de Foix, 1608–1789* (Toulouse, 1904).

101. Appolis. "Une Assemblée administrative sous un régime féodal dans le monde contemporain: Le Trés Illustre Conseil Général des Vallées d'Andorre," *Schweizer Beriträge zur Allgemeinen Geschichle,* Vol. XV (1957), 191–98.

102. Louis de Carné, *Les États de Bretagne* (2 vols.; Paris, 1862).

103. H. Sée, "Les États de Bretagne au XVIᵉ siècle," *Annales de Bretagne,* X (1894–95), 3–38, 189–207, 365–93, 550–76.

104. Armand Rebillon *Les États de Bretagne de 1661 à 1789* (Rennes, 1932).

105. There is an unpublished study of this period in the library of the *faculté*

to have more knowledge of Richelieu's relation with the estates. He was governor of Brittany and displayed more interest in this province than others. One may suspect that such a study would reveal that the cardinal was less unfriendly to the provincial estates than has been imagined.[106] Rebillons' study of the sources of the estates of Brittany makes it unnecessary to mention them here.[107]

Normandy.—The estates of Normandy has the distinction of being the only important provincial assembly for which there is a history from its origins until its demise around the middle of the seventeenth century. In accomplishing this difficult task, Prentout was aided by the fact that the documentation had been reduced to manageable proportions through the loss of the archives of the estates and by the fact that he could utilize the work of Charles de Beaurepaire who had made several specialized studies on the estates and had published many volumes of documents.[108] Prentout's work is excellent in most respects. He employed both the chronological and institutional approach so that the reader is given a clear picture of the slow evolution of the estates and its relation to the crown as well as a view of its composition, procedures, and functions. Prentout's work does, however, have one serious defect. He relied too narrowly on sources specifically on the estates and neglected other related materials such as the unpublished correspondence of the royal officials and the rec-

des lettres in Rennes. It is Besnier, "Les États de Bretagne de 1598 à 1643." I have not yet seen this work.

106. See especially the Archives du Ministère des Affaires Étrangères, mémoires et documents, France, MSS. 1504–6.

107. Rebillon, *Les Sources de l'histoire des États de Bretagne* (Rennes, 1932). Special attention should be called to Charles de La Lande de Calan, "Documents inédits relatifs aux États de Bretagne de 1491 à 1589," *Archives de Bretagne*, Vol. XV (2 vols.; 1908–9). Since Rebillon wrote, several articles have been published in local journals on individual meetings of the estates.

108. H. Prentout, "Les États provinciaux de Normandie," *Mém. de l'ac. nationale des sciences, arts et belles-lettres de Caen*, N.S., Vols. 1–III (1925–27). As Prentout includes a bibliography of the sources and published works on the estates of Normandy there is no need to repeat them here. However, special attention should be called to the eight excellent volumes of documents published by Charles de Robillard de Beaurepaire, *Cahiers des États de Normandie sous le règne de Charles IX; Henri III; Henri IV; and Louis XIII et de Louis XIV* (8 vols.; Rouen, 1876–91. Included are not only the *cahiers* of the estates, but other important documents. See also M. Baudot, "La Réprésentation du tiers-état aux États provinciaux de Normandie," *Mém. de l'ac. des sciences, arts et belles-lettres de Caen*, N.S., V (1929), 127–47.

ords of the king's council. This neglect is not very serious for the sixteenth century, perhaps, because the quantity of such material is not too great, but his failure to consult such huge collections as the Bellièvre and Séguier papers in the Bibliothèque Nationale and the Richelieu and Mazarin Papers in the Archives du Ministère des Affaires Étrangères seriously reduces the value of the last portion of his work. There is still need for a study that will provide a satisfactory explanation of why the provincial estates of Nomandy ceased to meet during the middle third of the seventeenth century.

The Estates in the Newly Acquired Territories.—During the reigns of Louis XIV and Louis XV the territory of France was expanded in the direction of the Low Countries and the Holy Roman Empire, and the island of Corsica was acquired. Nearly all the newly acquired provinces had estates. In some instances the French monarchy permitted them to continue to exist; in others it did not. An interesting study could be written explaining the factors that led to the divergent policies of the crown. In addition, there is still need for further research on some of the individual estates.[109]

There were several representative institutions in the territories acquired by France at the expense of the Low Countries. The most important of these was the estates of Artois. This institution has been the subject of an excellent study by Hirschauer from its origins until the French conquest in 1640.[110] For the next twenty-one years the estates was inactive, but it was revived by Louis XIV in 1661 and met frequently from that time until the Revolution. The archives of the estates offer a rich source for the study of the estates of this period.[111]

The estates of Walloon Flanders (or of Lille as it was sometimes called) was favorably treated by Louis XIV and met regularly

109. Since I do not plan to carry my own research on the provincial estates beyond the reign of Louis XIII, I have not visited the archives in the newly acquired provinces and have not made as careful a search for published works as I have elsewhere.

110. Charles Hirschauer, *Les États d'Artois de leurs origines à l'occupation française, 1340–1640* (2 vols.; Paris, 1923).

111. The archives are located in AD, Pas-de-Calais. There are two studies on the estates after the French occupation, but François Filon, *Histoire des États d'Artois depuis leur origine jusqu'à leur suppression en 1789* (Paris and Arras, 1861), is superficial; and G. Bellart, "L' Organisation et le rôle financier des États d'Artois de 1661 à 1789," *Positions des thèses de l'École des Chartes* (1956), pp. 23–28, is a descriptive study published as an abstract.

until the Revolution. Its activities have been the subject of a brief superficial study by Melun. A newer work exploiting the archival sources would be welcome.[112] The estates of Cambrésis was equally well treated by the French kings and has been better treated by the historians, no less than three studies having been made of its activities.[113]

The large and important provincial estates in the eastern territories acquired by France displayed less capacity for survival, although the vicissitudes of the Thirty Years War were often as much to blame as the French crown. The estates of Lorraine and Bar, for example, met for the last time in 1629, years before the French conquest. Duvernoy has provided us with an excellent study of the history of this institution until 1559, but except for an article on the assembly of 1626 nothing of value has been done on the last seventy years of the history of the estates.[114] The archives seem to provide ample sources for a study of this period and it would be of special interest to find out why the estates ceased to be convoked at the very time the existence of so many of the French provincial estates was threatened. There were also separate assemblies for the duchy of Bar.

The estates of Alsace underwent a crisis beginning in 1627, but the institution enjoyed a brief revival after the Thirty Years War when assemblies were once more frequent. The French acquisition

112. A. Melun, "Histoire des États de Lille," *Mém. de la soc. impériale des sciences, de l'agriculture et des arts de Lille,* ser. 2, Vol. VII (1860), ser. 3, Vol. I (1864), ser. 3, Vol. II (1865), ser. 3, Vol. IV (1867), ser. 3, Vol. VI (1868), ser. 3, Vol. VII (1869). There seems to be adequate material for a history of these estates in AD, Nord, ser. C, AC, Lille, AC, Douai, and elsewhere. For these and other estates of the region the Archives Générales du Royaume de Belgique and the manuscript collection in the Bibliothèque Royale de Belgique at Brussels should be consulted for the period before the French conquest and AN, H^I, for the period after the conquest.

113. Marc-R. Vilette, *Les États généraux du Cambrésis de 1677 à 1790* (Cambrai, 1950); A. Wilbert, "Les États du Cambrésis," *Mém. de la soc. d'émulation de Cambrai,* XXXI (1872), 247–308; and A. Durieux, "Les États provinciaux du Cambrésis," *Mém. de la soc. d' émulation de Cambrai,* XLI (1886), 131–245.

114. Émile Duvernoy, *Les États généraux des duchés de Lorraine et de Bar jusqu'à la majorité de Charles III* (Paris, 1904). R. Taveneaux, "Les États généraux de Lorraine de l'année 1626," *Annales de l'Est,* ser. 5, II (1951), 15–36. See these two works for bibliographical material. The archives of the estates do not appear to have survived, but the departmental archives, especially of Meurthe-et-Moselle, and the communal archives of the province contain many documents. Attention should also be called to the Lorraine collection in the BN.

quickly terminated its activity, the last meeting being in 1683. There is an adequate study of the estates of Müller.[115]

The estates of Franche-Comté had a long and active history that was abruptly terminated by the French conquest in 1674. Clerc has given us a somewhat romanticized chronological political history of its activities that could be improved upon.[116] His failure to describe how the estates functioned as an institution or to exploit the social-economic data that this institution provides opens further possibilities for research. Four volumes of documents located in the Bibliothèque Nationale have been published, and additional material may be found in AD, Doubs, and the communal archives of the province.[117]

The archives of the estates of Comté Venaissin are among the oldest and richest in France with registers of deliberations dating back to 1404.[118] The early history of the estates until 1594 has been studied by Giraud and its final years, 1774–1791, by Mouret, but no one has yet exploited the rich opportunities offered by the intervening one hundred eighty years which saw several brief periods of French rule.[119]

The climate of opinion had changed so much by 1768 when France acquired Corsica that provincial estates were actually established on the island modeled somewhat after those of Languedoc. Villat has devoted some attention to this institution in his general study, but there seems to be an opportunity for further work both here and on an earlier representative assembly.[120]

Other Representative Institutions.—There are several other types of representative institutions that merit consideration, the most important of which was the general assemblies of the clergy. This institution was born at Poissy in 1561 and met periodically until the Revolu-

115. Friedrich W. Müller, *Die elsässischen Landstände. Ein beitrag zur geschichte des Elsasses* (Strassburg, 1907).

116. Édouard Clerc, *Histoire des États généraux et des libertés publiques en Franche-Comté* (2 vols.; Lons-le-Saunier, 1881).

117. Adolphe de Troyes, *La Franche-Comté de Bourgogne sous les princes espagnols de la maison d'Autriche. Les Recès des États* (4 vols.; Paris, 1847). See also A. Thiboudet, "Trois recès inédits des États de Franche-Comté," *Mém. de la soc. d'émulation du Jura*, Vol. XXXVII (1873).

118. The archives of the estates are in AD, Vaucluse (Avignon), ser. C.

119. Joseph Girard, *Les États du Comté Venaissin depuis leurs origines jusqu'à la fin du XVIᵉ siècle* (Paris, 1908), extract from the *Mém. de l'académie de Vaucluse*, Vols. XXV–XXVI (1906–7). François Mouret, *Les Assemblées de pays du Comté Venaissin à la veille de la révolution française* (Nimes, 1952).

120. Louis Villat, *La Corse de 1768 à 1789* (2 vols.; Besançon, 1924–25).

tion to vote "free gifts" to the crown. It has been the subject of several collections of documents and many studies, the most important being those of Serbat, Blet, and Lepointe.[121] The assemblies of the clergy in the individual dioceses, however, have received scant attention and studies of several of them would be welcome.[122]

In view of all that has been said about the contributions of Calvin and Calvinism toward representative government, it seems strange that so little research has been done on the French Protestant assemblies where the reformer's influence was presumably most strongly felt. These assemblies were of two types, the synods and the political assemblies, both being organized at the national and local level. At the base of the synod was the consistory of the individual churches, above the consistories were the colloquies, above the colloquies were provincial synods, and above the provincial synods there was a national synod, each type of assembly being composed of both pastors and elders. Several collections of documents concerning the national synods have been published, but there is no detailed modern study of the national or local meetings.[123]

121. Louis Serbat, Les Assemblées du clergé de France. Origines, organisation, développement, 1561–1615 (Paris, 1906). Pierre Blet, Le Clergé de France et la monarchie; étude sur les assemblées générales du clergé de 1615 à 1666 (2 vols.; Rome, 1959). Gabriel Lepointe, L'Organisation et la politique financière du clergé de France sous le règne de Louis XV (Paris, 1923). For sources and secondary works see Blet, II, 433–49.

122. The procès-verbaux and other surviving documents on the assemblies of the clergy of the individual dioceses are generally in the departmental archives, ser. G. For an example of such a study see Appolis, "Les Assemblées financières du clergé dans un diocèse français au XVIIIe siècle," Anciens pays et assemblées d'ètats, XXIV (1962), 177–90.

123. The acts of the national synods have been published in English by John Quick, Synodicon in Gallia reformata: or the Acts, Decisions, Decrees and Canons of those Famous National Councils of the Reformed Churches in France (2 vols.; London, 1692); and in French by Jean Aymon, Tous les synodes nationaux des Églises réformées de France (2 vols.; La Haye, 1710). Élie Benoist, Histoire de l'édit de Nantes (5 vols.; Delft, 1693–95), contains many documents. The French Protestant movement in general has been studied by John Viénot, Histoire de la réforme française des origines à l'édict de Nantes (Paris, 1926); and Histoire de la réforme française de l'édit de Nantes à sa révocation (Paris, 1934). Jacques Pannier, L'Église réformée de Paris sous Louis XIII, 1610–1621 (Strasbourg, 1922); and L'Église réformée de Paris sous Louis XIII de 1621 à 1629 (2 vols.; Paris, 1931–32), are valuable for the periods indicated. M. Reulos, "Synodes, assemblées politiques des réformés français et théories des états," Anciens pays et assemblées

The political assemblies of the French Protestants have been nearly as neglected, for the often-cited work of Anquez is inadequate in many respects.[124] Fortunately, there are signs of renewed interest in these institutions.[125] The holdings of the departmental archives concerning the Protestants are on the whole disappointing,[126] but there are numerous and valuable manuscripts in the Bibliothèque Nationale,[127] the Paris library of the Société de l'histoire du protestantisme francais, and to a lesser extent the Bibliothèque Mazarine. Loutchitzki has published the *procès-verbaux* of the political assemblies for the period before 1570[128] and Barthélemy for 1620–1622.[129] Professor Gordon Griffiths is now preparing an edition of most or all of the *procès-verbaux* for the intervening years.

Conclusion.—There remain, then, many opportunities for research on the French provincial and local estates and on other types of assemblies. Even those whose interests turn more toward social-economic history can find much of value in the archives of the estates while those who lean more toward political-constitutional history can find no better place to turn. It is to be hoped that the estates will soon be made to yield their all too well-kept secrets of the French monarchy.

d'états, XXIV (1962), 97–111, rejects the idea that Calvinism deeply influenced the organization of French Protestant assemblies.

124. Léonce Anquez, *Histoire des assemblées politiques des réformés de France, 1573–1622* (Paris, 1859).

125. R. Kingdom, "Calvinism and Democracy: Some Political Implications of Debates on French Reformed Church Government, 1562–1574," *The American Historical Review*, LXIX (1964), 393–401. G. Griffiths read a paper before the American Historical Association in 1962 entitled: "Tradition and Reform in the Estates of France and the Low Countries in the Sixteenth Century."

126. There are a few exceptions. See, for example, AD, Gard, C 845, C 846, C 865, C 866, C 1919–C 1922, etc.

127. See especially *Nouvelles acquisitions françaises*, MSS. 7176–97, which contain a number of documents including the *procès-verbaux* of the general political assemblies from 1572 to 1625.

128. J. Loutchitzki, "Collection des procès-verbaux des assemblées politiques des réformés de France pendant le XVIe siècle," *Bul. de la soc. de l'histoire du protestantisme français*, Vol. XXII (1873), Vol. XXIV (1875), Vol. XXVI (1877), and Vol. XLV (1896). The *Bulletin* is also of value for the synods.

129. A. de Barthélemy, "Actes de la assemblée générale des églises réformées de France et souveraineté du Béarn, 1620–1622," *Archives historiques du Poitou*, V (1876), 1–473.

STUDIES IN THE HISTORY OF PUBLIC CREDIT OF GERMAN PRINCIPALITIES AND TOWNS IN THE MIDDLE AGES

by Matthew M. Fryde

Columbia University

Studies in the History of Public Credit of German Principalities and Towns in the Middle Ages

I

IT WAS rightly stressed recently by Dr. E. Miller that the nature and scope of government action in relation to economic affairs are problems of medieval history which still await detailed investigation.[1] It is well known that financial history is the especially neglected stepchild of economic history,[2] and that the financial history of Germany in the middle ages is most neglected. It is relatively easy to discover the causes of the unsatisfactory state of this branch of German historiography. The explanation *per se* also can serve to a certain degree as a justification for the present work.

After the beginning of the thirteenth century the constitutional development of the German Reich and of Western powers began to differ increasingly.[3] The peculiarities of German feudalism as com-

*I wish to express my profound gratitude to the staff of the Columbia University Libraries, and in particular to Miss Mary Lou Lucy and Miss Anne McCabe for their assistance and cooperation.

1. Edward Miller, "Economic Policies of Governments," *Cambridge Economic History of Europe*, III (Cambridge, 1963), 290.

2. In this respect the authoritative statement by Alfons Dopsch, in his article "Finanzwissenschaft," *Vierteljahrschrift für Sozial- und Wirtschaftsgeschichte*, XIV (1918), 509 ff., deserves to be cited. Walter Lotz, *Finanzwissenschaft* (Tübingen, 1917; 2d ed., 1931), p. 19, pointed out: "Vor allem besitzen wir bis heute noch nicht eine die verschiedensten Kulturgebiete berücksichtigende Geschichte des Milieus der Finanzliteratur, eine zusammenfassende Forschung nach ersten Quellen über die Geschichte der Finanzverwaltung und der Einnahmen und Ausgaben. Versuche sind allerdings vorhanden aber noch vieles Material harrt der Verarbeitung, und über vieles besitzen wir nicht einmal Material."

3. A. Schulte, *Der Deutsche Staat, Verfassung, Macht und Grenzen, 919–1914* (Stuttgart, 1933), pp. 70 ff., Heinrich Mitteis, *Lehnrecht und Staatsgewalt* (Weimar, 1933; reprinted Darmstadt, 1958), pp. 448 ff., "Das Reich war, verglichen mit England oder Frankreich, *zu wenig Lehnstaat;* oder genauer gesagt, zu wenig feudaler Machtstaat. . . . Das Reich erlitt einen dauernden Substanzverlust an spezifisch Territorialfürsten abwanderten"; Mitteis, *Der Staat des Hohen Mittelalters* (3d ed.; Weimar, 1948), pp. 400 ff., 501 ff., "An die Stelle der *zentripetalen* trat die *zentri-*

pared to its Western forms must, of course, be taken into consideration.[4] To quote Barraclough, one has to recognize that "the centralized machinery of administration, which in England was in formation in the days of Henry II, had no parallel in Germany, and it
was only later and haltingly that a similar organization was formed
in the principalities."

Following the fall of the Hohenstaufen dynasty and the Great
Interregnum the age of princes brought out clearly the complete
victory of the principle already recognized in the *Confoederatio cum
principibus ecclesiasticis* (1220) and in the *Statutum in favorem principum* (1231/32).[5] The results are known; at the end of the process of

---

fugale Wirkung"; Mitteis, *Deutsche Rechtsgeschichte,* ed. Heinz Lieberich (5th ed.;
Munich and Berlin, 1958), pp. 178 ff., G. Barraclough, *The Origins of Modern
Germany* (2d ed.; Oxford, 1952), pp. 245–46. Hermann Conrad, *Deutsche Rechts-
geschichte,* I. *Frühzeit und Mittelalter* (Karlsruhe, 1954), pp. 427 ff.

4. We cannot enter here into a detailed discussion of the specific character of
German feudalism. It is sufficient to stress that it differed in many respects from
feudalism in England and differences are to be found between the feudal system
in the western and the eastern parts of the German territory. It is well known
that it is impossible according to the modern approaches of contemporary historians to give a precise definition of feudalism which would be valid for all
European countries and cover all epochs. One has to accept the existence of a
variety of feudalisms. Cf. Mitteis, *Lehnrecht und Staatsgewalt,* p. 2, "Ebensowenig
wie es 'die' Gothik, 'die' Scholastik, 'die' Mystik usw. gibt, *ebensowenig gibt es
das mittelalterliche Lehnrecht als solches.* . . . Es gibt eine Mehrheit von Lehn-
rechten." See also James Westfall Thompson, *Feudal Germany* (Chicago, 1928),
pp. 292–94, 296–99, 312; G. O. Sayles, *The Medieval Foundations of England*
(Philadelphia, 1950), p. 199; Max Weber, *Wirtschaft und Gesellschaft,* ed. F.
Winckelmann (4th ed.; Tübingen, 1956), pp. 148 ff.; Otto Hintze, "Wesen und
Verbreitung des Feudalismus," *Sitzungsberichte der Preussischen Akademie der
Wissenschaften,* Phil.-Histor. Klasse (Berlin, 1929); F. L. Ganshof, *Feudalism*
(London, New York, and Toronto, 1952), pp. xvii–xviii; Marc Bloch, *Feudal
Society,* trans. L. A. Manyon (Chicago, 1901), because of its special methodological
approach cannot be referred to without some reservations. See, however, pp. xix ff.,
441 ff. The recent study by Otto Brunner, "Feudalismus: Ein Beitrag zur
Begriffsgeschichte," *Abhandlungen der Akademie der Wissenschaften und der
Literatur in Mainz,* Geistes- und sozialwissenschaftliche Klasse, 1958 (Wiesbaden,
1959), p. 592, on the whole agrees with the prevailing theory.

5. The evaluation of the role of these privileges granted to the princes in
shaping the structure of medieval Germany recently became a subject of revisionism
which cannot be discussed here. See K. Hampe and F. Baethgen, *Deutsche Kaiser-
geschichte in der Zeit der Salier und Staufer* (9th ed.; Leipzig, 1946), pp. 285 ff.;
Mitteis, "Zum Mainzer Reichslandfrieden," in Mitteis, *Rechtsidee in der Geschichte*
(1957), pp. 416–17.

decentralization and of the forming of territories, i.e., of *Landesherr-schaften,* the rulers of which—lay or ecclesiastic—became *domini terrae,* about 300 *Länder* came into being, each with its own independent financial structure and organization.

Whatever were the consequences of these great events, insofar as the unity of the old Empire is concerned, the new "age of princes" and the network of territories with independent political life, constitute per se a radical turning away from the old feudal state. Gradually, instead of a *Lehnstaat,* a *Beamtenstaat* was coming into being. During the era of romantic dreams in the first half of the nineteenth century, the disappearance of the strong German Empire in the middle of the thirteenth century was lamented by many German patriots. The historian of the financial institutions must accept, however, the sober statement of Alfons Dopsch, who, in his review of Lotz' textbook of public finance (see n. 7) pointed out that one should not see in the process of disruption in the thirteenth century only negative elements, and that in the sphere of the development of financial institutions important positive results were achieved by the principalities. His words deserve to be quoted in order to be remembered:

> that which the kingdom did not succeed in accomplishing in the Empire, the territorial lords now accomplished in the smaller circle of the German territories: the domination of feudal power and the founding of an unified administration dependent upon the princes. Here in the territories advances were also made in fiscal administration which elsewhere were the product of monarchy.

Dopsch's view is accepted by many eminent contemporary German scholars, among them Planitz, Th. Mayer, and Mitteis. It is obvious that a historical analysis of medieval finances in Germany cannot be restricted to the examination of the finances of the Empire but must also be largely based on the study of the financial development of the principalities—if not of all of them at least of the most important ones. This is by no means a simple task in view of their great number and variety. No wonder that such an all-embracing presentation is not yet available, and most probably will not be completed in the near future.

An ambitious undertaking was made forty years ago by Miss Elisabeth Bamberger, who attempted to set up the general picture of the financial development of German principalities during the period 1200–1500. Whatever the good qualities of her study, "Die

Finanzverwaltung in der Deutschen Territorien des Mittelalters 1200–1500"[6]—and there are many—this scholarly work cannot be considered even an adequate brief outline of the financial history of the German principalities. Yet it would be entirely wrong to minimize the great importance of Miss Bamberger's contribution, for it constitutes not only an incentive for a more detailed approach by historians but is a valuable basic guide which deserves careful attention and recognition. To avoid all possible misunderstanding it is imperative to stress that the present brief essay devoted to the history of three principalities by no means pretends to fill up the existing gap. It should be considered only as an attempt to add some new elements to already available descriptions of the finances of the principalities with special emphasis on public credit.

As a result of the eclipse of the imperial power in the thirteenth century, the principalities—the *Landesherrschaften*—gradually became consolidated and in many respects overshadowed the German kings. While royal financial resources failed to expand, the financial organization and wealth of some German principalities were constantly growing. Yet it would be erroneous to assume that the financial structure of the principalities, even if the best organized and administered among them are visualized, was in the thirteenth through fifteenth centuries even distantly similar to that in France or in England. To explain this phenomenon historians took two opposite approaches. Wilhelm Lotz stressed the backwardness of the finances of German medieval rulers compared to those of France or Britain. His statement was criticized by Georg von Below and Alfons Dopsch, while Elisabeth Bamberger supports Lotz's backwardness thesis. A well-balanced, scholarly treatment of the matter was recently given in the second edition of the well-known work of Gerloff and Neumark, *Handbuch der Finanzwissenschaft,* by the great historian and recognized authority Theodor Mayer.

As to Miss Bamberger's view, she refuses to consider the financial organization of the German medieval territories in the fourteenth century as equal to those in France or in England. This is quite understandable, because the political structure of German principalities was somewhat primitive compared with England or France. She concludes her investigation as follows:

6. *Zeitschrift für die gesamte Staatswissenschaft,* LXXVII (Tübingen, 1922–23), 168–255.

One should not wish to place the German territorial states on an equal level with the French and English states. In a garment that fits a giant a dwarf must necessarily suffocate, and if the dwarf grows and the old garment becomes too constricting he is smart enough to get another one.[7]

Bamberger's arguments are convincing: the development of the finances of several of the territories shows clearly that in the fourteenth and fifteenth centuries gradual progress and improvement was achieved. Before we proceed to the analysis of the development of public credit, a few words must be said about the general structure of finances of the territorial rulers,[8] with special emphasis on the peculiarities of organization in Bavaria, Brunswick, and Württemberg.

After the fall of the Hohenstaufen the *ministeriales* in many cases became organs of the administration serving the *domini terrae*, i.e., of the *Landesherren*. They were holders of an office—*Amt*—and therefore such an "officer" was called *Amtmann*.[9] The new institution of

7. See W. Lotz, *Finanzwissenschaft,* p. 5; Below's review in *Weltwirtschaftliches Archiv* (1919), pp. 7 ff., and that of Dopsch in *Vierteljahrschrift für Sozial- und Wirtschaftsgeschichte,* XIV, 509 ff., reprinted in Dopsch, *Verfassungs- und Wirtschaftsgeschichte des Mittelalters* (Vienna, 1928), pp. 359 ff.; Bamberger, *op. cit.,* pp. 52–54; Theodor Mayer, "Geschichte der Finanzwirtschaft vom Mittelalter bis zum Ende des 18. Jahrhunderts," in W. Gerlof and F. Neumark, eds., *Handbuch der Finanzwissenschaft* (2d ed.; Tübingen, 1952), I, 244 ff. Mayer stresses that "Das Reich verlor alle unmittelbaren Einnahmequellen, die ganze Finanzhoheit und die Exekutive lagen fortab in den Händen der Reichsfürsten. Diese verstanden es die Eingänge aus den finanziellen Hoheitsrechten so zu steigern, dass diese in vielen Territorien schon im 13. Jahrhundert die Erträgnisse aus den landesfürstlichen Domänen überragten. . . . Im Territorialstaat wurden die Grundlagen ausgebildet, auf denen sich in politischer und technischer Hinsicht die moderne Finanzwirtschaft entwickelt hat." See also Karl Bosl in B. Gebhardt, *Handbuch der deutschen Geschichte,* I (8th ed.; Stuttgart, 1954), pp. 659–60, 678–84; Mitteis, *Deutsche Rechtsgeschichte,* pp. 148 ff.

8. The best short outline is the above mentioned essay by Miss Elisabeth öffentlichen Machtmitteln ("Regalien" im weitesten Sinne, die zu den späteren Bamberger. It is to be regretted that for some reason she passed over many territories, such as Brunswick, Cologne, Würzburg, Mainz, etc., thus limiting her synthesis to a narrow basis.

9. The institution of *ministeriales,* which is considered by many as a typical German institution, and in particular their origin, remains still, to quote E. E. Stengel (1926), one of "der heikelsten und dunkelsten Probleme der älteren deutschen Ständegeschichte." The appearance of the monumental work of Karl Bosl, *Die Reichsministerialität der Salier und Staufer. Ein Beitrag zur Geschichte des hochmittelalterlichen deutschen Volkes, Staates und Reiches* (Schriftenreihe der

Amtsleute constitutes a radical retreat from the feudal system, and the territory ceased to be a typical feudal state. Gradually a state ruled by "officers"—*Amtsleute*—came into being, each of them exercising his administrative (and also judicial) power over a certain district.[10]

Bavaria, like Salzburg and Tirol, was one of the territories where the feudal forces of administration were overcome very early. Already in the first quarter of the thirteenth century the territory of Bavaria was divided into thirty-four districts, each under an *Amtmann*.[11] In Bavaria (as well as in part of Tirol) financial administration and judicial power were concentrated in one hand.

In the northeastern parts of the territory colonized by the Germans, the functions of the Bavarian and Tirolian judges were taken over by the *Vogt* (*advocatus*), who was also in charge of collecting the revenues. It is a well-established fact that at the end of the fourteenth century instead of the title *Vogt* we find the title *Amtmann* in these territories.

In the territories between the Elbe and the Rhine, except in isolated cases, financial administration was separated from the judicial.[12] In southwestern territories the old internal institutions were preserved longer than in other parts of the old Empire, and they were influential for a longer time. Of course, there was a great difference to be observed in various territories of southwestern Ger-

---

Monumenta Germaniae Historica, Vol. X [2 vols.; Stuttgart, 1950–51]), gave incentive to new investigations. Yet the explanation of the origin of *ministeriales* is not available. See Heinrich Dannenbauer, *Grundlagen der mittelalterlichen Welt* (Stuttgart, 1958), p. 329. As to the *Amtmann*, it should not be understood in a modern sense. The medieval *Amtmann* is not our "officer" or "civil servant." See Erich Bayer, *Wörterbuch zur Geschichte* (Stuttgart, 1960), p. 20.

10. Hans Planitz, *Deutsche Rechtsgeschichte* (Graz, 1950), pp. 136 ff., and literature quoted in Otto Brunner, *Land und Herrschaft* (4th ed.; Vienna and Wiesbaden, 1959), pp. 357 ff. The *Amtmann* is sometimes called *Pfleger, Drost*.

11. E. Rosenthal, *Geschichte des Gerichtswesens und der Verwaltungsorganisation Bayerns*, I (Würzburg, 1889), 49 ff., 52; Bosl, *Geschichte Bayerns*, Vol. I: *Vorzeit und Mittelalter* (Munich, 1952), pp. 119–21; Bamberger, *op. cit.*, p. 169. For the Austrian territories see Dopsch, ed., *Die landesfürstlichen Urbare Ober- und Niederösterreichs* (Vienna, 1904, pp. LXXXVI, CXXXI ff., idem., *Zur Geschichte der Finanzverwaltung Österreichs im 13. Jahrhundert. Mitteilungen des Instituts für österreichische Forschung*, XVIII (1897), 238, reprinted in Dopsch, *Verfassungs- und Wirtschaftsgeschichte des Mittelalters*.

12. Bamberger, *op. cit.*, pp. 175–76. On *Vogt* see Richard Schröder, *Lehrbuch der deutschen Rechtsgeschichte* (6th ed.; Leipzig, 1919), I, 663 ff.

many; yet there was a general propensity everywhere to separate financial from general administration. Thus the basic elements for a modern structure were clearly coming to light.[13] In some territories, as for instance in Austria, an integration which would lead to a concentration of all functions of financial administration in only one hand never took place.[14]

In Bavaria a special officer—*Vitztum*—came into being. In 1255 there were already four officers of this kind who were also in charge of finances officiating in Munich, Langenfeld, Straubing, and Pfarrkirchen. The *Vitztum* was placed between the *Amtmann* and the prince. In the fifteenth century his functions were taken over by a *Rentenmeister (Kastner)*. In his hand also was concentrated the administration of the domanial property. In Württemberg, where the counts used the services of their councilors *(Räte)*, mostly noblemen, an *Obervogt* was placed at the head of more important districts. He had as assistant an *Untervogt,* who did not belong to the nobility. By the side of the *Vogt* there sometimes existed a special financial officer called *Keller.* The *Vogt* and the *Keller* constituted the nucleus of the local administration in Württemberg, and they also administered financial matters.[15]

13. The general line of development is correctly outlined by Bamberger, *op. cit.,* pp. 180–81. "In dem Augenblick, in dem in festbegrenzten Sprengeln ein Vogt, Pfleger, Amtmann, Drost die oberste Administrativ—, Gerichts—und Militärgewalt in sich vereinigt, ein Richter ihm für die Gerichtsverwaltung zur Seite steht, und ein Kastner, Kellner, Rentmeister, Schosser die Finanzgeschäfte besorgt, hat die Organisation bis auf weiteres ihre Entwicklungsmöglichkeiten erreicht und ist an dem Punkt angelangt, an dem sie bis ins 19. Jahrhundert beharren sollte."

14. A. Luschin von Ebengreuth, *Österreichische Reichsgeschichte des Mittelalters,* (2d ed.; Bamberg, 1914), I, 303: "Die österreichische Finanzverwaltung entbehrte während des Mittelalters einheitlicher Einrichtungen sowie der Vereinigung zu einem höheren Ganzen und umfasste im günstigsten Falle die Einnamequellen eines Landes." For details concerning the offices of general secretary *(Landschreiber)* and "commissioner for taxes" *(Hubmeister),* see K. Schalk, *Österreichs Finanzverwaltung unter Berthold von Mangen, Blätter des Vereins für Landeskunde von Niederösterreich,* Vol. XV (1881), *Quellenbeiträge zur älteren Niederösterreichischen Verwaltungs- und Wirtschaftsgeschichte; ibid.,* Vol. XXI (1887); Dopsch, "Zur Geschichte der Finanzverwaltung Österreichs im 13. Jahrhundert," in his *Verfassungs- und Wirtschaftsgeschichte des Mittelalters,* pp. 386 ff.

15. Bosl, *Geschichte Bayerns,* I, 120. It should be stressed that sometimes, even at the end of the medieval period, the holder of the *Amt* called *Pfleger* was a judge and at the same time a financial officer *(Kastner)*. See Rosenthal, *op. cit.,* I, 349–50. For Württemberg, see V. Ernst, "Die direkten Staatssteuern in der Grafschaft Württemberg," *Württembergisches Jahrbuch für Statistik und Landeskunde*

The taxes (*Bede*) were often collected directly by the *Amtmann* or his assistants when they were visiting house after house; sometimes the tax was brought by the taxpayers to the office of the tax collector. In some northeastern territories the rulers collected taxes with the help of feudal lords. In many cases the collection was made with the assistance of the communities. This method appears in various forms, and the method of self-administration in the collection of taxes deserves special attention. The community itself appointed at its own expense the man in charge of collecting taxes, and the community was free in the choice of procedures to be adopted. In particular, a special committee could be set up to fix the tax for the members of the community. This second function was much more widespread than the cooperation and help in collecting the taxes. Württemberg, and to some extent Bavaria, can be cited as examples.[16] The assignment and collection of taxes in the towns was as a rule always made by the community.

Central financial administration was controlled by the territorial ruler (*Landsherr*), who was, of course, free to appoint assistants. His treasury—the *camera*—was the center of his financial administration. It received revenues collected over the territory of the principality. Thus the whole financial system revolved around the ruler's *camera*. In Bavaria the local officers, the *Vitztums*, collected the revenues and delivered them to the chief treasurer (*Kammermeister*) of the *camera*, whose functions and power were, however, limited. The nomination of local officers and the control of the revenues were in the hands of the territorial ruler, and certainly the chief

---

(1904), Heft 2, p. 59; F. Ernst, *Eberhard im Bart. Die Politik eines deutschen Landesherrn am Ende des Mittelalters* (Stuttgart, 1933), pp 16–20; A. Dehlinger, *Württembergs Staatswesen in seiner geschichtlichen Entwicklung bis heute,* II, (Stuttgart, 1953), 754 ff. It should be stressed that neither the *Vogts* nor the *Kellers* were officers in the modern sense. They can be regarded rather as a kind of contractors, who administer the revenues and the expenses in a district freely and independently. F. Ernst, *op. cit.,* p. 20, "Beamte im heutigen Sinn sind weder Vögte noch Räte des Grafen. Die Vögte und Keller sind in gewissem Sinne Unternehmer." P. F. Stälin, *Geschichte Württembergs,* I (Gotha, 1887), 130 ff.; Bamberger, *op. cit.,* pp. 187–88 n. 6.

16. V. Ernst, *op. cit.,* p. 60; E. Baasch, *Die Steuer im Herzogtum Bayern bis zum ersten landständischen Freiheitsbrief (1311),* Diss. (Marburg, 1888), pp. 8, 35. L. Hoffmann, *Geschichte der direkten Steuern in Bayern vom Ende des 13. bis zum Beginn des 19. Jahrhunderts* (Staats- und Sozialwissenschaftliche Forschungen, hrsg. von G. Schmoller, IV. 5 [Leipzig, 1883]), 1–41.

treasurer was not in a position to decide freely and independently upon the use of the money. It is difficult to say whether the clerk— the *Kammerschreiber*—in Bavaria was in charge of keeping the financial records. Miss Bamberger pointed out that at present historians do not have sufficient material to allow them to draw a clear-cut conclusion, and she is opposed to the opinions voiced by Rosenthal.[17]

In the northeastern German principalities in the colonized territories and in all small principalities, a central treasury *stricto sensu* did not develop prior to the fifteenth century. As a rule the man in charge did not enjoy the status of a permanent officer; the treasury was in the care of the chief scribe—the *Protonotar* (*Notarius camerae*)—who was in most cases an ecclesiastic, and who, because of his knowledge of Latin, was absolutely irreplaceable by a less-educated person. The *Protonotar* was instrumental, of course, in completing all documents of a financial character. He also participated in the work of commissions checking the financial accounts, records, and documents, and he paid visits to the local centers where monies were collected, in order to inspect them. Yet it would be a mistake to consider the *Protonotar's* office as a central office of the financial administration.[18] As to the mutual relations between the *Notarius camerae* and the treasurer (*Kammermeister*), it can be firmly established that the latter was subordinate to the *Protonotar*.

Gradually the use of writing spread to the local centers of financial administration. In Tirol customs were recorded by 1240. In Bavaria writing was used in the *officia* at the end of the thirteenth

17. Bamberger, *op. cit.*, p. 197 n. 4.

18. G. Mehring, "Beiträge zur Geschichte der Kanzlei der Grafen von Wirtemberg," *Württembergische Vierteljahreshefte für Landesgeschichte,* N.F., XXV (Jhg. 1916), 329; B. Krusch, "Die Entwicklung der herzoglich Braunschweigischen Zentralbehörden, Kanzlei, Hofgericht und Konsistorium bis zum Jahre 1584," *Zeitschrift des historischen Vereins für Niedersachsen* (1893), p. 94. Bamberger, *op. cit.*, pp. 201–2. Recently warnings were given not to apply modern standards to the medieval chanceries. See A. von Brandt, *Werkzeug des Historikers. Eine Einführung in die historischen Hilfswissenschaften* (Stuttgart, 1958), p. 113. " 'Die Kanzlei' eines mittelalterlichen Herrschers oder Dynasten ist häufig nicht mehr als ein Geistlicher . . . der das Schriftwerk als 'Notar' selbst oder mit Hilfe von Schreibergehilfen ('Ingrossisten'), oft nur nebenamtlich neben seinem geistlichen Hauptamt, verrichtet. Nur in grösseren Verhältnissen, so namentlich und am ersten an der päpstlichen Kurie, dann auch schon an . . . der werdenden Territorien des Spätmittelalters entwickelt sich ein grösserer, fester Apparat, meist mit einem Kanzler an der Spitze. . . ."

century. The primitive methods used in the accounts of the Bavarian *Vitztums* in 1293–1294 were later replaced by a system of recording which can be compared with the principles adopted by modern accounting.[19] As compared with such an advanced technique most other principalities were far behind, and even in the middle of the fifteenth century in many places all financial reports were made orally. Later when computations in the *camera* began to be based exclusively on written calculations the use of Arabic numerals long remained unknown.

The use of the Roman notation was, of course, one of the factors contributing to confusion and mistakes. It must be remembered, however, that even in Florence as late as 1299 merchants were forbidden to use Arabic numerals because the municipal officers in charge of the books did not know them. In France and England the new numerals were rarely used until after the mid-fifteenth century.[20]

We cannot here expand the present brief discussion of medieval techniques of calculation, or the use of the wax tablet and abacus, and in particular of its most popular form, the line abacus (sometimes called a calculating table, or a "table," or—in England—a "counter"). It is sufficient to say that the line abacus was very popular in Germany in the fifteenth and sixteenth centuries, i.e., when its use had already died out in Italy. A few words must be said, however, about tallies, closely connected in the medieval financial administrative practice with the abacus.

The tally is an ancient invention. It was a piece of wood, i.e., a wooden stick, with notches or scores cut along the edges to designate numbers. If the tallies were used by the officers in charge of finances, the notches represented sums of money. The tallies also served as receipts, the stick commonly having been split. Thus each party had a record, as the notches were cut before the tally was split. A larger notch represented, of course, a larger number. In the mid-

19. Rosenthal, *op. cit.*, pp. 285, 286; E. von Oefele, "Rechnungsbuch des oberen Vizedomamtes Herzog Ludwigs d. Strengen, 1291–1294," *Oberbayerisches Archiv für vaterländische Geschichte*, XXVI (1865–66), 272 ff.; O. Stolz, "Über die ältesten Rechnungsbücher deutscher Landesverwaltungen," *Historische Vierteljahrschrift*, Vol. XXIII (1926); Bamberger, *op. cit.*, pp. 202 ff.; Mayer, *op. cit.*, pp. 262–66.

20. H. Hankel, *Zur Geschichte der Mathematik im Altertum und Mittelalter* (Leipzig, 1874), p. 341; J. Tropfke, *Geschichte der Elementar-Mathematik*, I³ (Berlin and Leipzig, 1930), 37; F. Cajori, *A History of Elementary Mathematics* (2d ed.; New York, 1961), p. 121. See also G. F. Hill, *The Development of Arabic Numerals in Europe* (New York, 1915); D. E. Smith and L. C. Karpinski, *The Hindu-Arabic Numerals* (Boston, 1911).

dle ages the tallies were used to keep accounts. In Germany the tally was known as *Kerbholz; incisio* or *incisura* (in German *Kerbe*) and *tallia* were originally identical expressions for the early German tax: *Bede.* Later the term *tallia* fell from use in Germany.[21]

It is commonly assumed that the lack of order in the accounting of revenues led in Germany as in other European countries to the development of the widespread use of assignments on revenue not yet paid into the treasury, and in some cases not yet even collected by the collector in charge. The system of satisfying creditors by giving them these assignments was certainly unfortunate and undoubtedly contributed to confusion in handling the accounts of revenues of the territorial rulers. But it would be a mistake to assume that the medieval system of assignments on revenues was the main cause of precarious conditions of the finances of the principalities, as is claimed by many historians. Thus, one of the leading German authorities, R. Schröder, says bluntly that the "system of assignments . . . brought about the ruin of the entire financial administration."

21. Du Cange, *Glossarium mediae et infimae Latinitatis,* new edition, ed. L. Favre (1883–87; reprinted 1954–55) , VIII, 16; I, 46; IV, 326; VII, 16, 18, gives the following explanation: "tesseram lignea . . . in duas partes fissa, in quarum utraque debitum continetur, transversaria quadam caesura denotatum, altera penes emtorem vel debitorem, altera penes venditorem vel creditorem remanente." On the role of tallies in medieval financial administrative practice and in computation by the treasury we are well informed by the famous *Dialogus de Scaccario* (completed in the seventies of the twelfth century) . See the edition by Charles Johnson (New York, 1950), with a bibliography and a table reproducing specimens of tallies. See also B. Lyon, *A Constitutional and Legal History of Medieval England* (New York, 1960) , pp. 159 ff. For Germany, G. von Below, "Die älteste deutsche Steuer," in *Probleme der Wirtschaftsgeschichte* (2d ed.; Tübingen, 1926) , pp. 625–26. A. Wagner and H. Deite, *Finanzwissenschaft,* I, Part III (2d ed.; Leipzig. 1910) , 77–78; Lotz, *Das Aufkommen der Geldwirtschaft im staatlichen Haushalt* (Berlin, 1908) . On the abacus and computation, F. Unger, *Die Methodik der praktischen Arithmetik in historischer Entwicklung vom Ausgang des Mittelalters bis auf die Gegenwart* (Leipzig, 1888) , pp. 38, 66; M. Cantor, *Geschichte der Mathematik,* II (2d ed.; Leipzig, 1900) , 215 ff.; D. E. Smith, *History of Mathematics,* II (New York: Dover Publ., 1958) , 156–95, on computation in Germany (p. 194) with valuable bibliographical notes. On the use of methods of computation following the general patterns even in the relatively advanced financial offices of the German medieval towns and especially in southern Germany (Bavaria) , L. Schönberg, *Die Technik des Finanzhaushalts der deutschen Städte im Mittelalter* (Münchener volkswirtschaftliche Studien hsg. von L. Brentano and W. Lotz, 103 [Stuttgart and Berlin, 1910]) , pp. 123 ff., 131 ff., 139 ff. Interesting details on reckoning tables in Germany are to be found in Miss Lao Genevra Simons, "Two Reckoning Tables," *Scripta Mathematica,* I, No. 4 (1933) , 305–9.

Schröder's opinion represents the views shared by Theodor Mayer and others.[22] Some historians identify the assignments on revenue with pledging. Even such a serious scholar as G. von Below goes so far as to share this assumption. According to him, "pledges were joined to a system of assignments at the local collection places and of anticipation of income to produce an unsatisfactory type of tax administration."[23]

This view, which makes the system of assignments on revenue responsible for all the evils—and there were many—of the medieval financial administration everywhere, and in particular in the German territories, must be rejected. This has been done already by Miss Bamberger.[24]

E. B. Fryde reached the same conclusion in respect to the assignments in medieval England. The institution of assignments in all of the countries concerned, including England, was based on the same principle, and the same technique was used in handling the assignments. In his polemics against A. B. Steel, E. B. Fryde pointed out that although historians have been inclined to criticize the whole system of assignments of future revenues to discharge current obligations, and of compelling crown creditors to collect money locally instead of paying it to them at the center, it must be recognized that despite all inconveniences, in the fourteenth century constant anticipation of revenue was unavoidable and enabled the king to live beyond his ordinary income.

Thus, both Miss Bamberger and E. B. Fryde approach the medieval system of assignments on revenue in the same way. Yet Miss Bamberger

22. Schröder, *Lehrbuch der deutschen Rechtsgeschichte*, p. 592; E. Löbe, "Die oberste Finanzkontrolle des Königreichs Sachsen in ihrer organischen Entwicklung von den ältesten Zeiten bis auf die Gegenwart," *Finanz-Archiv*, II, No. 2, 9; Mayer, "Beiträge zur Geschichte der tirolischen Finanzverwaltung im späten Mittelalter," *Forschungen und Mitteilungen zur Geschichte Tirols und Voralbergs*, XVI, XVII (1919–20), 156, "Der Krebsschaden für die Finanzgebarung war aber das Anweisungssystem." Similar opinions are quoted by Bamberger, *op. cit.*, pp. 205–6 n. 3.

23. von Below, *Territorium und Stadt. Aufsätze zur deutschen Verfassungs-Verwaltungs-u. Wirtschaftsgeschichte.* (Historische Bibliothek, ii [Munich, 1923]), p. 286; *Probleme der Wirtschaftsgeschichte* (2d ed.; 1926), p. 656.

24. *Op. cit.*, pp. 205 ff., "Mit Unrecht macht man aber das Anweisungssystem als solches für die ständige Finanznot der Territorialherrn verantwortlich." "Dieses Anweisungssystem für die Misswirtschaft in den mittelalterlichen Territorien verantwortlich zu machen, heisst. . . . Ursache und Wirkung vollständig verkennen." E. B. Fryde, "Materials for the Study of Edward III's Credit Operations, 1327–48," *Bulletin of the Institute of Historical Research*, XXII (1949), 128; XXIII (1950), 8–10.

goes further. She finds many favorable aspects to that system, which she considers as a kind of check circulation with all of its positive effects, decreasing the costs and risks and increasing the possibilities of quicker use of the revenues, often to be collected in distant territories.

The financial penury of so many medieval rulers, which led to heavy indebtedness, requires a few brief remarks. The revenues of the majority of these rulers were ordinarily insufficient to cover the expenses, and certainly did not allow for the accumulation of reserves which could be used during the periods of urgent need. A continuous supply of money could not be secured. The taxation of their subjects was one of the most difficult tasks confronting medieval rulers, and for a very long period taxes were regarded as something extraordinary. Even in the sixteenth century, Jean Bodin would accept the taxes only in cases of emergency.[25]

In a few isolated cases financial penury resulted from the ruler's financial irresponsibility. Yet it would be a mistake to attribute the poor state of the finances chiefly to an alleged general system of reckless expenditures by the princes—as Miss Bamberger assumes (*op. cit.,* p. 207). One has to agree, however, with her other statement that the chaotic conditions of the finances of the principalities resulted from the lack of a good financial administration (*ibid.,* pp. 207 ff.). Another factor was lack of control. When in the fifteenth century, in some principalities, such as Bavaria,[26] Saxony, and Baden, an efficient control of the activity of the officers was established, an important step toward financial stability was achieved.

The financial entries regularly made in books, records, registers, *urbaria,* etc., are to be found in some principalities, as in Tirol, Bavaria, Saxony, and Baden, yet the role of these documents should not be overemphasized. Only for Tirol is there sufficient material available to allow us to visualize to some extent the total financial activities during a given period. There is no such material available for other principalities. It was rightly stressed by F. Ernst, in his study of one of the most brilliant rulers in Württemberg, that even for the fifteenth century we are only informed of the methods of the financial administration, and we are unable to grasp the basis and substance of the financial policy of the territorial rulers because of lack of sources.[27]

25. For details, see E. B. Fryde and M. M. Fryde, *Cambridge Economic History of Europe,* III (Cambridge, 1963), 431 ff.

26. Rosenthal, *op. cit.,* pp. 291, 297 ff., 719.

27. F. Ernst, *Eberhard im Bart, Die Politik eines deutschen Landesherrn am Ende des Mittelalters,* pp. 65–66.

Speaking of the financial records of the German medieval principalities, it might be interesting to investigate the question of whether, and to what extent, the financial administration of these principalities was modeled upon the financial technique of German towns. Such a question seems to be justified in view of the fact that in German historiography it is assumed (by von Below, W. Lotz, J. Landmann, B. Kuske, T. Mayer, H. Mitteis, and others) that the German medieval cities, by the forms and methods of financial administration, and in particular by their technique of public borrowing, influenced the financial systems of the territorial rulers.[28] This view finds some partial—and only partial—confirmation in special circumstances (it is not applicable to England and France), but the character of the influence should not be oversimplified. It cannot be denied, of course, that all cultural development is closely connected with the progress made in the urban sector of a given territory. Therefore it would be rather difficult to deny the influence of the financial technique as developed by the municipal administration upon the financial practices of the rulers of the principalities in a land like Germany in the fourteenth and fifteenth centuries; yet in order to reach a precise formulation as to the true character and extent of the influence it is absolutely necessary to examine the evidence available in each individual case and reject any hasty generalization.

28. This general concept has already been formulated by Herder in his *Ideen zur Philosophie der Menschheit,* Part IV, where he pointed out that the cultural and economic development of the German principalities was influenced by the model of the cities; von Below's standpoint is to be found in "Die städtische Verwaltung des Mittelalters als Vorbild der späteren Territorialverwaltung," *Historische Zeitschrift,* N.F., Vol. XXXX (1895); Lotz, *Finanzwissenschaft* (2d ed.), pp. 32 ff.; B. Kuske, "Die Entstehung der Kreditwirtschaft und des Kapitalverkehrs," in B. Kuske, *Köln, der Rhein und das Reich* (Cologne and Graz, 1956), p. 116; Mayer, "Geschichte der Finanzwirtschaft vom Mittelalter bis zum Ende der 18. Jahrhunderts," *Handbuch der Finanzwissenschaft,* I, eds. Gerloff and Neumark, 267, 272, ". . . stand das Finanzwesen in den deutschen Städten des Mittelalters auf einer verhältnismässig bedeutenden Höhe und hat durch seine Verwaltung, besonders aber wegen der Entwicklung des Steuerwesens und der Ausbildung des Kreditwesens vorbildlich auch gegenüber den Territorien gewirkt." J. Landmann, "Geschichte des öffentlichen Kredites" *Handbuch der Finanzwissenschaft,* III (2d ed.; Tübingen, 1958), 7, ". . . die spätere Umbildung der privaten Fürstenschuld zur öffentlichen Staatsschuld besteht zu einem guten Teil in der Übernahme, Anpassung und Abwandlung der vorbildgewordenen Formen des städtischen Kredites." Mitteis, *Deutsche Rechtsgeschichte* (5th ed.), p. 153, "Die neuen Staaten suchten Anschluss an die Geldwirtschaft, die nahmen sich die städtische und kirchliche Finanzpolitik zu Vorbildern."

The existence of regular financial records seems to provide us with a test if we are seeking to establish the fact of borrowing methods of recording from the cities. Yet in a great many cases such a test is very difficult or even impossible to make. It should be realized that in the middle ages administrative practice in Germany was, as we stressed already, for a very long period not acquainted with writing and recording. Thus, any kind of examination is impossible. Even when the municipal accounts are available the decision concerning the possibility of influence is difficult.[29] The oldest extant municipal accounts in the towns of the principalities, in which we are presently interested (Brunswick, Bavaria, and Württemberg), date from 1354 (the City of Brunswick), 1360 (the City of Heilbronn in Württemberg), and 1377 (the City of Nuremberg in Bavaria). If we take, for instance, Nuremberg, it was an imperial town (*Reichsstadt*). The customs and mint, once owned by the German kings, were in the hands of the municipal administration in the second decade of the fifteenth century. Hypothetically it can be admitted that the use of financial accounts could have spread from Nuremberg to the Bavarian principalities. These could, if they wished, follow the example of other cities, not necessarily located in the territory of Bavaria. The same can be said of Württemberg and Brunswick. Thus, a direct influence of a specific municipal financial administration cannot be traced, but the general role of the municipal model is quite possible.

In the sphere of public credit the influences of the city are, however, not so simple. The forms of credit operations of German princes and those of German towns have been studied in another place[30] and

29. For the municipal accounts see the following works by R. Knipping, "Die mittelalterlichen Rechnungen der Stadt Köln," *Mitteilungen aus dem Stadtarchiv von Köln*, Heft 23 (Cologne, 1893), pp. 187–222; *Die Kölner Stadtrechnungen des Mittelalters*, II (Publikationen der Gesellschaft für rheinische Geschichtskunde, 15 [Bonn, 1897 –98]); "Ein mittelalterlicher Jahreshaushalt der Stadt Köln 1379" (Festschrift für G. von Mevissen [Cologne, 1895]); L. Schwörbel, "Die Rechnungsbücher der Stadt Köln 1351–1798," *Mitteilungen aus dem Stadtarchiv von Köln*, Heft 21 (1892), pp. 1–42; P. Sander, *Die reichsstädtische Haushaltung Nürnbergs 1431– 1440* (Leipzig, 1902); Schönberg, *Die Technik des Finanzhaushalts der deutschen Städte im Mittelalter*, pp. 87–155; further bibliography in *Cambridge Economic History of Europe*, III, 669–71. On use of writing see F. Rörig, "Mittelalter und Schriftlichkeit," *Die Welt als Geschichte*, XIII (1953), 29–41. Of importance is the recent publication, Ernst Pitz, "Schrift- und Aktenwesen der städtischen Verwaltung im Spätmittelalter. Köln-Nürnberg-Lübeck. Beitrag zur vergleichenden Städteforschung und zur spätmittelalterlichen Aktenkunde," *Mitteilungen aus dem Stadtarchiv von Köln*, Heft 45 (Cologne, 1959), pp. 88 ff., 93 ff., 195–206, 334–57.

30. E. B. Fryde and M. M. Fryde, *Cambridge Economic History*, III, 430–553.

therefore no further explanations are necessary. It is sufficient here to stress the difference of the two forms. That municipal medieval financial technique was of importance for the modern territorial financial administration in Germany cannot be denied.

Much older than the financial accounts and records showing the state of revenues and the sums spent by the princes are the registers that listed the revenues to be expected and to be collected from various sources. These are the *polyptychon*, (also called *Urbar* or *Salbuch*), register of taxes, i.e., of *Bede*, or of customs duties etc. Among these documents the *Urbars* are most probably the oldest. The oldest Bavarian *Salbuch (Urbar)* available is of 1221–1228, the next oldest of 1280. The oldest *Urbar* from Württemberg is dated 1350. The *Urbars* were primarily records of revenues completed by the administration of seignorial estates, but often they also contained revenues from various sources, for instance customs duties, judicial fees, etc. Although by no means a complete record of the revenues of a prince, the *Urbar* nevertheless constitutes the first effort to estimate the amount of expected revenues.[31] Whatever their documentary significance, the *Urbars* were of some help to the officers in charge of financial administration and, as such, were highly valued in the middle ages.

It cannot be our aim to investigate in full the problem of whether and to what extent we are allowed to regard the princely household ordinances (*Hofordnungen*) of the middle ages as rudimentary forms of modern budgets.[32] The ordinances regulated life at the court of a

31. On *Urbars* and *Codices traditionum*, see Planitz, *Deutsche Rechtsgeschichte*, pp. 79, 191; Bayer, *Wörterbuch zur Geschichte*, pp. 431, 487; R. Klauser and O. Meyer, *Clavis mediaevalis* (Wiesbaden, 1962), pp. 255–56; O. Stolz, *Grundriss der Österreichischen Verfassungs- und Verwaltungsgeschichte* (Innsbruck and Vienna, 1951), pp. 176, 216–17, 250; H. Quirin, *Einführung in das Studium der mittelalterlichen Geschichte* (2d ed.; Brunswick, 1961), pp. 106, 322; O. Herding, "Das Urbar als Orts- und zeitgeschichtliche Quelle besonders in Württemberg," *Zeitschrift für württembergische Landesgeschichte*, X (1951), 72 ff. *Urbar* (in Latin *Urbarium*) is derived from an old German word, *erbern*; *Salbuch* is composed of *Sal (Sale, Salung)*, having the same meaning as the English word "sale." The term is very old as follows from the text in *Cod. Trad. Nideraltacensis*, No. 4, "Invenitur scriptum in libro nostro, quod dicitur 'Salpuch.'" On the role of *Urbars* in the financial administration see Josef Susta, "Zur Geschichte und Kritik der Urbarialaufzeichnungen," *Sitzungsberichte der philos.-historischen Klasse K. Kais. Akademie der Wissenschaften*, Vol. CXXXVIII (Vienna, 1898).

32. The early history of budgets, even of rudimentary budgets, of German medieval principalities is not yet available. Lotz, *Finanzwissenschaft*, pp. 103–6, although by no means inclined to accept lightheartedly the existence of real bud-

territorial ruler. This was their main aim. They contained, however, elements belonging to a budget, to be sure, of a primitive form, yet setting up the expected expenses and revenues. But these financial plans, if set up, were not observed, and the princes freely changed their orders concerning both the collection of revenues and the kind and amount of expenses. Miss Bamberger accurately said of these financial schemes that "all these estimates . . . have something in common. They were made in order not to be held to."[33]

gets in the middle ages, considers the *Urbars*—household ordinances of the princes and other financial records and accounts taken together—as antecedents of budgets to a certain degree: "Im übrigen scheint es, dass als Vorläufer eines die gesamten öffentlichen Einnahmen und Ausgaben umfassenden Sollbudgets teilweise buch-mässige Registeraufnahmen für wichtige wiederkehrende Einnahmem sich zuerst entwickelt haben: für die domanialen Einnahmen die Landbücher, Urbare usw, . . . ferner die Schossregister und sonstige Listen der Steuerpflicht. Trat zu solchen Aufzeichnungen des Einnahmesolls allmählich eine Buchung der wiederkehrenden Ausgaben . . . so konnte im öffentlichen Haushalt allmählich eine planmässige Fürsorge für die Zukunft, eine Art von Wirtschaften mit einem Solletat, entstehen. . . . Es muss Surrogate für einen förmlichen Solletat sehr zeitig gegeben haben und es genügt nicht, festzustellen, wann jeweils ein Solletat im modernen Sinne urkündlich zuerst nachzuweissen ist." Hans Spangenberg, *Hof- und Zentralver-waltung der Mark Brandenburg im Mittelalter* (Leipzig, 1908), p. 423, enumerates various efforts in German principalities to set up rudimentary budgets, but rejects the possibility of an adoption in these principalities of budgetary procedure *stricto sensu* in the fourteenth and in the first half of the fifteenth centuries. Dopsch in his review-article of Lotz's book in *Vierteljahrschrift für Sozial- und Wirtschaftsgeschichte*, XIV, 509 ff. (reprinted in Dopsch, *Verfassungs- und Wirtsch-aftsgeschichte des Mittelalters*, pp. 374 ff.), is rather critical of Lotz's evaluation of the role of *Urbars*. He thinks that the preserved documents are more important, showing the settling of accounts by the prince with his officers (*Amtsmännern, officiales*). Mayer, in his article cited above (*Handbuch der Finanzwissenschaft* [2d ed.; 1952], pp. 261–62), rejects the idea that the *Urbars* of territorial rulers in Germany can be considered rudimentary budgets, whatever their importance. He stresses that "doch wird man sie noch nicht als Voranschläge (Sollbudgets) der Einnahmen bezeichnen können. Dazu fehlt ihnen die Vollständigkeit."

33. Bamberger, *op. cit.*, pp. 223 ff., 226. On the household ordinances (*Hoford-nungen*) see H. B. Meyer, *Hof- und Zentralverwaltung der Wettiner in der Zeit einheitlicher Herrschaft über die Meissnisch–Thüringischen Lande, 1248–1379* (Leipziger Studien aus dem Gebiet der Geschichte, IX [Leipzig, 1902]), 3; Span-genberg, *Hof- und Zentralverwaltung der Mark Brandenburg im Mittelalter*; G. Schapper, *Die Hofordnung von 1470 und die Verwaltung am Berliner Hofe zur Zeit Kurfürst Albrechts im historischen Zusammenhange behandelt* (Veröffent-lichungen des Vereins für Geschichte der Mark Brandenburg [Leipzig, 1912]); A. Kern, *Deutsche Hofordnungen des 16. und 17. Jahrhunderts* (Denkmäler der deutschen Kulturgeschichte, ed. G. Steinhausen, Abt 2. B. 1, 2 [2 vols.; Berlin,

The oldest extant Bavarian household ordinances date from 1293 and 1294. They were issued by the three sons of Henry XIII (1253–1290), the ruler of Lower Bavaria, namely by Otto III, Louis III, and Stephen I. In April, 1295, the same dukes were jointly detained (*obstagium*) for debt at Regensburg. In the above-mentioned ordinances each of the dukes, long harassed by heavy debts, solemnly promised not to take money from a *Vitztum, Amtmann,* customs officer, abbot, and so on, nor to borrow money without the knowledge of the other brothers. Financial matters were strictly regulated in the ordinances; even the number of guests allowed to be invited was limited.[34]

The financial means at the disposal of medieval princes were basically composed of revenues from their domains, *regalia*, taxes, excises, customs duties and, in cases of an urgent need, loans. The role of these resources varied greatly between territories and no generalization of their valuation is possible. Thus, for example, in some of the principalities excises were a major source of revenue, while in others taxes were of greater importance. On the whole, however, it can be maintained that the ordinary revenues from the domanial property gradually became quite inadequate.[35] One of the main causes of this phenom-

---

1905–7]) ; M. Hass, *Die Hofordnung Kurfürst Joachims II von Brandenburg* (Ebering's Historische Studien, No. 87 [Berlin, 1910]) ; S. B. Fay, "The Hohenzollern Household and Administration in the Sixteenth Century," *Smith College Studies in History,* II, No. I (October, 1916), 1–64; S. Adler, *Die Organisation der Zentralverwaltung unter König Maximilian I* (Leipzig, 1886) ; Mayer, *Die Verwaltungsorganisationen Maximilians I, ihr Ursprung und ihre Bedeutung* (Forschungen, z. inneren Geschichte Österreichs, ed. A. Dopsch, I, 14 [Innsbruck, 1920]) .

34. The text of the ordinances, which differ only in that the ordinance of 1294 is more detailed, is included in the collection *Quellen und Erörterungen zur bayrischen und deutschen Geschichte,* VI (1861), 12, 53 ff. For details see M. J. Neudegger, "Die Hof- und Staatspersonaletäts der Wittelsbacher in Bayern," *Beiträge zur Geschichte der Behördenorganisationen in Bayern* (6 vols.; Munich, 1887–98), Vol. III.

35. See K. D. Hüllmann, *Deutsche Finanzgeschichte des Mittelalters* (Berlin, 1805), pp. 1–53, and *Geschichte der Domainen-Benutzungen* (Frankfurt on the Oder, 1809), both works still of importance for the student of the domain in medieval Germany. See also W. Roscher, *System der Finanzwissenschaft,* Part 1 (5th ed.; Stuttgart, 1901), pp. 37–86, with valuable historical notes; Lotz, *Finanzwissenschaft* (2d ed.), pp. 796 ff. His point of view is clearly formulated: "Blicken wir auf die geschichtliche Entwicklung zurück, so ist im Mittelalter das landwirtschaftliche Kammergut ausschlaggebend für die Macht des Fürsten, solange er Schwierigkeiten findet, eine über das ganze Land erstreckte Besteuerung durchzuführen." See also Mitteis, *Deutsche Rechtsgeschichte* (5th ed.), p. 153.

enon was the constantly increasing cost of warfare and the growing necessity to hire mercenary troops. The principalities were undergoing a profound transformation in this respect. Yet it should not be forgotten that during the later medieval period revenues from the domain consisted not only of material products but also of money, the amount of which in normal conditions could be regarded as having been sufficient to cover the needs of a medieval ruler at the beginning of the thirteenth century.[36]

The revenues from the domains being insufficient, taxes gradually became an important element of the princely finances. Medieval taxes constitute payments other than of a feudal character or origin; the meaning of the medieval term is, however, different from the modern one. It denoted primarily assistance rendered by the subjects to their ruler (*stiura, stiure, steora, stuofa, bede, bete, petitio, precaria, exactio*). These taxes were ordinary and extraordinary (*schoss*). The last-mentioned were considered uncommon in the thirteenth century; yet during the fourteenth and fifteenth centuries they came to be levied regularly, and in the sixteenth century they were a firmly established form of taxation. In some territories the ordinary tax lost its original character as an instrument of princely taxation. The moden tax developed from the form once considered extraordinary. The revenues from the taxes were often assigned and sometimes farmed. The assigning must be sharply distinguished from the farming, the difference being that, unlike the assignee, the farmer did not have to account for everything he had received. Anything over a fixed charge constituted his gain.[37]

As to excises, they were indirect taxes, in most cases, imposed upon alcoholic beverages. The excise was called *Ungelt* or *Ungeld* (*indebitum*) and it was an important source of princely revenues, con-

36. On the role and origin of taxes in the medieval German principalities see Wagner and Deite, *op. cit.*, pp. 66 ff.; von Below, *Probleme der Wirtschaftsgeschichte* (2d ed.), pp. 522–662; Mayer, *Handbuch der Finanzwissenschaft*, I, 244–55, where various theories concerning the origin of taxes (of Eichhorn, Lamprecht, von Below, Zeumer, Dopsch, Waas, O. Brunner, and others) are discussed. The works of von Below and Mayer contain excellent bibliographical data.

37. See A. Waas, *Vogtei und Bede in der deutschen Kaiserzeit*, Vol. II (Arbeiten zur deutschen Verfassungs- und Wirtschaftsgeschichte [Berlin, 1919–23]); Brunner, *Land und Herrschaft. Grundfragen der territorialen Verfassungsgeschichte* (4th ed.), pp. 273 ff.; F. Kogler, "Das landesfürstliche Steuerwesen in Tirol bis zum Ausgange des Mittelalters, I: Die ordentlichen landesfürstlichen Steuern," *Archiv für Österreichische Geschichte*, Vol. XC (1901).

stituting sometimes forty per cent of the total (for instance in Austria in 1438). The excises were of particular importance in municipal finances, yet their role in the finances of the principalities cannot be neglected.[38]

Regalia (iura regalia) denote primarily all kinds of sovereign rights and prerogatives of a ruler. The term became popular during the investiture quarrel. The steps taken in 1111 during the discussions between the German king and the pope, and in 1158 on Roncaglia fields were followed by a further development of the concept of regalia on German soil. Following the establishment of the rule of the domini terrae (Landesherren) as sovereign princes, many of the regalia were appropriated by them. A difference should be made between regalia maiora and regalia minora; to the last-named belong financial rights (customs duties, mint, market, etc.). The regalia became an important source of financial revenues in various territories. Thus, in some principalities the customs duties furnished 20 to 25 per cent of the total revenues. The revenues from regalia were often pledged by the princes.[39]

The exclusive right to issue coins, possessed primarily by the German kings, passed gradually to many territorial rulers as the result of grants (since the tenth century), or by usurpation.[40] Frederick

38. Dopsch, "Die ältesten Akzise in Österreich," Mitteilungen des Instituts für Österreichische Geschichtsforschung, XXVIII (1907), 651 ff. (reprinted in Dopsch, Verfassungs- und Wirtschaftsgeschichte des Mittelalters, pp. 506–15); on the origin of the German term Akzise see K. H. Rau, Grundsätze der Finanzwissenschaft (5th ed.; Leipzig and Heidelberg, 1864), II, 238 n.; Roscher, op. cit.; II, 27 n.

39. K. Bosl in Gebhardt, Handbuch der deutschen Geschichte, I, 650–51; Conrad, Deutsche Rechtsgeschichte, I, 309–76; H. Thieme, "Die Funktion der Regalien," Z.R.G., Germ. Abt. 62 (1942); Stolz, "Der Regalienbegriff," Vierteljahrschrift für Sozial- u. Wirtschaftsgeschichte, XXXIX (1952), 152 ff.; J. Ott, "Der Regalienbegriff im 12. Jh.," Z.R.G., Kan. Abt., Vol. XXXV (1948); H. Troe, Münze, Zoll und Markt und ihre finanzielle Bedeutung für das Reich vom Ausgang der Staufer bis zum Regierungsantritt Karls IV (Stuttgart, 1937). Older literature of importance: J. Falke, Die Geschichte des deutschen Zollwesens (Leipzig, 1869); F. Friedensburg, Münzkunde und Geldgeschichte der Einzelstaaten des Mittelalters und der neueren Zeit (Munich, 1926); Theo Sommerlad, Die Rheinzölle im Mittelalter (Halle, 1894); E. Wetzel, Das Zollrecht der deutschen Könige von den ältesten Zeiten bis zur Goldenen Bulle (Gierkes Untersuchungen, 43 [Breslau, 1892]).

40. Schröder, Lehrbuch der deutschen Rechtsgeschichte, pp. 571–74; J. Kulischer, Allgemeine Wirtschaftsgeschichte des Mittelalters und der Neuzeit (2d ed.; Munich, 1958), I, 325–26, ". . . wächst die Zahl der Münzherren ins Ungemessene. Nicht bloss die Pfalz-und Markgrafen und Bischöfe, sondern auch Äbte und ihre Vogte, ja jeder Edelherr und Junker schlechthin massen sich das Münzrecht an." A.

II was compelled to promise the territorial rulers that without their consent no new mints would be established on their territories, thus leaving the king a free hand to do so only in the imperial land.[41] Finally, in the Golden Bull of 1356, Charles IV recognized that the sole control over minting lay with the princes, who also received the right to issue gold coins—a right already possessed by Bohemian kings.[42]

While speaking of coinage in Germany, one has to realize that during the twelfth, thirteenth, and first half of the fourteenth centuries a spectacular increase in trade, already growing steadily since the beginning of the tenth century, took place. The changes were of such importance that some historians speak of a Commercial Revolution in the late thirteenth and early fourteenth centuries.[43] The impact of the expansion of trade on the wider use of coinage is obvious. No less evident is that the necessity for so many mints, spread over the territory of Germany, lay in the imperfect means of communication in many regions of that territory. Another great stimulus to the increase of coinage in Germany was the extensive exploitation of silver mines

---

Luschin von Ebengreuth, *Allgemeine Münzkunde und Geldgeschichte des Mittelalters und der neueren Zeit* (2d ed.; Munich and Berlin, 1926), pp. 241 ff., 244 ff.; K. Th. Eheberg, *Über das ältere deutsche Münzwesen und die Hausgenossesschaften besonders in volkswirtschaftlicher Beziehung* (Schmollers Forschungen 2.5 [Leipzig, 1879]), pp. 23 ff., 33 ff., 55; Troe, *op. cit.*, pp. 15–17.

41. *Confoederatio cum principibus ecclesiasticis, 1220*, c. 2.; *Statutum in favorem principum*, 1231/32, c. 17.

42. K. Zeumer, ed., *Die Goldene Bulle Kaiser Karls IV* (Vienna, 1908), p. 25, c. 10, §§ 1, 3; see Conrad, *op. cit.*, pp. 370 ff. It should be pointed out that Baldwin of Luxembourg, the archbishop of Trier, whose rule was characterized by successful financial administration and the use of Jewish financiers, was the first to achieve full independence in issuing coins. This was granted him by his brother, Emperor Henry VII, the *alto Arrigo* for Dante. (See the monograph devoted to a great episode in the life of Henry VII by W. M. Bowsky, *Henry VII in Italy: The Conflict of Empire and City-State, 1310–1313* [Lincoln, Nebr., 1960], p. vii). The privilege of Henry VII was extended substantially in 1346 by Charles IV. Thus the archbishop of Trier possessed unlimited sovereignty in all monetary matters prior to the Golden Bull of 1356.

43. R. S. Lopez, "The Trade of Medieval Europe: The South," *Cambridge Economic History of Europe*, II (Cambridge, 1952), 289 ff., points out, speaking of the Commercial Revolution, that "no other economic upheaval has had such an impact upon the world, with the possible exception of the Industrial Revolution of the eighteenth century." See also R. S. Lopez and I. W. Raymond, *Medieval Trade in the Mediterranean World. Illustrative Documents Translated with Introduction and Notes* (Records of Civilization, LII [New York, 1955]), 6; H. L. Adelson, *Medieval Commerce* (Princeton, 1962), pp. 68 ff.

in Rammelsberg, in Harz, in Freiberg, in Saxony, and in Kutna Hora (Kuttenberg) in Bohemia.[44]

As to the customs duties, it is worthwhile to stress that the medieval term *theloneum* or *teloneum* (in German: *Zoll*) had a larger meaning than the modern one, as it denoted all kinds of duties connected with the circulation of goods and the functioning of the markets. The term was also used in the towns for indirect taxes. In this area of the king's *iura regalia,* too, the territorial rulers were eager to infringe as much as they could upon the royal rights; yet until the middle of the fourteenth century they were less successful than in the matter of coinage. The *Confoederatio cum principibus ecclesiasticis* of 1220 gave the territorial rulers the right to participate in the regulation of customs duties insofar as it affected their territory, yet the provisions of the arrangement of 1220 did not at first gain great importance, as they were of practical value only for one of the electors. In this respect the Golden Bull of 1356 did not considerably increase the rights of the electors (the position of the archbishop of Trier having been privileged, however). Only in 1380 did some other electors acquire the right to decide upon the introduction of new customs duties in the Reich. Whatever the formal character of existing constitutional clauses, their real role should not be overestimated, since after the thirteenth century the German kings were not strong enough to be able to impose their strict control on the territorial rulers in matters of customs duties.[45]

A few brief remarks have to be made on the early development of taxation in Bavaria and Württemberg. The history of Bavarian taxes from the very beginning shows specific features which were preserved for a long period.[46] The first mention of a Bavarian tax is dated 1215, the amount paid having been 20,000 pounds of pfennigs (one pound having 240 pfennigs). The purpose of this tax was to release from cap-

44. Troe, *op. cit.*, p. 2; K. Kretschmer, *Historische Geographie von Mitteleuropa* (Munich and Berlin, 1904), pp. 395 ff.; K. Th. von Inama-Sternegg, *Deutsche Wirtschaftsgeschichte*, III, part 2 (Leipzig, 1901), 140 ff.; Planitz, *Die deutsche Stadt im Mittelalter* (Graz and Cologne, 1954), pp. 195 ff.

45. Troe, *op. cit.*, pp. 116–20.

46. L. Hoffmann, *Geschichte der direkten Steuern in Bayern vom Ende des 13. bis zum Beginn des 19. Jahrhunderts*, p. 1, pointed out that "Eine Geschichte der direkten Steuern für Baiern zu entwerfen, bietet vielleicht weniger Schwierigkeiten als für andere deutsche Länder," and that "Jedenfalls war die historische Entwickelung eine verhältnissmässig einfache und leicht zu überblickende."

tivity Duke Louis I (1183–1231), who in 1214 fell into the hands of the counts of Limburg and Jülich.[47] The next known fact of taxation is dated 1255. A "cattle tax," which was in fact a property tax, was imposed in 1302. It can be presumed that the tax was paid by the nobility alone, although the towns could also have contributed to it. In 1307, all three Estates, the aristocracy, the clergy, and the town population, consented to the payment of a tax. The Bavarian dukes were—as we shall see later—in a very difficult financial situation, and therefore they resorted to taxes, although this financial remedy was considered at that time as something extraordinary. In the following years taxes were levied from time to time in some of the Bavarian duchies, e.g., in 1311, 1322, 1331, 1335, 1358, 1365, 1383, 1385, 1390. If we examine the tax levied in 1390 in Upper Bavaria, it is found that the tax constituted about 20 per cent of the revenues of estates owned by the nobility, Church, and towns; the total sum paid was about 75,000 florins. The towns (including the marketplaces) paid 37,000 florins, the nobility 14,000 florins, and the monasteries and ecclesiastic institutions 24,000 florins.[48]

A general historical presentation of Bavarian taxation cannot be attempted within the compass of the present essay. It is necessary, however, to mention the tax ordinance (*Steuerordnung*) of 1396, which students of Bavarian medieval finances consider as having been of the greatest importance. We find here not only what is to be paid as a tax, but also who the taxpayers are, who the tax collectors are, who controls their activities, and who is to use the sums collected.[49]

47. *Monumenta Germaniae Historica, S.S.*, XVII, 632; S. Riezler, *Geschichte Bayerns*, II, 44; Baasch, *Die Steuer im Herzogtum Bayern bis zum ersten landständischen Freiheitsbrief (1311)* (Marburg, 1888), pp. 45–46.

48. L. Hoffmann, *op. cit.*, pp. 10–11. It should be noticed that following the debasement of currency in the fourteenth century and the uncertainty as to the real content of silver in a pound, i.e., in 240 pfennigs, tradespeople in Germany began to count in Italian gold currency, while otherwise, and in particular in local exchange, silver currency was used. This dualistic system continued until the beginning of the sixteenth century, when full-value silverthalers were issued. For details see Inama-Sternegg, *op. cit.*, III, part 2, pp. 363 ff., and another most competent study by the same author, "Die Goldwährung im deutschen Reiche während des Mittelalters," *Zeitschrift für Sozial- und Wirtschaftsgeschichte*, Vol. III (1894); Kulischer, *op. cit.*, I, 315 ff. (with valuable bibliographical notes); L. Hoffmann, *op. cit.*, pp. 7–11.

49. The text of this important source was published by G. von Lerchenfeld, *Die altbayrischen landständischen Freiheiten mit den Landesfreiheitserklärungen*

As was already mentioned, during the thirteenth century the collection of taxes was as a rule done by a judge and his sergeants, and also sometimes by the cashier *(Kastner)*. In the documents we find names of various *officiati* in charge of finances: *Vicedominus* or *Vitztum, Iudex, Kastner,* etc., no difference being made in their ranks. Thus, Duke Ludwig promised the monastery in Neustift (near Freising in Upper Bavaria) in 1212, "ut nec nos nec quispiam judicum nostrorum steuram aut jus advocati accipiat." In another charter, the same duke said: "ut nullus officialium nostrorum, judicum, magistrorum censuum seu preconum, aliquid exigat." Duke Otto, in a charter, stated, "ab omni exactione steure, seu qualibet alia prestatione, que per vicedominos aut alios officiales nostros fieri consueverunt." From these and similar charters it follows who was in charge of collection of taxes *(steura, stiura, steora,* later called *exactio, petitio, collecta, tallia,* etc.). Without entering into an analysis of the mutual relationship among the various officers we shall only emphasize that the collection of taxes was accomplished by officers *(Amtsleute, officiales)* and that the highest judge in charge of collection of taxes was the *Vicedominus*.[50] This administrative technique was gradually replaced during the fourteenth century by a quite different one, and the change—to be observed, of course, not only in Bavaria—was of great importance.

By 1356 the collection of taxes was done not by the *officiales* but by the Estates. The finances of Duke Ludwig V (1349–1361) of Upper Bavaria–Tirol were in a desperate state from the very beginning. In the first year of his rule he was compelled to ask the Jews in Munich to help him release his horse pledged to a certain Bauernfeind in Munich. In 1356 the Estates were ready to rescue the unfortunate duke provided that he would accept their direct collection of the tax (a cattle tax) to be levied. The duke had no other choice but to agree. The Estates elected a body composed of sixteen members, eight having been appointed by the towns and marketplaces. The role of the *officiales* of the duke was reduced to that of assistance.

The new system of collection became permanent, and the above-mentioned ordinance of 1396 follows the new patterns. This time the body set up by the Estates was composed of twenty-one members: one

---

(Einleitung L. Rockinger [Munich, 1853]) . The slightly abridged and modernized text is given by L. Hoffmann, *op. cit.,* pp. 11–14. See also the lucid comments in Riezler, *op. cit.,* III (1889) , 731, 732–33.

50. Baasch, *op. cit.,* pp. 32 ff.; for the quotations from the charters see *Monumenta Boica,* IX, 574; XI, 536; XIII, 240.

Vitztum (Vicedominus), named by the duke, four prelates, eight persons selected by the nobility and the councilors, and eight by the towns. The assessment of the tax in the landed estates owned by the duke was done by the *officiales,* while the nobility, prelates, and towns were left in charge of their own taxes. The right of the Estates to fix the taxes degenerated in the fifteenth century into a total emancipation of the nobilty and prelates from the obligation to pay taxes, and the full financial burden was loaded onto the shoulders of the peasantry. Instead of checking ducal willfulness and fiscal oppression, the Estates misused the idea of the ordinance of 1396 and created a new source of fiscal tyranny, not opposed by the dukes.

It can be said that the Bavarian taxes were a major source of revenue. Thus, Duke Ludwig the Rich of Bavaria–Landshut (1450–1479) received the sum of 73,000 Rhin. Guldens in 1464. Duke George the Rich of Bavaria Landshut–Ingolstadt (1479–1503) received taxes in the amount of 100,270 florins in 1490.[51]

The tax in Württemberg, known as "ordinary tax" (*Gewöhnliche Steuer* or *Vogtsteuer, Bedesteuer,* etc.) existed from the thirteenth century to the fifteenth century as the sole direct tax. It was paid annually, mostly in cash, but sometimes in kind, directly to the central administration of the counts of Württemberg. The peculiarity of the technique of assessment of the tax was that each community fixed the amount to be paid in absolute independence, taking as its basis for assessment the land and the buildings owned by the members of the community. Later, other elements, such as capital and rents, were taken into consideration. In some localities, in addition to that ordinary tax, a special tax called *Speisung* was levied.

The "offices" (Ämter) levied a special annual tax called *Landschaden* from 1440 to 1514. The total was fixed for the whole territory of Württemberg and was meant as compensation for expenses made by the count himself or his court as well as by the *officia,* and such a fixed total amount was apportioned among the *officia,* each of them freely dividing the sum concerned according to his own discretion.

In time of great need and to enable the ruler to repay debts, extraordinary taxes were levied, called *Schatzung* or *Schatzsteuer.* The first tax of this kind was collected in 1425, and then again in 1448, 1463, and 1470. The ordinance of November 19, 1470, prescribed how the assessment of this tax should be made.

51. Riezler, *op. cit.,* pp. 732 ff.

At the end of the fifteenth century, a new extraordinary tax was introduced. Its assessment was based on a system adopted by the *Landschaden* tax, which was mentioned earlier, i.e., the total to be collected was fixed by the financial administration in advance and later repartitioned among various *officia*. These divided the sum concerned among the communities, which finally distributed the sum to be levied among the individual taxpayers. The primarily extraordinary tax became in Württemberg—as in many other principalities—a regular periodically collected tax after the sixteenth century.

A special tax—*Landsteuer*—was levied in connection with the so-called Tübingen Settlement of 1514 in order to repay the heavy debt of 500,000 florins, to which we shall return later in the section devoted to public credit in Württemberg. In addition to the above-mentioned taxes, some taxes of minor importance like the *Schlossgeld* were levied from time to time, and excises were imposed.[52]

The *Statutum in favorem principum* of 1231/32, together with the imperial decision (*Reichsspruch*) of May 1, 1231, created a legal basis for further development of the role of the Estates in the principalities. In the *Reichsspruch* the princes were referred to for the first time as *domini terrae* and it was ordered by the king that they were not allowed to promulgate and enact *constitutiones vel nova iura* without the consent of the *meliores et maiores terrae*, i.e., without the consent of the privileged upper classes of their territories.[53] The intervention of

52. Chr. F. v. Stälin, *Wirtembergische Geschichte*, III (Stuttgart, 1856), 722 ff.; K. Weller, *Württembergische Geschichte*, p. 82; E. Marquardt, *Geschichte Württembergs* (Stuttgart, 1961), pp. 60 ff.; F. Ernst, *Eberhard im Bart. Die Politik eines deutschen Landesherrn am Ende des Mittelalters*, pp. 65 ff.; F. Winterlin, *Geschichte der Behördenorganisation in Württemberg*, I (Stuttgart, 1902), 31 ff.; Dehlinger, *Württembergs Staatswesen in seiner geschichtlichen Entwicklung bis heute*, II, 753 ff., 825 ff.

53. The text of the *Reichsspruch* of May 1, 1231, contains the following sentences of great importance, ". . . nobis . . . petitum fuit diffiniri: si aliquis dominorum terrae aliquas constituciones vel nova iura facere possit, melioribus et maioribus terre minime requisitis. Super qua re requisitio consensu principum, fuit taliter diffinitum: ut neque principes neque alii quilibet constituciones vel nova iura facere possent, nisi meliorum et maiorum terre consensus primitus habeatur." See Mitteis, *Deutsche Rechtsgeschichte*, pp. 154 ff.; F. Hartung, *Deutsche Verfassungsgeschichte vom 15. Jahrhundert bis zur Gegenwart* (6th ed.; Stuttgart, 1950), pp. 61 ff., and his article, "Herrschaftsverträge und ständischer Dualismus in deutschen Territorien," *Schweizer Beiträge zur Allgemeinen Geschichte*, X (1952), 163–77 (reprinted in Hartung, *Staatsbildende Kräfte der Neuzeit, Gesammelte Aufsätze* [Berlin, 1961], pp. 62–77). Hartung's view is opposed to that of

the Estates took place most commonly when the finances of the prince were in a bad state and radical steps had to be taken to bring relief in order to avoid a situation which could also be dangerous for the Estates.

It should not be forgotten that the *meliores et maiores terrae* were very close to the ruler in his private life and that often they were his main creditors, and that sometimes the sources of the princely revenues were specifically pledged to them. Hence, the members of the privileged Estates were directly interested in putting the finances in order. The assemblies of the Estates were almost exclusively devoted to deliberation concerning the levy of taxes. It was said rightly: *Landtag ist Geldtag*. Gradually these interventions of the Estates in the financial administration of the principalities led to a "financial dualism"; the prince did administer the *Camerale* and the Estates the *Contributionale*. It was only rarely that the princes dared to impose taxes without the consent of the Estates. Thus, two separate financial powers developed, each of them compelled to be reconciled with the existence of the other, each with a separate treasury: *Kammerkasse* and *Landeskasse*.[54]

It should be pointed out that the development toward dualism was

---

Spangenberg, *Vom Lehnstaat zum Standestaat* (Munich, 1912), based predominantly on material pertaining to Brandenburg, and to that of Brunner, *Land und Herrschaft*, devoted mainly to Austria. Hartung is not inclined to accept the too favorable attitude toward the role of German medieval Estates adopted recently by F. L. Carsten, *Princes and Parliaments in Germany from the 15th to the 18th Century* (Oxford, 1959), and in Carsten's article in *Die Welt als Geschichte*, XX (1960), 16–29. Hartung's standpoint is similar in many respects to that of G. Oesterreich in Gebhardt's *Handbuch der deutschen Geschichte*, II, 345–47. We think, however, that Oesterreich goes too far when he asserts that the Estates were defending the interests of "des gemeinen Mannes gegen Übergriffe." It might be that in some cases such a defense really took place but the generalization made by Oesterreich is not well grounded. We have seen that the financial policy of the Estates led to a fiscal oppression of the "little man." Bamberger, *op. cit.*, p. 246, has taken a sober point of view which is far from the enthusiastic approach of other historians toward the role of the Estates in shaping the princely finances.

54. Mayer, *op. cit.*, p. 246; Mitteis, *op. cit.*, p. 155. The coexistence of the two powers was rightly described by Mitteis: "Den Höhepunkt erreichte die landständische Verfassung am Ausgang des Mittelalters. Jetzt stehen sich vielfach geradezu zwei Staaten im Staate gegenüber, ein fürstlicher und ein ständischer Apparat; Fürst und Stände haben gesonderte Truppen, Behörden, Kassen, diplomatische Vertretungen."

by no means uniform in all principalities. On the contrary, great differences are to be observed in this respect.

In Bavaria, Duke Otto III of Lower Bavaria–Landshut promised, together with his two brothers, to renounce taxes in the future and to grant the right of lower jurisdiction to the prelates, nobility, and towns. The price for these concessions was an agreement by the Estates to levy a tax which would enable the dukes to repay heavy debts. The development in Bavaria was marked by continuity and uniformity. The privilege of 1311—the famous First *Freibrief* of 1311—was confirmed many times during the next two centuries.[55] Yet it would be a mistake—as was stressed recently by F. Hartung—to assume that the *Freibrief* of 1311 or the others issued between 1311 and 1565 strongly influenced the development of the Estates. In each *Freibrief* there is a statement that the promises made by the duke had not been kept, that a new tax had become imperative, and that it would be the last one to be imposed.

The role of the Estates in the management of the financial matters in Württemberg was quite different. While in most of the great principalities the Estates were called by the fourteenth century and sometimes even earlier, in Württemberg the first occurrence of activities of the Estates took place in 1457 and the questions to be discussed were connected with dynastic problems. The role of the Estates in financial matters began only much later, following a great crisis which led to the rebellion of Armen Konrad in 1514. The financial aspect of that crisis will be discussed later.

In the territory of the duchy of Braunschweig-Lüneburg the Estates attained a certain role in financial matters as early as in the fourteenth century in various principalities. It would be sufficient to refer here to the famous *Sate* agreement of 1392, which will be studied later.[56]

When all sources of revenues—and among them the debasement of currency sometimes played an important role—proved to be quite insufficient to cover all princely expenses, the only way left was to resort to selling property and borrowing.

The older generation of historians was inclined to regard the medieval period as a primitive stage in the development of public credit.

55. L. Hoffmann, *op. cit.*, pp. 7–10; Hartung, *Staatsbildende Kräfte der Neuzeit*, p. 73.

56. For details concerning the role of Estates in financial matters in Tirol and Brandenburg see *Cambridge Economic History of Europe*, III, 520 ff.

Such an attitude was a legacy of Bruno Hildebrand's theory of stages of economic growth in Europe—an assumption which is rejected by historians today.[57] Among the arguments once widely used was that in view of the fact that the debts of medieval rulers were almost invariably regarded as their personal obligations and that the continuity of indebtedness was an institution which came into being only with the introduction of modern funded debts, it was impossible to speak *stricto sensu* of state debts, i.e., of public credit, in the middle ages. It is, of course, imperative to differentiate between the medieval and modern forms of public credit, yet it would be absolutely wrong to apply to medieval credit the particular test mentioned above. It was stressed recently by E. B. Fryde and M. M. Fryde that

> the presence or absence of the funded debt cannot be a valid criterion of the importance of the credit transactions of the territorial rulers at any time or place in medieval Europe. The treatment of the debts of medieval rulers as personal obligations of the princes who contracted them was an inevitable consequence of the prevailing, purely personal, conception of sovereign power. But the practical consequences of this must not be exaggerated. In reality, rulers repeatedly assumed responsibility for the debts of their predecessors. . . . There is no evidence that the temporary character of princely obligations deterred financiers from advancing money to medieval governments.

The form and methods of public credit in the middle ages having been analyzed by the above-mentioned authors, it is superfluous to enter here into a detailed discussion of that matter.

57. A detailed presentation of various theories of stages of economic growth is given by B. F. Hoselitz in B. F. Hoselitz *et al, Theories of Economic Growth* (Glencoe, Ill., 1960), pp. 193–238.

II

THE LAND which in modern times is known as the duchy of Brunswick, was in the hands of various mighty dynasties, such as the Brunos, the counts of Northeim (or Nordheim) and the counts of Supplinburg from the tenth century to 1127. After a long process of various changes the territories ruled by these counts were united in 1127 under Henry the Proud (1108–1139), the duke of Saxony and Bavaria and the head of the Welf family, when he married Gertrud, the daughter of the German king Lothair III of Supplinburg (1125–1137). Subsequently, these lands became part of a large duchy ruled by Henry's son, the famous Duke Henry the Lion (1129–1195) until his downfall in 1180 when he was placed under imperial ban and deprived of all his territories. In 1181 he received back, however, part of the land lost, namely the allodial property, which consisted of a large part of Brunswick and Lüneburg.

Around this center a larger duchy gradually developed. The sons of Henry the Lion (Henry, Otto, and William) divided it in 1202 but it was soon reunited. Otto the Child (d. 1252), the son of William, assumed the title of a duke of Brunswick-Lüneburg (dux de Luneborg et de Brunswic). Emperor Frederick II recognized his title and created him duke of Brunswick and Lüneburg. Otto acquired (1236) the allodial lands of the count of Osterburg and other territories (1246), part of which were lost in 1264. Otto the Child was the ruler who restored to some extent the old glory of the Welfs. The territories united under his rule were subsequently divided in 1267 between his sons Albert and John.[1] Albert (d. 1279) received the duchy of Brunswick, Wolfenbüttel, Grubenhagen, Göttingen, and other lands.

1. K. Kretschmer, *Historische Geographie von Mitteleuropa* (Munich and Berlin, 1904), pp. 226–29; H. Rössler and Günther Franz, *Biographisches Wörterbuch zur deutschen Geschichte* (Munich, 1953), pp. 94, 327, 653 ff., 881; W. Havemann, *Geschichte der Lande Braunschweig und Lüneburg*, I (Göttingen, 1853), 118 ff., 142 ff., 210 ff., 363 ff.; O. von Heinemann, *Geschichte von Braunschweig und Hannover*, I (Gotha, 1884), 159 ff., 247 ff.; Gebhardt's *Handbuch*, I, 322–24; F. Güterbock, *Der Prozess Heinrichs des Löwen* (Berlin, 1909); J. Haller, "Der Sturz Heinrichs des Löwen," *Archiv für Urkundenforschung*, Vol. III (1911); for further literature see Dahlmann-Waitz, *Quellenkunde der deutschen Geschichte* (9th ed.; Leipzig, 1931), No. 6629, and Mitteis, *Deutsche Rechtsgeschichte*, p. 88.

He was the originator of the older line of Brunswick. John (*d.* 1277) received Lüneburg, Celle, and other territories, including Hanover.

Albert's sons, Henry, Albert the Fat, and William, again divided the duchy of Brunswick. Henry (*d.* 1322) was the founder of the line Brunswick-Grubenhagen, so named after a castle, Grubenhagen, in the neighborhood of the town of Einbeck.[2] Albert the Fat (*d.* 1318) was the originator of the Göttingen line. He received various territories including Göttingen and Calenberg, and in 1292 also the land of Brunswick-Wolfenbüttel, once ruled by his deceased brother William (except for some territories inherited by Otto of Lüneburg). Further divisions of the lands of the duchy took place later. After Duke John's death in 1277, his son Duke Otto of Lüneburg, surnamed the Stern, added new territories to his inheritance, often through purchase. Thus in 1282 he bought a castle from the count of Hallermund for 1100 marks of silver. He bought the county of Wölpe (Welpe, Wilipa, Wilpia) in 1302 from Count Otto von Oldenburg for 6,500 marks of Bremen silver. These transactions attest to his financial abilities and efficiency. In 1389 the Lüneburg lands went to the dukes of Brunswick of the older line.[3]

The relations between the dukes belonging to various lines were by no means harmonious. Numerous feuds and wars contributed greatly to the poor state of the ducal finances, which were, except in some isolated cases, in precarious condition.

We are informed of the extreme financial difficulties of Dukes Albert and John, the sons of Otto the Child. These difficulties resulted from war expenses. The war of the dukes against the count of Holstein ruined the finances of the dukes, and they were absolutely unable to find the necessary means to repay their heavy debts. The usual remedy, the pledging or selling of estates and borrowing from the Jews, proved insufficient. Duke John was compelled to accept onerous personal obligations toward his creditors and to spend some time in custody (*obstagium*). He was only released in 1263 when the sums required were collected through a tax levied on the saltworks by the City of Lüneburg at his earnest supplication. In his appeal of April 22, 1263, Duke John stated that "verum est, frater noster, Dux, in

2. G. Max, *Geschichte des Fürstentums Grubenhagen*, I (Hanover, 1862), 3 ff., 485 ff.; K. Brüning, *Niedersachsen und Bremen* (Handbuch der historischen Stätten Deutschlands, II [Stuttgart, 1958]), 104–5, 158; bibliographical notes, 490–94.

3. For details see Havemann, *op. cit.*, pp. 460 ff.; Kretschmer, *op. cit.*, pp. 228, 229.

recessu suo a terra patrie reliquid nos quibusdam pro persona sua debitis obligatos, pro quibus persoluendis quasi captiuj ab emulis honoris nostrj aduersariis detinemur." On April 28, 1263, the unfortunate duke pointed out that "quia cum nos grauibus debitis obligati de quibus nullam uiam persoluendi potuimus inuenire. sed inimicis nostris captiui pro ipsis debitis iacebamus." In the first of these documents we also find an admission that "et eciam apud Judeos propositum minime haberemus." It is interesting to note that Duke John asked the town of Lüneburg to help him "nullo de Jure sed speciali de gracia." No wonder that under these circumstances Duke Albert I, the brother of Duke John, decided to abandon his plans in Denmark where he acted as governor on behalf of Queen Margaret and returned to Brunswick-Lüneburg.[4]

The financial difficulties of Duke Albert I did not end here. Following the unfortunate issue of the battle near Besenstedt (between Halle and Wettin) on October 27, 1263, where Duke Albert was defeated by the army of Margrave of Meissen, he was taken prisoner and remained in captivity a full year. To release other members of Albert's force, it was necessary to pay a ransom of 8,000 marks of silver; and to regain their freedom, the dukes of Brunswick-Lüneburg were compelled to cede various towns and castles to the victors.

The finances of the dukes, and in particular their borrowing, cannot be studied apart from two factors, which in certain periods played an important role. One of them is the towns, the other is the early development of the organization of the Estates.

The towns in the territory of the duchy of Brunswick-Lüneburg

4. H. Sudendorf, *Urkundenbuch zur Geschichte der Herzöge von Braunschweig und Lüneburg und ihrer Lande* (hereinafter quoted as *U.B. Braunschweig-Lüneburg*), Vol. I (Hanover, 1859), Nos. 56, 57; see also O. von Heinemann, *op. cit.*, II, 15, where the story is briefly told without reference to the *Urkundenbuch Braunschweig*. It is imperative to stress that, while for the history of public credit in the middle ages, in the important towns located within the territory of the old duchy of Brunswick-Lüneburg (i.e., for Brunswick, Lüneburg, Hanover, and Göttingen) we possess not only publications (*Urkundenbücher*) containing numerous charters but also other sources of information, in respect to the public credit of the duchies, *U.B. Braunschweig-Lüneburg* is the sole and exclusive source. Cf. the authoritative statement of A. von Kostanecki, *Der öffentliche Kredit im Mittelalter. Nach Urkunden der Herzogtümer Braunschweig und Lüneburg* (Schmoller's Forschungen, IX.1 [Leipzig, 1889]), 2. Kostanecki's study is the first special work devoted to the study of public credit in the middle ages and its importance in this respect can never be sufficiently stressed.

came into being in most cases during the twelfth and thirteenth centuries. It is known that the role of the Welfs in creating new towns was very important. The activities of Henry the Lion should be stressed especially.[5] Among the towns the following should be mentioned: Brunswick, Lüneburg, Hanover, Göttingen, and Münden. Two other important towns were also situated in the Welf territory. One of them, Helmstedt, arose around a monastery which for a long period exercised the lordship over the town. The dukes extended their lordship over Helmstedt to some extent, but became fully established there only in 1490. The history of the other town, Hildesheim, is closely connected with the history of the bishops of Hildesheim. As to Brunswick and Lüneburg, they were important centers, the first of a textile industry, the second of extraction of salt from the salt springs. Both became Hanseatic towns and played a great role in the financial history of the dukes of Brunswick-Lüneburg, and therefore they must be included in the presentation of the dukes' credit operations. The same applies to some extent to Hanover and Göttingen.[6]

Before the role of Estates is briefly examined, a few words must be said about different dynastic policies followed by the dukes of the Lüneburg line and those of the Brunswick line.[7] While in the last-named, divisions—and sometimes also reunions—of the land were often made, the dukes of Lüneburg were from the very beginning determined

5. Planitz, *Die deutsche Stadt im Mittelalter,* p. 139, rightly pointed out that "Den Stadtgründungen der Zähringer stehen die der Welfen an Bedeutung nicht nach . . . Heinrich der Löwe hatte offenbar als Schwiegersohn Konrad von Zähringen wichtige Anregungen zur Errichtung eigener Städte erfahren." The recently published study of J. Bärmann, *Die Städtegründungen Heinrichs des Löwen und die Stadtververfassung des XII Jahrhunderts* (Forschungen zur deutschen Rechsgeschichte, [Cologne and Graz, 1961]) was not accessible to me.

6. Havemann, *op. cit.,* I, 353–62. Planitz, *op. cit.* pp. 139–48; Kostanecki, *op. cit.,* pp. 6 ff.; Brüning, *op. cit.,* pp. 47 ff., 264 ff., 165 ff., 148 ff., 284 ff., 186 ff., 194 ff.; Dürre, *Geschichte der Stadt Braunschweig im Mittelalter* (Brunswick, 1861); O. Jürgens, *Geschichte der Stadt Lüneburg* (Hanover, 1891); E. Thurich, *Die Geschichte des Lüneburger Stadtrechts im Mittelalter* (Lüneburg 1960), pp. 12 ff., 37 ff. (with excellent bibliographical notes); G. Franke, *Lübeck als Geldgeber Lüneburgs. Ein Beitrag zur Geschichte des städtischen Schuldenwesens im 14. und 15. Jahrhundert* (Neumünster, 1935), pp. 1 ff., 9 ff., 21 ff., 27 ff.; W. Reinecke, *Geschichte der Stadt Lüneburg,* I (Lüneburg, 1933); A. Saathoff, *Geschichte der Stadt Göttingen,* I, (Göttingen, 1937), 15 ff., 36 ff., 43 ff.

7. G. Herden, *Entwickelung der Landstände im Herzogtum Braunschweig-Lüneburg vom 13. bis zum Ausgang des 14, Jahrhunderts* (Jena, 1888), pp. 6 ff., 30 ff.

to avoid divisions. The development of the role of the Estates is better known in Lüneburg than in other duchies. As we shall see later, it was in Lüneburg that the spectacular event, the so-called *Sate*, took place, by virtue of which the duke was restricted in his activities by the Estates. We shall also have the opportunity to examine the less-known but by no means less interesting limitation of the power of Duke Otto Cocles of Göttingen.

The Welf lands belonged to principalities where the prelates, the nobility, and the towns, which later constituted the Estates of the duchies, already assumed power and rights in the thirteenth and four-teenth centuries at the expense of the dukes. It can be proved that the incentive for the formation of an organization of Estates was the assemblies of nobility called by the dukes eager to discuss some matters "cum consilio fidelium." In a document in 1263, Duke John of Brunswick mentioned "*fideles,*" this time including the "*ministeriales,*" and in a document of 1282, Duke Otto of Brunswick mentioned "*milites*" or "*ministeriales*" present.[8] It is certain that the term "*fideles*" was identical with that of "*meliores terrae*" of the decree of May 1, 1231, and thus the burghers were not included.

The rise of the cities created new conditions, especially in view of the constantly growing need of the dukes to acquire money. Sometimes they had to restrict themselves to exclusive deals with the burghers, but there are cases where the dukes were compelled to approach all three groups, i.e., the prelates, the nobility, and the burghers. Such a situation occurred in 1293 when Duke Otto of Brunswick and Lüneburg, together with his wife, sold the right to issue coins in Lüneburg "to prelates, noblemen, towns, and to all men of the duchy of Lüneburg."[9] The buyers enjoyed the right to nominate persons to supervise and control the issuing of coins. A similar transaction was completed on February 2, 1322. This time Duke Otto of Brunswick-Lüneburg sold the "mvnte vnde wesle to Honouere" (i.e., in Hanover) to

8. *U.B. Braunschweig-Lüneburg,* Vol. I, Nos. 57, 97.

9. *Ibid.,* No. 122, ". . . (nos) vnanimi consensu, habito consilio cum fidelibus consiliariis nostris, causa utilitatis nostre, monetam nostram in Lvneborch rationabiliter vendidimus . . . Abbatibus, prepositis, aliisque ecclesiarum prelatis, militibus, famulis vniuersisque in terra . . . in parrochiis . . . Et dilectis burgensibus, Ciuitatum, et oppidorum, Lvneburch, Vlsen . . . Ceterisque hominibus oppidorum et villarum in quibus moneta Lvneburgensis soluere consueuit . . . Renuntiauimus enim omni iuri, quod in dicta moneta. nos. et dilectus pater noster, dux Johannes, et progenitores nostri a prima fundatione ciuitatis Lvn [i.e., Lüneburg, M.M.F.], habuimus."

the noblemen, the city of Hanover, and to the population. ("Den herren vn den Ridderen vnde der Stat to Honouere vnde deme gancen lande.") [10]

Transactions of this kind and the more usual financial problems led the dukes to approach not only the two privileged groups but also the burghers. The towns were bound—whatever their policy to secure freedom and self-government—to watch carefully the attitude and the policy of the dukes, almost constantly involved in all kind of feuds and wars. It is obvious that the towns could not remain neutral and that it was in their interest to prevent an occupation by the enemy. Hence, the towns were compelled in many instances to assist the dukes financially and rescue them from difficult situations. As we shall see, the finances of the towns were endangered and even ruined as a result of the financial help extended to the dukes.

It would be, however, an oversimplification to assume that because of these relations between the dukes and the towns (Brunswick, Lüneburg, and Göttingen) the process of forming a full-fledged organization of the Estates was substantially accelerated. The institution of rendering homage to the duke assuming the reins of government was a major factor in this development.[11] The towns were the economic and financial centers of the duchies, yet politically they were weak,[12] and, despite some spectacular success achieved from time to time, were unable to secure a lasting influence on ducal policy even in financial matters.

The relations between the towns and the dukes followed the usual patterns: the dukes in constant need of money were compelled gradually to give up their *regalia minora,* mostly through pledging them to the towns. In this way the City of Brunswick acquired from Duke Magnus his part in the mint for a period of five years,[13] and in 1369 for an indefinite period.[14] The right to mint coins in Lüneburg was

10. *Ibid.,* No. 357. See also No. 358, where the sons of Duke Otto confirmed the transaction.

11. Herden, *op. cit.,* pp. 42 ff.

12. See the lucid presentation by H. Preuss, *Die Entwicklung des deutschen Städtewesens,* I: *Entwicklungsgeschichte der deutschen Städteverfassung* (Leipzig, 1906), 95. The author stressed that "In seltsamer Weise kontrastiert diese politische Ohnmacht der deutschen Städte mit der fortdauernden wirtschaftlichen Blüte des städtischen Bürgertums."

13. *U.B. Braunschweig-Lüneburg,* Vol. II, No. 265.

14. *Ibid.,* Vol. III, No. 404. The sum received was "vor veftich lodighe mark brunsw wichte vn witte," i.e., 50 marks of *argentum legale* of Brunswick. On the

sold by Duke Otto and his wife Mechtild on January 6, 1293.[15] On April 30, 1351, Duke Ernst, the son of Duke Albert, sold the mint and other rights to the burghers and the council of Göttingen with the right to repurchase, i.e., in fact, the duke pledged the mint.[16] It was pledged again on May 28, 1357, for a period of seven years for 314 marks of silver[17] and for twenty-five years on July 13, 1382. This time Duke Otto III (1367–1394) asked for an additional two hundred marks, increasing the sum of the pledge from 314 to 514 marks. The City of Göttingen paid the amount requested and received a written promise that he would never issue coins. It is worth mentioning that this promise was strictly observed by the duke and his successors.[18]

As to the pledging or selling by the dukes of their right to customs duties, the buyers were primarily wealthy burghers. Later, however, the customs duties came into the possession of the towns. Part of the customs duties was pledged by the Dukes Magnus and Ernst of Brunswick to a burgher of Brunswick on January 25, 1360.[19] On March 30, 1360, Duke William of Lüneburg assigned to a burgher of Lüneburg the right to collect the "Tollen vppe der sulten to luneborch," i.e., the right to collect the tax on salt of Lüneburg for a period of four years against payment of the considerable sum of 3,000 marks of pfennigs of Lüneburg.[20]

The main goal of the towns in the duchy of Brunswick-Lüneburg was, as in other medieval German towns, to come into possession of the office of the bailiff (*Vogt, advocatus*), i.e., of the bailiwick (*Vogtei*). The *Vogts* were appointed by the dukes and exercised judicial power and functions.

---

currency in Brunswick see Otto Fahlbusch, *Die Finanzverwaltung der Stadt Braunschweig seit dem grossen Aufstand im Jahre 1374 bis zum Jahre 1425. Eine städtische Finanzreform im Mittelalter* (Gierke's Untersuchungen, 116 [Breslau, 1913]), pp. 178–90.

15. See nn. 9 and 10.

16. *U.B. Braunschweig-Lüneburg*, Vol. II, No. 393

17. *Ibid.*, Vol. III, No. 23; cf. G. Meinhardt, *Münz- und Geldgeschichte der Stadt Göttingen* (Göttingen, 1961), pp. 12 ff.

18. *U.B. Braunschweig-Lüneburg*, Vol. VI, No. 9; Meinhardt, *op. cit.*, p. 12; Saathhoff, *op. cit.*, I, 71. On currency in Göttingen see Meinhardt, *op. cit.*, pp. 13–20, 184 ff., and the works referred to (bibliographical notes pp. 193–99).

19. *U.B. Braunschweig-Lüneburg*, Vol. III, No. 97

20. *Ibid.*, No. 110. The role of salt and saltworks in the finances of the dukes of Lüneburg and the town Lüneburg will be disscussed later. On the mark of Lüneburg see A. Luschin von Ebengreuth, *Allgemeine Münzkunde und Geldgeschichte* (2d ed.; Munich and Berlin, 1926), p. 168

The City of Brunswick came gradually into the possession of the *Vogtei*.[21] The first known *Vogt* officiated in 1147. The dukes of Brunswick had been compelled, since 1299, to share the rule of the City of Brunswick with the dukes of Grubenhagen and, since 1345, with the dukes of the Göttingen line. The dukes did not reside permanently in the town and were not in a position to control events. Constant, however, was their need of money, hence the necessity to apply for financial help to the City of Brunswick. As, since 1299, rule over the city was divided, not one but two *Vogts* officiated in the city. Under these circumstances their authority was greatly reduced, especially because often they were not unanimous. From the beginning of the fourteenth century the city tried to reduce the power and competence of the *Vogts*. We cannot enter here into details, and it is sufficient to stress that gradually their power was substantially reduced.

While being a nuisance to the town, the *Vogtei* ceased to be of importance to the dukes. The time came for the *Vogtei* to be disposed of by the dukes. The part of the *Vogtei* owned by the dukes of the Göttingen line came into possession of the city as Duke Otto the Mild, acting in his own name and as guardian of his two younger brothers Magnus and Ernst, assigned it for 100 marks to the council of Altstadt, which was a part of the City of Brunswick. After Otto's death Dukes Magnus and Ernst confirmed on February 15, 1345, the transaction made by Otto, yet reserved for themselves the right of repurchase.[22] When Duke Magnus II confirmed once more, in 1371, the transaction of pledging, the *Vogtei* was already, in fact, owned by the town. The *Vogts* became officers of the City of Brunswick.

The town Lüneburg is mentioned for the first time in 956, when King Otto I gave to the Michaelis monastery "teloneum ad Luniburc ... qui ex salinis emitur."[23] It is well known how great was the im-

---

21. On *Vogts* in Brunswick see Dürre, *op. cit.*, pp. 63, 130–31, 142, 264–68, 284, 286–90. Dürre refers to his article "Die Stadtvogtei zu Braunschweig," *Archiv des historischen Vereins für Niedersachsen* (1847), pp. 171–93. In twelfth-century documents the *Vogt* appears under the name *advocatus*. During the reign of Duke Otto the Child he is called *judex*, and in documents written in German, *der Vogt* or *unsers Herren Vogt*.

22. *U.B. Braunschweig-Lüneburg*, Vol. II, No. 95: "Nos magnus et Ernestus fratres duces in Brunsw. recognoscimus publice per presentes. Quod dilectis Consulibus nostris ... ciuitatis brunsw pro sexingentis et nonaginta marcis puri argenti et ponderis brunswicensis ... dimisimus aduocaciam nostram in brunsw sicut inclitus princeps. dominus Otto dux ... ipsis eandem vendidit ac dimisit."

23. Cf. Thurich, *op. cit.*, p. 17.

portance of the saltworks of Lüneburg for the economic development of the town.[24] The saltworks were no less important in the process of the gradual emancipation of Lüneburg from the ducal supremacy, as the dukes were bound to respect the financial power of the salt magnates and of the City Council which they dominated.[25]

It can be assumed that the saltworks were at first owned exclusively by the dukes. At the turn of the twelfth and thirteenth centuries, most probably, some private owners also existed. They could be noblemen and prelates. Since the middle of the thirteenth century the administration of the saltworks passed gradually from the dukes to the wealthy burghers who constituted the ruling majority of the City Council. To what extent the dukes were dependent on the new plutocracy is drastically shown by the promise made by Duke John of Lüneburg on July 15, 1273, to a group of owners of a saltwork, composed of Cistercian and Benedictine monasteries and the council of Lüneburg, to fill up a newly opened saltwork with earth and never again to open a new one. Needless to say, the duke was financially rewarded for such a concession.[26] The ruling group in Lüneburg was prepared to pay for further privileges to be granted by the dukes, and the financial administration of the duchy of Lüneburg had no choice but to accommodate itself to the existing state of affairs.[27]

By the middle of the fourteenth century the *Vogt* in Lüneburg was compelled to share his power in some spheres of activities with the City Council,[28] and on November 6, 1369, Dukes William and Magnus pledged the *Vogtei* in Lüneburg to the city ("den Ratmannen vnser

---

24. E. H. L. Krause, *Zur Entwicklungsgeschichte der Lüneburger Saline* (Lüneburg, 1890) ; L. Zenker, *Zur volkswirtschaftlichen Bedeutung der Lüneburger Saline* (Hanover and Leipzig, 1906) ; H. Heineken, *Der Salzhandel Lüneburgs mit Lübeck bis zum Anfang des 15. Jahrhunderts* (Eberings Histor. Studien, No. 63 [Berlin, 1908]) .

25. Thurich, *op. cit.*, p. 23; Brüning, *op. cit.*, p. 266; Franke, *op. cit.*, pp. 3–5; Zenker, *op. cit.*, pp. 21 ff.; Heineken, *op. cit.*, p. 19.

26. Von Heinemann, *op. cit.*, II, 21; Thurich, *op. cit.*, pp. 23–24.

27. K. Friedland, *Der Kampf der Stadt* Luneburg *mit ihren Landesherren. Stadtfreiheit und Fürstenhoheit im 16. Jahrhundert* (Quellen und Darstellungen zur Geschichte Niedersachsens, LIII [Hildesheim, 1953]) , 9, gave the following formulation: "Geldzahlungen der Stadt, Gewährung von Rechten durch den Fürsten," which quite correctly describes the mutual relations between the dukes of Lüneburg and the ruling group in the city.

28. *U.B. Braunschweig-Lüneburg*, Vol. III, No. 330. The document in question is dated September 20, 1367; cf. Herden, *op. cit.*, p. 29; Thurich, *op. cit.*, pp. 30 ff.

Stad tu luneborch de nu sint vn eren nacomelinghen vn vnsen menen borghern al vnse macht vn recht de we hebben inder voghedige vn indeme richte") for 1,500 pounds of pfennigs of Lüneburg for a period of four years.[29]

We can now consider the main trends in the financial and, in particular, in the credit policy of the dukes in their duchies.

According to A. von Kostanecki [30] about three hundred obligatory letters issued by various dukes between 1293 and 1405 are known. The peak was reached during the period 1369–1373, when Duke Magnus the Younger of Brunswick-Lüneburg issued forty obligatory letters totaling 37,000 marks of silver. The duke was engaged in bitter fights against his enemies[31] and the war required considerable sums. Yet the financial calamities of the duchy started long before the reign of Magnus the Younger.[32]

Following the death of Duke Otto on August 30, 1344, the reign of the duchy of Brunswick went to his brothers Magnus I (the Older) and Ernst, who ruled jointly until April 17, 1345, when they divided the duchy. Duke Ernst received the territory of Oberwald around the City of Göttingen, the city, and several towns, while Duke Magnus took the rest of the duchy with its capital—Brunswick—and other towns.[33] During their joint reign the dukes continued their late brother's policy of pledging. They confirmed Otto's pledging of the *Vogtei*, and the

29. *U.B. Braunschweig-Lüneburg*, Vol. III, No. 426. The normal relations between the City of Lüneburg and the dukes became strained and finally broke during the War of Lüneburg Succession (1369–88), i.e., during the war between Duke Magnus Torquatus of Brunswick's older line and Duke Albert of Saxony, who received the duchy from the Emperor Charles IV following the death of Duke William of Lüneburg in 1369. Magnus was defeated in the battle at Roggendorf (in Mecklenburg) in 1369, and in 1371 the citizens of the City of Lüneburg destroyed the ducal castle. Duke Magnus was killed in the battle at Leveste on July 25, 1373, fighting against Count Otto of Schaumburg. Duke Albert of Saxony was mortally wounded and died in 1385 during the siege of the castle Ricklingen. Following the battle at Winsen, fought on May 28, 1388, between the successors of Duke Magnus and Duke Albert, the dukes of Brunswick firmly established their rule in the duchy of Lüneburg. The importance of the events of the period 1369–88 for the financial history of Lüneburg will be dealt with later.

30. Kostanecki, *Der öffentliche Kredit im Mittelalter*, pp. 56 ff.

31. See n. 29.

32. A genealogical table of the dukes is to be found in *U.B. Braunschweig-Lüneburg*, II, vi.

33. The duchy of Lüneburg, divided after the death of Otto the Child, returned to the Brunswick line only in 1389.

same day they pledged the castle Asseburg (pledged once by Duke Otto to the brothers Burchard and Günzel of Asseburg) as well as some other objects to the burghers and to the City of Brunswick ("vsen leuen borgheren deme Rade, vn der stad to Brunsw") for 1,470 marks of silver (*argentum legale*) of Brunswick.[34] On February 15, 1345, the dukes confirmed the debt of their brother Otto, who had borrowed 100 marks of silver from the City of Brunswick, and promised to repay it within one year or to raise the sum for which the castle Asseburg was put in pledge to 1,570 marks of silver.[35]

In connection with Magnus' preparation for the war with the archbishop of Magdeburg, he embarked on the road of selling and further pledging. Some of these transactions made since December 13, 1345, can be mentioned. On December 13, 1345, Duke Magnus pledged one-half of the castle Jerxheim to Günzel of Asseburg and to Henry and Ludolf of Wenden for 400 marks of silver, and the village and *Amt* (*officium*) Dettum to the same persons for another 400 marks.[36] Assignments of revenues from taxes were also made.[37] On June 2, 1346, Duke Magnus I and his son Duke Magnus II (who shared the reign of the duchy with his father) undertook to pay on May 20, 1347, to Duke Ernst of Brunswick-Göttingen, 400 marks of silver which they owed to him; otherwise they agreed to be obliged, together with their burghers, to *obstagium* in the City of Brunswick.[38] To finance the war against Magdeburg the duke of Brunswick made the greatest sacrifices and sold or pledged many castles and sources of revenue. He was compelled to continue this policy even after the end of the hostilities.[39] It should be noted, however, that in spite of his financial difficulties Duke Magnus continued to spend lavishly for all kind of pious purposes. He is rightly surnamed Magnus the Pious.

As a result of the war considerable debts were accumulated and

34. *U.B. Braunschweig-Lüneburg*, Vol. II, No. 97.

35. *Ibid.*, No. 98.

36. *Ibid.*, Nos. 144, 145.

37. *Ibid.*, p. xviii, Nos. 166, 167, 169, 175, 178, 179. All these transactions took place between May 14 and July 15, 1346.

38. *Ibid.*, No. 171. It should be noted that, although the City of Brunswick was allocated to Magnus I in accordance with the division of the territory of the duchy Brunswick-Lüneburg made on April 17, 1345, the dukes of the Grubenhagen line and those of the Göttingen line continued to exercise some sovereign rights over the city. Thus, after 1345 the City of Brunswick had three dukes as lords. This explains why the *obstagium* should have taken place in Brunswick.

39. *Ibid.*, Nos. 195, 196, 203, 207, 216.

new pledging became imperative.[40] How precarious was Magnus I's situation is clearly attested by the transaction of February 25, 1348, when Duke Magnus I and Magnus II were compelled to sell the castle Campen, villages, and other sources of revenues to the Dukes Otto and William of Lüneburg for 1,250 marks of silver. Campen was a most important castle and the dukes would not wish to sell it under normal circumstances. But these circumstances were far from normal. As a matter of fact, the dukes owed a considerable amount of money to the brothers Ludolf and John of Honlege. The date of payment was fast approaching. Duke Magnus and his son could expect to be compelled to start *obstagium* at the request of the brothers Honlege. Thus no choice was left them but to sell the castle. On the day when this transaction was performed, i.e., on February 25, 1348, Duke Magnus and his son satisfied one of their creditors by assigning to him 50 marks of silver to be paid by the buyers of the castle Campen.[41]

Needless to say, the poor state of the ducal finances necessitated further borrowing and pledging. We are relatively well informed as to one transaction which sheds light on the methods and technique of ducal borrowing in the mid-fourteenth century. This time the dukes borrowed on June 24, 1349, from von Cramm and von Salder, the sum of 315 marks of silver to be repaid in 1352.[42] The rate of interest was fixed at 10 per cent and the interest was to be paid out of the revenues from the customs at Linden. For the repayment of the debt revenues were selected from specific sources enumerated in the document. Various objects were pledged by Duke Magnus I to the bishopric of Hildesheim. It should be noted that relations between Duke Magnus and the bishop of Hildesheim were by no means harmonious and hostilities could be expected in the not too distant future, despite family ties existing between the respective rulers.

It is quite understandable that under these circumstances Magnus I was eager to recover from Hildesheim the possession of the above-

40. *Ibid.*, pp. xxx–xxxii. Instead of quoting from numerous documents attesting to a long chain of mass selling and pledging of various objects, a summary (p. xxxii) of the contents of these documents as completed by H. Sudendorf, the editor of the *Urkundenbuch*, is referred to: "Die Folgen des Krieges machten sich noch fortwährend sehr bemerklich. Herzog Magnus sah sich genöthigt, von einer Verpfändung und Veräusserung zur anderen zu schreiten, um das zur Fortführung der Regierung erforderliche Geld, weil der Krieg alle Einkünfte vorweggenommen und verzehrt hatte, herbeizuschaffen."

41. *U.B. Braunschweig-Lüneburg*, Vol. II, Nos. 245, 247. See also No. 248.

42. *Ibid.*, Nos. 320, 321, 322.

mentioned pledged sources of revenues. He borrowed 315 marks of silver with the intention of completing the deal with Hildesheim and redeeming the pledged objects. Another problem was that of providing the new lenders, i.e., von Cramm and von Salder, with a satisfactory guaranty. In order to accommodate them Magnus and his son handed over objects pledged to sixteen noblemen, mostly councilors of the dukes, officers, and *Vogts,* who also appear as sureties. They were empowered by the dukes to collect custom duties and use these funds for payment of interest. The revenues from the other objects pledged were to be used for the repayment of the capital. The dukes also authorized the above-mentioned commission of sixteen noblemen to nominate and appoint a special *Vogt* in case of necessity. In addition to the guaranties and securities, in case of default the dukes and, if necessary, their guarantors, were obligated to take up an *obstagium* in Brunswick and remain there in custody of the creditors until the debt was settled.

We have discussed the transaction with von Cramm and von Salder at length in order to prove that the technique of credit operations used by the dukes was by no means primitive; onerous personal obligations had to be accepted and the dukes had to endure humiliating contracts in their own land. It is also worthwhile to stress that in the contract between the dukes and von Cramm and von Salder the interest to be paid was explicitly mentioned. Whether 10 per cent was the real rate or not, cannot be established. It is known that even in the case of loans to princes it is wrong to deny all practical importance to the antiusury legislation. Therefore, illicit interest was rarely mentioned and all kinds of devices were used to disguise its presence.[43]

The expected war against Archbishop Otto of Magdeburg did not materialize and a relatively peaceful period contributed to a temporary improvement of the ducal finances. It even became possible to redeem the castle of Asseburg pledged in 1345 for 1,470 silver marks by Otto the Mild to the City of Brunswick. The castle—one of the strongest in the duchy—was of vital importance to the City of Brunswick for its paramount role in the system of defense of its trade routes.[44] The recovery of Asseburg most probably took place prior to May 1, 1349.[45]

The payment of 1,470 marks of silver had been a serious drain on

43. Cf. E. B. Fryde and M. M. Fryde, *op. cit.,* p. 431.

44. Brüning, *op. cit.,* pp. 16–17. Asseburg was situated on the most important route to Leipzig and Vienna.

45. *U.B. Braunschweig-Lüneburg,* II, xxxvi.

the dukes' finances and it is quite understandable that they were compelled to pledge various objects again. On November 11, 1349, Duke Magnus I pledged to Hermann von Salder, his wife, and relatives, the castle Hessen for 555 marks of silver. Other pledges followed, among them that to the City of Helmstedt on April 10, 1351, of the *Vogtei* in that city, and of some other regalian and proprietary rights for 200 marks of silver of Brunswick.[46]

Between 1346 and 1356 various other credit operations took place. The lenders were the burghers of the City of Brunswick. Thus, on January 5, 1346, the duke received 110 marks, on March 16, 1348, 90 marks, on June 18, 1348, 100 marks, on June 15, 1355, 350 marks, on June 24, 1355, 30 marks, and on February 9, 1356, 70 marks. In most of these cases the objects in question were formally sold with the stipulation that they could be repurchased, hence the real character of the operation was pledging.

The financial assistance of the burghers and the City of Brunswick continued to be of great importance to the duke. With this help Magnus I could recover the castle Hessen pledged to von Salder and, most probably, also the custom duties at Linden, pledged to von Cramm and von Salder. This transaction was probably completed on March 22, 1355, as it can be concluded from a new pledging of the castle Hessen together with a village, the *Vogtei*, etc., to the City of Brunswick. The time limit for the redemption of the objects pledged was three years. In case of default, 30 marks of silver were to be collected from the custom duties at Linden.[47]

If we examine carefully the various known transactions it can be concluded that, though each new contract attests to only a small decrease in the duke's indebtedness, the total decrease is of some significance.[48] Whatever the improvement of the ducal finances, it was only of temporary character, and soon new feuds and wars created new complications.

During the late fifties and early sixties of the fourteenth century, the borrowing, pledging, and selling was kept, on the whole, within usual—one could say normal—dimensions. But it should not be for-

<hr>

46. *Ibid.*, Nos. 339, 389.

47. *Ibid.*, Nos. 151, 251, 272, 512, 505. From document No. 505 we learn that Duke Magnus had sold, with the right of repurchase, a certain village with the *Vogtei* and other regalian rights, giving up the right to collect taxes and to request services. Similar exemptions were often made by the duke (Nos. 512, 541).

48. *Ibid.*, p. xxxviii.

gotten that Magnus I needed money to help his son Albert, provost at St. Paul in Halberstadt, to become archbishop at Bremen. This seat was promised to Albert if Archbishop Gottfried of Bremen should resign, as was envisaged. We cannot go into details of the story. Suffice it to say that as the result of the diplomatic maneuvers a coalition against Albert was created in August, 1359. Naturally, Duke Magnus I could not fail his son and he made all necessary military preparations for the approaching hostilities. In 1361, following the resignation of Archbishop Gottfried of Bremen, Pope Innocent VI designated Albert for the see. Yet the see was already occupied by Count Moritz of Oldenburg. Only after a military action against him did he abandon the seat, and Albert became the archbishop of Bremen (1362). The new archbishop had to borrow money in order to extricate himself from financial distress. Among the lenders was Duke Magnus II who together with Duke William of Lüneburg forwarded 4,150 silver marks to Archbishop Albert.[49]

In 1367 a great coalition of dukes and other *domini terrae,* among them Archbishop Dietrich of Magdeburg and Bishop Albert of Halberstadt, directed against Bishop Gerhard of Hildesheim, came into being. Duke Magnus I joined this coalition. On September 3, 1367, the army of the coalition was defeated and many noblemen were killed or taken prisoner.

Among the prisoners were Bishop Albert of Halberstadt and Duke Magnus I.[50] Their ransom was set at 7,000 marks. It can be assumed that the duke had to provide 3,000–4,000 marks. The only way to obtain this sum again was pledging. Hence it became imperative to request a considerable loan from the City of Brunswick. The city was ready to aid the duke and on November 11, 1367, in return for 2,500 silver marks Duke Magnus I pledged for a period of three years his castle Asseburg with various regalian rights and in addition some vil-

49. A history of Brunswick-Lüneburg which would satisfy the modern standard of historical writing is not available. The works of Havemann and von Heinemann provide us only with scanty material. As to the sources, they are not sufficient to give an account of all financial efforts made by Duke Magnus in connection with the action that he undertook to assist Albert. It can be assumed that the sums spent were considerable. See *U.B. Braunschweig-Lüneburg,* III, xiv–xxiv. Among the sums received following the pledging in 1360 were 1,200 marks, 300 marks, and 700 marks. The sum borrowed by Archbishop Albert of Bremen is mentioned in a source noted by Havemann, *op. cit.,* p. 474 and n. 1.

50. We follow v. Heinemann, *op. cit.* (p. 89), while Havemann, *op. cit.* (p. 477), and some other historians assume that not Magnus I but his son fell into the hands of the enemy.

lages and other objects. The city had paid, however, only 2,300 marks, the balance, i.e., 200 marks, having been reserved to cover the future cost of new construction to be made in the castle.[51] The same day Duke Magnus sold with right of repurchase, i.e., pledged, the *Amt* (*officium*) in Dettum for 400 marks. Other pledging transactions on February 2 and February 29, 1368, brought 635 marks. We are also informed by the *Hemelik rekenscop* (secret report) of 1406 that Duke Magnus pledged the castle Wolfenbüttel for 3,800 marks as a partial security for the ransom to be paid to the bishop of Hildesheim. Magnus was aware that the amount could not be paid at the fixed date, and there was great danger that the Wolfenbüttel castle would be lost to Hildesheim and become a stronghold in the hands of Bishop Gerhard. The City of Brunswick had no choice but to provide the duke of Brunswick with the money, take over the castle, and hold it in pledge.[52]

The resulting war debts were embarrassing and often cumbersome for Duke Magnus I. The situation changed after a settlement made between him and his son Magnus on May 25, 1368. The stipulations of this arrangement are known and we need not here consider the details.[53] Of greater importance was the fact that Magnus II was named on September 14, 1368, by Duke William of Lüneburg as his successor in the principality, and he took over the obligation to repay the debts of Archbishop Albert of Bremen—a payment guaranteed by Magnus I.

Magnus I died in July, 1369, and Duke William of Lüneburg died in November. The problem of succession in that duchy became an important factor in shaping the duchy's history for the relatively long period of nineteen years (1369–1388).[54] The wars of that period necessitated strenuous financial efforts by the rulers concerned and they also involved the main cities of the duchy Brunswick-Lüneburg in financial trouble. The financial history of these wealthy towns, and in particular the history of their systems of borrowing, had always been closely connected with ducal finances. During these crucial nineteen years, and after 1388, they became interwoven to such an extent with the history of the credit operations of the dukes and other rulers that it becomes necessary to devote some attention to the main phases of borrowing by the cities of Brunswick and Lüneburg.

The City of Brunswick was composed of five towns: Altstadt, Ha-

51. *U.B. Braunschweig- Lüneburg*, Vol. III, No. 338.
52. *Ibid.*, Nos. 339, 344, 349, 350; Vol. IV, No. 16. On *Hemelik rekenscop* see n. 57.
53. *U. B. Braunschweig-Lüneburg*, Vol. III, Nos. 363, 364; cf. pp. xxxvi–xxxvii.
54. See n. 29.

gen, Neustadt, Altewiek, and Sack. In 1269 a general council (*Gemeiner Rat*) was created by the first three towns. Later Altewiek and Sack were included. The internal structure of the city government and the relations between the five component parts underwent various changes due to ducal intervention or revolt of the population. The council gradually lost its original aristocratic character. The participation of the guilds and artisans grew constantly. Yet the role of the patricians always remained important.[55]

The wealth of the burghers of Brunswick and the great role the city played in the medieval trade was briefly mentioned above. In the middle of the fifteenth century Brunswick became one of the most splendid towns in Germany. It could impress even such a highly educated man as Aeneas Sylvius (later Pope Pius II) who, in his writings, gave a vivid description of the comfort of life in Brunswick. The city was striving to become immune from the ducal interference with municipal affairs and in this endeavor it was, on the whole, successful. This goal could be achieved because of wealth which gave to the City Council and the burghers real power in their dealings with the dukes as sovereigns of the city. The dukes lived, as we know, in a state of almost permanent financial penury and could be rescued only by willing lenders. Thus, a way for a *do ut des* policy was paved and other logical prolegomena for a fruitful coexistence of a wealthy town and a poor ruler were available. They determined historical reality. As a matter of fact, Brunswick nearly reached a status similar to that of an imperial town, insofar as its self-government and its financial administration are concerned. It was not in the city's interest to go too far and become a *Reichsstadt*. It should be noted that already in 1263 the dukes had transferred the seat of their government from the City to Wolfenbüttel, where they remained for many centuries.

Prior to 1269, each of the towns (*Weichbilder*) had its own finan-

55. Dürre, *Geschichte der Stadt Braunschweig im Mittelalter*, pp. 278–313. Dürre asserts that Brunswick was one of the old German cities that already had a municipal council composed of *consules* in the second half of the twelfth century. On the municipal government of Brunswick see also *Die Chroniken der deutschen Städte vom 14. bis ins 16. Jahrhundert, VI, Die Chroniken der niedersächsischen Städte. Braunschweig,* I (2d ed.; Göttingen, 1962), xiii–xxxv. On the financial administration prior to the revolt of 1374, see H. Mack, *Die Finanzverwaltung der Stadt Braunschweig bis zum* Jahre 1374 (Gierkes Untersuchungen, XXXII [Breslau, 1889]), pp. 18 ff. On the period 1374–1425, see Fahlbusch, *op. cit.,* pp. 6 ff; Kostanecki, *op. cit.,* pp. 42–55; v. Heinemann, *op. cit.,* p. 145; Brüning, *op. cit.,* p. 49.

cial administration. Then it was decided to discuss in common all matters pertaining to Altstadt, Hagen, and Neustadt and that the elected council should be in charge: "consules super causis civitatis universae." A common cash office was set up, to which each of the towns contributed. The agreement of November 18, 1269, prescribed how the collected funds should be used: "Redditus eciam et collectus totius civitatis ad communes usus et expensas reponentur in unum, et ex una et communi bursa civitatis comoda disponantur." Borrowing too was concentrated in the hands of the newly created common council (*Gemeiner Rat*), as follows clearly from the agreement of 1299 between Dukes Albert and Henry and the council: "Se hebbet ok dat geloved und gesworen, alle de schult de se nu schuldich sin und schuldich werden to user nod und der stad noet dat se de mit sumpder hand endrechtliken gelden schullet, und ok den tins, den de stadt vorkofft hefft, to erer noet, den scullen se geuen endrechtliken, bet dat se den wedderkoppen."[56]

The debts contracted by the City of Brunswick in the first half of the fourteenth century and in the fifties and sixties of that century were not very high, as is manifest from the most important source available, namely from the *Hemelik rekenscop,* i.e., secret report, completed in 1406, probably by one of the city councilors.[57] It is true that in view of the practice of concentrating all payment connected with the service of debts contracted, i.e., of two forms of annuities—life annuities (in Brunswick called *Leibgedinge*) and perpetual annuities (called *Weddeschatz*)[58]—during two terms in the year, a shortage of

56. The texts of the agreements of 1269 and 1299 are available in *Urkundenbuch der Stadt Braunschweig*, I (L. Haenselmann, ed. [Brunswick, 1861]). Cf. Kostanecki, *op. cit.*, pp. 42–43; Mack, *op. cit.*, pp. 24–26, 30 ff. As to the term *redditus* Mack translated it rightly as *Schoss und Zinseinkünfte* with reference to Du Cange and other dictionaries. From the glossary completed by K. Schiller in *Chroniken der niedersächsischen Städte*, I, 483–523, we take the translation of a term used in the quoted sentence into modern German: *endrechtliken-einträchtiglich*.

57. The text is to be found in *Chroniken* . . ., VI, 133–207. For the history of this document see pp. 123–32.

58. On municipal annuities see B. Kuske, *Das Schuldenwesen der deutschen Städte im Mittelalter* (Tübingen, 1904), pp. 11 ff., 27 ff.; H. Buchner, *Zur Entwicklung des städtischen Kredits in Deutschland im Mittelalter und im 16. Jahrhundert* (Munich, 1925), pp. 19–23, 34. Kuske, "Die Entstehung der Kreditwirtshaft und des Kapitalverkehrs," *Kölner Vorträge hsg. von der Wirtschafts- und Sozialwissenschaftlichen Fakultät der Universität Köln*, Vol. I (Leipzig, 1927), (reprinted in Kuske, *Köln, der Rhein und das Reich. Beiträge aus fünf Jahrzehn-*

available funds occurred systematically and periodically. Hence, borrowing money could not be avoided. But on the whole the indebtedness arising from the selling of annuities was not burdensome. Data is not available for the whole period directly preceding the eventful years at the beginning of the seventies. It can be established, however, that the total paid by the city in 1355 was about 145 marks (including both types of annuities), i.e., only about 6.5 per cent of the total municipal expenses. At the end of the sixties Brunswick's total indebtedness was 1,587 marks and 2 farthings according to the *Hemelik rekenscop*. This capital required an annual payment of 148 marks, 3 farthings.[59] Even if we do not consider the sum of debts as precise, there is no doubt that the amount does not differ considerably from that in 1355. It can be admitted, in accordance with the results of Mack's investigations, that the debt remained stationary almost until the end of the sixties.[60]

When did the burden of debts begin to rise? The question is of paramount importance, for it is known that the rebellion of 1374 in Brunswick was the result of debts contracted by the city during the preceding period—let us assume during the previous seven years.[61]

It is well established that the increase of public debt in a given territorial unit is very often functionally determined by war preparations and war expenses and in particular by military defeat. The City of Brunswick was so closely tied to the ducal administration that each grave political shock the dukes suffered was bound to cause severe repercussions—including financial ones—in the municipal administra-

---

ten wirtschaftsgeschichtlicher Forschung [Cologne and Graz, 1956], pp. 108–11):
E. B. Fryde and M. M. Fryde, *op. cit.*, pp. 529 ff.; Although predominantly interested in the legal aspect of the life annuities, W. Ogris, *Der mittelalterliche Leibrentenvertrag. Ein Beitrag zur Geschichte des deutschen Privatrechts* (Munich, 1961), is of importance for all students of the role of the annuities in the middle ages. The sale of annuities constituted the most usual form of medieval municipal borrowing in Germany. No wonder that they were long regarded erroneously as a purely German institution.

59. *Chroniken* . . . , VI, 135; Mack, *op. cit.*, p. 106, n. 3, stresses correctly that the exact date is not given by the *Hemelik rekenscop* and that the year in question cannot be 1367.

60. Mack, *op. cit.*, p. 107.

61. The rebellion of 1374 and its financial causes will be studied later. It is worthwhile, however, to refer to the authoritative statement of Mack *(op. cit.,* p. 106), who is fully aware that whatever the shortcomings of the financial administration of Brunswick, they cannot be regarded as the real cause which plunged the city into the abyss of an enormous indebtedness, leading to the rebellion of 1374.

tion. Such a heavy blow was the victory of Bishop Gerhard of Hildesheim over Duke Magnus and his allies on September 3, 1367. We have
noted that the city could not refuse to help Duke Magnus financially.[62]
As a result municipal debts rose rapidly, for the city was unable to
provide the needed amount—3,800 marks—from the ordinary revenues.
It pledged the castle Hessen for 1,000 marks and received 2,800 marks
from the sale of perpetual annuities, probably at a rate of 8 per cent.
Such a rate can be found in one of the existing registers of sale of
annuities. According to that source, in 1370 Brunswick sold annuities
for 400 marks, 200 marks, 150 marks, and three times 100 marks. In
1371 the sum of annuities sold was 150 marks, in 1372, 50 marks. In
all these cases the rate on the annuities was 8 per cent. In 1370 the
total indebtedness of the city rose to 5,400 marks.[63]

Other calamities of Duke Magnus contributed to the further deterioration of the finances of the City of Brunswick. It is therefore
necessary to return to the events of 1370–1373 and to analyze their
impact on ducal financial policy. Only after a brief examination of
these events is it possible to explain how the rising indebtedness of the
City of Brunswick caused a revolt in 1374.

Dukes Rudolf, Wenzel, and Albert of Saxony-Wittenberg were
confirmed on March 3, 1370, in their rights to the duchy Lüneburg
given them in fief by the Emperor Charles IV. The cities of Lüneburg
and Hanover were ordered on June 29 to render homage to the dukes
of Saxony-Wittenberg. Duke Magnus II (Torquatus), a man of
violent character unable to resort to the means and devices of clever
diplomacy, did everything to complicate his already difficult situation.
One of his greatest errors was his handling of affairs in the City of
Lüneburg, in connection with a financial matter of the greatest
importance.[64]

Among the not too numerous staunch supporters and followers of
the emperor in the northern parts of German territory was Duke Albert of Mecklenburg. As a result of a feud between Magnus II and
Albert, following the defeat of Magnus' army at Roggendorf on No-

---

62. See n. 52.
63. *Hemelik rekenscop*, cap. 3; Dürre, *op. cit.*, p. 157; Mack, *op. cit.*, pp.
107–8.
64. Chronicle of the City Notary Nicolaus Floreke, in *Chronicken der deutschen Städte*, XXXVI (Stuttgart, 1931), 11 ff. (Other editions of this important
source are cited by W. Reinecke in his Introduction on p. 7); Havemann, *op. cit.*,
pp. 479–83; von Heinemann, *op. cit.*, pp. 90 ff.

vember 29, 1369, a great number of Magnus' vassals were taken prisoner. On June 19, 1370, the sum of ransom to be paid on November
11 of the same year was set at 3,000 marks of silver.[65] Duke Magnus,
unable to pay this sum, decided to extort it from the municipal council of Lüneburg. At first the city rejected Magnus' demand. Nor could
the council accept Magnus' seizure of the parts owned by clergymen of
Mecklenburg in the salt works of Lüneburg. Magnus also asked the
municipal council to hand over all revenues from the saltworks, to
which revenues the monasteries in Mecklenburg, Schwerin, and Holstein were entitled.[66]

Duke Magnus could not forget the humiliation. His relations with
the City of Lüneburg became increasingly strained. In August, 1370,
Magnus was prepared to use arms against the city and soon he carried
out his plans. He asked the councilors to come, and extorted from them
by threats acceptance of the occupation of the city gates and towers
by the ducal garrison. He went so far as to consider jailing the city
councilors, but gave up this plan. Instead he asked the city to pay the
exorbitant sum of 20,000 marks but finally was satisfied with the promise of 7,000. In addition Lüneburg was compelled to surrender various
privileges granted it by Duke William, which were received at the
expense of about 1,000 marks.[67]

The city was unable to pay the promised sum out of its own re-

65. *U.B. Braunschweig-Lüneburg*, Vol. IV, No. 31.

66. *Chroniken* . . . XXXVI, pp. 11 ff.; H. Heineken, *Der Salzhandel Lüneburgs
mit Lübeck bis zum Anfang des 15. Jahrhunderts*, pp. 60–61; O. Hoffmann, *Der
Lüneburger Erbfolgestreit* (Halle, 1896), pp 20–22; Franke, *Lübeck als Geldgeber
Lüneburgs*, p. 27; von Heinemann, *op. cit.*, pp. 91 ff.

67. The text of a draft of a declaration of Magnus on August 22 and 25, 1370,
is preserved. *U.B. Braunschweig-Lüneburg*, Vol. IV, No. 39: "We Radman vnde
meynen Borghere der stad to Luneborch. bekennet openbare in dessem breue, dat
alle de vriyheyt priuilegia, vnde Breue myd alle eren articulen. vnde rechtecheyt, de
vns vnse gnedeghen heren. her Wilhelm. vnde Junchere Lodewich. herteghen to
Brunswich. vnde to Luneborch. gheuen vnde beseghelet hebben scollen van stun-
den an doet wesen vnde eweghen doet blyuen. vnde nene macht macht meer
hebben. . . ." On August 25, Duke Magnus declared that he was compelled because of his difficult situation ("we van nod weghene") to ask the City of Lüneburg for financial help for the release of the imprisoned men, and that the councilors and burghers of Lüneburg promised to pay the previously mentioned sum
("Des hebben dhe suluen vse Ratman. vnde borghere, vse noed ane zeen . . . vnde
hebben vns ghetwidet also. dat se vns gheuen souen dusent lodeghe mark . . .").
Cf. pp. xx–xxi. The list of privileges canceled is given in No. 38; the renounce-
ment of the city in No. 39.

sources and the only way available was to ask the saltworks to contribute to the fund needed. This was exactly the remedy rejected by the council when it had been requested by Duke Magnus. Now the council was compelled to try to use the same dreadful device. The duke promised to help the councilors in their taxation of the saltworks, and a special draft was made of Magnus' declaration. In this draft Magnus refused to promise in a categorical form not to levy a similar tax (*Bede*) in the future, and he preferred a milder expression. The councilors became suspicious and asked that the sum be reduced from 7,000 to 6,000 marks. Agreement was reached, and on August 25 the document was signed, after the necessary amendments were made. The same day the city handed Magnus a letter in which it obliged itself to pay him the sum of 6,000 marks of silver. The city had to pay 200 marks within the coming week and another 800 marks on September 29. Further, the city was obliged to pay 3,000 marks to the Duke of Mecklenburg before the coming November for the release of prisoners, to pay the City of Brunswick 1,000 marks on December 25, 1370, and another thousand on April 6, 1371.[68]

Magnus treated the City of Lüneburg—to use the expression of Sudendorf—as a conquered town.[69] To be sure, it paid homage[70] to him, in accordance with the settlement of August 25, 1370, although it was ordered by the Emperor Charles IV to do homage to the new rulers appointed by him, i.e., to the dukes of Saxony-Wittenberg. The city was eager to fulfill all promises of payment. But it was unable to pay the 200 marks before September 1, 1370, and this payment was made together with that of another 800 marks on September 29, 1370. As we know, it was by no means an easy task for the city to provide the necessary funds, and recourse to borrowing was unavoidable.

The list of loans includes the following sums borrowed by the city:

68. *Ibid.*, No. 41. In the text of the letter concerned we read: "We Radman vnde de gantze gemeynheyt der Borghere, der Stad to Luneborch, bekennen openbare in dessem Breue, dat we dem dorchluchteghen vorsten, hern Mangno . . . Schuldich sin van rechter schult Ses dusent mark lodeghes Suluers. . . ."

69. Sudendorf, *ibid.*, p. xxi, describes the situation in the following words: "Herzog Magnus hatte die Stadt wie eine eroberte behandelt, hatte sie aller Macht und Herrlichkeit entkleidet und hoffte, sie auf jenen unbedeutenden Standpunkt, dem sie längst entwachsen war hinuntergedrückt zu haben. Kein Widerstand zeigte sich mehr, keine Klage wurde laut, nur dumpfer Schweigen herrschte." Needless to say the brutalities of Magnus stirred a wave of anger in the towns of the duchy.

70. The text, *ibid.*, No. 42.

October 15, 1370	borrowed	150 marks of Lün. pfen. from Johann von Brokele
October 31, 1370		330 marks of Lün. pfen. from Albert Kulen
November 6, 1370		1,800 marks of Lün. pfen. from the abbot and the monastery of Rheinfeld
November 11, 1370		100 marks of Lün. pfen. from Johann Grundis in Lübeck
November 11, 1370		1,008 guilders of Lübeck from various burghers of Lübeck
November 11, 1370		1,000 marks of Lün. pfen. from various burghers of Lübeck

Some of the loans were interest free, one was contracted on the basis of a rate of 6 ⅔ per cent interest, another at 8 ⅓ per cent, and all the others at 10 per cent. Most onerous was the loan from Reinfeld. Here it was stipulated that in case of default of payment of 150 marks on November 11 of each year, the double amount should be paid on December 25 of that year. The annuity could not be made redeemable before the period of time between November 11 and December 25, 1376.[71]

The City of Lüneburg was long under obligation to comply with the order issued by the emperor to recognize the dukes of Saxony-Wittenberg. In January, 1371, the situation became acute and on the last day of that month the city took the decisive step and informed

71. *Ibid.*, p. xxv. On the role of Lübeck as financier of Lüneburg see Franke, *op. cit.*, pp. 34 ff. Cf. also *Urkundenbuch der Stadt Lüneburg*, ed. F. W. Volger (Lüneburg, 1872–77), (hereinafter referred to as *U.B. Lüneburg*), II, 647. Cf. the text revealing the credit operations in which the abbot and the monastery appear as lenders, *U.B. Braunschweig-Lüneburg*, Vol. IV, No. 53. In this interesting document the *consules* of Lüneburg declare that "Religiosi viri abbas et conuentus monasterij in reyneuelt, Cystersiensis ordinis . . . volentes vtilitati et necessitati sue et ipsius monasterij prouidere. Nos igitur consules predicti pecunijs ad vtilitatem et perpetuam releuationem nostre ciuitatis indigentes . . . vendidimus eisdem abbati et conuentui et eorum successoribus centum quinquaginta marcarum redditus pro Mille. octigentis marcis. . . ." It is known that the Church did not object to the creation of annuities in the initial stages of their development and, as a matter of fact, clergymen and monasteries did much to popularize them. Even when restrictive measures were demanded by some writers on Canon Law, the Church could not bring itself to condemn the sale of annuities, considered to be lawful even prior to the declaration made by Pope Martin V. For details see E. B. Fryde and M. M. Fryde, *op. cit.*, pp. 530–31, and the books there cited. The payment on November 12, 1370, of 3,000 marks of ransom to Duke Albert of Mecklenburg is confirmed by the document he issued. See *U.B. Braunschweig-Lüneburg*, Vol. IV, Nos. 56, 57. On November 13, 1370, Duke Magnus attested to having received from the City of Lüneburg 4,000 marks (*ibid.*, No. 59).

Duke Magnus that it must obey the imperial orders. On February 1 the city destroyed the ducal *Burg* in the city and on February 2, Duke Albert of Saxony entered the town. Other cities, Hanover among them, followed the example of Lüneburg.

Like Brunswick the City of Lüneburg[72] was a wealthy and splendid town. Its saltworks were for centuries the main source of wealth of its burghers. First owned by the dukes of Lüneburg, they were gradually assigned and later sold to private persons. Their participation in the exploitation of the salt springs and saltworks took various legal forms which cannot be studied within the compass of the present essay. It is sufficient to say that while the extraction and trade of salt was in the hands of the population of Lüneburg, the financial interests were represented by a large spectrum of financiers and investors, many of them situated outside Lüneburg. They derived annual rents from their parts in the salt industry in Lüneburg. These parts as well as rents or other revenues could be assigned, pledged, or sold. The payment of rents was secured by revenues from the saltworks specially earmarked for this purpose. These *Sülzrenten*[73] were a peculiarity of Lüneburg, yet

72. For the general history of Lüneburg, cf. Jürgens, *Geschichte der Stadt Lüneburg* (Hanover, 1891) ; U. Wendland, *Aus Lüneburger 1000-jähriger Vergangenheit* (Lüneburg, 1956) ; W. Reinecke, *Geschichte der Stadt Lüneburg.* For the history of salt industry and trade, L. Zenker, *Zur volkswirtschaftlichen Bedeutung der Lüneburger Saline;* Heineken, *Der Salzhandel Lüneburgs mit Lübeck bis zum Anfang des 15. Jahrhunderts;* W. Kaiser, *Die Geschichte der Unternehmung und des staatlichen Einflusses in der Salzindustrie Hannovers und Westfalens bis zum Ende des 18. Jahrhunderts* (Cologne, 1938) ; Franke, *op. cit.*

73. For *Sülzrenten* cf. Kostanecki, *op. cit.;* Ogris, *Der mittelalterliche Leibrentenvertrag,* p. 57. As an example of such a rent the text *U.B. Lüneburg,* No. 151, p. 94, of 1287 (as referred to by Ogris) can be given. It contains a donation of a *Sülzrente* to the monastery of Rheinfeld, "Quod nos Gherardus . . . Alhedihis uxor ejus et Bruno, ejusdem Alheidis filius . . . redditus duorum Chororum salis annuatim . . . humiliter optulimus tali modo, quod nos prenominati tres eisdem perfruamur, quandiu viximus." The rents, primarily paid in salt, later were paid in money. (Franke, *op. cit.,* p. 5) "Wer Anteil an der Sülze erworben hatte, Pfannen- oder Chorusgut, gehörte der Gemeinschaft der Salineninteressenten an, einer Universitats, die im juristischen Sinne Eigentümer der Sülze war. Diese Anteile hafteten zwar ganz bestimmten Siedehäusern, Pfannen oder anderen rententragenden Objekten der Sülze an, waren aber, seitdem die Sülzmeister die Siedung übernommen hatten und die Rente nicht mehr in Salz sondern in Geld gezahlt wurde, zu eineim Anteil des gesamten Gewinnes am Salzwerk geworden." Franke's remark deserves to be compared with the explanation provided by Kostanecki (*op. cit.,* p. 36), who failed, however, to reach Franke's precision. K. T. von Inama-Sternegg, "Zur Verfassungsgeschichte der deutschen Salinen im Mittelalter," *Sitzungsberichte*

other forms of financing and lending were by no means excluded. It is worth noting that among the persons deriving their revenues from the Lüneburg salt industry and trade in one way or another, a predominent role was played by the monasteries and ecclesiastical institutions referred to in the medieval charters and chronicles as "salt prelates" (Sülzprälaten).[74]

Already in 1200 there were fifty-four saltworks in Lüneburg. The revenues from the salt industry reached a very high level in the fourteenth century and Lüneburg at that time was one of the great industrial centers in Germany. There were periods during which all northern Germany from the Oder to the Rhine was supplied with salt by Lüneburg. The city survived periods of industrial depression and even a great financial catastrophe at the end of the fourteenth and middle of the fifteenth centuries, both caused by excessive debts.

Duke Magnus died the next day after the fight at Leveste (July 25, 1373). Lüneburg's debt already reached 12,033 marks of pfennigs at the end of 1372, insofar as it was represented by letters obligatory. If other forms of debts are added the total was considerably higher. A long period of wars ended following the battle at Winsen on May 28, 1388, when the Ascanian cause supported also by the City of Lüneburg suffered a heavy defeat. The way was open for the rule of the Welfs in Lüneburg. The loans contracted during the unhappy period of hostilities were a great blow to the stability of Lüneburg's municipal finances. The following figures will illustrate the increase in indebtedness.

---

der Kaiserlichen Akademie der Wissenschaften, I (Vienna, 1886), 26, considers that the Pfannherren did constitute a sui generis association. The term Pfanne (Lat. panna) denotes primarily a kitchen utensil (pan), i.e., a broad shallow container used in cooking. In the salt trade it also denoted a unit of measurement. The term Pfanne was used predominantly in this sense. See the useful comments in J. Freydank, Die Hallesche Pfännerschaft im Mittelalter (Halle, 1927), p. 36, where a document of 1179 is quoted, containing the following sentence: "contulimus ecclesiae . . . tantum porcionem de puteo salinarum, ut ad coquendum salem quatuor inde panne instruantur. . . ." It is interesting to note that the Hallesche Pfännerschaft which is 1,000 years old, was in modern times reorganized as an Aktiengesellschaft, i.e., a corporation.

74. The role of the Sülprälaten in the history of public credit in Lüneburg will be examined in connection with the so-called Prälatenkrieg. In a document of November, 1377, U.B. Braunschweig-Lüneburg, Vol. V, No. 121, the names of numerous monasteries, chapters, and clergymen are given. Cf. also Kaiser, op. cit., p. 36.

During 1371 new loans contracted amounted to 16,533 marks of pfennigs, half of this sum provided by financiers from Lübeck.[75] The financial reputation of Lüneburg suffered heavily; borrowing money became extremely difficult even in Lübeck which was closely connected to the old center of the salt industry by various financial and commercial ties.[76] While in 1371 the total sum of new loans contracted in Lübeck by the City of Lüneburg was 8,000 marks, the total in 1372 was only 633 marks. It should be pointed out that the prices of salt and of saltrents (*Sülzrenten*) declined at that time. The moneylenders in Lübeck were prepared, however, to lend money to the City of Lüneburg if sufficient guarantee and security could be found. Thus in April, 1374, when the City of Lüneburg with the consent of the dukes pledged the salt tax (which did not belong to the city), moneylenders in Lübeck made favorable financial offers. The Lüneburg 10-percent saltrents were an excellent investment for them. The pledging was completed on July 22, 1375.[77] The sum of the pledge was fixed at 5,300 marks, yet it could be raised to 7,000 marks, the original annual rent having been 530 marks. The definite contract was perfected on September 29, 1375, and a special consortium of eighteen creditors was created.

The improved financial opportunities resulted from the city's new policy of securing financial assistance from the partners in the saltworks. Until 1370 the City Council was wont to make compulsory deductions of a certain percentage from its revenues to cover the war expenses. This procedure was always opposed by the "salt prelates," especially by the cathedral chapter in Lübeck. On July 13, 1374,[78] a compromise solution was found: the city ceased to deduct the sums from the rents and agreed to submit the whole matter to arbitration. On January 28, 1375, the arbitration court decided that the deductions should be made in order to render financial help ("hulpe") to the City of Lüneburg in view of its difficult situation ("des hebbe we de noth hort vnde bekant"). This financial help was to continue until 1378.[79] It is worthwhile to note this event, for in later periods the "salt pre-

---

75. *U.B. Braunschweig-Lüneburg*, IV, xci; Franke, *op. cit.*, p. 38.

76. *Ibid.*, p. 38.

77. *U.B. Braunschweig-Lüneburg*, Vol. V, No. 62; Franke, *op. cit.*, p. 42.

78. The text of the agreement reached in *U.B. Braunschweig-Lüneburg*, Vol. V, No. 27.

79. *Ibid.*, No. 47.

lates" declined in a most categorical manner to participate in financial measures aimed at repayment of heavy debts.

The war against the dukes of Brunswick-Lüneburg, in which Lüneburg was involved, brought a new colossal increase of municipal debts. We shall not go into details. It is enough to say that the debts rose to 100,000 marks of pfen. in 1377, which made a new arrangement with the "salt prelates" imperative. The settlement took place on November 25, 1377. This time the payments to be made by the "salt prelates" were nearly doubled and a special commission was created to control and supervise the levying of the sums to be deducted and the repayment of the debts. It was composed of the abbot of the Cistercian monastery in Reinfeld, the provost of the Premonstratensian monastery in Heiligenthal, the provost of the Benedictine monastery in Lüne, the bursar of Scharnebeck, four councilors of Lüneburg, and four burghers of that city.[80] In the oath then sworn, the councilors also agreed that the settlement could be submitted to the pope for approval: "Presentibus rogamus petimus et consentimus vt premissa omnia et singula cum executorum deputacione meliori modo quo fieri poterit per sedem apostolicam confirmentur." The financial assistance was to be extended over a period of ten years.

The repayment of the municipal debts proceeded in an efficient manner. Yet the total municipal debt was still very high in 1385, amounting to 60,000 marks of pfennigs. New and more energetic measures became necessary. A new agreement as to financial assistance was reached with the "salt prelates" in October, 1385. As mentioned before, in 1273 the destruction of a newly discovered salt spring was decided on and performed. In 1385 the exploitation of this old salt spring, once filled with earth, was renewed in order to increase revenues. The moment was favorable for a new deal with the prelates and this time, indeed, they did not oppose the financial projects of the City Council. The new settlement is dated October 27, 1385, and it was planned to apply its provisions over an eight-year period. In the document in question the total sum of the municipal debt was stated to be 60,000 marks of pfennigs ("De summe der schulde, dar me de hulpe to don schal de is LX dusent mark penninge"), and it was decided that it was to be repaid within the next eight years "mid deme tyntze vte dem nyenzoltwerke allene." Provision was also made for the measures

80. *Ibid.*, Nos. 121, 122; cf. Franke, *op. cit.*, p. 44, where *U.B. Lüneburg*, Vol. II, Nos. 898, 899, 900, 903, are also quoted.

to be taken if the debt was repaid earlier or if repayment of the total debt should require a longer period. At the same time it was ordered that no new salt springs were to be constructed in the future.[81] The repayment of the debt was to be supervised and controlled. Thus, a kind of a sinking fund was established and the monopolistic policy of the group exploiting the salt springs and saltworks was strongly protected.

The new measures differed in many respects from those of 1377, when the creation of a sinking fund *stricto sensu* was envisaged. In 1385 the repayment was coupled with the exploitation of a new salt spring. It could be expected that the new financial plan would succeed, but the war destroyed all hopes of reducing the debts. Following the defeat of Lüneburg at Winsen on June 11, 1388, the amount of indebtedness reached a total of 173,000 marks of pfennigs.[82] It should be realized that the rate of interest was usually 10 per cent. Thus the financial burden was very heavy.

81. *U.B. Braunschweig-Lüneburg*, Vol. VI, No. 131; cf. also Kostanecki, *op. cit.*, pp. 29–30.

82. We have mentioned the role of the moneylenders in Lübeck as financiers of the City of Lüneburg. It is not possible to give an adequate presentation here of these relations which were studied with great patience and skill by Franke. It might be useful, however, to mention briefly that the total of known credits extended by the moneylenders of Lübeck to Lüneburg, during the period 1360–90, was 58,437 marks of Lübeck. The burghers of Lübeck participated in this total with 49,621 marks, while the clergy and the ecclesiastic institutions lent 8,816 marks. Consider also the following table of the prices of the saltrents during the period 1366–1403. The price of a *Pfanne*, i.e., of a part entitling one to share in the revenue of the saltworks was:

In 1366	900 marks of Lübeck
In 1384	1200 marks of Lübeck
In 1386	1000 marks of Lübeck
In 1390	1432 marks of Lübeck
In 1392	950 marks of Lübeck
In 1394	910 marks of Lübeck
In 1404	1200 marks of Lübeck

As to the relationship between the mark of pfennigs of Lüneburg and the mark of fine silver, it should be pointed out that in 1325, Lübeck, Wismar, Rostock, and Stralsund made an arrangement with Hamburg and Lüneburg concerning the minting of a larger silver coin, equal to four pfennigs of Lübeck. At that time one mark of fine silver equaled three marks of pfennigs. Cf. Inama-Sternegg, *op. cit.*, III, Part 2, 396 ff.; W. Jesse, *Münz- und Geldgeschichte Niedersachsens* (Braunschweiger Werkstücke, Vol. XV [Braunschweig, 1952]) (not accessible to me).

Let us now consider the financial affairs of Dukes Bernhard and Henry who, after the battle of Winsen, became the rulers of the duchy of Lüneburg, including the City of Lüneburg. The dukes after Magnus II inherited ruined finances and were unable to repay debts. The duchy of Lüneburg was in a precarious economic situation as the result of two wars and feuds of the preceding stormy period. From whom could the dukes receive the financial help they so badly needed? It could be provided only by the Estates with the active participation of the towns.

The first and the most urgent problem was to recover the pledged Elbe custom duties. No less imperative was the need to regain the castles Hitzacker, Bleckede, Lüdershausen, and Rethem. On September 20, 1392, the hard-pressed Dukes Bernhard and Henry entered into a strange agreement with the Estates, in which the cities Hanover, Lüneburg, and Ülzen played a leading role. The agreement is known as *Sate*.[83] The Estates lent the dukes 50,000 marks of Lüneburg pfennigs, agreed upon the levy of a special tax (*Bede*) and surrendered to the dukes all documents of pledging, the value of which exceeded 60,000 marks of silver.[84] As a reward the dukes agreed to a serious limitation of their sovereign rights, among them the right to impose new custom duties or increase the already existing ones, and the right to levy taxes.

It was also stipulated in the *Sate* agreement that the dukes were not allowed to sell or pledge castles to persons who were not members

83. The word *Sate* is derived from *friedensate*. In the document concerned the word *zate* appears. *Sate* meant *Satzung*, i.e., statute or charter. The text is to be found in *U.B. Braunschweig-Lüneburg*, VII, No. 100; cf. also Nos. 97, 98, 99, 101, 103, 104. Cf. Havemann, *op. cit.*, I, 537–38; v. Heinemann, *op. cit.*, pp. 160–61; Friedland, "Die 'Sate' der braunschweig-lüneburgischen Landstände von 1392," *Blätter für deutsche Landesgeschichte*, 91 Jhg. (1954), pp. 110–29 (not accessible to me); Thurich, *op. cit.*, pp. 37–38; see also Kostanecki, *op. cit.*, p. 78.

84. Thurich, *op. cit.*, p. 37 n. 88, refers to a remark of Friedland (*op. cit.*, p. 116 n. 29), where Friedland examines the views of historians who assume that the dukes received, in connection with the *Sate* agreement, not only 50,000 marks of pfennigs but also documents of pledging. Thurich quotes a document, where the following is said: "leten en [i.e., the dukes] boven de vyftich dusent mark . . . mer wen sestich dusent mark." Cf. *Chroniken*, XXXVI, 50: ". . . leten desulven heren boven de veftichdusent mark penninge leddich unde los mer wen sestich dusent mark penninge, de me uns rechter schult van der herschop Luneborch wegene schuldich was, alse de breve, de we van der herschop Luneborch darup hadden. . . ." Cf. also *U.B. Braunschweig-Lüneburg*, Vol. V, Nos. 14, 73, 81, 162, 163; Vol. VI, Nos. 2, 124, 138, 153, 155, 158, 256; Vol. VII, No. 235, where the objects pledged and the sums paid are enumerated; and Vol. VII, No. 162.

of the *Sate*. Other drastic limitations on the power of the dukes were included in the agreement. To guarantee the execution of the *Sate,* a committee consisting of representatives of the Estates (including councilors of the cities of Lüneburg, Hanover, and Ülzen) was set up to control the fulfillment of the provisions of the *Sate* agreement. We are not concerned here with the institutional aspect of this extraordinary arrangement. It should be stressed, however, that it could be planned and enacted only because of the heavy indebtedness of the dukes of Lüneburg and their failure to extricate themselves from a financial catastrophe.[85] As a matter of fact, the dukes did not have the slightest intention of observing the *Sate*. The rift between them and the Estates became greater every day and finally, in February, 1396, an open war broke out. Peace was restored only on October 21, 1397. In the instrument of peace *Sate* is not mentioned at all, which is, of course, highly significant.[86]

It is no less significant that on the same day, October 21, 1397, a new financial transaction was made, whereby Dukes Bernhard and Henry of Lüneburg pledged the castles Harburg and Bleckede with the villages, the castle Lüdershausen, the three respective *Vogtei,* as well as various other objects and regalian rights to the cities of Lübeck, Hamburg, Lüneburg, and Hanover for at least ten years for the total of 19,200 "mark pennynge alze to lubeke to hamborg vnd to luneborg ghenghe vnde ghue synd." The payment of this sum was to be made in the following way: the lenders undertook to pay 12,000 marks to three of the dukes' creditors, to whom the castles were once pledged, and 4,000 marks to the dukes themselves. The last sum was to be used to redeem two other ducal castles from pledge.

We see that the long period of feuds and wars between the dukes of Lüneburg and the cities did not essentially affect the existing order: the dukes continued to live in permanent financial distress and the cities continued to lend them money.

85. It is interesting to note that on July 26, 1393, King Wenzel accepted the *Sate* agreement. See *U.B. Braunschweig-Lüneburg,* Vol. VII, No. 186; cf. No. 200. In No. 186 the German king inserted a significant clause: "Volumus tamen et decernimus quod non obstantibus premissis. prescripta pacis ordinacio et omnia in ea contenta perinde valeant et valere debeant ac si dicti duces Bernhardus et Heynricus tempore date dicte ordinacionis ipsum ducatum luneborgensem a nobis in feudum suscepissent et de eodem debite fuissent investiti." The confirmation came, following the action undertaken by the Estates.

86. *Ibid.,* Vol. VIII, No. 195.

Let us now return to the credit operations of the dukes of Brunswick and to those of the City of Brunswick.[87] In November, 1373, Duke Ernst, the brother of the deceased Duke Magnus II, was involved in a feud with Archbishop Peter of Magdeburg. The City of Brunswick took part in the fighting on the side of Duke Ernst. The duke and many knights and burghers of Brunswick were taken prisoner, following the defeat on November 10, 1373, on the Elme. On April 16, 1374, the ransom of 4,000 marks was fixed for the release of the prisoners. The City of Brunswick was compelled to pay this amount and, in addition, to spend 600 marks in order to restore various material losses. As the result of these expenses the municipal debt rose to 9,987 1/2 marks.

The City Council was in an awkward position. It did not know how to solve the problem of repayment of the debt. The direct tax—*Schoss*—had for a long period been increased year after year, and the councilors believed that no further increase was possible. The remedy they intended to apply was an indirect tax on grain, the *Scheffelpfennig*. It was obvious that the envisaged taxation would affect the price of bread. Whatever the special circumstances which were beyond the city's control, there is no doubt that the financial administration in the city was poorly organized, and one can even speak of mismanagement. As long as no extraordinary events occurred, the population of Brunswick did not realize how weak were municipal finances. The burghers were unable, however, to understand the causes of the financial breakdown.

Before the new financial plan could be discussed by the councilors, a violent insurrection broke out in which the guilds took the lead. The chronicles give various explanations of this revolution. While the *Hemelik rekenscop* relates that the fighting started because of false rumors that the leaders of the guilds were seized by the council, the *Schichtboick (Shigtbok)* states that they were disturbed by the high level of debts which had accumulated despite heavy taxes, and they started to quarrel with the councilors. It is not excluded that the

87. *Chroniken,* VI, 137 ff., 313–409; Dürre, *op. cit.,* pp. 151–68; Havemann, *op. cit.,* pp. 528 ff.; v. Heinemann, *op. cit.,* pp. 103 ff.; Mack, *op. cit.,* pp. 106 ff.; Fahlbusch, *op. cit.,* pp. 6 ff. See also W. Mehl, *Die Braunschweiger Schicht von 1374 und ihre Nachwirkung in anderen Städten* (Berlin, 1909), pp. 8–21; H. L. Reimann, *Unruhe und Aufruhr im mittelalterlichen Braunschweig* (Braunschweiger Werkstücke, Vol. XXVIII [Braunschweig, 1962]), pp. 45–84. The last named work does not contain new material or points of interest for students of the financial history of the City of Brunswick; a valuable bibliography is to be found on pp. 136–142.

council threatened to use force. The atmosphere of Brunswick was so charged with discontent that even very slight causes were sufficient to bring about a formidable explosion. Crowds of men poured out of their houses onto the streets. The movement soon gained in scope and intensity. Several members of the City Council were slain, others fled. Buildings and records were destroyed. Wherever a document of a loan or an annuity was found, it was burned by the infuriated crowd.

The new city government did its utmost to prevent the financial collapse which seemed to be unavoidable. The council attempted to improve relations between Brunswick and the Hanse, from which the city was expelled after the revolution of April, 1374. Brunswick was readmitted only in 1380. The most important problem for the new City Council was to establish the amount of debts outstanding— by no means an easy task in view of the mass destruction of the records. It was also imperative to relieve the financial burden resulting from the administration of castles pledged to the city by the dukes.

The technique of pledging castles by the dukes has already been described. We know also that the castles were of great importance for the protection of the trade routes. Yet it is a matter of fact that the administration of these strongholds was expensive and that a considerable amount of money was immobilized by the city as a result of loans connected with the pledging of these castles—about 20,000 marks in 1373.[88] The city could not rid itself of the castles for it was not permissible to pledge them to princes and lords outside the duchy, and the local noblemen were financially not strong enough to forward money to the city and accept the castles in pledge. A compromise solution could be sought: to keep some of the castles and to return the others to their owners. Yet this solution required, of course, the owners' cooperation. But they could not make such a deal either prior to 1374 or immediately after the revolution of that year. Only in 1395–1396 could a radical step toward this goal be taken. Several castles held in pledge by the city were redeemed by their owners. As a result the city received 5,400 marks in cash, which amount could be used to repay the most urgent and oppressive debts.[89] In the following years further progress was made in the recovery of funds immobilized in the castles.

88. *Chroniken*, VI, 346: "des hadden se wol twintich dusent mark an sloten unde an vesten." Cf. Mack, *op. cit.*, p. 9.

89. *Hemelik rekenscop*, cap. 17, 18; cf. *Chroniken*, VI, 151–52; Fahlbusch, *op. cit.*, p. 15.

The reform of the technique of assessment of the direct tax (*Schoss*) was another change which contributed greatly to the improvement of the municipal finances. Confidence in the city's credit capacity rose gradually. It became possible to reduce the rate of interest of annuities from 10 per cent to 8 per cent, then to 7 per cent, and later even to 4 per cent.

Thirteen years after the revolution the city's debts were much higher than in the eventful year of 1374. As a matter of fact, the sum had more than doubled. The peak of indebtedness was reached in 1389.[90]

In 1374 the total indebtedness was	9,987	marks
In 1387	22,088	marks
In 1389	29,512	marks

As already mentioned, in 1380, Brunswick was readmitted to the Hanse. The energetic action of the council could proceed in the new favorable conditions with chances of success. And indeed, the next years brought a marked improvement in the municipal finances of Brunswick.[91] The city was again in a position to lend money to the dukes. In 1411–1412, Duke Henry owed 300 guilders to Brunswick and 700 to Duke Bernhard.

The debts decreased considerably after 1389. After 1410, however, they started to rise again. The amount of debts was:

In 1406	8,159 1/2	marks
In 1413	10,420	marks
In 1416	11,268	marks

A further deterioration of the municipal finances took place in connection with extensive borrowing by the dukes of Brunswick during the war of 1420–1421 against the bishop of Hildesheim.

The lesson of 1374—when heavy indebtedness, mismanagement, and mishandling of financial affairs by the City Council caused the revolution—was forgotten after a time. In 1445 debts rose to such a high level that it became necessary to double the rate of the tax (*Schoss*). To mollify the population, concerned with the financial problems and dangers, the councilors and leaders of the guilds decided to issue a proclamation, the so-called *Grosser Brief*. Issued on July 19, 1445, it aimed at a reorganization of the city government. Among its provisions three paragraphs (14, 15, and 16) were devoted to financial matters.

90. Kostanecki, *op. cit.*, p. 45.
91. *Ibid.*, pp. 51–54; Fahlbusch, *op. cit.*, pp. 163 ff., where details are given.

Of special interest is § 14 which stipulated that in the future the city was not allowed to sell perpetual annuities or life annuities without the consent of a special commission to be nominated for the control of borrowing.

Financial matters in the duchy Brunswick-Göttingen were dealt with by the ruling dukes in the same manner as by the dukes in Brunswick or in Lüneburg, i.e., pledging and borrowing were the basic elements of the ducal financial policy. On April 30, 1351, Duke Ernst pledged the mint and exchange to the City of Göttingen for a period no less than six years for 200 marks "lodeghes suluers, gottingischer wichte vn weringhe."[92] On May 28, 1357, these regalian rights were pledged again—this time for seven years—for 314 marks. Duke Otto III pledged them again in 1382 for 200 marks. The dukes never redeemed the pledged rights.

Duke Otto III (later called Otto der Quade) was one of the staunch enemies of the towns in Germany. His main problem was how to check Göttingen's propensity to become more and more independent. Yet he failed to achieve this aim: every year the city became more independent, while Duke Otto III became more dependent on Göttingen's financial power.[93] He had no choice but to pledge the office of the *scultetus*. The sum he received is not known. Sometimes he was compelled to borrow even such relatively small sums as 20 marks. How limited was his credit is seen from the fact that when on June 24, 1378, he borrowed 100 marks from his city, this was done for a period of only one month. The list of Otto's transactions of borrowing and pledging is of considerable length. When he died on December 13, 1394, he left debts which could not be easily repaid.

Otto's son Duke Otto IV (named Cocles) was the last person able to cope with the old and new financial troubles. He repeatedly borrowed money from Duke William of Brunswick, to whom he promised the succession. Otto Cocles was continually hunted by his creditors. In a desperate mood and tired, he decided in June, 1435, to renounce his reign. The next month he assigned the rule of the duchy to a committee composed of four representatives of the nobility, five representa-

---

92. *U.B. Braunschweig-Lüneburg*, Vol. II, No. 393; see also Saathoff, *Geschichte der Stadt Göttingen bis zur Gründung der Universität*, pp. 52 ff.; on money and currency in Göttingen see G. Meinhardt, *Münz- und Geldgeschichte der Stadt Göttingen*, pp. 13–19.

93. Saathoff, *op. cit.*, p. 68.

tives of the towns, and a *Landvogt* to be nominated with his approval. The Estates agreed to repay Otto's debts and to redeem the objects pledged, while Otto himself undertook to repay his debts up to the amount of 1,200 guilders. The Estates were obliged to provide the duke with various commodities for the ducal household and to pay him 200 Rhinish guilders annually in four instalments, which sum could be increased later if conditions allowed. Further, the Estates undertook to provide the duke with a complete set of winter and summer clothing. The ducal seal had to be delivered to the councilors and kept by them in a chest. Each of the members of the council was to receive a key to it.[94]

The agreement between Duke Otto IV and the Estates met with the opposition of Otto's relatives. Duke William of Brunswick expressed his readiness to give 10,000 guilders for the repayment of Otto's debts on condition that reign in the duchy Brunswick-Göttingen be surrendered to him. William's cousins in Lüneburg agreed to this proposal. Before reaching a settlement with William, Otto succeeded in receiving the consent of the Estates in 1436 to lend him 6,000 guilders. At the same time a new tax (*Bede*) of 6,000 guilders was agreed upon. The sums to be collected from the *Bede* were pledged to the Estates, which were empowered to deduct them from the loan extended to Otto. In addition, the original loan of 6,000 guilders was secured by the pledge of Otto's castles in Münden and Sichelnstein. This somewhat complicated transaction is an interesting example of a combination of a tax and a loan. The respective clause of the agreement deserves to be quoted. The Estates declare here: "We bekennen . . . dat we . . . mit unsen eddeln und erbaren mannschoppen, steden, landen und luden umme beteringe, nud und fromen willen der gen, unser lande und lude overkomen syn, so dat se uns eyne bede geven up myn oder mer 6,000 fl., darup we myt erbarn mannschoppen und steden unses landes gereyde eyne summe goldes geborget hebben, und auch bynnen kort eyne summen goldes borgende werden, de men von der bede betalen schal." It should be added that the City Council of Göttingen was empowered to collect the tax and the sums were to be deposited with the council.

The above-mentioned credit operation did not contribute essentially to the improvement of Duke Otto IV's financial situation, and he

---

94. Ibid., pp. 94–95; cf. Havemann, *op. cit.*, pp. 680 ff.; v. Heinemann, *op. cit.*, pp. 83–84.

continued to be harassed by his creditors. On April 18, 1437, he resigned and retired to the castle in Uslar. Duke William obligated himself to provide Otto annually with a certain amount of various commodities and to pay him 300 Rhinish guilders a year. Otto died in Uslar on February 6, 1463, the last member of the Göttingen line of the Welfs.[95]

A few words need to be said concerning the public credit operations of the City of Göttingen. In the fourteenth century the city reached the status comparable to that of an imperial city. Rule was exercised by a City Council. It is worth mentioning that the councilors contributed 1/10-1/6 of the tax *(Schoss)*. The weak point of the city's financial administration was the sale of annuities which, at the beginning of the sixteenth century, nearly caused bankruptcy. In the accounts for the year 1499-1500 the revenues from the sale of annuities were 2,471 marks, while the total paid out to the holders of these annuities was 2,241 1/2 marks. It should be pointed out that revenues for that year totaled 7,451 marks, while expenses totaled only 4,299 1/2 marks. This account can be compared with that for the year 1399-1400, when the revenues from the sale of rents were 887 marks and the expenses were 1,110 1/2 marks. Despite this unfavorable financial balance, the total revenues for the year 1399-1400 were 2,784 marks and the expenses were 2,459 marks.[96]

During the first two decades of the sixteenth century a marked deterioration took place in the municipal finances in Göttingen and extensive borrowing became necessary. The increased indebtedness was the result of numerous feuds fought by Duke Erich I with other lords, and of the struggle between the duke and the city. We cannot here follow the march of events. Peace was made between the duke and the city on December 29, 1511, and the city was compelled to pay 1,400 guilders at once and 5,000 guilders within a few months. Another cause of financial trouble was the sale of life annuities which had long since ceased to be a lucrative source of income. About 1,400 guilders had to be paid annually to the owners of these annuities. Mismanagement must certainly also have been a factor in the rapid deterioration of municipal finances.

95. Kostanecki, *op. cit.*, pp. 78–80, where the main source contained in G. Schmidt, *Urkundenbuch der Stadt Göttingen* (Hanover, 1867), Vol. II, No. 176, is quoted; cf. Saathoff, *loc. cit.*, pp. 94–95.

96. The accounts for the respective years are published in full by Saathoff, *op. cit.*, pp. 130 ff.

Whatever the causes, the debt rose steadily. In 1513 it amounted to 90,000 guilders and the annual interest rose to 4,000 guilders. It became imperative to find new sources of revenues. The City Council decided to mint new coins (so that one guilder should contain 24 shillings) and to levy a new excise on beer and flour. The proposal stirred great excitement among the citizens of Göttingen, especially among the members of the guilds. The opposition was rather inclined to accept the new currency, but absolutely opposed the new excise duty. When rioting began the council was ready to yield on some points, yet it was too late, for it could no longer master events. The councilors were compelled to resign and a new City Council was set up composed of members of the guilds. Six new treasurers were appointed by the guilds, and their activities were to remain under the constant control of the guild representatives. Several former councilors were to pay fines from six to 500 marks. The former treasurers fled from Göttingen and their property was confiscated.

The City Council, facing colossal debts and unable to find the necessary funds to proceed with their repayment, took the way of negotiation with the creditors with the aim of persuading them to be satisfied, for the time being, with smaller amounts and agree to reduce the rate of interest. The creditors had little choice. On December 15, 1515, a committee of eight members in charge of the repayment of debts was appointed. The sum of 2,000 guilders was originally fixed for each forthcoming year to serve as the fund for repayment of debts, but it was impossible to continue in this way. The payment of interest was postponed till Easter, 1516; for six years the owners of life annuities had to be satisfied with only one-half of the annual payment; the creditors entitled to 5 per cent interest were forced to accept the repayment of the capital within a twelve-year time limit, with the proviso that no interest be paid them. Should they refuse to accept such a proposal or should the capital be too great, the rate of interest would be reduced to 2 per cent. It is worth noting that several creditors, such as the burghers of Einbeck, created serious complications for Göttingen. Other creditors, such as those in Magdeburg, sometimes had to wait a full year for the payment of the amounts due them. On the whole, the procedure of repayment of the old debts worked well. In 1529 the indebtedness was reduced to 33,000 guilders.[97]

97. The financial matters are dealt with by Havemann, "Der Haushalt der Stadt Göttingen am Ende des 14. and während der ersten Hälfte des 15. Jhdts.,"

The finances of the City of Lüneburg were in a very poor state after a long period of war. The debt rose from about 320,000 marks of Lüneburg pfennigs in 1431 to about 597,000 in 1442.[98] Among the primary causes of this tremendous increase in debts were the wars and feuds in which the city or the dukes were involved, and the necessity of extending financial help to the dukes.

Another element must also be taken into consideration. Since the very beginning of its independent financial policy the City of Lüneburg was concerned with extraction of salt and trade in salt. To protect the free movement of this commodity on which the city's wealth depended, it was necessary to protect the trade routes. To achieve this goal, the City of Lüneburg was compelled to accept in pledge the castles Winsen, Rethem, Welpe, Brome, and Artlenburg. This necessitated a considerable financial effort, while the cost of administration of the castles was very expensive. The construction of defensive works around the city also required considerable amounts of money. Another serious drain on the municipal finances was the payment of large sums to local and foreign dukes in order to make them suppress and prohibit the transportation to Lübeck and Wismar of salt produced in places other than Lüneburg. Unable to repay its debts, the city had no choice but to pay interest on interest.[99]

Duke Otto (called Otto von der Haide) died on June 1, 1446, and was succeeded by his brother Frederick I (called Frederick the Pious). During his reign an event of the greatest significance took place in the City of Lüneburg: the *Prälatenkrieg,* so called because of the role played in the conflict by the ecclesiastic owners of the salt rents.[100]

Zeitschrift des Historischen Vereins für Niedersachsen, (1857), pp. 204–26. The history of the eventful year 1514 is given by Saathoff, *op. cit.,* pp. 167–71; cf. v. Heinemann, *op. cit.,* pp. 233 ff.

98. Havemann, *op. cit.,* p. 697; see also *Chroniken,* XXXVI, 272, 288 n., 322, 381.

99. *Ibid.,* pp. 106, 116, 199, 260 ff., 281, 287, 304, 318 ff., 324 ff.; Havemann, *op. cit.,* p. 696.

100. The main sources are the chronicle written in 1455 and 1456 by the burgomaster Hinrik Lange. It was edited by Leibniz under the title "Henricus Lange de origine belli praelatorvm Lvnebvrgici" in G. W. Leibniz, *Scriptores Rerum Brunsvicensium,* III, (Hanover, 1711), 222 ff., now included in *Chroniken,* pp. 163–256; *Die Chronik des Anonymus vom Prälatenkrieg,* written in 1476, now included in *Chroniken,* pp. 280–336, and "Historia der uneinicheit zwischen dem olden und nigen rade to Luneborg, anno 1450 ex parte veteris *senatus* per dominum Theodoricum Doring conscriptum," included in *Chroniken,* 343–86. Cf. v. Heinemann, *op. cit.,* pp. 186 ff. The list of ecclesiastic participants in the saltworks includes a

Soon after the death of Duke Otto, the City Council approached the prelates asking them to contribute to the repayment of the debts double the amount they had agreed upon in the past, i.e., to put at the disposal of the City Council 50 per cent of their revenues.

The majority of the prelates expressed their willingness to cooperate with the city. The minority, however, found an energetic leader in the person of Dietrich Schaper, provost of the Benedictine monastery in Lüne. Schaper also found support among some groups of burghers, and even among clerks of the municipal administration. In view of the failure to reach a positive solution in the negotiations conducted with the prelates in 1447–1448, the City Council sought opinions from various universities and doctors of law, and finally appealed to the pope.[101] The prelates did the same. Finally, thanks to the intervention of the bishop of Verden and a legate sent by the Holy See, a settlement was made on June 1, 1450, to the effect that the prelates would pay ten marks from each *pan* (*Pfanne*) of salt and five marks from each *Wispel* (*Chor*). The solution was accepted on condition that these payments would be sufficient.

When in 1451 it became obvious that the fixed contribution was too small, the City Council attempted to persuade the prelates to contribute a single large sum. The prelates refused and a group of burghers took their side. Both parties appealed again to Rome. The Holy See instructed Dietrich Dompnitz, dean of Halberstadt, to investigate and decide the case. His decision was that the prelates were not obliged to contribute more than the payments fixed in the settlement of June, 1450. The council appealed to Rome against this sentence. Pope Nicholas V decided in favor of the prelates in a bull and ordered that the sums due the prelates but retained by the council be returned to them, otherwise the council would be put under the ban of the Church. Other severe censures were foreseen in the bull.

The council refused to obey. The excommunication of the City of Lüneburg followed, with all its consequences. All churches were closed and the population was excluded from the communion of the Church. When the city sent its burgomaster, Albert von der Mölen, to Rome in order to appeal against the imposed ban, he was imprisoned. The City Council answered, at the end of December, 1453, by seizing the

---

great many of the most important monasteries and ecclesiastic institutions (see *U.B. Braunschweig-Lüneburg*, Vol. V, No. 121).

101. *Chroniken*, pp. 162 ff., 247 nn. 1 and 2, 248.

property of the salt prelates. Another papal bull followed in 1454. The City Council appealed to the Ecumenical Council.

On October 28, 1454, the City Council called a meeting of esteemed burghers. The burgomaster defended the council's policy, while the burghers pointed out that the city could no longer endure the severe censures of excommunication. These arguments made a strong impression upon the councilors. New efforts were made to reach a settlement with the prelates, but nothing was achieved. On November 14, 1454, a committee composed of sixty members was elected by the population and the City Council was asked to turn in the keys of the city. After a certain period of hesitation the council resigned on November 23, 1454. The next day a new City Council was elected by the committee with the approval of the prelates. As could be expected, the new council concluded an agreement with them. The former councilors were assured that no harm would be done them. Contrary to this promise, the new City Council, in which Schaper played a leading role, ordered the confiscation of the property of the former councilors. The burgomasters and seven former councilors were imprisoned. One of the burgomasters, Johann Springintgut, died in prison.

The new council did not succeed in solving the difficult problem. In the meantime Emperor Frederick III ordered the new council to resign and the old council to be restored. Yet the councilors refused to carry out the order. But the mood of the population had now changed. On November 2, 1456, the committee of sixty was expelled from the town hall by a crowd of burghers, and the old councilors were asked to return from Lübeck where they had found refuge. The members of the committee of sixty and the members of the Council nominated by that committee had to pay 15,000 Rhinish guilders to the imperial fisc, restore the property of the old councilors, and pay an indemnity to the family of Springintgut. Two leaders of the insurrection were sentenced to death and executed on October 25, 1457. The conflict with the prelates was finally settled only in 1472, when the prelates agreed to pay thirty-six marks and eighteen marks respectively from each of the units of their salt production.

The conflict of Lüneburg is an interesting episode of the pre-Reformation period in Germany. Its causes, as we have seen, were of a specific character. The *Prälatenkrieg* was, in fact, only a financial quarrel between one group of plutocracy, dominating the City Council of Lüneburg, and another wealthy group, the *Sülzprälaten*. To what extent this violent clash of interests can be considered an early manifestation of the discontent which led to the explosion in the second decade of the sixteenth century, is beyond the scope of the present investigation.[102]

(To be continued)

102. The state of affairs in Germany during the pre-Reformation period is presented by W. Andreas, *Deutschland vor der Reformation* (6th ed.; Stuttgart, 1959). The student of the financial history of that period might also consider the statement by P. Joachimsen, *Die Reformation als Epoche der deutschen Geschichte* (Munich, 1951), p. 44, where the revolution of 1509–14 in German towns are mentioned. Joachimsen assumes that in some cases the movements constituted a continuation of fighting between the guilds and the patriciate which took place before 1509. Yet according to Joachimsen the main causes were financial: 'Es ist die Finanzwirtschaft des Rates und die Steigerung der Lasten, die sich aus den vermehrten Aufgaben des Gemeinwesens, sowohl für seinen Schutz nach aussen wie für die Polizei im Innern, nicht zum wenigsten auch aus den Auflagen des Reichs ergaben. Sie erschienen dem gemeinen Mann unverständlich. Der Rat soll Rechenschaft ablegen. Die Gemeinde will in finanziellen Dingen die Aufsicht führen und ihren Einspruch einlegen können.' The conflict in Lüneburg was, of course, of a quite different nature.